TOOLS OF THE MIND

TOOLS OF THE MIND

techniques and methods for intellectual work

V. STIBIC

NORTH-HOLLAND PUBLISHING COMPANY
AMSTERDAM • NEW YORK • OXFORD

ISBN: 0 444 86444 X

Publishers:

NORTH-HOLLAND PUBLISHING COMPANY
AMSTERDAM • NEW YORK • OXFORD

Sole distributors for the U.S.A. and Canada:

ELSEVIER SCIENCE PUBLISHING COMPANY, INC.
52 VANDERBILT AVENUE
NEW YORK, NY 10017

1st reprint 1983

PRINTED IN THE NETHERLANDS

Abstract

Most professionals gained in their school years and university studies wide background knowledge and thorough training in their specific fields of science or technology, but were not taught on how to study and work efficiently. This book describes the basic techniques and methods of intellectual work: the organization of one's own workplace; the gathering, storage, management and retrieval of information for personal use; the traditional and modern methods of text processing, in particular the practical use of a word processor by a professional for more challenging tasks than simple typing of business correspondence; personal computing by means of pocket calculators, personal computers and terminals; some basic techniques and methods of graphical presentation, and techniques of communication by traditional and new means, including electronic mail and computer conferencing. Suggestions and recommendations on how to employ simple as well as sophisticated tools are demonstrated in a number of examples. The first chapter characterizes the basic principles of efficient personal work, the trends and prospects of development of technical means and their usage, and includes critical remarks and warnings concerning misunderstanding or misuse of the old and new 'tools of the mind'.

V. Stibic:
Tools of the Mind - Techniques and Methods for Intellectual Work
1982, Amsterdam-Oxford-New York: North-Holland Publ. Co
296 + xiv pages, 160 figures, 375 references; subject index

PREFACE

The schools which I attended provided me for life with certain fundamental knowledge and an enormous volume of detailed facts about kings, battles, butterflies, aorists, laws, crystals, mercantilism, conic sections and many other things. For the former I am grateful, but as regards the latter I forgot the majority of it, and have felt much better ever since - as jolly old Jerome Klapka Jerome would say. I do not complain. On the other hand, I do blame all my schools because they never tried to teach me how to learn and how to work.

Much has changed and improved in the educational system since that time. I am happy to hear from my younger friends that they, or their children, learn more about the sense of history than about the dates of battles, and more about the life and behaviour of animals than about their classification, Latin names and appearance. Techniques of education have also improved essentially - it is a pleasure to see modern instructional devices in schools, audio-visual means in public libraries, or the excellent methods of subject teaching in the television courses. Unfortunately, one thing has not changed: students, though well prepared as concerns general knowledge and their specialist fields, are given no advice on how to work efficiently, how to organize their work, how to read, listen and study, how to gather, store and organize information, or how to use modern technical means to save time and effort and to improve their own productivity.

Just as in the time when I was a student, they have to find their own way by chance and by trial and error. Some manage this problem excellently, but the majority remain at a low level in terms of the organization and style of their work, which often contrasts strikingly with the high accomplishments in their special fields of activity. For example, a biologist works in his laboratory with the most modern equipment and methods of 1982, but when he returns to his writing desk, he uses technical means and methods that do not differ essentially from those of his counterpart in, let us say, 1932.

The subject of the technique of intellectual work first began to attract my interest in my early student years when I found in my father's library a reprint of the lectures entitled 'How to work', given in 1898 by T. G. Masaryk, the great philosopher and humanist, first president of the democratic Czechoslovakia, who as a university professor taught already before 1900 his students how to study and to work. This triggered my inquisitiveness and search for newer and more detailed literature. My study specialization and later activity in the field of industrial planning and accounting and office mechanization was closely related to the problems of organization of personal work: many an industrial method, simplified and adapted, could be transplanted into the personal sphere. My easy access to computers has seduced me time and again to investigate their usefulness as tools in the sphere of personal work. Fortunately, I have also close contact with specialists in 'small mechanization', comprising the use of card indexes, planning boards, calculating machines, dictating equipment etc. I learned very much from them, and have never considered the computer of our time as a means that offers the best solution in all situations. Also in my Philips years I had the opportunity to use in my research work the most advanced computers, but again I worked in the environment where attention is given to 'small' devices that support a professional in his daily work - remember the Philips dictating machines, word processors, office computers and microcomputers or telecommunication means. Often I encounter people who - fascinated by the vision of the 'office of the future' and the telecommunication techniques of tomorrow - infringe the elementary rules of effective work or forget to use some simpler technical means that are very practical. What about an author of a visionary report on the new means of communication, who writes his own drafts in longhand; what about a book on office of the future, published without an alphabetical index; what about an abstracting journal that presents abstracts with a delay of one, two or even more years and then makes them online available in seconds; what about... the enumeration could be very long.

Indeed, we live in a time of promiscuity of technologies. The computers and means of telecommunication develop in a fast tempo, offering ever wider possibilities; nevertheless, we have not yet reached the age of paperless work. The sophisticated technology is intermingled with simple tools and even with the plain paper-and-pencil techniques, and applications of advanced methods contrast with cases of ignorance of the elementary principles of effective work organization and mechanization. The situation is similar to the times when automobiles and carriages were to be seen in the streets side by side, and when the roads were adequate for horse-and-buggy and not yet really suitable for motor vehicles. In such a situation, it is not easy to gain orientation and to determine an optimal personal style of work. I myself learned very much from my own faults and from disappointments that inevitably followed whenever my enthusiasm and expectations were exaggerated.

The present book aims to give an overview of the heterogeneous activities of a professional over a spectrum broader than that of his narrow specialist field, and of the wide assortment of available technical means and methods. It tries to characterize their principles, features, possible applications, advantages, week points, limits and dangers, and offers suggestions and recommendations that make the individual choice easier. For a detailed study of special questions - such as programming of personal computers, operation of a word processor, details of graphical presentation etc. - the reader must make use of more specialized literature. The 'references' section of this book helps him to locate such specific works.

I am indebted to many friends and colleagues at Philips Corporate ISA (Information Systems and Automation) in Eindhoven and at Philips Data Systems in Apeldoorn for reading selected parts of the text and for their helpful criticisms. My friends at the Technical Universities in Eindhoven and in Delft I am obliged for their help, advice and for suggestive discussions. I am also grateful for the linguistic help given by Mr. R. Speed of the Philips translating office who carefully checked the text and translated many a sentence into English that is less deviating from standard than was my original draft. Acknowledgment and appreciation are expressed to the staff of the North-Holland Publishing Company in Amsterdam: to Drs. W. Dijkhuis, Senior Editor for the computer and information science section, I am indebted for his advice concerning the structure of the book and also for the suggestion of its title; to Dr. R. L. Hunsucker who as Publishing Editor read the final version, for many an improvement of the text.

The author

Zeebruggestraat 21
5628 NH Eindhoven
The Netherlands

TABLE OF CONTENTS

1 - TOOLS AND METHODS OF INTELLECTUAL ACTIVITY

From the very beginning of his existence man has been using *tools* to amplify the power of his muscles, to improve his skill and dexterity. The production tools - from those primitive implements used in the prehistoric age, down to the modern machinery in automatic factories of our time - influenced fundamentally the development of man and the course of his history. Apart from tools amplifying his physical power and improving his skill, man uses also tools that augment his mind, amplify his mental power and help him in many aspects of his intellectual activity.

11 - The field of intellectual activity

The concept of *intellectual activity* is rather vague, and we shall not attempt to define it precisely. It is often understood to be the opposite to physical work, however, the boundaries between the two are not always sharp enough and, moreover, by no means all activities which are not physical merit the description 'intellectual' - think of many simple, repetitive clerical jobs.

For our purposes, intellectual work can be characterized as working with information - accepting, evaluating, organizing, storage, retrieval, handling, processing, original creation and output of information: an intellectual worker is handling symbols rather than things, his activity is for the most part non-repetitive, it is heterogeneous, there are few strictly defined rules that could be followed mechanically. The work is partly or prevailingly abstract and it contains to some degree an element of creativity. The typical components of intellectual work are:

Organization, personal planning and accounting. Every professional has to organize his own work and workplace, he has to plan his activities, to schedule his tasks, appointments and other events, he must record important facts and events, and often he also has to plan, record and evaluate his activities, costs and income in the form of personal budgeting and accounting. We describe the organization of the workplace in chapter 2; planning, scheduling, budgeting and accounting in chapter 3.

Information management. Everybody receives information from his environment, has to select relevant information, store it if it is worth storing, and organize it; he must try to establish some system to enable him to retrieve information when it is needed. Effective use of existing sources of information, from the traditional (libraries, books, journals, abstracting journals) to the modern (SDI services, online information systems, viewdata etc.), is essential for professionals of any vocation. We describe these methods and techniques in chapter 4.

Word and text processing. Writing letters, memos, notes, reports, internal communications etc. is an activity that concerns every professional; many also write articles, books or other publications. The need to write, dictate, correct, edit and update texts - often containing tables, figures, schemes or indexes - is quite common. We consider the questions of how to organize and mechanize these activities in chapter 5.

Computing. Also the need for computing is quite general; the intensiveness and the nature of computations differ considerably according to the profession - the need for computation varies from the modest requirements of, say, a teacher in a non-technical field to the special requirements for sophisticated and voluminous computations of a physicist or an expert on the national economy. In chapter 6 we restrict our attention to the problems of personal computing.

Graphical presentation. For many professionals, graphical presentation is an integral component of their work: consider the technical drawings of an engineer, the synoptic maps of a meteorologist, the flow-charts of a systems analyst etc. In what follows we do not describe such special applications; it is not the aim of this book to teach a designer or architect how to make technical drawings by the modern CAD (Computer Aided Design) methods, nor to teach, say, a statistician how to present statistical data in graphical form. On the other hand, nearly every professional needs, from time to time, to present and to analyze data graphically, either simply in order to improve his own insight into complicated structures or relations of data, or in order to present ideas in a form more easily acceptable by his audience. Selected forms of graphical presentation and the respective technical means are described in chapter 7.

Communication is an inherent part of any intellectual activity. It includes accepting information from the environment, exchanging opinions with others, presentation of one's own ideas and work-results in written or spoken form, all this either directly between two persons face-to-face, via communication facilities, at meetings, brainstorming-sessions, congresses and conferences, or by publication. Chapter 8 deals with this subject.

Special activities. A substantial part of professional's intellectual work is done using specific methods and techniques of his vocation, often at workplaces that are equipped with quite special tools - in laboratories, experimental workshops, hospitals, studios etc. We shall not, of course, concern ourselves with such specific activities of particular professions, but shall concentrate on the technique of desk work which is common to all professionals.

The types of work mentioned above are not, in practice, strictly discrete nor need they be performed exactly in a fixed sequence. Often, they are mixed, many are iterative. Also, their proportions are quite individual, depending on the profession, function and personal style of the individual concerned.

Communication, for instance, accounts for much more than 50 %, sometimes more than 75 %, of the working time of a manager. Computation may take a considerable part of the working time of a physicist. The structure of the working time of a professional may also change essentially depending on his current activity: in the case of a researcher, it differs when he enters a new field of research, when he is immersed on detailed research-work, and when he is preparing a publication based on its results. It might be worthwhile for everybody to analyze his own spectrum of work and to try to answer the question: how much time do *I* spend on communication, on information organization, on writing, computing etc.? The answer can encourage an individual to reorganize his activities, and give them better support by technical means.

Accumulated knowledge and experience, a good memory, a sharp intellect coupled with an ability for association, deduction and induction, imagination and creative thinking are some of the decisive qualities of an intellectual worker. These abilities cannot be replaced even by the most sophisticated modern technical means - on the other hand, they can and must be supported and stimulated by suitable tools.

12 - Man and his tools

The earliest tools amplified the physical power and dexterity of man. The first machines merely replaced the crude muscle work in simple activities such as the pumping of water or grinding of corn. Later, machines appeared that were able to perform more and more complicated operations requiring power, skill, precision, dexterity and diligence: think of a loom or a printing press. For hundreds of years, certain machines exhibited some - albeit rudimentary - elements of *automation*: machines able to perform repetitive work without continuous control by man (e.g. mills), and even machines self-controlled by simple forms of feedback (a windmill turning automatically to face the wind by means of a fan-tail mechanism, Watt's centrifugal governor). The first machines able to work according to a *rigid program* also appeared early: the Jacquard's loom, controlled by punched cards at the end of the eighteenth century or the sophisticated astronomical clock even in the Renaissance. Mechanical automatic machinery such as automatic packing machines, automatic lines for filling bottles, automatic production and assembly lines, etc., proliferated in the first half of the present century. The creation of machines controlled by a *flexible program* had to wait for the advent of electronics. In our age of microelectronics they have achieved a flexibility and a degree of automation undreamed of in the past.

The typical categories of tools and machines are classified by Amber and Amber in their fine book 'The Anatomy of Automation' [ref. 10]. The authors describe nine categories of tools characterized by their essential features and by the human abilities that they can replace - the crude muscle work, skill, dexterity, diligence, attention, evaluation, self-learning, considering and creativity.

Tools supporting intellectual activity

The first tools used outside the sphere of production, intended to support human brain power, appeared a very long time ago. Simple writing and drawing tools for recording information, and the first scientific and technical instruments for measurement and observation, are thousands of years old, and even the first tools for counting and calculation (for example, the abacus) were known in the ancient East as well to the Greeks and Romans. However, the development of these types of instrument was incomparably slower, and their use was far not so common as the use of production tools. Firstly, the need to mechanize intellectual activities was nowhere near as crucial to everyday life as the mechanization of the physical work; secondly, the task of mechanizing activities such as computing or writing was much more difficult, and almost impossible to achieve by means of the available technology.

The first invention to have a wide impact on the technique and style of intellectual work was that of printing in the middle of the 15th century. The invention and practical design of the first calculating machines by Pascal (1642) and Leibnitz (1671) was a modest beginning for tools that have immensely improved man's computational power. The 19th century saw the birth of many devices still widely used today: the first typewriter was designed by Mitterhoffer in 1864, adding and calculating machines were improved and were soon able to print, the punched card machines of Hollerith have been used in large statistical jobs since 1887. At the same time, the basic inventions in the field of telecommunications, the telegraph and telephone, were emerging.

The first half of the 20th century brought many improvements - the electric typewriter, bookkeeping machines, automatic calculating machi-

CHAPTER / activity	1 writing and drawing tools	2 forms	3 card index	4 peek-a-boo cards	5 filing devices	6 planning board	7 microfilm	8 reproduction equipment	9 tape recorder	10 dictating machine	11 slide/overhead projector	12 film	13 closed-circuit tv	14 teletext, viewdata	15 telex, teletex, facsimile	16 telephone, videophone	17 videorecorder, DOR	18 typewriter	19 word processor	20 plotter	21 graphical display	22 pocket calculator	23 programmable calculator	24 personal computer	25 terminal/mainframe
3 PLANNING/ACCOUNTING																									
personal planning		*	*			*														+	+			*	*
scheduling		*	*			*															+			*	*
alerting						+																+		*	*
Critical path method		+				+														+	+			*	*
budgeting, accounting		*																				+	+	*	*
diary, log		*								+								+	*					*	*
4 INFORMATION MANAGEMENT																									
studying	*	*	*	+	+		+	+	*	*	+	+	*	*			*	+	+		+	+	+	*	*
computer-aided instr.																					+			*	*
notes	*	*	*		+			+	+	*								*	*					*	*
filing, storage		+	*	+	*		*	+									*	+	+					*	*
classif., indexing			+																					+	*
retrieval		*	*	*	*		*							*			*		+					*	*
5 TEXT PROCESSING																									
drafts	*	+						*	+	*								*	*					*	*
correcting, editing	*							*										*	*					*	*
reproduction, print							*	*										+	*					*	*
mailing			*	+				*							*			*	*					*	*
6 PERSONAL COMPUTING																									
simple calculations																						*	*	*	+
advanced computing																				+	+	+	*	*	*
modelling, simulations																				*	*		+	*	*
programming		+																					*	*	*
7 GRAPHICAL WORK																									
drawing	*	+						*												*	*			*	*
graphs and schemes	*	*				*		*												*	*	+	+	*	*
designing	*							+												*	*	+		*	*
8 COMMUNICATION																									
personal communication		+						+		*					*	*		*	*					*	*
preparation of present.	*					*		*	*	*	+						+	+	+		+			+	+
presentations	*							*	*	+	*	*	*	+			*				*			*	*
preparation of confer.	*		+			*		*	*	*	+							+	+		+			+	+
conferences	*							*	*	+	*		*		*	*	*		+		*			*	*
brainstorming	*								*	*	*					+	+				+			+	+
publishing	*						*	*		+				+			+	*	*	*	*			*	*

Fig. 12.1 - A professional's activities and technical means

There are many specialized tools that are helpful in the heterogeneous activities of a professional. They are beginning to be integrated into multifunctional units - a universal work station of the future is the ultimate solution.

∗ usable as a main tool *+ as auxiliary tool or not fully adequate aid*

nes, improved types of punched card equipment, dictating machines, cheap and efficient reproduction techniques, and many others. All these machines were used mainly in the office; their chief applications were relatively simple, repetitive clerical operations in bookkeeping, invoicing, statistics, correspondence etc. Their penetration into the professional's work room was - with the exception of the telephone and typewriter - slow and limited. The machines were used as support more for a clerk than for a professional. Consequently, the professional's place of work in the middle of this century was equipped typically only with a telephone, a typewriter, a slide rule, and a few simple devices such as a card index, letter files and small office appliances (fig. 22.1).

The simple tools available in the first half of this century did not essentially change the work style or the productivity of a professional: they merely mechanized isolated elementary operations (writing, adding, multiplication, reproduction) in the traditional work process. The highly productive automatic devices (the punched card systems) of the time were limited to mass jobs in large companies and organizations; only in exceptional cases were they employed by a professional for technical or statistical computations.

The basic trend of development in this field of technology was the *differentiation* of machines. From a few basic types, there grew a wide assortment of specialized machines and devices supporting the professional in his diversified activities (fig. 12.1).

A plain typewriter of the beginning of this century differentiated into many types - from the small portable machine to the standard mechanical office typewriter, electrical typewriter and many variants of typewriters with quite special functions. Many types of calculating and accounting machines as well as special-purpose machines for invoicing or addressing appeared, and the traditional set of punched card machines was extended by a number of special machines for specific functions such as collating, interpreting, reproducing or calculating.

Very early, the first signs also of a reverse trend appeared: the trend to *integration* of machine functions.

Multi-functional production machines have been known for a long time. Also in the field of office machines, integration of functions appeared early: the Moon-Hopkins billing machine from the beginning of the present century combined the functions of a typewriter and a calculating machine. A punched card tabulator was able to compute simultaneously in several counters, to print-out the items, and to store the sums. Some reproducing machines are able to print and sort in one run. The invoicing machine is a combination of typewriter, calculating machine and accounting machine.

In the era of mechanical machines, integration of functions led to the creation of a machine of new, specialized type, often intended to be used for a specific purpose - remember the invoicing machine. Thus, integration of functions in the past resulted in further differentiation in machine types: a multi-functional machine was often a single-purpose machine.

The radical change came with the advent of the computer. From that point the main trend reverted definitively from differentiation to integration, with dramatical consequences for the effectiveness of mechanization, and for the style of work involving the new tools. Understanding the principles and impacts of integration is essential for an effective use of modern techniques in the office as well as in the personal work sphere. It can also help in comprehending the present changes in the technology of information processing, storage and transmission, and its future prospects.

13 - Integration of machines, functions and applications

Integration brings about the effect of *synergy*: the total effect of integrated operations is greater than the sum of the effects of the same tasks, performed separately. In a simplistic form, this can be expressed by the crazy equation $1 + 1 = 3$. If two operations are combined, then the total time is less than the sum of both operation times; often, some operations can be eliminated, or slow operations can be replaced by faster ones. In data processing, slow and arduous manual input operations are saved if several jobs are integrated - the same input data are used for more tasks, interim results are transmitted in the machine-readable form from operation to operation, results are stored and can be used again with minimum effort.

In the above-mentioned simple case of the integration of typewriter and calculating machine, the figures typed-in by the typist were printed-out by the typewriter and simultaneously counted up by the adding mechanism. The number was typed-in only once, the printed and added numbers could not differ as a result of a typist's error. In a computer, very long strings of operations can be performed; the ratio between the volume of input data and the volume of fast automatic operations shifts in the favour of the latter, and the overall processing-performance increases accordingly.

Integration of machines

Several machines having similar functions can be mounted in a common housing, and their operation can be unified and streamlined. An example of this is the integration of telephone, intercom and dictating equipment in a common housing. Instead of three units of different sizes, shapes, colours and - more important - with different keyboards and ways of operating, one unit has now been created, the functional elements have been unified and adapted according to the principles of ergonomics. The whole thing is easier to operate, the interconnections (telephone with dictating unit, intercom with telephone) are built-in and easier to handle, and the integrated unit is not only more functional, but is also handsome.

Integration of machine functions

The advent of computers and terminals was the big break in regard to the traditional differentiation of office and professional's tools. Indeed, the computer is the most universal machine ever made. From the very beginning of its existence, it was able to take over the functions of many different devices - it replaced adding and calculating machines, accounting machines, punched card equipment, addressing machines, card index, typewriters; now it can even be used as a drawing device or a projector. A big step towards integration was the *convergence of*

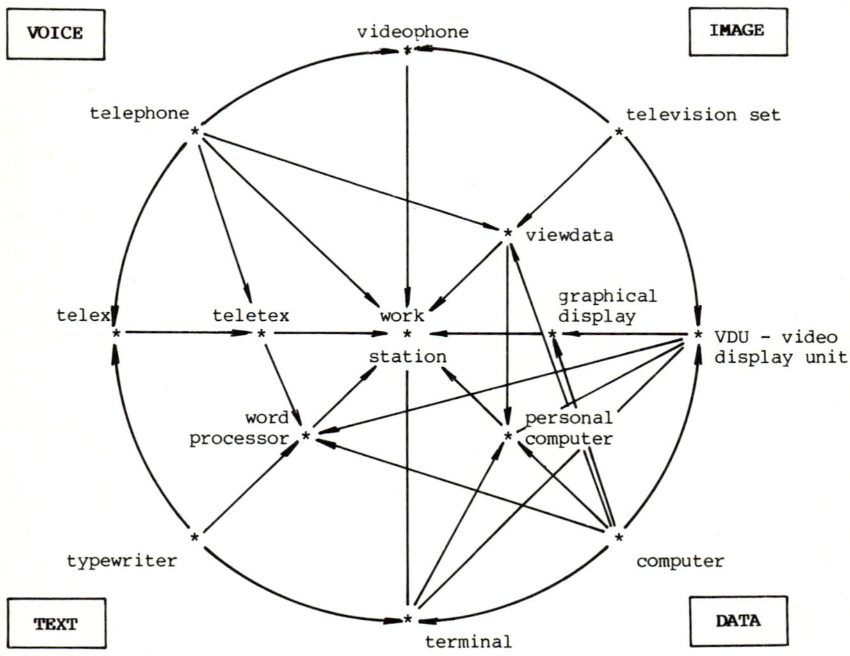

Fig. 13.1 - Integration of technologies of information processing and transmission

For many years the technical means of information processing and transmission were specialized and incompatible. Step by step they are converging.

computing and communication. The first approach was the dislocated terminal enabling remote conversational online systems to be built. Further development allows communication between a number of stations within a company (terminals, word processors or personal computers), and likewise with the outside world via public or private telecommunication networks. Another essential step is integration of the processing, storage and transmitting of information in the form of *text, data, voice and image.* The modern means are able to combine more than one form of information. From our point of view the development from a number of specialized machines to a *universal work station* - able to accept, process, store and transmit information in all four forms (text, data, voice, image) - is essential (fig. 13.1).

Integration of software

The early application software offered by the computer manufacturers was a conglomerate of isolated, incompatible programs solving special tasks. Later, more flexible programs, adaptable to a user's specific requirements, were written, and program packages solving complex tasks, particularly in the field of business data processing (wage administration, invoicing, sales statistics, production scheduling etc.) appeared.

Even so, the first programs in non-business applications were isolated and rigid: the early programs for processing library indexes required a rigid input data structure (a fixed number of record fields, exact record format, obligatory separators etc.), and they also produced a pre-defined output that was not adaptable by the user. Modern software in this field - if it is not designed for a specific application - has the form of a modular system consisting of compatible, flexible programs allowing the user to define his own data structure, his own variant of processing and his own type, form and layout of output data - for example, a set of indexes adapted in content and form to his individual needs.

A similar development is badly needed also in the sphere of personal computing, word processing and other activities of a professional. A system of personal software and not a conglomerate of incompatible programs, is the goal. We present a sketch of such modular, flexible, compatible personal software in fig. 67.1.

No longer will we have an isolated program for storage and retrieval of addresses, another isolated program for personal documentation, another for planning, diary keeping and accounting etc.; all the programs should form a modular system so that it is possible to use the retrieval module for search both in the personal documentation file and in the directory file or in the chronological records of the diary. Similarly, the addresses from the directory file must be easy to use, say, in letters typed by the word processing module. A flexible sort and merge program must be able to use any of the records as input. Output of the retrieval run must be usable as input for processing a KWIC index by means of the indexing program (compilation of personal selective bibliographies), etc.

Integration of applications

Little needs to be said on this topic if we do not wish to repeat what has been said above, and what will be said in the following sections about specific fields of a professional's work-technique (though some basic principles have, obviously, to be repeated and emphasized time and again). Some programs to mechanize isolated activities might help. In particular, word processing and personal computing are both large sectors of the activities of many a professional, that can be tackled immediately and - initially - without relations to other fields of his work. However, the final goal is a *complex mechanization* of all (mechanizable) personal activities by means of hardware with integrated functions, and by means of a system of software consisting of a set of compatible programs. Such a system has a much greater effect than isolated processing - we have explained the principle of synergy above.

14 - Tools and methods

The *techniques* influence the *methods*. Simple tools do not change working-methods: they merely make old jobs easier and improve performance, but the work itself remains basically unchanged. With more sophisticated techniques, more radical changes in methods are possible and even inevitable.

If a calculating machine is used by somebody performing complicated calculation, then the method of computation, its algorithm, remains unchanged. The machine mechanizes only isolated multiplications or divisions in a long chain of manual operations; it remains an auxiliary means situated at the fringe of the stream of manual operations.

Even a dictating machine requires some changes in the style of dictation (see section 53), and mechanized retrieval requires different structure and content of the input data, different indexing methods and essentially different search strategy from an old-style card index. Work mechanized by means of advanced techniques no longer resembles - and in most cases, should not resemble - the traditional procedure. It is - as we note several times in a special context in the subsequent chapters - a frequent misunderstanding that the new technique is being used simply to replace the old one.

Imitation of old manual techniques or *anthropomorphization* of techniques - technical solutions simulating human work - arise due to inertia of human thinking and a limited imagination unable to forsake the old manual methods when trying to mechanize them.

By way of an extreme example, let us recall some of the abortive inventions aimed at simulating human activities by mechanical devices, ignoring the fact that a machine has its own specific properties and idiosyncrasies. Brunton's locomotive with legs, at the time of Stephenson, is a typical case which because of its quaintness has not been forgotten. Mr. Hawkins' Polygraph (fig. 14.1) tried to mechanize the copying of documents by simulating manual rewriting (of course, a sheet of carbon paper turned out to be a better solution). Less striking cases of the simulation of manual procedures in mechanized operations are frequently encountered in practice. For example, output-data displayed on the screen of data processing systems are often nothing more than slavish imitations of pre-printed forms; the designers treat the screen as a paper form, characterized by its fixed pre-printed fields. They ignore the specific property of a screen, i.e. its flexibility (fig. 14.2).

The inevitable changes of methods in mechanized processes compared with the traditional methods result from the fact that the machine is able

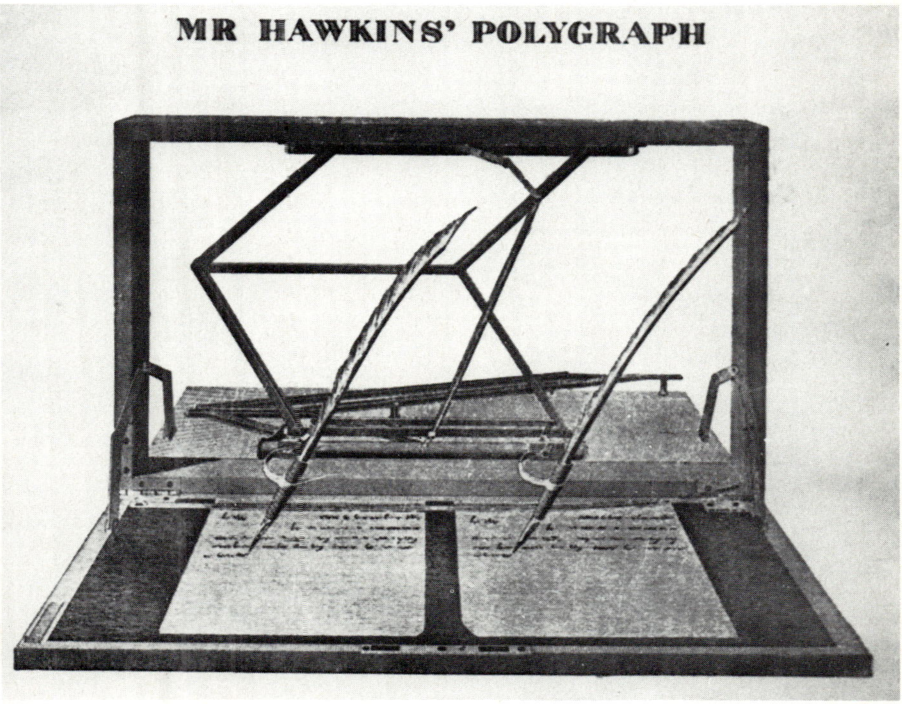

Fig. 14.1 - Anthropomorphization - a wrong solution to a technical problem by simulating an old manual technique

Mr. Hawkins tried to mechanize the copying of documents by a complicated mechanism simulating manual re-writing. Instead, a sheet of carbon paper was the solution. We encounter often the use (or misuse) of modern technical means that simply simulate the old techniques. Not all cases are as striking as Mr. Hawkins' polygraph, but the error is of the same nature.

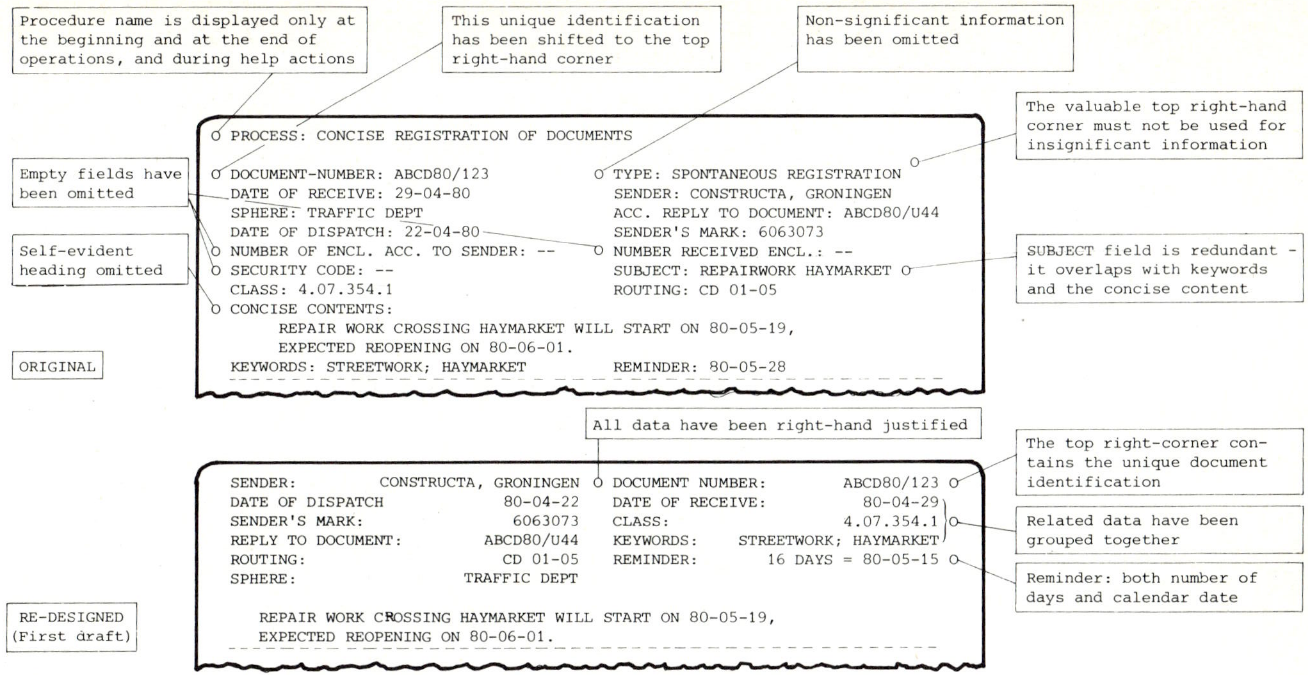

Fig. 14.2 - An example of misleading tradition: pre-printed form is transplanted uncritically to the screen

This example is less striking than Mr. Hawkins' polygraph (fig. 14.1), but the output on a screen suffers from a similar fault: the screen-layout simply imitates the layout of a traditional pre-printed form.

to perform some operations much more easily and faster than man, while, on the other hand, it is unable to perform effectively, or at all, other operations that are quite easy for a human being.

An industrial product has first to be fundamentally re-designed before its production can be effectively automated. For instance, pre-processed material should enter the production in continuous form (not cut into pieces), shaping is replaced by forming, parts are no longer assembled by screws but by pressing together, etc. A chair made by automatic production differs essentially from a chair made by a cabinet-maker: it differs in the material, technology used and finally in its shape and form [ref. 10-Amber].

In the case of computerization, the re-design of jobs and change of methods are dictated among other things by the contrast between the slow input on the one hand, and the fast internal operations on the other. Consequently, we need to limit the input data, to store the repetitively used data in the computer memory, to use the data for every useful purpose and

FIELD	INPUT	STORED	OUTPUT
DATE	80-05-28 80/05/28 28.5.1980 28. 5. 1980 28-05-80	800528 (binary)	80-05-28 (default) 28. 5. 1980 (variant) 28 May 1980 (variant) etc.
	May 28th, 1980 28. V. 1980 28 mei 1980 etc.	not accepted	
DEPT	patent department patent dept. octrooien en merken octrooiafdeling O&M	51978 (binary)	O&M (default) patent dept. (variant) 51978 (variant) etc.
	patents pat. dept. O/M O+M etc.	not accepted	

Fig 14.3 - Flexibility of data is allowed in modern user-friendly systems

In a traditional mechanized system, each data element had to be entered in a stricly uniform, standardized version. The date had to be written in a prescribed form, in a certain sequence and with a certain interpunction. A personal name had to be typed in a given form (e.g. surname, comma, space, first initial, colon, space etc.); otherwise it was either not accepted or mutilated by the system. A modern user-friendly system gives more freedom to the user, it is able to accept more than one form of data, it formalizes them into a standard version and asks the user to correct his input only if it deviates too much or is ambiguous [ref. 10-Stibic].

from many points of view. Too simple jobs, isolated small jobs, one-off jobs are less suitable for effective automation.

During the fifties and sixties when computers entered the field of business data processing, the early applications were subjected time and again to criticism: too often the old jobs were merely being transferred from the punched card equipment to a computer; no consideration was given to the fact that the computer is able to do more, that it is able to store large volumes of data and to use them repetitively, that its internal operations are fast but input is slow, that it can take over logical decisions, that its output can be reduced from complete lists to a selective print-out of items requiring human attention and triggering human actions, and that the application of computers should move from the trivial isolated accounting, invoicing, statistics etc. to complex mechanization of clerical work, and finally to planning, scheduling and management support. Much time was needed before these principles were generally accepted. Similarly, in the following chapters we shall have many an opportunity to show how the use of a word processor, a personal computer, graphical display, electronic mail, computer conferencing, and the other new techniques, requires a profound change in the methods, habits and style of work.

The modern technical means make it possible to use methods that earlier were either unknown or prohibitive. In other cases they revive old methods that had been abandoned and forgotten, sometimes for decades. They make these feasible and advantageous again, usually in changed and improved forms. We could speak of a *spiral of development*: techniques and methods are surpassed by the development, and are seemingly forgotten. With the advent of new technical means they reappear in an improved form. The spiral returns to its starting point, but at a higher level. Again, in the following chapters we shall find concrete cases, e.g. in the field of document classification and indexing, graphical methods etc.

Another significant difference between manual and mechanized operations follows from the fact that, in the former case, all operations are performed by man; they are under his *control*. Any irregularity, exception or error is visible and can be corrected by man during the process. In contrast, an automated process consists of long strings of operations automatically performed by the machine according to a program; any error or exception remains invisible to man, and it could trigger a chain of wrong actions and decisions, and perhaps end in disaster. The processing has to be protected by inserted checks and screenings of both the input data and interim results in a form not known and not needed in manual processing.

In a text typed on a typewriter no typist would underline, by mistake, a whole paragraph instead of just its heading, and no typesetter would set a whole page in the large letters used for the chapter titles. In automatic typesetting, an omission of a mark 'end of underlining' or 'begin small letters' would cause the machine to underline a whole page or to print it out in the very large letters used only in the chapter headings. A wrong instruction controlling the letter size of a telephone directory in a large German town a few years ago caused the whole edition of a telephone directory to be set in smaller letters than intended, and a million users had to struggle with addresses and numbers that were scarcely legible.

Automatic equipment, in particular the computer, is fast, precise and highly reliable. Unfortunately, it does not have the intelligence and background knowledge of man, nor his ability to think, decide, associate or improvise. This fact is often forgotten by the designers of computerized systems, as well as by their users. This is another symptom of anthropomorphization.

Fortunately, the development of modern technical means is characterized by higher and higher *intelligence* embodied in their programs. Only a few years ago, mechanization required perfect formalization of input data and processing. While input interpreted by man allowed a wide degree of flexibility and some lack of formalization, the input data for a computer had to be filled in according to quite exact rules and standards. Any deviation - even in punctuation, orthography or abbreviating - was not tolerated and such data caused an error in processing. At present, the automated procedures are becoming more flexible and user-friendly.

A modern user-friendly data processing or information system is able to accept data in less strictly standardized form; the user is free to fill in input data elements in various forms, spellings, punctuation, abbreviations etc. The computer formalizes them automatically into the standard versions, screens them for validity, and only in cases of doubt does it ask the user to correct or specify the input (fig. 14.3). The system helps the user in all further steps of processing: it prompts for actions, displays a 'menu' of potential choices, informs the user about the progress of work; it displays warnings and gives recommendations, comments or explanation if the user asks them or if he apparently needs help [ref. 10-Shneiderman, Smith, Stibic].

At the moment, only a few information systems can be called user-friendly in all respects. Development over the next few years will undoubtedly bring about a significant improvement.

15 - Tools support intellectual activity

Technical means, firstly, improve performance. They allow us to do old things faster and more efficiently. They save time - particularly in trivial activities - and leave more time over for more challenging activities. Secondly, the advanced technical means make it possible to use methods that earlier were unknown, technically impossible or economically prohibitive. They improve the methods and style of work and, directly or indirectly, stimulate and support creative activities of man.

Tools save time - old things are done more efficiently

It is not necessary to explain that technical means improve efficiency - in the following chapters we mention factor 10 to 80 improvements in speed of calculation by means of a pocket calculator in comparison with computing without technical means, or performance improvement of dictating, 1:3, by means of a dictating machine compared with drafting in longhand. Time spent on re-typing texts is saved by a word processor, the performance of computers and graphical displays is incomparably higher than of any traditional technique, etc.

The plain fact that technical means save time and disburden man from various chores that would consume his time and energy is an indirect contribution towards improving human creativity. Indeed, unimportant chores, administrative work, and daily tasks often take priority over serious creative work.

It is crazy, but it is true: we *must* write a quarterly report, we *must* answer a letter even though unimportant, we have to accept telephone calls, solve administrative problems, or attend a departmental meeting - not only have we to do all these activities, but many of them must be done on a certain day, at a given hour and minute. They cannot be delayed. On the other hand, reading, studying, thinking, contemplation, evaluation, thoughtful discussions and productive brainstormings are not subject to a rigid plan or schedule; they can and usually must wait. Hundreds of trivial chores have to be given priority, creative work can only be done if time remains. We all recall Parkinson's law [ref. 10]: the time devoted to problems is in inverse proportion to their importance !

It is difficult to combat this plague of small, trivial activities. *Delegation* of tasks may help to some extent. A radical solution, occasionally preferred by many a professional, is to leave his office for some time and to solve a special task in the *isolation* of his home (if it helps) or in a quiet resort away from both home and the office; communication should be made as difficult as possible. Another solution, chosen in some research institutes, is the method of '*block-time*', i.e. setting aside a part of the day as a time when no telephone calls, visits or other contacts are allowed. A nice solution, but not one that is always possible. The technical means can help, at least partly: they help us to master our many chores more efficiently, some of them even automatically. Some of the new means can help us to redistribute work time. We are thinking here primarily of electronic mail, which can gather incoming messages without causing repeated interruptions, and makes it possible to answer them at a suitable moment. This prevents the working day being interrupted by telephone calls - if not fully, then at least to some extent. Saving time on trivial jobs means more time for creative work.

Technical tools improve methods - new things can be done

The influence of techniques on methods has been explained in the preceding section. New technical means make it possible to employ methods that have been unknown, impossible or prohibitive earlier.

Think of the many methods that appeared after the advent of computers: the Critical Path Method of planning and scheduling; the KWIC index; the online retrieval; automatic indexing of documents and the free text search; interactive graphical display; computer conferencing; paperless publishing etc. Many of these are in common use, some are at the very beginning of their existence. We have also mentioned above the reviving of some methods that, though known for decades, could not find wide acceptance, as they are too arduous when done manually. New technical means bring about their renaissance, often in modernized form - think of some excellent graphical methods that were rather difficult in the time of paper-and-pencil methods but are easy with the help of a graphical display. The warning against using new means as surrogates of the old techniques has been mentioned above, and it will be repeated time and again in what follows.

Technical means support problem-solution and decision-making

In many situations the solution of a problem can be found following a number of logical steps of the type 'if... then... otherwise... provided... etc.'. A complicated problem can then be split into a larger number of simpler decisions leading step by step to the solution. In such a case, the logical thinking can be supported by simple devices such as *flow-charts* or *decision tables* (see section 75). When the algorithm of a logical or numerical problem has been defined, and the input data can be formalized, then a problem can be solved by a computer: the intellectual work, once stored in a program, can then be performed repetitively in a mechanical way.

Medical diagnosis - in the past based only on the knowledge and experience of the physician - can now be obtained by means of a computer program (representing concentrated knowledge and experience formalized in a large number of rules) that accepts the data on the symptoms and biomedical measured data as input, and prints out the name(s) of the most probable disease(s) as output. Similarly, a managerial decision on whether to concentrate or decentralize warehouses supplying a network of stores in a certain territory can be solved by employing the methods of operations research quite objectively. In both cases, the computer can either find an optimum solution, or merely make a suggestion (a list of diseases in descending order of their probability, several suboptimal solutions to the storage problem) from which man choses one, evaluating also some imponderable factors and criteria.

Sometimes, a complicated problem has to be solved or a decision taken, when the input data are known merely with some degree of probability - this is a common feature in solving military or business strategic problems. In these situations also the methods of *operations research* can be employed and the best solution can be found by means of a computer.

As early as the beginning of the 19th century some far-sighted men had been aware of the fact that finding a solution in a complicated situation when a great number of factors have to be taken into consideration, and most of them can be only estimated with some degree of probability, could be based on computation. Carl von Clausewitz in his classical work 'Vom Kriege' (1832) mentions that the decisions of a commander in chief, based on a large number of factors, could be solved by means of mathematical methods. He also cites Napoleon's words 'many of the questions about which a general has to make a decision would raise problems of mathematical calculation not unworthy of the power of Newton or Euler' [ref. 10-Clausewitz, Rapoport p. 157].

Furthermore, the computer is able to find a solution in situations where the algorithm leading to a solution in a number of logical steps is unknown. The enormous performance of computers enables a large number of trials to be automatically generated by randomly varying the input data or conditions; each of the variants is evaluated, and if there is a criterion of success or failure, then the best variant found is presented by the computer as a suboptimal solution. This is the principle of the simulation by *Monte-Carlo method* making it possible to find a solution by 'organized chance'.

In simpler situations, the conditions and input data can be modified and varied manually in a *trial-and-error* style. Again, it is the task of the intellect, reasoning and evaluation of man to consider possible variants, to reject or accept any of them, to vary the conditions further, and finally to come to an acceptable solution. The computer does not replace the human intellect, nonetheless it is an excellent instrument for supporting it.

Support of creativity and inventiveness

Conceiving new ideas, finding new solutions, creating original products of any kind, inventing and discovering are the highest activities of man. They cannot (yet) be taken over by a machine, though some significant results (musical composition, graphical design) have been achieved, and research in the field of *artificial intelligence* promises further progress. At present, technical means can help indirectly. They can support creative activity by gathering, organizing, pre-processing, analyzing and by visualization of information, thus improving our insight and making the human mind fertile to original conclusions and ideas.

Creative activity has not yet been fully analyzed and explained scientifically. Its mechanism remains to a large extent undiscovered. It is known that the moment of creativity often comes unexpectedly, sometimes in rare situations or triggered by an incidental event, but that it nearly always happens in a prepared mind (Pasteur: 'The chance prefers a prepared mind'), when information has been accumulated, a problem has been stated, when the originator has, in the past, tried to solve it time and again without results, considering various points of view, combining the known factors and trying many possible ways to find a solution. In an unexpected moment, a solution might be clearly seen by the human mind as a product of the brain's unknown power to combine facts subconsciously and to recognize a correct solution. Koestler in his fine book 'The Act of Creation' [ref. 10] speaks about subconscious comparison of two matrices of concepts that match at a given moment, giving in one position the searched (sometimes unsearched, unexpected) solution.

Examples cited in the literature are usually based on famous stories about great historical inventions and discoveries (the 'eureka' of Archimedes in his bath, Newton's falling apple, James Watt's pot lid, the sudden solution to a complicated mathematical problem occurring to Poincaré at the very moment when he was stepping into a bus etc.); however, the same marvellous process that ends with the flash of an idea at the most unexpected moment and triggered by quite trivial events occurs everyday on less momentous occasions: a designer trying to solve a technical problem, a systems analyst striving to find an elegant and most economic solution to a non-conventional data processing problem, rarely arrive at a solution in a number of logical steps. They define their problem, combine various facts, try to find a clue, consider many variants, feel their way with uncertainty and, after some 'incubation period', the solution is visible in a second. *Probatum est.*

In such a subconscious process, technical means cannot help directly. Nonetheless, they can create advantageous conditions for the 'moment of creation', helping to initiate the unknown process in the dark space of the human brain. Gathering isolated pieces of information, sorting and organizing them into a transparent form, graphical presentation of logical structures and quantitative relations, factor analysis, modelling and simulating, experiments in the trial-and-error mode, are all activities that improve our insight into a problem, stimulate ideas, help us to draw conclusions and trigger associations which ultimately lead to discoveries, inventions and other creative acts.

Let us imagine Mendelejev trying to find a law in the diversity and affinity of chemical elements known at the time: he noted the elements on small pieces of paper, and by shifting and re-arranging them according to chemical and physical properties of the elements was able to see - after trials and errors - his periodical system of the chemical elements. Similarly, plotting sets of data and comparing curves can reveal much more than the plain reading of columns of numbers. The mechanical sorting and repeated re-arranging of data on the blood coagulation of hundreds of patients brought Dr. Janský to the conclusion that there are only four blood groups, known today as A, B, AB and O. Sorting historical data by means of computerized indexes and arranging them by time, place, person or event, is a quite mechanical procedure, yet it might trigger the flash of a new idea, the discovery of relationships hitherto concealed.

Mechanical sorting, graphical presentation, computerized correlation analysis, simulation and experimenting - to name only the basic methods - are ways in which the technical means support the human brain and improve the chance of the flash of a new idea occurring. In the last few years, sophisticated methods have appeared that are capable of doing much more than simply sorting, arranging, modelling or visualizing information. The computer is able to analyze large volumes of data and to draw conclusions in a way that resembles human generalization and inductive thinking, i.e. it formulates common rules and laws based on accumulated, organized and evaluated experience

Prof. Slamecka describes [ref. 10] his MARIS system of knowledge organization in the field of medicine which makes it possible to analyze and evaluate information accumulated from a large number of individual anamneses. The system comes to generalized conclusions and is able to answer questions such as 'What are the probable complications after a certain type of operation on a certain type of patient?', or 'How would this case probably be treated by a certain surgical team in a certain hospital?'.

Solving complicated problems through methods of operations research and other sophisticated computerized calculations is outside the limited sphere of personal computing and outside the scope of this book. Nevertheless, simpler tasks of this type can be solved also by personal computers.

16 - Use and misuse of tools

It is no rare exception for advanced techniques to be misunderstood and misused by their users. The correct application of advanced techniques has always to be learnt, including their special features, change of methods and habits. The extremely fast developments of the last few years are increasing this danger. Changes in technology come too rapidly, they require too far-reaching adaptations in methods and style of work, the possibilities are too varied, the presentation of new products by manufacturers and dealers is persuasive, and practical experience is limited.

Inadequate use of tools

A widespread fault is to use technical means for too limited purposes: employing a multifunctional technical device merely for a few simple operations, usually only for those that had been performed by traditional techniques, although the new device is able to perform more.

Too many people have pocket calculators with many functions but use only the four trivial arithmetic operations, and even ignore the advantageous multiplication or division by a constant factor. Word processors, as mentioned in chapter 5, are generally considered to be typewriters that enable corrections to be made more easily. Many a personal computer is used only for a few tasks whereas it could serve its owner in many other jobs.

One of the basic rules for the rational employment of technical means is: analyze your real needs for technical help and try to find means that can best support you. Investigate all the functions that a new tool offers, evaluate objectively which of them might be useful in your case (either immediately or later); do not ask new tools to do only what you have been in the habit of doing with older equipment (even a pocket calculator offers many excellent functions that were never employed in the past because they were too arduous - think of the linear interpolation of curves mentioned in chapters 6 and 7 etc.); do not hesitate to learn and make practical use of the new features.

Use of advanced technical means for small, isolated jobs

Integration of applications (see section 13, and specific examples in the subsequent chapters) is an important method of increasing the effectiveness of personal applications of word processors, personal computers and terminals.

In specialist journals, advertisements and commercial literature, we often find announcements about programs for personal use (personal planning, diary-keeping, accounting, documention etc.). Many of them are written by hobbyists; the programs might be elegant and witty, but many of them obviously originated in a concrete situation as ad hoc solutions to a specific problem; they are inflexible, unadaptable and usable only as small, isolated and incompatible units. Each of these programs has its own data structure, its own command set, its own input and output formats. All in all, such a conglomerate of programs from various sources cannot improve one's personal work technique, and can only increase confusion without contributing any positive effect.

Use of inadequate tools

It is a mistake to use complex tools for primitive jobs. The opposite mistake is to try to use inadequate means for tasks to which they cannot bring the required performance and quality. Advertisements and publications often encourage exaggerated expectations resulting in machines with insufficient parameters, being used for too pretentious jobs. This particularly concerns the personal computers in the lower price classes.

In the following chapters, we mention a number of cases in which a personal computer is unable to do the job properly. In chapter 3, we warn of network-planning programs that only allow (due to the small memory capacity of a cheap computer) a limited number of nodes and activities, so that such a program is scarcely of any practical use - a small problem can be solved without a computer, while a larger problem is not processable due to hardware limits. A miniaturized 'retrieval system' exists that is capable of accepting no more than 180 very short abstracts with a limited number of keywords, and that takes - even if the inquiry consists of only three terms - 3½ minutes to search one hundred records; another system is realized on a microcomputer able to store 20 (twenty) documentation records on one floppy disk. Such systems are in fact advertised, published and demonstrated; they are practically useless. Chapter 5 discusses poor word processing systems on cheap (sometimes not so very cheap) personal computers that are able to store only short documents, that in addition to other insufficiencies cannot find a two-word compound if its components occur in two consecutive lines, etc. Again, the respective personal computer is offered as a machine capable of word processing - true, but many a user is later disappointed.

Hobbyistic approach to personal computing

Computer development in the fifties and sixties was an evolution 'from big to small' with regard both to hardware and applications. The large computers used in large scientific and business applications were followed by smaller and cheaper machines capable of mechanizing smaller tasks in smaller organizations. Because of this historical development, the approach to systems analysis and programming was professional: a methodology was developed and strict formal rules were respected in all phases of work; software development was planned and coor-

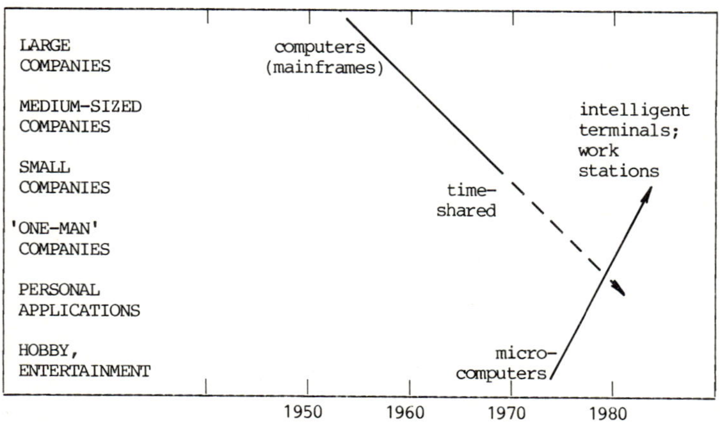

Fig. 16.1 - 'From large to small' and 'from small to large'

During the fifties and sixties, the computers developed from the large systems and applications to smaller ones. The development of microcomputers went in the reverse direction: from the smallest and simplest hobby computers, to modest personal computers and to larger configurations. Similarly, the applications shifted from hobby and entertainment to more practical and more intricate tasks.

dinated. The advent of personal computers followed a reverse trend: it went *'from small to large'* - from primitive hobby computers, limited in performance, memory capacity, peripherals and software, to larger personal computers of improved performance, with larger internal and external memories, extended peripherals, programming facilities in higher-level languages, and utility and application programs (fig. 16.1).

History again influences the style of use: The hobbyistic background can be felt in many directions: software for personal computers is growing over an immensely wide terrain, it is being created mainly by many thousands of hobbyists, without planning and coordination, stimulated by personal initiative, curiosity, desire to play and experiment, and enthusiasm. These, although undoubtedly positive, aspects are mostly associated with a lack of background knowledge, an amateurish approach to applications, a lack of feeling for practical usefulness, and a tendency to small-scale, inflexible, special-purpose, ad hoc solutions. Large manufacturers of personal computers have until now mostly neglected systematic, coordinated development of software for personal use.

Never have computer manufacturers had such vast external programming capacities as today. The efforts of thousands of hobbyists and other users need only be coordinated and encouraged, for instance in the form of competitions: prizes could be awarded for the best solutions for a certain program or program module to meet given specifications, i.e. able to form a compatible part of a system. Architects have been accustomed to such an approach for many years.

Lavish use of technical means

Cheap and easily available sources of material, energy or service tend to be used lavishly. This is also true of the use of technical means. If they offer cheap, fast and easy operations, then they are called upon unstintingly.

Sometimes, the difference between personally written and dictated letters is striking: the latter are more eloquent as it is easier to speak than to write. Easy and cheap copying results in an unreasonable number of copies being made and distributed to a much larger number of addressees than necessary. Similarly, the enormous capacity of a computer line-printer is often misused for producing printed output in immense quantities, thereby increasing the problems of information pollution.

This danger cannot be underestimated in connection with the advent of new technical means for a professional. For example, electronic mail will bring about many advantages, but the ease of sending a message or, moreover, of distributing it to many receivers simultaneously by pushing a button, might cause a further source of information pollution.

A deluge of electronic messages coming from all sides is a terrifying vision: the 'electronic box' of tomorrow not only will contain hot news, announcements, regulations, directives, memos, communications and other messages from the company management and many departments, messages and inquiries from peers and colleagues, SDI information from various sources, but might also include a spate of individually addressed commercial advertisements and individualized offers of all kinds. Shall we be forced to build into our electronic mail system of the future an information filter or 'information killer' that automatically deletes information of a certain type or coming from certain senders, doing the same job automatically that we do now when we sort out and throw away certain publications, leaflets and advertisements without reading them ?

Vulgarization of technique: frivolous use of intelligent machines

There is a real danger that advanced technical means will be misused for trivial applications. Personal computers, word processors, viewdata and many other inventions of the recent years offer many possible uses: these differ in aim, complexity, ease of introduction, but also in attractiveness. Of course, there are many users who immediately grasp the unique chance that the new means offer, and who are able to use them intelligently and rationally from the first moment. Being aware of the prospects, they see these means as an excellent help in their work, they develop their application step for step towards a complex system of personal administration, knowledge organization and information management, personal computing, text processing or education. A large number of personal computers are now employed for the data processing in the smallest, or even one-man, companies.

On the other hand, there is a wide class of trivial applications for the new technical means that are enormously seductive to a large population of users. For example, the personal computer, has resulted in an enormous popularity of *computer games.* No doubt, in principle, these are harmless and have certain positive functions as a means of teaching beginners and children how to approach a computer. Many of the games train manual dexterity, speed of perception and reaction, and logical thinking. However, some facts must not be ignored: firstly, when a personal computer is treated as a black-box, then playing a game has no educational value in the field of computers in the same way as watching television does not improve our knowledge of television technology; secondly, a new, time-consuming element has been created that might improve, but is more inclined to degrade the way in which the free time is used. According to an absorbing cover story in the Time magazine by J. Skow [ref. 10], in 1981 about $ 5 . 10^9$ and about 75000 man-years were spent by the 'video-game addicts' playing the machines installed in the arcades.

Compared with the royal game of chess with its strict logical rules of classical beauty, some computer games are nothing better than low-taste amusement. A typical example is the amazingly large and ever-increasing number of war games in which intellectual exercise is replaced by cheap optical and acoustic effects, and simulated killing is the final goal. What of the advertised computer-simulated battle between the commando of American sergeant Buck Paddoka and Feldwebel Kurt Reich and his squad of German infantrymen, fighting with rifles, grenades, bayonets and bazookas in the ruins of a French town? Indeed, the example is far from unique.

It is striking that at the top of the lists of applications of viewdata we find *jokes, games* and *puzzles* - another symptom of the intensive use of this marvellous new instrument for rather trivial applications.

Surprisingly, it is by no means only young people who are crazy about computer games: In the journal Byte [vol. 6, no 3, p. 246] a short paragraph states that Federal auditors had found 456 non-authorized files (including several hundred games, jokes etc.) created by the 200 employees of the Nuclear Weapons Research Center in Albuquerque, using the facilities of their terminals for personal purposes. It is no rare exception to encounter similar misuse of these tools on a surprise visit to offices equipped with personal computers.

Symptoms of the degradation of new techniques are striking. We fully agree with Toffler [ref. 10], who enthusiastically writes about the possibilities of a new style of work in the microelectronic age. The new devices might essentially improve our work and life style. Indeed, they *might.* Within a few years, they will deploy all their power and ability to free us from arduous chores, to give us more time for thinking and contemplation, for informal contacts and exchanging of information; they will be able to pre-process data for human decision-making and even take over some types of decisions; they can model difficult situations and help to find optimal solutions; they can improve insight into a subject, select and present information from vast resources of knowledge, store and organize acquired pieces of information and become our personal systems for organization of knowledge; they can essentially improve our methods of learning; they can enable us to work at home and at a freely chosen time, to communicate over a distance and in many forms. Yes, the technical means are able to do this all. The question is: shall the majority of users be able, willing and interested to make use of all these fascinating opportunities ? The danger that they shall not is by no means hypothetical. As Weizenbaum [ref. 10] and others point out, there are eminent technical devices that in the past had a similar chance to become important tools to improve national culture, education, information and intelligent entertainment - but they have fallen short in their missions.

Radio stations are broadcasting music that is devasting the musical taste of millions; those few stations broadcasting mainly classical music, such as BBC 3 or Hilversum 4, are cultural oases, and - according to statistics - they are not the most popular stations. *Television,* technically perfect in image and sound, could also be able to bring culture, education, objective information and good entertainment into every home, but it has not come up to expectation. In countries where it is a commercial enterprise, it has become a university of violence, crime and bad taste. In totalitarian countries, it is a medium of disinformation and political propaganda. Merely in democratic countries with high cultural traditions where television has remained under government control (such as in West Germany) has it retained high standards, but it still has to make concessions to the taste of the mass viewer. According to a Belgian television expert, *cable television* reduces the cultural influence of television: experience shows that light entertainment is generally preferred, and there is then always an opportunity of finding such a programme in a large number of channels; they distract attention from the higher-value programmes being transmitted simultaneously. *Video-recording* offers a unique opportunity to own the best films, television programmes, or educational materials. Instead, we hear of alarming experiences in Sweden, where the video-recording market has grown faster than in other European countries: the prevailing customers are teenagers and the recordings mostly bought are films about violence, cruelty, crime and pornography that would never pass the most tolerant censorship of a public television.

It may happen that the perfect technical means and excellent information networks of the future will be degraded to instruments for answering trivial inquiries (news, weather, sport...), advertising, electronic shopping and banking, games, puzzles and quizzes, and that only a minority will appreciate them as tools for improving work style and promoting the quality of life.

2 - THE WORKPLACE

The *workplace* has a significant influence - either positive or negative - on the effectiveness of intellectual work. A quiet, well-lit and air-conditioned, adequately spacious room, equipped with all the necessary tools, all within easy reach, helps to make work smooth and efficient.

The work environment differs, of course, substantially from person to person. It depends on the profession, function, field of interest and even on the individual style of work and personal taste. Everybody has to design his own workplace according to his specific requirements and within given constraints that may be either local (often, we have to work in the only room available) or financial. In what follows we do not describe the organization of such special work environments as the workplaces of professionals in laboratories, observatories, hospitals etc.; only occasionally do we comment on the use of some special technical means (such as dictating equipment) outside the traditional workplace characterized by a writing desk and its surroundings.

21 - The work room

We need not emphasize that the *work room* of a professional should be quiet. The *noise level* should not exceed about 45 dB (compare: a whisper, 30 dB; soft music, about 40 dB; the human voice, 60 dB). Above this threshold noise has a negative influence on intellectual work, while simple mechanical work begins to be disturbed at about 70 dB. It is well known that continuous noise (the hum of many voices and machines in an acoustically well-designed open-plan office or 'office landscape', the steady and rhythmical noise of machines or street traffic) is less disturbing than irregular, unexpected and distinct noise of the same intensity (a conversation, ringing of telephones in a small room). Consequently, a semi-partitioned area in a large open-plan office (or 'office landscape') might be more agreeable than a joint workplace for two or more persons in a smaller room.

Many people like *background music* when working. It can stimulate and sometimes can also create an acoustic barrier against disturbing noise. The right sort of music must be carefully chosen, otherwise it will add a new source of distraction. Non-stop, rhythmical music without abrupt changes of intensity or rhythm, without singing, is the most acceptable to most persons; evergreens or light classics are generally preferred.

In the USA some radio stations broadcast good non-stop background music interrupted only twice an hour for two or three minutes by short news bulletins and advertisements. In Europe, radio is no good as a sort of background music: music is continuously interrupted by announcements and chat, and the majority of sounds diffused could scarcely be called music. We have then to use our tape recorder as a source of background music to stimulate but not to disturb.

The work room should also be isolated from *optical disturbances* - for example, there should be no traffic in the field of vision of the worker. Low walls in an open-plan office isolate not only against acoustic but also against visual distraction. A separate room, well protected from both acoustic and optical disturbances, is the solution preferred by most professionals. The *dimensions* of a work room are limited only by personal requirements (and status) of the professional, and by local constraints. Large companies and organizations usually set down their own standards for employees in different functions.

The *illumination* of a workplace is an important factor. The work room should be light but protected from direct sunshine either by its orientation or by sunblinds or awnings. Natural light should never come from behind or from the right-hand side (or from the left-hand side if one is left-handed). Permanent focussing of the eye over a distance of 30-40 cm, typical of desk-work, is tiring for the eyes. Occasional re-focussing by looking for a moment over a longer distance is a physiologically motivated compensation. The outlook should be as close as possible to the normal field of sight so that it is only necessary to lift the eyes. A window situated less than 90° from the normal viewing direction - provided it is not dazzling - is the best solution except for workplaces at display screens: the screen must never be situated with a window as a backgroung, as the light contrast would be too great. On the other hand, the screen should never be placed with a wall immediately behind it.

Artificial light must have sufficient intensity: for the general illumination of a normal office, about 500 lux, for drawing offices and for office landscape about 1000 lux are recommended. Many persons dislike general illumination of the whole work room and prefer local illumination of the workplace only; it helps work concentration and makes the milieu more intimate and pleasant. In this case the general illumination is either switched off or, better, dimmed. *Dimming* of the general illumination is necessary if we are using a display unit or a microfilm reader. The level of the general illumination should then be reduced to about a half (about 250 lux) so that the contrast between the light intensity of the screen and the environment should not exceed the admissible ratio of about 1 : 10. It is convenient if the switch or dimmer of the general illumination is situated at the workplace within arm's reach.

Lack of light at the workplace is rarely encountered, but often the light sources are badly situated so that they radiate light in the wrong directions. Some parts of the workplace are thus overlit and others underlit, or unpleasant reflections occur. In particular, fluorescent lamps attached to the ceiling often cause reflections on horizontal surfaces (writing desks, coated paper, rulers) and keyboards. A local source of light from the left-hand side (right-hand in the case of left-handed persons) is usually the best solution. Nonetheless, designers of furniture and machines should avoid polished surfaces; in particular, the keys of the keyboard must not shine.

The *temperature* should be kept at a level personally accepted as agreeable - the standard values for offices are about 20°C. According to FEA (US Federal Energy Administration), the thermostat in offices should be set to 20°C in the winter, and to 27°C in the summer.

The *colour of walls* should be light and soft; dark or sharp colours should be avoided. Light green or yellow are nearly always suitable. They are the colours generally recommended by psychologists for rooms where intellectual work is done. Green is generally considered to be 'cool', yellow to be 'warm'. Also a neutral light grey may be used. If we work with a terminal or microfiche reader, we prefer rather darker (but not too dark) tints, in particular in the background of the display, as the light reflected from the walls should not be too much greater than the light level of the screen.

Individual *taste* (or advice from others) can help make the workplace not only functional, but also more cosy: a good painting or piece of sculpture, flowers or photographs can change an impersonal, strictly functional work room into a pleasant and stimulating working environment and give the workplace the personal touch.

22 - The work space

By the term *work space* we mean here the smaller part of the work room where a professional does most of his work and the area within reach of his arms. Even though he occasionally or quite regularly works in the 'field' (think of an archeologist, geologist, botanist etc.), in a laboratory, lecture room etc., he always returns to his 'central' work place that has hitherto been represented by his *writing desk* and its surroundings. Here he reads, writes, dictates and draws, and it is from here that he communicates via his telephone or intercom. This work space has changed significantly in the last few decades, and it will change ever more in the near future. It has developed from a simple writing desk with a telephone, a few office appliances and a filing cabinet at hand, to the highly technicized workplace of today that includes a number of special devices (typewriter, dictating machine, interphone, microfiche reader, personal computer or terminal), and finally it will develop to the universal work station of the future, as we schematically show in fig. 22.1.

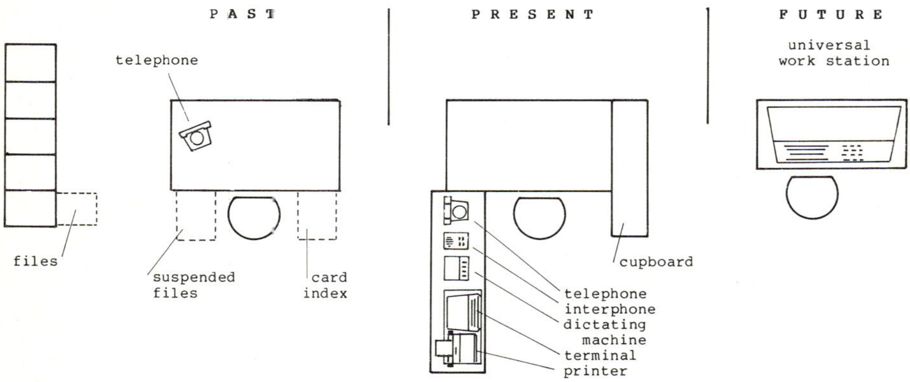

Fig. 22.1 - Scheme illustrating workplace development

The workplace of a manager or professional has developed from a simple writing desk with telephone to the highly technicized centre of today.

The basic rule for designing a functional work place is: *Keep your work space as small as possible !* The ideal is that all tools, papers, documents, communication equipment and frequently used devices are within arm's reach. Every piece of equipment must have its fixed place so that they do not have to be moved when they are needed: a microfiche reader, a typewriter, dictating machine etc. should always be on stand-by and not require troublesome and time-consuming handling. If your dictating machine is stored in a cupboard, it will never be used. Also small tools must have their fixed places so that they can be reached with a simple hand movement and without searching.

We must learn to apply the basic principles of *ergonomics.* Although this science is many decades old, has been intensely applied in the design of such specialized workplaces as cockpits, control rooms and factory workplaces, and is beginning to be employed in the design of terminals, word processors and other special office tools, it has until now been

Courtesy Bild-Archiv der Österreichischen Nationalbibliotheek, Wien

Fig. 22.2 - St. Luke at his functional reading desk

St. Luke certainly did not use the terms 'functional workplace' or 'ergonomics' yet his rotatable two-level desk was a very practical device indeed.

neglected in many of our daily work situations. In practice, we encounter in offices far too many infringements of the elementary rules of ergonomics: standing up and walking across a room time and again to fetch a document, having to move machines and equipment when they are needed, opening of heavy drawers just to find a clip or pin, etc.

There are plenty of good and less good solutions for organizing a workplace according to the principles of ergonomics. We have to find the best available to suit our own specific situation as determined by the local conditions and our own configuration of technical equipment and sources of information. Figures 22.4 to 22.6 give some suggestions.

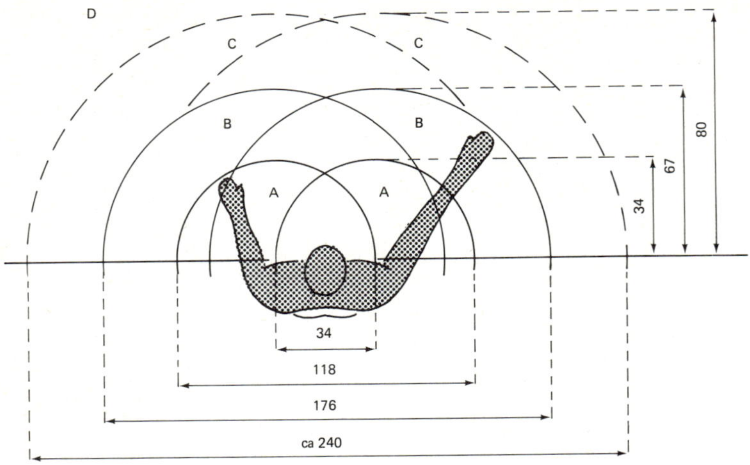

Fig. 22.3 - Work areas of a sitting man

The limits are valid for a normal man and must generally be reduced by 10 % for a female worker. They should be individually adapted; try to ascertain the boundaries of your own work areas A, B, and C. Areas A and B should contain the work-in process and very frequently used documents or devices, area C (maximum reach of hands when stretching or leaning) should contain things that are used repeatedly, but not frequently.

For example, if we situate our writing desk with its left or right side against a wall, we gain large capacity storage space within easy reach. The vertically structured *shelves* make it possible to store the many devices, office appliances, handbooks, dictionaries, directories etc. that are frequently needed, as close to us as possible. They are always visible (not hidden in drawers; no searching is needed), they are accessible in a single movement of the hand, and no heavy drawers need to be opened. Instead of installing shelves on a wall (fig. 22.4), we can situate a *bookcase* with open shelves at the side of the writing desk. Modular office furniture makes it easy (fig. 22.5, 22.6), sometimes in quite simple and cheap form.

Technical equipment must not be placed on top of a writing desk. It needs a special lower table that can best be situated at right angles to the main desk, thus creating an L-shaped working desk. The typewriter or word processor, terminal, telephone, intercom, calculator, dictation machine etc. then have their fixed places and they are on stand-by at all times (see fig. 22.1, 22.7, 26.1, 26.3).

We can also learn from the modern design of the *work cells* (figures 22.7 and 22.8) that are typical of an open-plan office. We shall certainly be

Fig. 22.4 - Example of a workplace

Author's 'compact' workplace with a word processor; frequently used documents (files, dictionaries, directories, handbooks) and small items are within arm's reach on the wall shelves; the telephone, tuner, tape recorder and dictating machine are also directly accessible. The clock, timer, alerting device and a magnetic board with selected data and reminders are within the field of vision.

Courtesy Pohlschröder Büroeinrichtungen, Dortmund, Germany

Fig. 22.5 - Modular office furniture makes it possible to build up a 'compact workplace'

The most frequently used documents are again within arm's reach. Part of the vertical surface serves as a planning and information board. Note the ideal location of the fluorescent lamp (light from the left-hand side, no shadows, no desk surface occupied) and the plug-socket.

Courtesy VOKO - Franz Vogt & Co., Giessen, Germany

Fig. 22.6 - Another example of a 'compact workplace'

able, perhaps at minimum cost, to create a well designed, ergonomically friendly work environment either in a private office or at home.

Many examples and practical suggestions can be found in the specialist journals dealing with office organization. Published projects from the best architects can give you ideas, solutions or elements to help you design your own pleasant and functional work environment. The traditional layout - a large writing desk in the centre of the work room - is the worst possible solution. It might be tolerated in the prestige offices of the top managers whose work consists mostly of communication, informal contacts and meetings, reading and signing papers, and who use technical means through the intermediary of their secretaries and assistants.

Surprisingly, even in large and well organized companies there is a lack of systematic advice and help concerning the organization of workplaces for managers and professionals. While ergonomists help to organize workplaces on an assembly line or special workplaces in the offices where simple repetitive work is performed (telephone exchanges, typing pools, word-processing centres, mail rooms...), the creative worker is left alone without any help and advice. He is given a room, a few standardized pieces of furniture, an elementary set of office appliances and he is expected to organize his workplace in a do-it-yourself manner. Sometimes he succeeds, sometimes not. A function of 'office organizer' is needed, and it would undoubtedly pay off in a short time.

It is to one's advantage to utilize the vertical surfaces in the work room such as the walls or outside surfaces of furniture, as *information boards.* Ergonomics teaches us that movement of the eyes is the most economical action. Why hide frequently used pieces of information (telephone numbers, codes, addresses, project numbers, account numbers, timetables, postal rates, organization schemes etc.) in files or drawers when we can easily have them in our field of vision ?

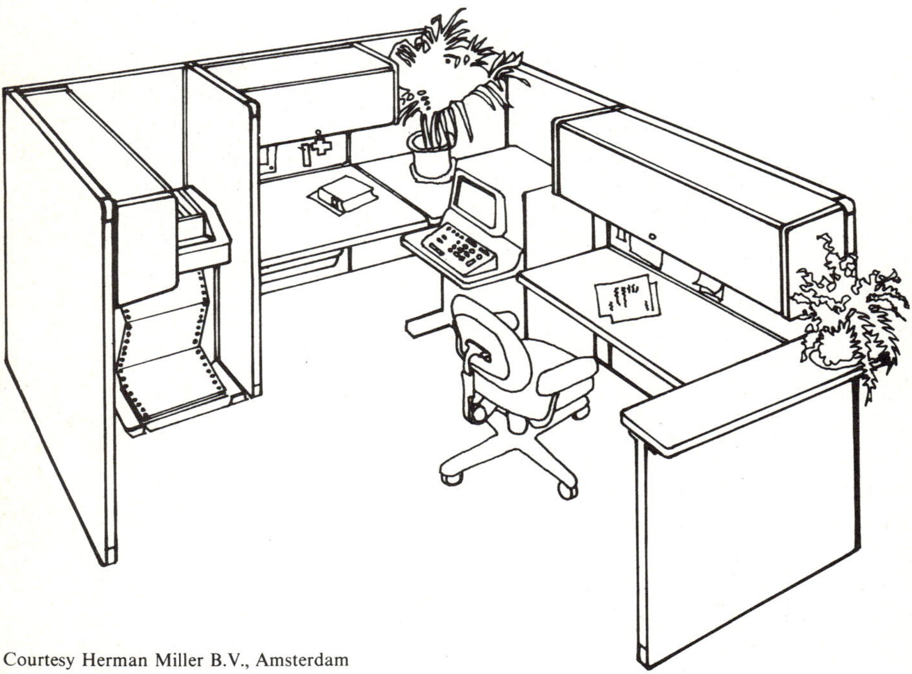

Courtesy Herman Miller B.V., Amsterdam

Fig. 22.7 - Workplace in a semi-closed form

Example of a 'work cell'. Work cells are mostly used as semi-closed units in large offices, but their design may inspire also those who design their own personal workplace.

Courtesy König & Neurath, Büromöbelsysteme, Karben b. Frankfurt/Main, Germany

Fig. 22.8 - Another examples of 'work cells'

Modular elements of office furniture (here the DELTA-2 system) can be combined in many variants. The work area is designed according to the principles of ergonomics. It is as small as possible, but all things needed are within hands' reach. Again, the valuable space above the top of the writing desk is not wasted.

Also a *blackboard* is a practical aid for quick sketches, drawings, drafts or schemes, charts and graphs. It helps to visualize ideas in graphical form. As we emphasize in chapter 7, graphical presentation makes ideas easier to comprehend ('one drawing is worth a thousand words'), secondly a graphical presentation simultaneously watched by all the participants in a discussion helps to concentrate the attention of the whole group on the point.

23 - The writing desk

Until the universal work station arrives, the *writing desk* will remain the centre of the activities of most professionals. Its design and organization influence strongly the effectiveness of work done behind it.

Technical development, which has been so fast in the field of computers, telecommunication and reproduction techniques, has hardly influenced the design of writing desks. Compare the 'old-timer' (fig. 23.1) with a typical, seemingly modern desk of today, and you must admit that although the desk of the twenties was perhaps ugly, it was certainly functional. Perfectly designed modern desks are to be found at office equipment exhibitions and in specialist journals, yet most of the desks that are encountered in offices and work rooms violate the fundamental principles of ergonomics. In fig. 23.3 we show frequent faults found in a typical writing desk.

The dimensions of an office desk according to European standards are 152 × 87 cm. Larger desks are chosen only for prestige (higher function

Courtesy Marts-Meubels, Purmerend, The Netherlands

Fig. 23.1 - A functional 'old-timer'

This desk, a descendant of the 18th-century secretaire, appeared before World War I. It became very popular in Europe under the name 'American writing desk' in the twenties and thirties. It might be considered ugly but it was very functional; from the point of pure utility, it is much better than most of the writing desks of today. It is on its way back in a somewhat modernized form (fig. 23.2), but for customers who are sentimental about the past, it has until now been produced in its original form.

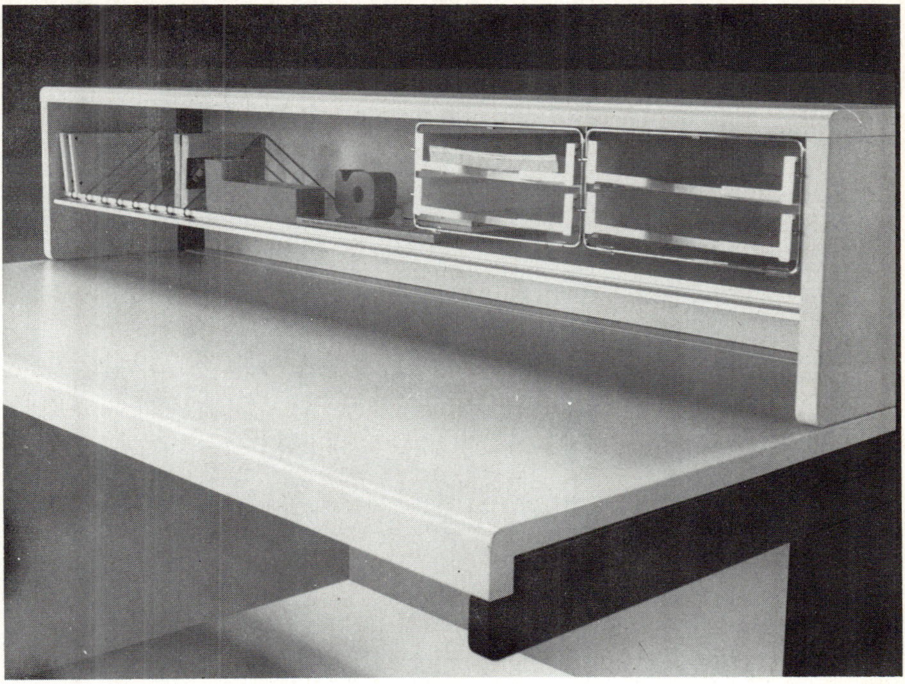

Courtesy König & Neurath, Büromöbelsysteme, Karben b. Frankfurt/Main, Germany

Fig. 23.2 - A modern version of a secretaire or 'American' desk

The space above the desk top within arm's reach is too valuable to be wasted

= larger desk = less desk work) or for special purposes. If we adhere strictly to the principle that the top of the desk should never be used for storage of piles of papers and documents and that no apparatusses, machines, lamps, trays, office appliances etc., should be placed here, then a rather smaller writing desk might be quite sufficient. The standard height of an office writing desk is 78 cm.

In the past, the personal efficiency manuals recommended fixed arrangement of papers and appliances on the top of a desk. Nowadays, the basic rule should be that ONLY the work-in-process may be placed on the desk top: no papers and no documents other than those really needed at the moment, no telephone, no lamp, no photographs, no calendar, no pen trays, no office appliances, no card index boxes, no clock. Only the IN and OUT trays may be tolerated at the corner(s) of the work place; a better solution however is to fix them above the desk top or to place them beside the desk but within arm's reach, of course.

We must admit that it requires a lot of self-discipline to stick to the principles mentioned above. All too often we encounter writing desks cluttered by piles of documents, books, scattered pieces of paper, and equipment and appliances, all in such a terrible disorder as to

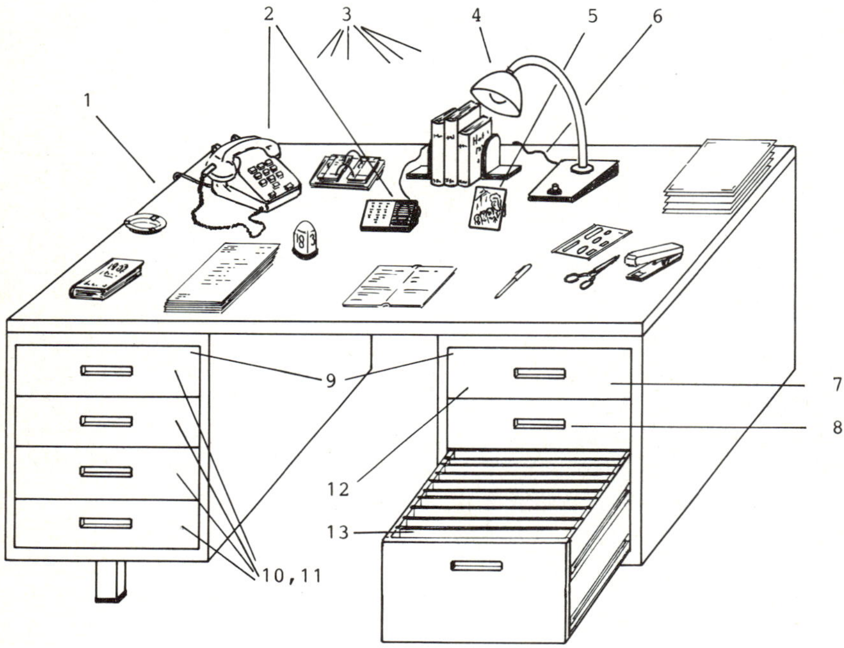

Fig. 23.3 - The inconvenience of many seemingly modern writing desks is striking

Many designers of office furniture think more of appearance than utility (as also do many architects). In our drawing, faults 1 to 5 are due to the user, 6 to 13 due to the designer.
[1] The desk in the middle of the room - there is no storage space at reach of hand
[2] Telephone, intercom and dictating machine must be placed on an auxiliary table
[3] The lack of easily accessible storage space leads to overfilling the top of the desk
[4] The lamp must not occupy a space on the desk
[5] Calendar and photographs should hang on the wall
[6] A set of plug-sockets is missing - there are too many cables between the desk and the wall
[7] Drawers are difficult to open
[8] Shallow grooves instead of sturdy handles
[9] A flat drawer for small utensiles is missing
[10] All drawers have the same height
[11] Inflexible internal division of drawers
[12] There are no special drawers for cards or microfiches
[13] Suspended folders are in wrong position.

hamper effective work. We have to exert all our will power to avoid such a situation. There is, however, one indispensable condition: we must first create other facilities for storing all our papers, documents and tools within arm's reach. We often overload our desk simply because we have no other way of keeping certain frequently needed things within reach. The solutions presented in figures 22.4 - 22.6 offer a few ideas on how to keep the desk-top clear.

The top of the writing desk should be smooth, not too hard and non-reflective. A writing mat, in common use some time ago, is not functional; it tends to be a hindrance. The drawers, if any, must be easy to move and they must have sturdy handles, not simply shallow grooves. Their inside dimensions must conform to the paper formats used (the European standard for the inside width of drawers is 33 cm). Subdivision of the inner space must be possible, and it should be easily adaptable to individual needs. One or two drawers should be shallow (depth less than about 25 mm) and subdivided into a number of small compartments for the separate storage of many sorts of small items such as pens, pencils, pins, stamps, clips, drawing appliances, if these items have not been better placed at the fingertips on the 'second floor' above the desk top as mentioned below and shown in fig. 23.1 and 23.2.

One of the drawers can act as a paper-dispenser; frequently used sorts of paper and pre-printed forms are then easily available without searching. In many writing desks, one or two large drawers are adapted for the installation of suspended files. These can be used to store a limited volume of frequently used documents. Some folders can also be preserved for storage of papers and forms in place of the above-mentioned paper dispenser.

Sometimes, we store a card index or a collection of microfiches in one of the drawers. We either use a card-index box of the appropriate dimensions that can be fitted into the drawer, or simply adapt one of the drawers by suitable partitioning. The cards must be situated parallel to the movement of the drawer (fig. 23.3).

We mentioned above the old writing desk that made it possible to store some papers and frequently used items in small compartments at the top instead of in drawers (fig. 23.1). Such a solution, making use of a 'second floor', is ergonomically ideal: we need not open and close heavy drawers time and again nor search for the many things that are frequently used; they are always immediately to hand. This old idea has been revived in modern forms. Writing desks with an additional low set of shelves and with compartments at the top are now available (fig. 23.2).; a hobbyist joiner can easily add such a 'super-structure' to his old writing table. Otherwise, we can use the space at the side of a desk, as mentioned above.

24 - The furniture

Besides the writing desk, some additional furniture is needed in every work room. First of all, a *chair*, and this is more important for efficient work than many persons think. It should be comfortable, but it should also stimulate a healthy sitting position. Its height must be adapted to individual needs. Adjustable chairs are often standard equipment in offices; in the private sphere we prefer a fixed-height chair chosen to meet our personal requirements. A rotating chair is helpful if we work with card indexes or files in the drawers, and it is indispensable at an L-shaped desk. If the wings of the L are longer, then a chair with wheels is the best solution.

A *lower table* on which the technical instruments (telephone, dictating machine, interphone, terminal etc.) are situated, is usually an extension of the writing desk. Based on European standards for typewriter and terminal tables, its height is 70 cm, its breadth may be about 50 cm or more, and its length will depend on the number and dimensions of the equipment.

Another piece of furniture that is always needed is a *cupboard* or *case* with open shelves and/or drawers for storage of books, files, documents or appliances that are less frequently needed. As mentioned above, it can be (partly) replaced by a set of shelves on the wall. Location at the side of the writing desk is the best for reasons mentioned above.

Until fully electronical storage of information arrives, a *filing cabinet* will also be needed. A large *bookcase* with our library can be situated in the neighbourhood of the work place. Its distance is not crucial, as it is only occasionally accessed, and the frequently used books are situated to hand.

Much special *office furniture* is available on the market in many types and sorts, dimensions, qualities, colours, styles and prices. Specialist journals offer many a suggestion to help you make a good choice. A better overview can be gained at office equipment exhibitions (such as the well known SICOB held every autumn in Paris, the Efficiency Beurs held every other year in Amsterdam etc.), the specialized sections of general fairs (such as the Hannover Fair); one of the world's largest exhibitions of office furniture, Orgatechnik, is regularly held in Cologne. Besides many types of furniture in modern style, there are also writing desks, cupboards and filing cabinets in classical style; some of them are handsome and also functional. Perhaps before long there will also be a Louis XIV terminal on the market.

25 - Auxiliary devices

We do not intend to describe the many small auxiliary devices and office appliances that everybody uses in his daily activities. Most of them are generally known and need not be explained; others are used only by specialists (such as the special drawing instruments of a designer or architect) who also need no instruction on how to use them. In the section on document storage we shall make a few remarks on *storage devices.* They have improved considerably in the last few years. Practical and neat tools are now available - see, by way of example, the excellent plastic document boxes (fig. 42.1) produced in many bright colours that enable us to organize our document collection better, and also to brighten our working environment.

We strongly advise not to underestimate the small appliances; they may be cheap and simple, yet they can stimulate, or hinder, our work. These small and simple devices are also improving, and new types are appearing on the market. For example, a broad assortment of adhesive stickers is available in many shapes, types, formats and colours that are excellent for correcting, signalling, lettering, numbering and many other purposes. There are magnetic signals, also in many colours, shapes and formats, that can be used in combination with a magnetic board; self-adhesive plastic tapes are cheap and effective devices for marking books, files or boxes; fluorescent markers are replacing underlining in texts by marking that is visible but not reproducible; many sorts of graph papers are available with reproducible or non-reproducible pre-print; two-layer papers make it possible to erase the upper layer and draw again on the lower one, etc.

Every professional should check his 'small' requisites and consider whether to modernize them. A visit to a large specialized office-equipment shop or brief look at the office equipment section of a large special exhibition or fair (we have mentioned them above), and attention to the advertisements in specialist journals can yield suggestions for improving your technique of work.

Technical development brings about improvements and results in new sorts of auxiliary devices, but it also causes older devices to be discarded. Modern copying machines are removing the need for traditional carbon paper, word processors are eliminating many correcting devices such as white correcting papers, correcting stickers and solutions, graphical terminals are replacing graph papers and drawing instruments. The advent of the universal work station will cause all the small devices, now indispensible on any writing desk, to disappear; there will be no pens and pencils, paper, clips, no glue and scissors, no files - even the waste paper basket will be replaced by a simple ERASE command.

26 - Secretary's workplace

The importance of the help of a secretary will not diminish with the advent of sophisticated office technology; it will probably increase. Unfortunately, due to the ever-increasing staff costs on the one hand, and the falling costs of mechanical devices on the other, the number of people who can afford a personal secretary will steadily decrease. Some of the secretary's services will be centralized (dictating via telephone to dictating machines located in typing pools etc.), and more and more managers and professionals will be supported by electronic means that they will use in a do-it-yourself manner.

The happy minority who in the future will have the support of a personal secretary will then enjoy the advantages of both personal and mechanized service: a boss will either communicate with the system directly, or simply use his secretary as an *intermediary*. There will of course be hobbyists and enthusiasts who will be eager to operate their terminals and work stations themselves - at least sometimes. We can expect however that most managers and professionals - though equipped with their own personal stations - will prefer to give short, informal (often rather vague) commands to their secretaries and let them operate the word processor, terminal or work station; only the final output would then be

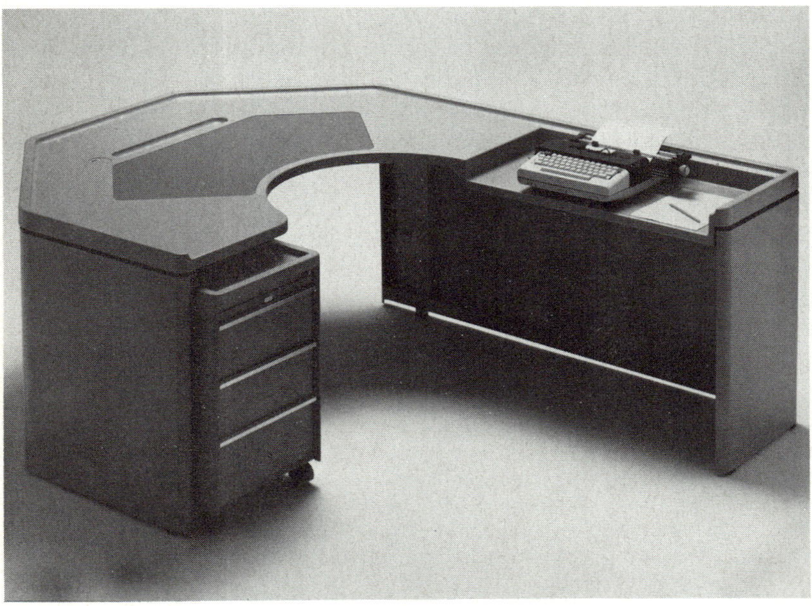

Courtesy Gispen Staalmeubel, Culemborg, The Netherlands

Fig. 26.1 - Secretary's special desk

An L-shaped desk (here a J-shaped version) consists of a higher wing for document handling, and a lower wing where typewriter, word processor, dictating equipment or other tools can be placed.

transmitted to the boss's display unit, while the most conservative will insist on a printed output.

Such a situation will not be new: from the biographies of top managers we know that they always delegated (and had to delegate) maximum activities to their subordinates. This was also the case with the use of technical means. For example, Jan Baťa, the owner of the world's largest shoe manufacturing concern, did not know how to dial a trunk-call - never in his life had he dialed a telephone call personally. General MacArthur - like marshal Joffre during World War I - had no telephone in his office, and he also rarely wore a wrist-watch: someone else could always tell him the time or alert him [ref. 20-Manchester p. 216, 446].

A typical *secretary's workplace* is characterized at the present time by a writing desk, a small typewriter-table (typically, in the well known L-shaped configuration), the traditional telecommunications equipment (telephone and intercom), dictating equipment (often missing), and a filing cabinet. This picture is beginning to change.

Courtesy TAB Products, Amsterdam

Fig. 26.2 - Secretary's workplace with a video display unit

Special furniture is designed for workplaces where alternatively traditional documents are handled, and a video display unit is employed.

The first major improvement is the advent of the word processor. Its function is extending in the last time: it becomes a teletex station allowing electronic mail to be received and sent, and it will change into a terminal able to communicate with a mainframe computer and to interrogate in-house as well as external information systems.

A universal work station of the future will be situated in the secretary's room and interconnected with a secondary station in her boss's room. This may significantly change the style of cooperation between the secretary and the boss (see also fig. 26.3).

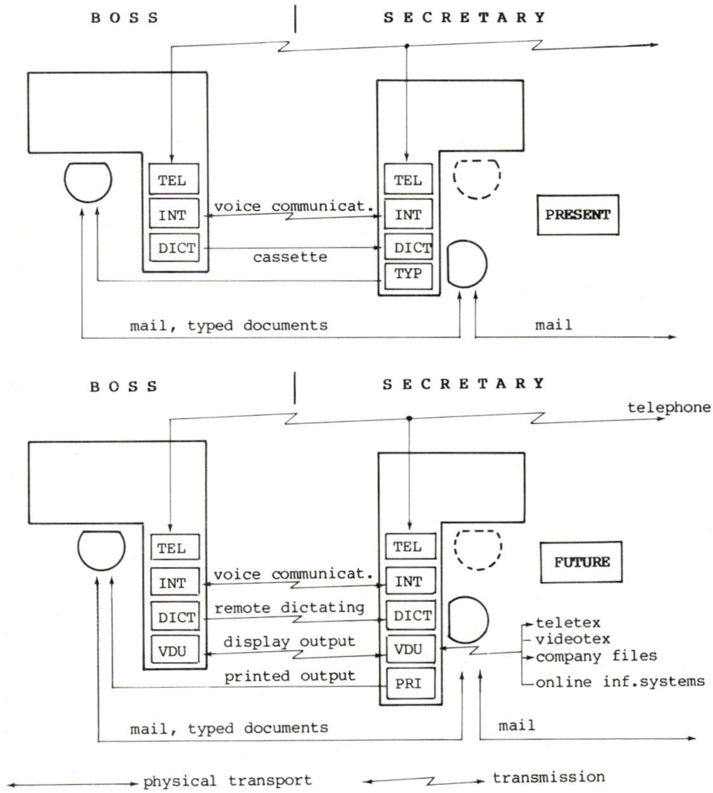

Fig. 26.3 - Communication between the boss and the secretary

Traditionally, the boss sends his longhand drafts to the secretary (the worst method), or he dictates to shorthand record (better), or he makes use of a dictating machine (best). The documents and tapes are transported physically. The future version: The boss can dictate in the traditional ways, but occasionally also via the interphone checking the typed text on his own screen. He can also use his work station for retrieval or for electronic mail in do-it-yourself mode, or he simply gives informal instructions to his secretary who operates the terminal and transmits the output on his screen, or sends him the hardcopy.

The secretary will be relieved of many simple, laborious activities (such as re-typing, correcting, searching for documents, finding addresses, repeated attempts to reach somebody by telephone etc.), but must become a highly qualified operator of complex technical means. Employing background knowledge, intelligence, initiative and skill of improvisation, the secretary will transform the informal concise commands and wishes of the boss into a set of precise instructions to a sophisticated information system. The new technical means will not down-grade secretaries, but the numbers of them will decrease.

27 - Workplace at home

In previous sections we tacitly assumed one place where the professional works - either his office in a company or other organization, or his private office. In his private sphere he is less bound by conditions, the local situation, the standards and time schedules of his employer, and he can better adapt his work environment to his own personal taste and wishes. A negative feature is that he cannot always afford expensive equipment such as special copying machines, an advanced word processor or a larger computer. Fortunately, technical developments are producing cheaper and increasingly effective tools that are now available for private use by an increasing number of persons: programmable calculators, personal computers with simple word-processing functions, cheap microfiche readers etc. are now within the reach of the average professional man, and many can afford quite sophisticated equipment. Moreover, many services are now available in online mode at reasonable prices (access to information systems, viewdata, online use of large mainframe computers via telephone line and terminal) or they can be used via special service centres (computing centres, microfilm service centres, copying centres).

Special problems occur when a professional is in the habit of working both in his office and at home. Some regularly take their work home, doing their normal work in evenings and weekends (a bad habit, indeed). Many are more selective: they take home only special types of work, for example reading and the study of special literature, reports, drafts or other texts, the preparation of lectures, writing articles and reports and other sorts of creative work requiring a high degree of concentration in an isolated, quiet environment.

The *work room*, its situation, organization and equipment must be adapted to the type of work involved. Splitting the activities between two separated locations causes many a problem. The technical equipment and files cannot be simply duplicated, so that some activities have to be done in one place only (e.g. online retrieval, copying). Before deciding on the location of the technical means and files we must first ascertain which type of work we intend to do only at the office and which we only intend to do at home, and that which can be done in both places; this helps us to decide which files, books and other information sources we need at which of the places, and what is the minimum equipment needed at home.

For example, those who are in the habit of studying and writing their special articles and reports at home, will store their special literature and private library at home, and they will also have their personal documentation at home while the administrative, commercial and other files will be kept only at the office. Information occasionally needed at the other place must then be transported or copied.

Modern techniques are making this problem of availability easier: dictating equipment makes it easy to create texts in a quiet milieu at home and have them transcribed in the office - only small cassettes need to be transported. A word processor installed at home and in the office makes it easy to transport a large volume of texts in the form of portable floppy disks (one disk contains more than 100 A4 pages); microfiche is also an ideal medium for keeping large volumes of information available in duplicate files and for storing large volumes of literature at home at minimum cost and minimum amount of space.

Also, improving communication techniques allow us more freedom in the selection of a workplace: a *terminal* at home connected via a telephone line to the mainframe computer makes large files remotely accessible. Security (if we are not working with confidential or secret files) can be adequately protected by simple means: access can be protected by an account number and a personal password, the contents can be protected against accidental tapping by a simple code, for example by a text-compressing algorithm. Sophisticated techniques (cryptographic methods) must be used if the data have also to be protected against deliberate tapping. For special categories of users, such as reporters, portable terminals with word processing functions are now available; they can be plugged in anywhere, and they transmit messages via a normal, acoustically coupled telephone.

A full-fledged *work station* of the future will eliminate most of the differences between work at the office and at home. It will allow many people to spend a considerable part of their time at home working under nearly the same conditions as if sitting in their offices.

The future prospects of *home work* are well known and have been discussed intensively. Toffler describes his vision of an 'electronic cottage' [ref. 10] in a very optimistic tone. Indeed, the prospect of working at home has many positive sides. First of all, the advantage of immense saving in the time and energy now spent on travelling between home and the office. *Information*, not the *man*, should be transported! Voice, picture, text and data communication with people, files and computers will obviate the need for personal presence. Another advantage is the chance to work in one's own milieu, and this could be quiet, attractive and stimulating.

Courtesy Philips Data Systems, Apeldoorn, The Netherlands

Fig. 27.1 - A personal computer, usable also as a terminal, makes it possible to work at home

Moreover, freedom to schedule working time according to one's own wishes and convenience is an excellent prospect for many. In contrast to these obvious advantages, there are some inevitable negative effects: for many individuals, it would be rather difficult to work without a rigid time schedule and work regime, and the home sphere could be a source of pleasure as well as distraction, frustration and interruption.

The wife, children, visits, home chores, dog and garden may be very disturbing elements. A semi-fixed *work regime* and an isolated location for the home work room might help - for example, the work room would best be situated on another floor from the living rooms. We can understand why Jules Verne worked in the tower of his house in Amiens, why Karel Čapek did his writing in the mansard room of his cottage, or why Joachim Fest, when writing his huge critical biography of Hitler, decided not to work at home but to rent, for a time, a small flat that enabled him to work in isolation.

Much more dangerous is the lack of personal contact with colleagues, peers, superiors and subordinates that is being replaced by impersonal electronic mail and computer conferencing. This could cause severe dehumanization and desocialization. Serious thought must be given to overcoming these dangers, for example by preserving some hours or days for traditional personal contacts and by thorough planning and organizing of informal meetings, brainstorming sessions, and social events.

3 - PERSONAL PLANNING AND ACCOUNTING

Technical means available for planning, scheduling, recording of daily events, accounting and evaluation of activities range from the simplest and cheapest, for instance a plain diary or notebook, to the more advanced techniques of planning board or appointment card-index, and finally to online planning and accounting by means of a terminal or a personal computer. Though the computerized methods are attractive, they are not available to everybody at the moment; fortunately, some simpler devices render competent service, and they even have the advantage of being portable.

31 - Planning

Paradoxically, we tend to concentrate our attention on the trivial daily chores and actions, and too often forget to think of the more important long-term actions. Hundreds of small things that must be done immediately consume our time and energy, and little remains to give attention to more distant tasks; deliberation about long-term tasks and actions, a clear definition of them, and statements of long-term goals are often delayed, sometimes *ad infinitum.* Of course, we are considering here merely *personal planning*; if the same person formulates and executes the plan, then a written goal definition and plan would not seem to be necessary. This is not true: it pays to think clearly about the goals, means, steps and terms, and to record the result in written form. It helps us to clarify our thoughts, it gives us a steady line for future actions, and it makes it possible later to compare the achieved results with the original goals.

Many a time, individuals or teams starting long-term activities will feel it pointless writing down their intentions and final goals. Everything seems to be clear and the planner knows (or thinks he knows) what the job is and what the goal is. During the following weeks, months or years, as the work progresses, as new information arrives and experience is gained, the aim changes slowly and imperceptibly, and the original idea becomes hazy. Undoubtedly, it would

```
      Task parameter
         Targets (from 1971) - the system should :
           HARPY system (1976) - the system did :

(1)   What sort of speech ?
         accept connected speech
           accept connected speech
(2)   How many speakers ?
         from many
           from five
(3)   What sort of speakers ?
         cooperative speakers of the general American dialect
           cooperative general American speakers
(4)   What sort of auditory environment ?
          in a quiet room
           in a computer terminal room
(5)   Over what sort of communication system ?
         over a good quality microphone
           over an ordinary microphone
(6)   How much training of the system ?
         allowing slight tuning of the system per speaker
           after substantial tuning of the system
(7)   How much training of the users ?

(19)  When should the system be operational ?
         demonstratable in 1976 with a moderate chance of success
           operational 13 August 1976
```

Fig. 31.1 - Long-term strategic targets and actual achievements

If you make a long-term plan, you should define your targets in the written form of a 'charter'. The goals are recorded, and can be compared with achievements. Here is an example of a list of targets and achievements of the HARPY speach recognition project [ref. 30-Medress].

1 9 8 2

activity	JAN	FEB	MAR
Textbook PC			
gathering of material	=======		
synopsis	===		
first draft	==	==============	
case studies		======	====
second draft			========
final editing			
ABC project			
feasibility study	==		=====
UNISER conference		X	
Lectures for THM			
preparation		=======	
slides		==	==
lectures			XX XX

Fig. 31.2 - Example of personal long-term planning in graphical form

Simple planning of activities in tabular or graphical form; a planning board makes it easy to adapt and signal the actual state of the work. A graphical display might also be used, but for a rather simpler form a word processor or personal computer can be employed.

be unwise to stick to the original plan if there are objective reasons for adapting it. But in any case, we must always have the original plan before our eyes, must be able to recognize the changes made and finally to compare the final results with the original goals.

A *long-range statement*, sometimes called a *'charter'*, requires no sophisticated technique. A short but clear definition on one sheet of paper may be sufficient. Preferably, such a 'charter' should be structured into well defined and objectively controllable items. The example in fig. 31.1 offers perhaps a useful suggestion. A project is defined here without technical details, yet the main properties of the planned product are described in a list of basic, exactly defined (as far as possible in the form of quantitative parameters) and controllable functions. After finishing the task, each item can easily and objectively be checked. Such a comparison of the completed task with the original intentions has an important side-effect: it teaches us to plan our future actions more realistically.

To achieve the defined goal, a number of specific activities must be performed. If their number is small, and sequence and relationships simple, we can keep the planning in our head; otherwise, some written form of planning has to be chosen in order to allow the actions, their sequence, interrelations, volume, time of start and end etc. to be recorded in distinct form. Again, there are many technical means available, ranging from a table on a sheet of paper (simple, but not adaptable), to a *planning board* or a *computer* or *graphical display*. The plain tabular or graphical presentation of the actions is sufficient in simple cases (fig. 31.2); in more complicated situations, a computational evaluation of their interrelations by the critical path method must be employed (see section 33).

32 - Scheduling

Scheduling is fitting specific jobs and activities into a general timetable considering the priority, sequence and terms of the tasks on the one hand, and the available capacity on the other hand. Methods of scheduling in industrial production have been known for decades; the need to plan and coordinate the production of many parts and products in industry stimulated development from the simple paper-and-pencil techniques to the systematic use of *planning boards* and finally to *online computer scheduling*. In the personal sphere the planning is much simpler, and sophisticated methods are rarely needed. Most individuals use a plain *diary* for their 'scheduling'.

There are many types, formats and pre-printed forms of diaries on the market from the small pocket-size for people with simple requirements, to the larger bound or loose-leaf books, specially printed (one week/page, one week/two pages, one day/page etc.), some of them with pre-printed hourly scale for graphical planning, others with special columns or fields for notes on visits and telephone calls, for daily recording of business expenses etc. A visit to a special shop will give you a sufficient overview of what is available and allow a choice.

A simple diary in the book form has one advantage over all the other, more sophisticated methods: it is portable. The diary is employed for the scheduling of work and events, as well as for recording actual work done and all happenings worth recording. It serves then simultaneously both as a planning device and as a log. Yet this traditional method of work scheduling can also be rationalized: we should create our own system of marks, symbols or abbreviations to save time and to make the diary clear, neat and more legible. By very simple symbols, it is possible to distinguish the activities planned and those actually done, and indicate their start, duration and end. Standardized personal abbreviations or graphical symbols should also be used for visits, telephone calls (if worth recording) and other frequently occurring sorts of activities. One of the many possible systems of such a 'personal shorthand' in a diary is presented in fig. 32.1.

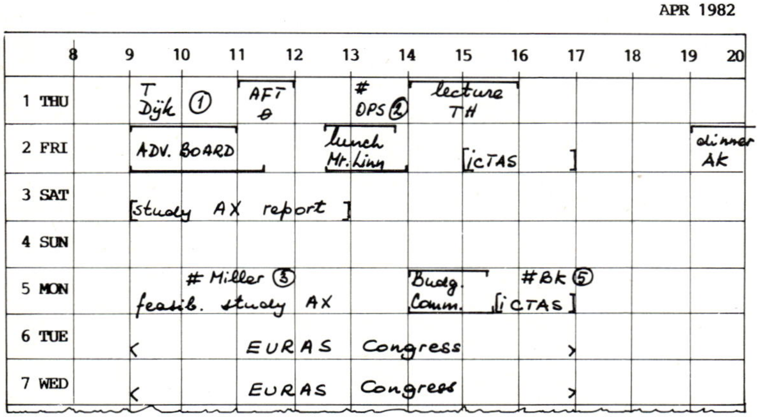

Fig. 32.1 - Diary in graphical form

A diary can also be kept in graphical form; depending on the number of activities, we use a pre-printed one page/one day, or one page/one week or only one page/one month (above). A system of 'personal shorthand' consisting of symbols and abbreviations allows us to keep the scheduling and recording concise and legible. Detailed remarks can be numbered and placed on the left-hand side (not in our figure).

A well-known scheduling device is a *planning board*; it is divided horizontally into time units (hours, days, weeks), and on the lines specific activities are marked by colour signs or strips. There are three basic types of planning boards suitable for personal use: a *pocket-strip board* has long horizontal pockets in which strips of hard paper can be inserted and, if needed, shifted horizontally; a *peg-board* is a large matrix of holes into which pegs of various colours and shapes can be inserted or in between which can be stretched coloured plastic strips - in the pre-computer age, these (rather expensive) planning boards were frequently used in workshop planning and scheduling. For personal use, an inexpensive but practical *magnetic planning board* might be the best solution (fig. 32.2).

We can buy such a board, but we can easily make one ourselves: we simply buy a sheet of iron for a few cents, and a set of magnetic marks that are available in special shops in many colours, sizes and shapes. We fix the iron sheet to the wall or other vertical surface in the field of vision, cover it with a sheet of paper (a rectilinear paper, graph paper or paper with a large pattern of lines and columns). Planning is done simply by putting magnetic symbols in the respective lines and columns, or by attaching pieces of paper with notes by means of magnets. At minimum expense, we gain an excellent planning instrument.

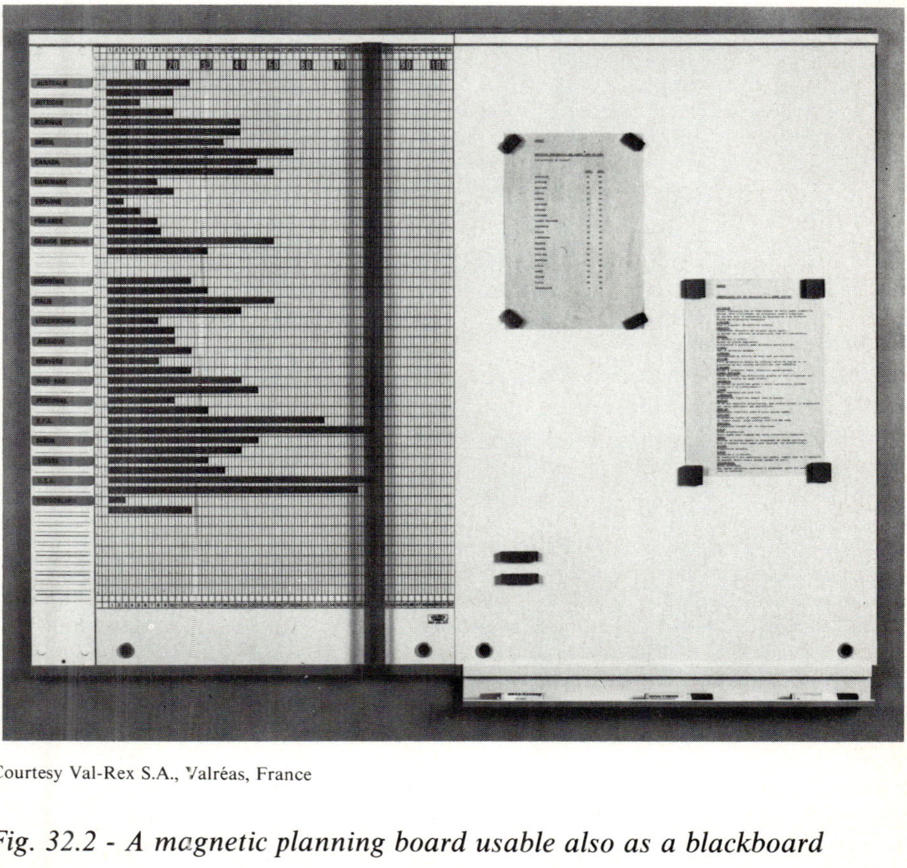

Courtesy Val-Rex S.A., Valréas, France

Fig. 32.2 - A magnetic planning board usable also as a blackboard

Easy legibility and adaptability are the advantages of planning boards of any type; the lack of a written record of the plan and of the actual events is their main disadvantage. Thus, this technique is often used for visualization of important events and actions, while a systematic log is kept in the traditional written form of a diary.

Another interesting technique is planning and scheduling by means of an *appointment card-index.* A set of 365 cards constitutes an 'eternal appointment calendar'. Fixed dates (jubilea, birthdays, recurring dates) are recorded directly on the respective day cards (sometimes even a few days in advance). Variable and one-off planning items are recorded on cards of the same format but of another colour and are stored just before the appointed day, or a few days before. Every day, in the morning, we remove the cards of daily appointments, sort them according to their priority, group them by type to make our work more effective and set up our work plan for the day.

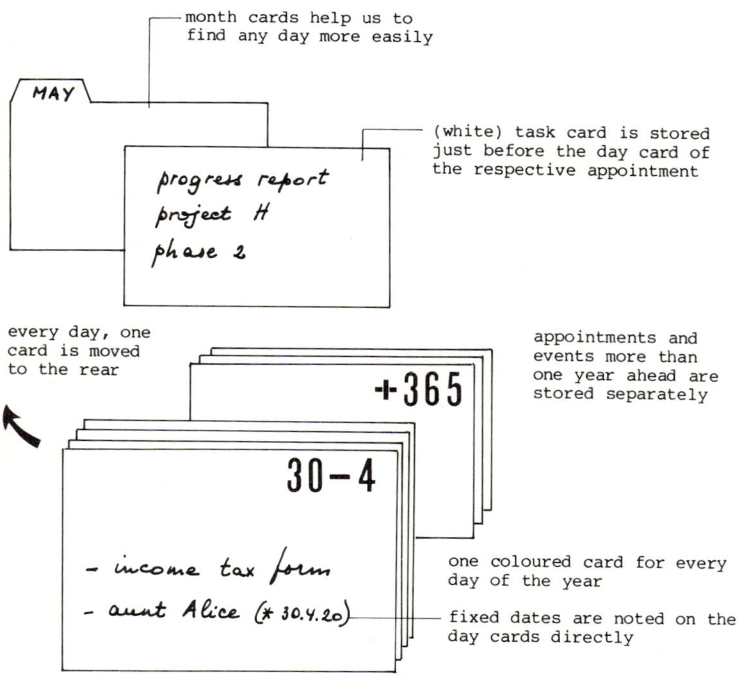

Fig. 32.3 - The 'eternal' appointment calendar in card-index form

365 cards (preferably in mini-card format) rotate once per year. Fixed dates are noted on the day cards, variable appointments and tasks are noted on 'task' cards and stored before the respective date of performing or alerting.

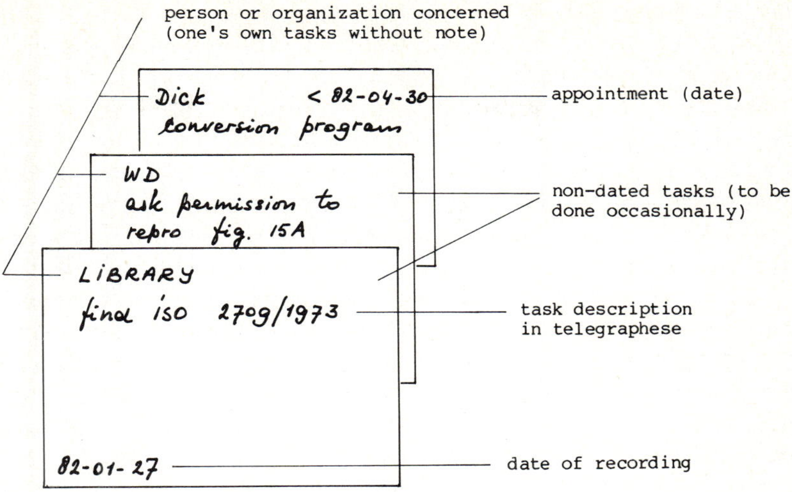

Fig. 32.4 - Task inventory on mini-cards

The user always carries a small plastic envelope with blank A8 (52 × 74 mm) mini-cards in his pocket. He notes tasks, dates, appointments etc.; he may store long-term tasks in an appointment calendar (fig. 32.3). Every morning, he checks the task cards, sorts them by priority and type. Before any appointment or visit, he sorts out the cards concerning the respective person or organization. Cards cost a few cents, recording takes a few seconds, yet this simple system can streamline activities and improve personal performance.

A simplified variant of the appointment card index can be used for noting *reminders.* We use a set of blank cards, preferably in a miniaturized format, that are kept in a small plastic box or soft pocket-sized case format. The tasks and other reminders are then recorded in telegraphese, one task per card; usually, we add one or two keywords, e.g. person concerned or date (fig. 32.4). Again, every day we review the tasks pending, sort out those that should be done today, arrange them according to their priority and sequence in which they should be performed.

If we plan to visit a person, company, library or warehouse, we sort out the cards for the respective tasks (points to be discussed with Mr. X, books we should like to read or borrow from a library, something we wish to buy etc.). The entire 'hardware' of such a 'system' costs a few cents, but it might sometimes be more effective than a sophisticated computerized alerting system, as it is portable (in your jacket pocket!). Only a wristwatch-sized terminal of the future will be able to compete with this simple technique.

Computerized scheduling is becoming available to an increasing number of people, as terminals of shared computers and personal computers are proliferating. We mentioned earlier some of the positive properties of the simple techniques (diary, planning board, appointment card, reminder card system); a computerized technique can only compete with them if it is able to offer some decisive additional advantages. Thus, not only do we expect from a computerized scheduling system that it should be able to accept data on planned tasks and actions, to arrange them in the proper sequence, and to display the plan, at best in a graphical form; a good scheduling program should also do rather more: it should contain some retrieval functions, for example it should make it possible to find all tasks for a given period, of a certain type, or concerning a certain person or organization (all meetings between given dates, all lectures in the next *x* weeks, all tasks concerning project *Y*, all questions to be discussed with Mr.*Z*); secondly, it should be able to weigh up the future task burden as a whole or by type of task (number of work hours planned for a certain task over a certain period); finally, it should be able to record data on actual work done and to assist with the time accounting, which we mention in section 37.

There are many programs available for various types of personal computers. We merely have to check the software list (if there is one), ask the advice of our computer supplier or members of our users' club, or try to find a suitable program via specialist journals. If we use a shared computer, we must first consult the computer centre as to whether there are programs for personal planning and scheduling available. Do not be surprised if the answers in the above-mentioned cases are disappointing. Let us hope that the general usefulness of a non-trivial program for personal planning and scheduling will stimulate the necessary software development.

In large companies and organizations there is also an urgent need for computerized *arrangement of meetings*. Every secretary knows how difficult it is to stipulate a date for a meeting when several people are invited. How many telephone calls it needs to find a date that suits all the participants ! A computer can easily scan the timetables of all the people invited and discover a date, using a special program that can take account of the priority of the meeting, priorities of personal scheduled tasks, and the possible substitution of some of the participants. This requires personal planning and scheduling to be stored in a common file, or that it should be available to external users; on the other hand, some degree of security is necessary, e.g. the personal planning content must be accessible only to the user and his secretary; the blocked and free dates should be revealed.

Undoubtedly, only very few persons will at present be using an advanced system of computerized personal planning and scheduling. The traditional systems are too easy and familiar, there is the lack of software already mentioned, the need to provide the system with all the input data (each activity item defined by name, type, date etc.) is not a pleasant task,

SUGGESTED CORRECTIONS, CHANGES AND IMPROVEMENTS IN THE MODULES OF THE ARD SYSTEM

```
*** highest priority
**  medium priority
*   low priority
+++ realized
```

NO	DATE	AUT	***	MODULE	SUGGESTION
1	80-06-12	SC	***	THA	redesign the record structure; extend the binary-half frequency counters
2	80-06-23	KD	**	INP	insert automatic screening of the journal name abbreviations (ISO standard)
3	80-07-01	KD	***	THA	check for duplicity of hash codes
4	80-07-15	HL	+++	SRT	extend the maximum number of records temporarily stored in the AB-field to 256
5	80-08-12	SC	*	RRD	adapt output layout conformly with the PRD/L-module (incl. parametrized R-field)

Fig. 32.5 - List of tasks, suggestions and ideas

During the planning, programming, testing, pilot run and application of a project many ideas come up that cannot immediately be put into effect but that must not be forgotten. They should be systematically recorded. A word processor, terminal or personal computer are ideal means to keep the record and to update it regularly.

IN	DATED	TYPE	CONTACT	
12-14	12-30	WRITE	DS	ask permission repro fig. 15
12-16		FIND	ONLINE	lit on history of automata
12-21	01-19	DRAFT		quarterly report ABC
12-21	01-26	VISIT	UNI	lecture A.B.Holm (14.30 h)
12-23		INQ	Brown,J.	recommendation of an interpreter
12-23		INQ	vdLaan	special daisy wheel for WP
12-23		FIND	LIB	Amber-Amber: Anatomy of Automation
12-28	01-07	VISIT	UNI	reception jubil. A.M. (17.00)
12-28	01-08	VISIT	ISA	annual meeting ISA (VN 15.30)
12-29		BUY		motor for tape-rec. code 4822 194
12-29		DRAFT		article 'Human use..' for Inf Sci
12-28	03-31	CHECK	Halderman	progress project-group C
12-28	02-15	DRAFT		suggestions on the team reorg.
12-29	02-11	FIND	LIB	biography of H.G.Wells
12-29		FIND		
12-30		FIND		
01-04		FIND		
01-04		INQ		
01-06		INQ		
01-08		ORDER		
01-08	02-02	VISIT		
01-08	03-01	COMP		
01-11	03-01	DRAFT		
01-11		BUY		
01-11		FIND		
01-12		INQ		
01-12	03-11	LECT		

12-29		BUY		motor for tape-rec. code 4822 194
01-11		BUY		Wahrig: Deutsches Wörterbuch
12-28	03-31	CHECK	Halderman	progress project-group C
01-08	03-01	COMP		factor analysis: the Q1 investigation
12-29		DRAFT		article 'Human use..' for Inf Sci
12-21	01-19	DRAFT		quarterly report ABC
01-11	03-01	DRAFT		message structure in EM-1
12-28	02-15	DRAFT		suggestions on the team reorg.
01-11		FIND	CSI	citations see ref. list 2
12-30		FIND	LIB	Weizenbaum, J.: Computer Power..
12-29	02-11	FIND	LIB	biography of H.G.Wells
01-04		FIND	LIB	Capek, K.: RUR
12-23		FIND	LIB	Amber-Amber: Anatomy of Automation
12-29		FIND	LIB	J. Reichardt: Robots
12-16		FIND	ONLINE	lit on history of automata
12-23		INQ	Brown,J.	recommendation of an interpreter
01-06		INQ	Dalh	terminology problems (see SC X1241)
01-04		INQ	Grünwald	comments to chapter 1

Fig. 32.6 - List of pending tasks updated and sorted by a word processor

The word processor or personal computer make it possible to create and update a list of pending tasks and to sort the tasks by date, type, or person (organization) concerned.

and the system is not portable. Yet the situation will change in the future. The often mentioned universal work station will become the central point of activities, including communication, of a professional. It will then be possible, and necessary, to make use of computerized planning; the input data will be recorded immediately while a message of the electronic mail is accepted or while the work is being done, the automatic alerting system will be an integrated part of the daily work regime, and the system will be able to record automatically, without arduous manual input, the data on the actual work and all events in the form discussed in section 37 on time accounting.

A computer or simply a word processor might also be effectively used to make and regularly update a general or special *list of pending tasks*; in fig. 32.5 we present an inventory list of ideas, suggestions and tasks concerning a particular project. A professional or a team records in this list all notes and remarks, especially those tasks that cannot be done immediately but must be recorded and have to wait to be checked, discussed, decided upon and performed later. Fig. 32.6 shows a list of personal tasks kept in chronological form by a word processor, and also sorted by type of task and by organization or person concerned.

Undoubtedly, the best solution would be to have no pending tasks at all, i.e. to perform tasks without delay. Frits Philips [ref. 30, p. 46] in his autobiography remembers that his father, Anton Philips, insisted that every task be performed immediately. This was not the wilfulness of a strong man. He said to his son: 'You must try to keep as few problems in your head as possible; if you want to act, then act immediately and you can forget the matter'. Indeed, the list of pending problems should be as short as possible; unfortunately, it never will be empty. Sometimes it is a problem of efficiency to accumulate tasks of the same type, and to perform them later in one single action.

33 - Network planning - Critical Path Method

Network planning - also known as the *Critical Path Method* (CPM) - was born after World War II when huge projects, particularly in the field of space research, involving a large number of activities, had to be planned, coordinated and managed. For each activity the earliest possible and the latest urgent dates must be found. These dates depend on the relations and sequence of activities: they are either dependent (action B cannot start before action A has been finished), or independent (action C may be performed earlier, simultaneously or later than action A). The interdependence of activities is usually drawn in the form of a *network chart* sometimes called 'arrow diagram' (fig. 33.1). Activities are symbolized by horizontal lines; their starts and ends are indicated by points, called events or nodes. Each activity is defined by a pair of numbers of its start and end nodes; if two or more parallel actions would be defined by the same pair of nodes, an auxiliary start or end point is added and connected by a fictive ('dummy') activity line (see in fig. 33.1 the activities

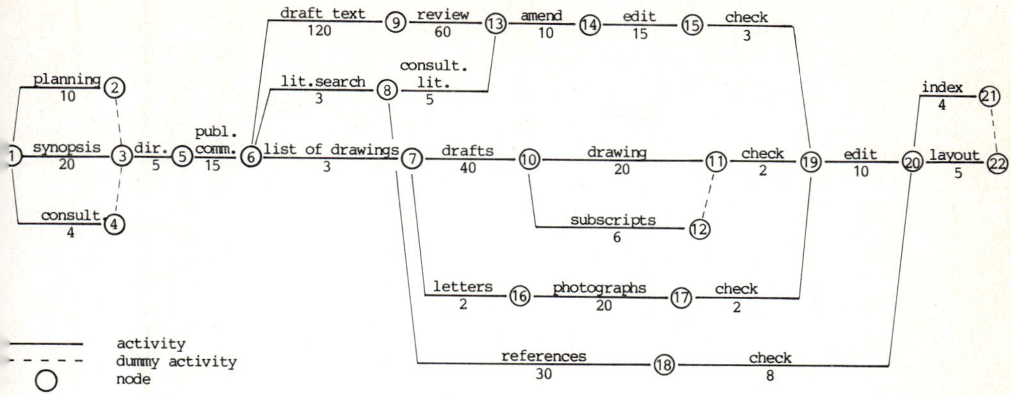

Fig. 33.1 - Example of a simple network plan

Activities are represented by horizontal lines, defined by the number of the beginning and end points. Workdays needed are noted under the names of activities.

2-3, 4-3, 12-11, 21-22). The length of lines does not express the time needed for the respective activity. The time is noted in the graph, or in a separate table. If two or more activities can be performed simultaneously (e.g. the activities 1-2 and 1-3 in our fig. 33.1), then the minimum total time needed is equal to the longest of them, and the shorter activity can start later, or - if it is started immediately - the finished work has to wait for the longer activity to be finished. In other words: for each activity there is an earlier date when it *can* start, and a later date, when it *must* start if it is not to delay the total project time. For a string of activities there is no such freedom: their 'can' and 'must' dates are the same. The sequence of these activities is the *critical path* of the whole project, and any delay of these 'critical' activities delays the project as a whole. Our schematic, rather simplified, example shows the principle of the critical path method better than a long narration (fig. 33.1).

The critical path method rapidly gained widespread popularity. In the last two decades, many forms and modifications of it have appeared, for example the well known PERT method that, among other things, defines each activity by a set of three values - optimistic, expected and pessimistic - and that bases its calculations on statistical probability of the start and end.

Drawing a network chart encourages a systematic approach to an action, it helps us to define and understand the relations between many activities; the simple fact that we must make an inventory of all the activities needed, and must think about their interrelation and sequence, is an impetus towards rationalization and streamlining of the whole work.

The crucial point is the calculation of the earliest possible and latest urgent dates for beginning each activity. In very simple cases, this could be done manually, but in practice it is always computerized. Programs for network planning are (or should be !) available in every computing centre.

Programs for network planning are also available for many types of personal computers provided their internal storage has a certain minimum capacity required by the program (example: in the case of a concrete program for the TANDY TRS-80 model I, the required core capacity is 48K bytes). Each program has its limits (maximum number of activities, and maximum number of nodes); the user must always check carefully whether the program offered for his computer allows him to process his specific planning problems. Larger network planning problems can also be solved in a service computing centre.

In quite simple cases - and these are predominant in personal planning - merely drawing a network chart without further computing might be helpful. To design it we need to make an inventory of all the actions needed, to think about their priorities, sequence and interrelations; if we compile such a scheme carefully, we have gained a guide to help us start each activity at the right moment - not too early, not too late.

There is also another simplified technique, that might be criticized as a violation of the orthodox rules of network planning but which is excusable in simple cases: the network chart could be drawn in a *time scale* (fig. 33.2). Then, the horizontal scale of the network graph represents time

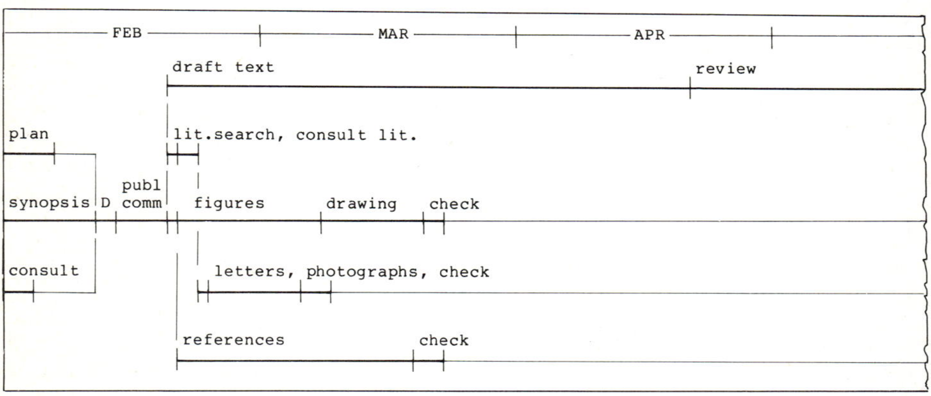

Fig. 33.2 - Network planning on a time scale

Normally, a network scheme is not drawn on a time scale (see fig. 33.1). However, in simple cases of personal planning, we may be permitted to infringe the rules and to draw a network on a time scale, abstaining from computation and limiting the planning to the graphical form. We must allow for the movable terms, and we must never use this mutilated form in complicated cases.

units (days, weeks, months), the length of activity lines is proportional to the total time available for the activity, and the proportion needed for realization of the activity is drawn in bold line or in a different colour. The activities on the critical path are then of course bold or coloured over their entire length. The manual design of such charts usually needs some trial-and-error sketching.

We have described here only the basic principles of the critical path method; a knowledge of these is sufficient for simple calculations. More detailed explanations can be found in the extensive literature on this subject; a few selected sources are cited in chapter 9, further detailed information can be easily found via abstracting journals, indexes and online systems (use keywords CRITICAL PATH, NETWORK PLANNING, CPM, PERT). Before using the available computer programs, the user should study the program documentation, the constraints, and the form of the input data; a schematic example of these is given in fig. 33.3.

activity	node numbers start	end	days
PLANNING	1	2	10
SYNOPSIS	1	3	20
CONSULTATIONS	1	4	4
DUMMY	2	3	0
DUMMY	4	3	0
DIR. DECISION	3	5	5
PUBLICATION COMMITTEE	5	6	15
DRAFT TEXT	6	9	120
REVIEW	9	13	60
LITERATURE SEARCH	6	8	3
CONSULT. LITERATURE	8	13	5
LIST OF REFERENCES	8	18	30
INDEX	20	21	4
DUMMY	21	22	0
LAYOUT	20	22	5

Fig. 33.3. - Example of input data for a critical path method computation

The data of the network in fig. 33.1 are used here as an example of the input for computerized processing.

34 - Alerting

The scheduling techniques mentioned in section 32 also have the alerting function: a diary, planning board or appointment calendar contains information about coming events and actions that have to be taken at a certain date and time. All these devices respond when they are interrogated. On the other hand, there are also *alerting instruments* that give automatic reminders.

The *alarm-clock* (nowadays also in wrist-watches) is the oldest invention of this sort. Another very old instrument for automatic count-down is the simple *timer*, which is of practical use not only in the kitchen but also in laboratory and on numerous other occasions. The electronics industry now produces a wide assortment of instruments to replace these older devices. The most popular at present are *pocket calculators* with watch, stop-watch, date and alarm or count-down functions (fig. 34.1). Similar instruments are also available in panel style (fig. 34.2); the device in fig. 34.3 also has an one-line text display, it can accept a number of data on coming events and required alerting times; at the preset moment it gives an acoustic signal, and simultaneously displays a short text; moreover, it acts as a clock and calendar and it can accept a limited number of frequently used telephone numbers, and dial them automatically.

The functions of alerting devices are improving and expanding, but the instruments mentioned are specialized and can only be used as isolated units. In the universal work station of the future the alerting, of course, will be integrated with all the other functions. We shall be able to store

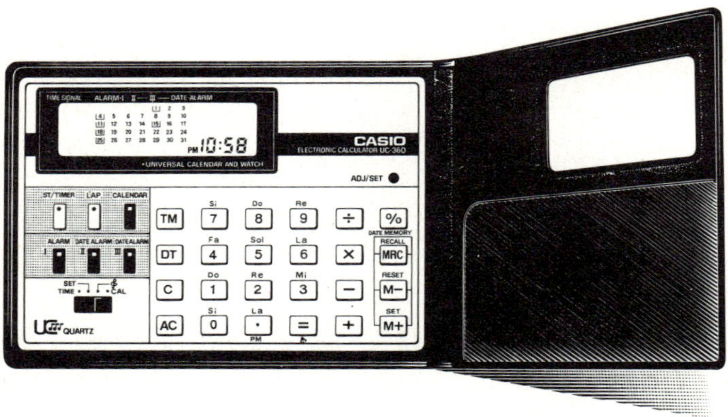

Courtesy Vroom & Dreesman, Amsterdam

Fig. 34.1 - Pocket calculator with stopwatch, alarm clock and calendar functions

The Casio UC-360 offers basic calculation functions, and it displays the precise time in hours, minutes and seconds, the days of the week and the date. The hourly time signal can be set or deactivated. The apparatus can be used as a stopwatch to measure times (also lap times) up to 24 hours with a precision of 1/10 second, and as an alarm clock with three pre-set alarms. The stored 200-year calendar makes it possible to find the day of the week of any date between 1.1.1901 and 31.12.2099. The date memory can accept two dates: on arrival of the pre-set date a sign blinks on the display for 24 hours and the pre-set melody can be played instead of the hourly time signal. Moreover, any significant days within 12 months can be set on the calendar (holidays, birthdays etc.); they are displayed in the calendar field. Acoustic alarms are given by a buzzer or one of the three pre-programmed melodies.

Courtesy Vroom & Dreesman, Amsterdam

Fig. 34.2 - A panel-style alarm clock

This clock/calculator keeps constant time (hours, minutes, seconds), it displays one-month calendar dates, and allows you to set three acoustic alarms. It has stopwatch and count-down functions, as well as a date memory feature.

a practically unlimited number of items containing text, date and time. At the preset moment we shall be alerted acoustically by a buzzer sound or by a message in voice form, and/or a text will be displayed.

What a pleasant prospect: our work station will remember all our appointments, meetings and other duties and it will remind us by its synthetic voice (some manufacturers offer a free choice between a male or female voice) that we have promised to deliver report X tomorrow, that we have to attend a meeting today at two o'clock, that we must not forget the birthday of aunt Alice or something else. Perhaps, after an initial period of over-enthusiasm, we shall limit the messages to the really urgent ones so as not to be reminded, reprimanded, disturbed and annoyed a hundred times a day, otherwise our helpmate might become a frustrating and hated instrument. We shall try to use it (by employing its communication and planning facilities) to streamline our work, to avoid splitting our work time into a large number of small actions

Courtesy Pelikan Nederland, Zevenaar, The Netherlands

Fig. 34.3 - Electronic clock, calendar, alerting and dialling device

Alerting and other information is given as a one-line message. The device is able to store 150 deadlines, appointments of up to 40 alphanumerical characters, as well as about 40 date-related memoranda (such as messages for secretary or staff members), and 200 telephone numbers with names and area codes of the addressees (up to 28 characters per item); the telephone numbers can be dialled automatically. The device also acts as a calculator, clock, calender or stopwatch with a count-down alerting function.

scattered throughout the day. We shall begin in the morning by displaying a list of tasks, reading the messages of the electronic post waiting in the 'electronic post box', we shall edit the list of duties for this particular work day, sort them into the most effective sequence, grouping similar tasks together as possible, so that only a few important alerting messages will remain.

35 - Diary and log

A traditional *diary* has two main functions: planning the future and recording past activities and events. The detail of the recording depends on the purpose of our diary and on the reasons why we keep a written record about our work. First, we may need to be able to recall later what has been done and when. Second, we often need to sum up and analyse our work over a certain period (how many days or hours we spent on a certain project, preparing a report etc.). Third, we sometimes need to reconstruct some activity (history of a negotiation or a project) for publication or other purposes; some people may also intend writing their memoires or autobiography in the (distant) future. In all these cases a good diary is a necessity. We must decide which events are important enough to be noted (we may be quite wrong, as we sometimes find out later), and we also should take care that any abbreviations and codes, that are quite clear at the moment when they are fresh in our memory, still remain understandable after a longer time. A list of abbreviations, codes, acronyms and symbols attached to a diary might be a valuable tool later, when we cannot recall who was meant by the abbreviation Blb and what was action PRD.

The required specificity of a diary influences the choice of its *form*; we mentioned in section 32 that we can use the detailed form of one day = one page allowing a very detailed record of all daily activities, or more abbreviated versions; in fig. 32.1 we presented a very concise form in which one A5 page was used for a whole month, and each day recorded on one line only. The user developed his own system of telegraphese and symbols. Some people prefer a combined form: a small pocket-size notebook for recording dates and appointments, and a large size (loose-leaf or bound) book for detailed chronological recording and comments.

Scientists and researchers traditionally prefer to maintain a *log-book* in which they write down chronologically the detailed progress of their laboratory or observatory work. Minute details about experiments, interim results, measurements, observations - sometimes seemingly irrelevant at the time - might be found to be of crucial importance later. If we do not like to spend too much time on written recording (often disturbing during laboratory work, but less reliable when done later) we can use a *tape recorder*, preferably a handy 'pocket memo' *dictating machine*; it can and should also be used for immediately recording notes on other occasions, for example notes on important discussions, phone calls, one's own remarks etc. The tapes can then be transcribed by the secretary, or filed as they are. In the latter case, the cassettes should be stored chronologically, carefully labelled with dates, and an index kept.

The universal work station will make the recording much easier than it is with present technical means: it will make it possible to store voice and text and to combine both in one record. A telephone conversation could then be stored and labelled with a number of keywords, partly automatically (day, time, number dialled) and partly manually (person, subject), and followed by a complete record. Similarly, short notes can be stored immediately and recalled at any time later by date, person, subject. Also, a detailed log could be stored chronologically in the form of a dictated or typed text, and any part of it will be retrievable later. Furthermore, the universal work station will be able to record some actions and events automatically - it will recognize what we are doing at a given moment (it 'knows' what project number we are working on, what files we are communicating with, what programs we are using at any given moment; this is sufficient information for it to recognize the type and aim of our activity, and the start, duration and end of the activity can easily be recorded automatically).

36 - Personal performance standards

Intellectual work is non-repetitive, heterogeneous and ever-changing. It can rarely be standardized, and if it can, then never as easily and exactly as the simple, repetitive jobs in production or the clerical jobs in an office. Nonetheless, if we wish to plan our activities, to make a realistic estimate of the time needed for a job, than we should try to quantify our performance in some typical activities.

The *performance standards* must be based on experience, and they must be periodically checked and updated. In fig. 36.1 we present - by way of example - a set of personal performance rates in a few typical types of work.

Everyone should ask himself the question: Do I know my average performance in my typical activities? If the answer is negative, he should try occasionally to measure his performance under varying conditions. This raises a second question: Can I consider my personal

ACTIVITY	PERFORMANCE	
careful proof-reading	7 min/page (a)	
study reading	3 min/page (a)	
normal reading	2 min/page (a)	
fast reading	1 min/page (a)	
fast scanning of abstracts	300 abstracts/hour	
speaking (lecture)	110 words/min	
dictating simple text	80 words/min	
dictating difficult text	30-60 words/min	
drafting/typing simple text	2 pages/hour	(a)
drafting/typing difficult text	1 page/hour	(a,b)
longhand	30 words/min	
shorthand	80 words/min	
typing from a legible source	250 strokes/min	(a,d)
word processor typing incl.coding	2.5 pages/hour	(a,d)
translating/dictating (e)	3 pages/hour	(a,e)

Fig. 36.1 - Personal performance standards help to estimate and plan our own work

Everyone should know his average throughput in typical operations. The performances in this table are an example rather than standards. Try to measure your own performance and replace the numbers in his table by your own personal standards. Use them to gain a critical evaluation of your efficiency in specific activities.

Notes :

[a] page of A4 format, spacing 1½, 40 lines/page, 60 characters/line, total 2400 characters (including spaces), i.e. about 400 words a page;

[b] including one's own editing and correcting;

[d] including online proof-reading, correcting, layout editing, and inserting codes for the photoelectric typesetting;

[e] dictated translation of a familiar subject into one's mother tongue.

performance satisfactory? A negative answer is an incentive for improvement. For example, there is a vast literature on fast reading techniques that can help us increase our reading speed to 600 or more words per minute - president Kennedy, as his biographer notes [ref. 30-Schlesinger, p. 104], was a fanatical reader, able to read even 1200 words per minute. Similarly, we should critically evaluate our speed of typing; in the present age of the proliferation of terminals and personal computers, everyone is expected to have a good knowledge of typing. It is becoming part of general education, and it should be taught at the age of ten or perhaps earlier. The urgent need for typing skill will diminish in the, rather distant, future when unlimited voice input will be the common form of communication with computers and word processors. The touch method, i.e. typing using all ten fingers without looking at the keyboard, should be learnt and mastered. Shorthand is not an obsolete skill; it can be helpful in many situations where a dictating machine cannot be used (in meetings, conferences, for personal notes). Unfortunately, to achieve an adequate speed, one has to learn long and hard and if the skill is not learnt at school early, then it may be difficult to find time and energy to learn it later.

To sum up, personal performance standards have two basic goals: Firstly, a knowledge and critical evaluation of them spurs us into improving our personal efficiency, secondly, they are most important for realistic planning and scheduling of various activities, helping us better to estimate what we can do and how long it will take.

37 - Time accounting

In project organizations, research institutes, consultant's offices etc., time devoted to specific tasks and projects is usually recorded for internal cost accounting and invoicing. The working hours of the employees are allocated to specific project or job account numbers and recorded on pre-printed sheets.

Some professionals, e.g. free-lance consultants, are in the habit of maintaining such simple time recording, since they, firstly, must invoice for their services, and secondly, they are interested in obtaining a general picture of time spent on various types of their activities; it helps them to estimate more precisely and realistically the work time needed for similar jobs in the future. All of us should maintain at least some - albeit quite simple - record of time spent on our activities. The task is quite easy if we are working continuously on one big job for a fairly long period of time. Otherwise, we should note - in our diary for example - the time spent on specific actions, and also the time needed for general ('overhead') activities such as general study, correspondence, travel time etc. A somewhat more formalized technique is time recording using special forms. Sometimes, the time is registered not only per *cost bearers* (in cost accounting terminology, the products or services) but also per *types of work*. An example of the classification of types of work as used in a service computing centre can be found in fig. 37.1.

Recording of work-time both per type and per project is much more difficult. Although a professional is working only rarely on more than one project simultaneously, the types of his activities are much more diversified. Recording work-time requires a good deal of discipline. Though condemned by everyone concerned, and though sometimes presenting 'exact sums of inexact data', the processing of the recorded data does give an insight into the structure of work time, and comes up with many a suggestion for improvements.

We cannot expect many professionals to be willing to record their work-time in the detail described above. Those who do find sufficient

0 MANAGEMENT, CONTROL, CLERIC.W. 01 management 02 meetings 03 long-term planning 04 short-term planning 05 accounting; budgeting 06 clerical work 07 secretarial work 08 drawing 09 other activities	**5 COMMERICAL ACTIVITIES** 51 commercial contacts, meetings 52 marketing 53 demonstrations 54 purchasing activities 55 56 sale promotional activities 57 business administration 58 59 other commercial activities
1 DESIGN, PROJECTS, PROGRAMMING 11 project management 12 feasibility studies 13 systems analysis 14 project design 15 programming 16 debugging; testing 17 project/program documentation 18 implementation; maintenance 19 other proj/progr activities	**6 CONSULTATION, ADVICE ACTIVITIES** 61 general consultations 62 special studies; expertises 63 64 committees; advisory boards 65 66 67 68 69 other activities
2 TECHNICAL ACTIVITY, MAINTENANCE 21 installation of hardware 22 preventive maintenance 23 maintenance; repairs 24 general repairs 25 technical diagnosis and analysis 26 hardware testing 27 testing of new devices 28 design 29 other technical activities	**7 STUDY, EDUCATION, TRAINING** 71 study; literature study 72 attending courses and lectures 73 attending congresses etc. 74 documentation 75 training 76 study trip 77 study trip abroad 78 free time for study purposes 79 other study, educ. & training act.
3 DATA PROCESSING 31 data preparation; input 32 screening & corrections of input 33 updating of databases 34 operating the peripherals 35 36 screening of output 37 38 evaluation of output 39 other DP activities	**8 AUXILIARY ACTIVITIES** 81 auxiliary work 82 travel time 83 errand time 84 waiting; lost time 85 86 87 88 89 other auxiliary activities
4 EDUCATION, TRAINING, PUBLISHING 41 organizing courses 42 preparation of courses 43 teaching; conduction courses 44 conduction of training 45 publishing 46 editing 47 translating 48 org. of excursions and visits 49 other educational activities	**9 HOLIDAYS, ILLNESS ETC.** 91 non-labour days 92 holidays 93 special holidays; extraord.holid. 94 maternity leave 95 special paid holidays 96 military service 97 illness 98 accident 99 other non-working time

Fig. 37.1 - Classification of activities

Example from a service computing centre with educative and commercial functions

courage and self-discipline can achieve quite interesting and informative results. Again, we must emphasize that the goal is not the recording, but the critical analysis and evaluation of the results, and the drawing of the right conclusions.

If we have doubts about our performance and the productive and unproductive work-time, we should occasionally try to make a one-day detailed *time-study*, an exact analysis of the working day. On a pre-printed form we record every (even short-time) action; we note the hour and minute we begin it and add a short description or abbreviation about the type of work. At the end of the day we summarize the times and sort them by type, distinguishing among productive time, overhead activities and wasted time. It is interesting to draw the results in graphical form. Often, we shall be surprised, and we shall have data to think about.

Detailed time studies of the working day of managers and professionals have been made and published. Prof. Mintzberg summarizes the results of several investigations in an absorbing article on the manager's job [ref. 30]: a study of a group of 56 U.S. foremen revealed that they averaged 583 activities per eight-hour shift; another analysis of the working time of 160 British managers discovered that they worked without interruption for a half hour or more only about once every two days. The working day structure of other professionals might be rather less disjointed, but it is never free from disturbances and interruptions at various times. Analysis of working time might reveal interesting facts. It can stimulate reorganization of the work regime and thereby lead to increased efficiency and less stress and frustration.

38 - Personal budgeting and accounting

Many persons keep some rudimentary form of *personal accounting.* It may consist of chronologically stored bank statements with short comments added to the income and expense items, and a file of invoices and other documents that are needed for tax and other purposes. In what follows, we describe a more systematic form of personal budgeting and accounting using either manual or mechanized bookkeeping techniques.

We avoid here a description of a complete accounting system in which all income and expenditure items, as well as all items concerning assets and liabilities, are recorded and processed according to the legal and financial standards prescribed for companies (including one-man companies). Such a perfect accounting system requires a knowledge of the double-entry accounting system, the forms of depreciation of assets, time allocation of costs etc. It is beyond the scope of this book to explain these principles. In this section, we shall describe simplified methods of personal budgeting and accounting, concentrating on the recording of income and expenditures.

The *accounting scheme*, used also in budgeting, depends on two factors: firstly, on the peculiarities of the profession and special requirements of the individual; secondly, on the requirements of the tax laws in the respective country.

The accounting scheme in fig 38.1 must therefore be considered simply as an example and one of many possible variants. Example 38.1 also includes assets and liabilities to make the scheme complete. For practical reasons the expense accounts might be separated into two categories: expenses that are tax-deductible, and those which are non-deductible - for example, specialist books and journals as opposed to light reading matter. Another solution is to keep one account (books and journals), to distinguish the specific items, and to summate the two groups separately.

Personal budgeting and accounting must be kept as simple as possible; nobody wants to spend too much time and effort on this activity. For *manual accounting*, a plain system of chronological records in a *journal* is the simplest way; if our expenses are paid both in cash and by bank or

0 ASSETS 01 real estate 02 house 03 car(s) 04 technical equipment 05 furniture, household. equipm. 09 other assets	**5 HOLIDAYS, SPORT, HOBBY** 51 holidays 52 sport 53 photo, film 59 other costs
1 FINANCIAL ASSETS & LIABILITIES 11 bank: current account 12 bank: savings account 13 cash 14 mortgage loan 15 shares 19 other fin.assets & liabilities	**6 CULTURE, EDUCATION, HEALTH** 61 books, journals 62 tapes, LP's, videotapes & disks 63 education, school, courses 64 theatre, concerts etc. 65 medical costs 69 other costs
2 BUSINESS EXPENSES 21 travelling expenses 22 office appliances 23 (bus.) entertaining expenses 24 professional organizations 25 professional literature 26 other business expenses	**7 FINANCIAL COSTS** 71 income tax 72 other personal taxes 73 insurance 74 interest paid 79 other financial costs
3 HOUSEHOLD 31 house: rent/mortgage 32 house repairs 33 house taxes & insurance 34 energy 35 telephone 36 household expenses 37 clothing 39 other household expenses	**8 EARNINGS** 81 salary 82 consultancies 83 cost reimbursement 84 author's fees 85 interest received 86 dividend 89 other earnings
4 TRANSPORT 41 car depreciation 42 fuel 43 car repairs and maintenance 44 car taxes and insurance 45 plane, train, bus 49 other transport expenses	**9 BALANCE** 91 capital account 92 profit & loss account

Fig. 38.1 - Example of a personal accounting scheme

Account classification is always adapted to individual needs, i.e. the specific structure of costs and earnings. In our example, the professional with a basic knowledge of accounting - undoubtedly under the influence of the classical Schmalenbach's Kontenrahmen - has chosen a two-digit decimal classification system of accounts. His originally manual system has easily been converted to a mechanized system by means of a personal computer.

TEXT	ACCT TYPE	X	CASH –	CASH +	CASH BALANCE	BANK –	BANK +	BANK BALANCE
rest. Windsor	36	1			210	62		4754
	42	3*	28		182			
	11	–				500		4254
	13	–		500	682			
med. handbk	25	3				82		4172
Pentax	04	6				811		3361

S	TYPE	X	#	–	+	TEXT
B	36	1		62		REST. WINDSOR
C	42	3		28		
B	11	–		500		
C	13	–			500	
B	25	3*		* 82		MED. HANDBOOK
B	04	6		811		CAMERA PENTAX

Fig. 38.2 - Personal bookkeeping entries in manual and computerized form

Manual records are kept in a cash/bank-account journal; its content is self-evident. Computer input is limited to the account number and amount; a short comment is added when needed. Asterisk ∗ denotes a tax-deductible item; at the end of the accounting period the computer prints out a list of all specified items. Abbreviations B and C mean payment by bank or by cash. Amounts are rounded-off; meticulous accounting in cents is pointless in a personal system.

CUMULATIVE BUDGET	CUMULATIVE ACTUAL	DIFFERENCE (100) –	DIFFERENCE (100) +	THIS MONTH	ACCOUNT
4 100	4 703		+6	651	21 TRAVELLING
620	515	-1		85	22 OFFICE APPLIANCES
1 505	1 220	-3		245	23 ENTERT. EXPENSES
350	251	-1		0	24 PROF. ORGANIZATIONS
800	1 180		+3	381	25 SPEC. LITERATURE
11 713	12 886		+12	3 142	2 TOTAL BUSINESS COST

Fig. 38.3 - Summary sheet of personal accounting

A personal computer can process the input data (fig. 38.2) into various forms of statement, for example into monthly and yearly summaries and balances; monthly data are extended by cumulative amounts (from the beginning of the year) and compared with the budgeted amounts.

cheque, the journal should be split into two parts (fig. 38.2). The entries in the journal are self-explanatory.

At the end of the accounting period (usually monthly) we simply summate the expenses and incomes per account (a pocket calculator with addressable memories might be helpful) and enter the sums on a pre-printed form on which also the budgeted amounts have been recorded (fig. 38.3). *Documents* worth storing (invoices needed later for tax purposes etc.) are filed by account numbers and chronologically within each account.

The perfectionist will notice that not only the types of expenses are important, but also their aim, and that both viewpoints are mixed rather unsystematically in our scheme in fig. 38.1. For example, the account 'hotel expenses' contains both business expenses and holiday expenses. If we classify expenses only by sort, we have no overview of the aims (we cannot summate business costs, holiday costs etc.), if we classify them by aim, we lose sight of the cost structure (if we split up the costs of a car among business, private and holiday expense accounts, where these are mixed with other cost types, we lose our overall view of the total costs of the car). A perfectionist may classify every cost item by its type (fuel, insurance, books and journals, medical costs etc.), and by aims (business, house, household, holidays, hobby...) as shown in fig. 38.4; this is not difficult in manual bookkeeping, and it costs almost nothing in a mechanized system.

Computerized personal accounting requires similar input data to the above-mentioned manual techniques: we must type-in the income and

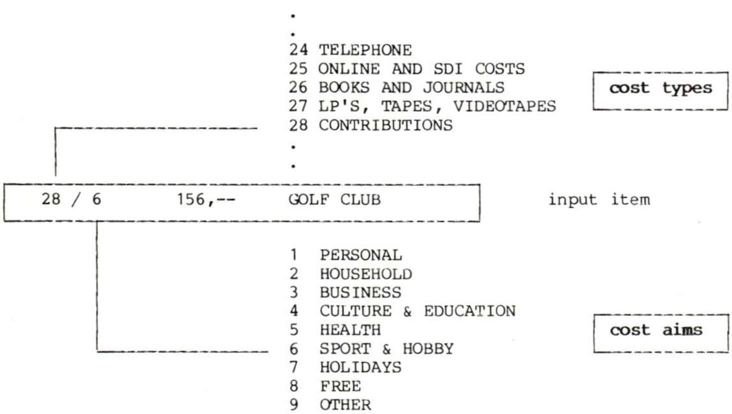

Fig. 38.4 - Cost classifications by cost type and aim

The classification scheme in fig. 38.1 is rather confusing as it distinguishes costs by type and by aim in an unsystematic way. Two separate codes offer more variants, more freedom and cleverer insight. Contributions to associations are always coded as cost type 28, but it is easy to distinguish contributions to professional organizations (28/3), to sport clubs (28/6), to cultural organizations (28/4) etc. A computer can produce sums by cost type, by aim or combination of type/aim.

expense items in their chronological sequence, each item comprising a short comment, the account number, sign (plus or minus) and amount. Again, there can be two (or more) journals, for recording cash and bank payments and receipts. The computer summates the incomes and expenses per account, and prints out a monthly or yearly summary sheet; it is also easy to add cumulative data from the beginning of the year, and/or sliding sums (sums of the last 12 months) to provide an excellent overview and comparison. The budgeted incomes and expenses are recorded at the beginning of the period and the system compares actual and budgeted amounts automatically (fig. 38.3).

There are many programs for personal computers to be found under the heading 'personal accounting' in software directories. Unfortunately, it is not easy to find out what their precise functions are: what accounting scheme they incorporate, whether it is fixed or flexible (adaptable by the user to his own specific needs), whether and how the tax deductible expenses are distinguished, whether the computer prints selective lists of tax-deductible expense items, what is the content and structure of input data, and what is the form of the output statements and statistics etc. Consulting the supplier of our personal computer, scanning the specialist journals or abstracting services, consulting members of a computer hobby club form the (not always easy) paths to such information. If you do not succeed, and if you consider personal computing a hobby, then sit down and write your own personal budgeting and accounting program.

Personal accounting also includes *asset accounting*. It is worth a little effort to keep a systematic overview of all your valuable assets, with the identification data. It can be kept in the form of a card index or in computerized form; a simple, regularly updated list can be also maintained by means of a word processor. We enter all valuable objects (car, cameras, television sets, tape recorders, pictures, antiques etc.); add the necessary data (date of purchase, price, location and identification marks such as serial numbers in the case of machines, sizes in the case of pictures etc.) as shown in fig. 38.5. Such a card index or list is very useful for realistic estimating of the total insurance value, and it might be invaluable in the event of damage to or theft of these properties.

Personal accounting must be as simple as possible. In contradistinction to the strictly employed principles in business accounting, we may introduce into our system the following three simplifications (that would be considered criminal acts by any professional accountant). The first of them is *aggregation* of small and less important items concerning the same type of expenses into one bookkeeping item. Secondly, all items may be *rounded-off* - for example, we omit cents and keep our accounting in whole money units only (if the money unit is lira, peseta or yen we round off to hundreds). Thirdly, some *imprecision* may be tolerated: we check our cash and bank balances daily; if there is a large difference, we are usually able to remember what the item is, but we do not waste time trying to identify the reason for small differences; we simply write them off to a special account 'accounting differences'. Indeed such simplifications are unimaginable in a business accounting system where absolute (formal !) precision is required; a personal accounting system however is to help, not hinder.

Some persons may consider personal budgeting and accounting or asset accounting as a waste of time unworthy of the creative man. Let it not be forgotten that even Goethe was in the habit of keeping personal records of his assets (including items such as 194 shirts with cuffs and 82 without, or 108 handkerchiefs) and he recommended accounting as a helpful tool for everybody; his statement on double-entry bookkeeping as 'one of man's greatest inventions' is often cited (particularly by accountants).

card in a card index

```
camera PENTAX-ME                        PHOTO
body 9533165
std objective 50 mm 2540360
bought 78-12-20 De Greef Tilburg    f 869
```

computer input

```
ITEM:     CAMERA PENTAX-ME
GROUP:    PHOTO
NO:       9533165
DATE:     78-12-20
PRICE:    869
ACCESS:   STD OBJ 50MM 2540360

ITEM:     TAPE RECORDER PHILIPS N2511
GROUP:    AUDIO-VIDEO
NO:       1304616
DATE:     77-11-25
```

Fig. 38.5 - List of assets in card-index and computerized form

A regularly updated list of valuable property items helps us to make more realistical estimate of the insurance value; in the event of loss or theft, this list serves as source of identification and price data.

4 - PERSONAL INFORMATION MANAGEMENT

Paradoxically, in the environment of abundant information, we often suffer from lack of information. Large volumes of badly needed information are hidden somewhere in books, journals, reports, patents and many other sources. On the other hand, we receive large volumes of information that we shall never use, or that arrives when we do not need it, that disappears without a trace and that cannot be found later when it is urgently required. We must manage the stream of information that we like to receive regularly (subscribed journals, abstracting journals, SDI services), and know where and how to search for information at a moment of need. New technical means help us to deal with these problems, but due to an ever-increasing volume of literature and data, the large volume of various sources of information, the overlap, the lack of standardization and availability, we find that orientation and access to information is increasingly difficult.

Effective *information gathering* from the existing diversified information sources via the various channels of information, using an adequate search strategy and technique, sifting, selecting, sorting, arranging, evaluation and storage of information is an art that must be learned and continuously improved. We have to build our own file of information. The ultimate goal is not a large volume of randomly accumulated information, but information systematically arranged and organized. Instead of simple information storage, *organization of knowledge* should become our ideal.

The need for personal documentation is not new. We are surely not surprised to learn that Jules Verne gathered and systematically stored information in the fields of geography, natural science and technology in his well organized collection of 20000 cards and excerpts. However, it is somewhat unexpected to find, upon visiting the country house of Jack London in Glen Ellen near San Francisco, 188 card-index boxes alongside the writing desk of this writer who had an image of sailor, trapper and adventurer.

41 - Information gathering

A rational strategy of information gathering is the first step to the organization of knowledge. It requires clear replies to the following questions:

- What is my main *field of interest*, and what are the peripheral fields ?
- Which types of *information sources* are relevant to me (books, journals, reports, patents, standards, statistics, commercial publications, dissertations etc.) ?
- Via which *channels* can I get the information needed (libraries, documentation centres, companies, government bodies, persons) ?
- Where do I find '*information about information*', i.e. which abstracting journals, SDI services, online systems, catalogues, bibliographies etc. are the best sources for me ?

The field of interest

It is often stated that we are living in an age of ever increasing specialization, sometimes we could say over-specialization. Essentially, this is true. However, there are many professions that still require a wide general knowledge: managers and teachers are typical examples. Their background knowledge must be broad and polythematic.

A manager needs to have a knowledge of organization, planning, budgeting and accounting, marketing, statistics and optimization techniques, but also some basic knowledge of the special technology of his branch, of psychology and personnel management etc. Similarly, not only must a teacher be a good specialist in his field, but his background knowledge has to be wide enough, and a special knowledge of methodology, pedagogy, practical psychology and modern educational techniques is also necessary.

Furthermore, the trend to over-specialization has in the last few decades been compensated by the growing integration and multidisciplinary character of many fields of science, technology and economics.

A researcher in the specific field of the nutrition of piglets can serve as an example of a super-specialist: he has only a few peers in the whole world, there are merely four or five journals and a few books that relate to his narrow field of interest. Nonetheless, there are fields in other disciplines that he must master: the general problems of the metabolism of mammals, the chemical composition of feed, chemical methods of analysis and measurement, basic and special laboratory techniques (including the use of radioactive isotopes for marking the feed elements), methods of multivariance statistics for evaluation of experiments, techniques of linear programming for optimization of feed rations and mixtures etc. Consequently, this super-specialist is interested in a number of peripheral problems in the fields of biology, medicine, chemistry, nuclear physics, mathematics and statistics.

Consequently, it is not always easy to define precisely one's field of interest, even in the case of a narrowly specialized professional.

Information sources

There are three levels of information sources. The *primary documents* (books, journals, patents, reports etc.) contain the original information. Their huge volume stimulated the creation of the *secondary sources* that contain 'information about information', and that make it easier to find primary sources dealing with a specific problem. The oldest form of these is catalogues in libraries and abstracting journals; the modern version is online information systems. Also a catalogue in a company archive and an index to correspondence are examples of secondary in-house information sources. The growing number of libraries, documentation and information centres, abstracting journals, online services etc. led finally to the advent of *tertiary sources.* They inform us about the secondary sources, their content, structure and availability (fig. 41.1).

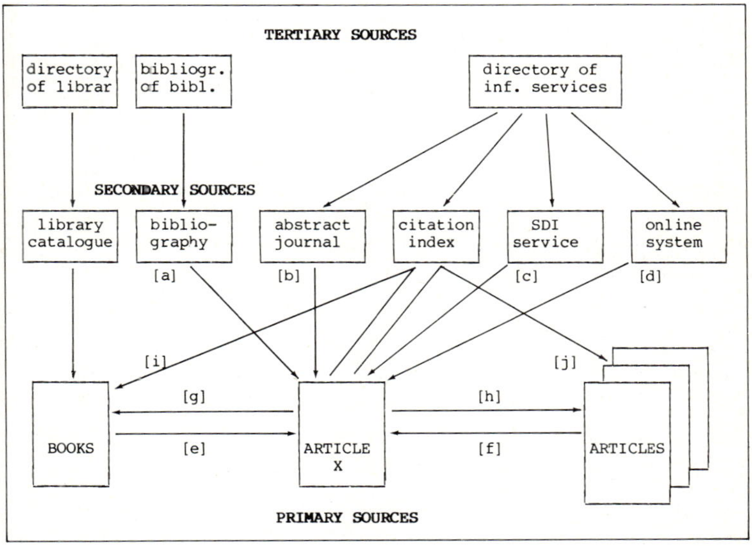

Fig. 41.1 - Scientific and technical literature is a network of documents

It is not an amorphous collection of isolated documents, but a network with many cross-connections. The article X in our scheme can be found by various paths: via bibliographies, abstracting journals, SDI and online systems [a,b,c,d], via citations in books and articles [e,f]; the article may, on the other hand, be used as a pointer to books and articles cited by its author [g,h]. By means of citations indexes it is possible to find all books and articles in which the article X has been cited [i,j].

Ways to information

There are many ways and means to *gather information.* We can never limit ourselves to only one, and we have to select the best combination of them. We offer a few recommendations below:

1. Visit a *library* or several libraries regularly; try to get some knowledge of its (their) collection(s), become acquainted with its (their) classification and indexing system(s) and search tools (catalogues, indexes, online indexes); periodically check the lists of new acquisitions or the new books display; browse occasionally through the collections; consult the librarians.
2. Find out which are the *core journals* in your field(s) of interest; scan them regularly cover-to-cover and read selected articles. Carefully scan the *book review* columns and abstracts of selected literature.
3. Find out other *journals* that contain relevant information in your main or peripheral fields of interest and scan them.
4. Do not forget *special publications*: reports, commercial publications, theses, dissertations, annual reports of companies and organizations, internal bulletins, government publications, patents, standards etc., relating to your special interest.
5. Do not overlook *non-traditional sources* of information: audio-visual aids such as courses on videotapes, collections of slides and microfiches etc.
6. Select one or more *abstracting journals* in your field of interest; master their systems of classification and concentrate your attention on selected class(es) most relevant to you; do not try to focus too sharply, as an abstracting journal can yield fast and broad orientation on the state-of-the-art on a wide front of a discipline.
7. Subscribe to an *SDI-service* - choose either a cheap standard interest profile ('topic' in the terminology of INSPEC), or order your own profile tailored to your own specific interest.
8. Use *online retrieval* when searching for specific information; find out which of the online data bases best cover your field of interest.
9. Keep informed about which *persons* and *organizations* (universities, research institutes, manufacturers, governmental bodies etc.) are active in your field of interest; also search sometimes via authors' or organizations'names (all recent publications by Mr. X, or recent reports of organization Z).
10. If you do not know which individuals and which organizations are active in a specific field, make use of *references* and of a *citation index.* Also a *Who's Who* directory of the respective discipline or special directories (there are directories of universities, libraries, research institutes etc.) can be useful. There are also lists of current projects and research activities in specific fields.

11. Do not underestimate *informal paths* to information, e.g. contacts with colleagues, peers, discussions at meetings and conferences, demonstrations of new products and systems.
12. Keep informed about the dates and places of *congresses, conferences and exhibitions* in your field of interest; scan their *proceedings.*
13. Learn to use *citation indexes* regularly; they can lead you from known relevant papers via citations (which author and which paper has cited the document) to newer works on the same or a similar subject; you also get an excellent insight into the literature of your specific field.
14. Spend some time occasionally on *browsing* through the collections of a library, through an abstracting journal or at the terminal of an online system; it might lead to unexpected discoveries of pertinent literature that otherwise would remain hidden. The effect of *serendipity* (finding something that has not been searched for) must not be underestimated.
15. Use non-bibliographic online systems and other services in your field - there are now about 200 of these available, and their number is growing steadily. Some contain technical data (example: a data base of electronic components), addresses of manufacturers and parameters of their products (example: the French DIANE system in the field of the building industry and machines), numerical data (economic statistics, market analyses), scientific and technological data (example: a metallurgical data base).
16. Do not ignore general and special *encyclopedias* and *handbooks*; they inform one about basic problems, make reference to classic and basic literature, and sometimes help us to start a search via online systems and citation indexes.
17. Consider public *viewdata systems* that are beginning to become generally available. At the moment, they yield rather general and popular information (news, weather, sport), but they might become a useful source of information about coming events (exhibitions, congresses, new books); in the future they will also be able to give more specific information on scientific and technical literature and facts.
18. Check whether the new online and off-line *newspaper information services* (example: the New York Times online system and its followers in many countries) can be useful to you. They give a fast overview of paragraphs and articles in newspapers and some weekly journals in all fields (politics, business, finance, culture, sport, social events etc.). These systems replace the old cutting services.

Even an experienced professional should from time to time check and update his strategy: the information services have changed rapidly in recent years. New journals, new abstracting services, SDI services, new audio-visual aids, new online data bases and retrieval systems are appearing continuously; also some traditional sources are now accessible in online form, libraries are starting to work as public terminals of online systems, reports and dissertations are now more easily accessible in the microfiche form at very low prices. The scene of the information market is changing continuously, and we must not always stick to methods and techniques that were effective some years ago.

42 - Physical storage of documents

The *physical storage of documents* or their photocopies is not a difficult problem. The storage devices are well known and in common use: books are stored on shelves; letters in files, in flat files or folders; journals, reports and other unbound literature in boxes; documents being worked on are temporarily stored in open letter trays or sorting cabinets. There are plenty of good and less good storage devices on the market - a visit to a specialist business equipment and stationery shop or to a special exhibition will suggest ideas.

Many persons stick to old-fashioned storage devices and means; they are influenced by their own habits or by the purchasing departments of their organizations that are often more

Courtesy Esselte-DYMO, Sint-Niklaas, Belgium

Fig. 42.1 - Document boxes

Boxes produced from impact-resistent plastic are practical for filing journals, catalogues, prospectuses, reports and similar documents that are difficult to store in traditional files or folders. The boxes are available in many colours - they brighten up the work place and improve orderliness.

price-oriented than efficiency-oriented, and cannot easily satisfy the specific needs of individual users. Indeed, an ugly and less practical paper flat file is a few cents cheaper than a handsome coloured plastic file with a transparent cover and interchangeable label, but improved orderliness at the workplace of a high-salaried professional is worth the small price difference.

It is necessary to look from time to time for any improvements in storage devices. By way of example, light plastic transportable *book racks* with removable partitions can improve order in small sets of repeatedly used dictionaries and directories. *Plastic boxes*, available in many bright colours, are excellent means for the storage of journals, reports and other thin and floppy publications (fig. 42.1). *Flat files* can be equipped to take a suspended folder rod so that they can be used as single portable units, and also be stored in suspension pocket files or in special drawers and cabinets.

Special devices are needed for such information carriers as microfiches, slides, magnetic tapes, computer output, floppy disks, tape cassettes, video-cassettes etc. Suppliers of these media can usually recommend and deliver appropriate storage equipment. New special storage devices improving tidiness, making search easier and offering better protection to the valuable information carriers are emerging all the time. For instance,

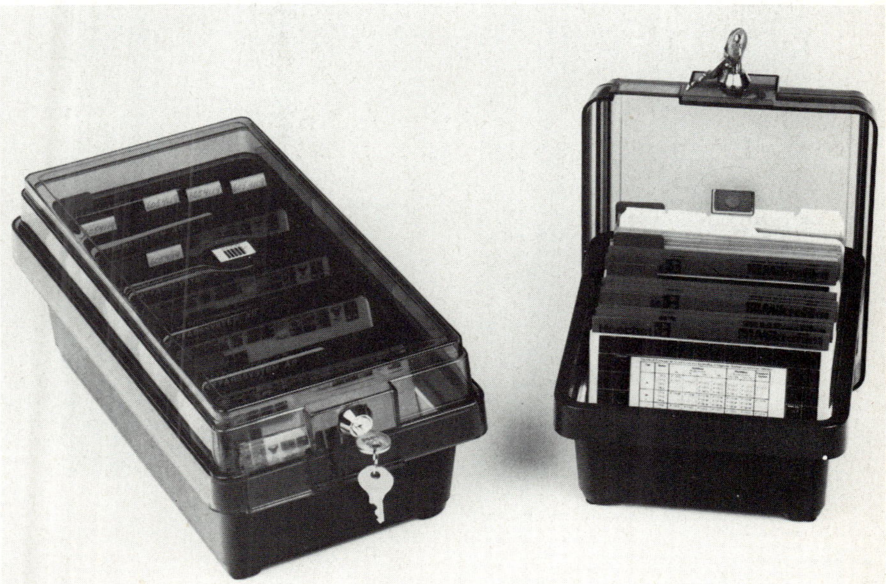

Courtesy ACCO Nederland, Cothen (U), The Netherlands

Fig. 42.2 - Storage of microfiches

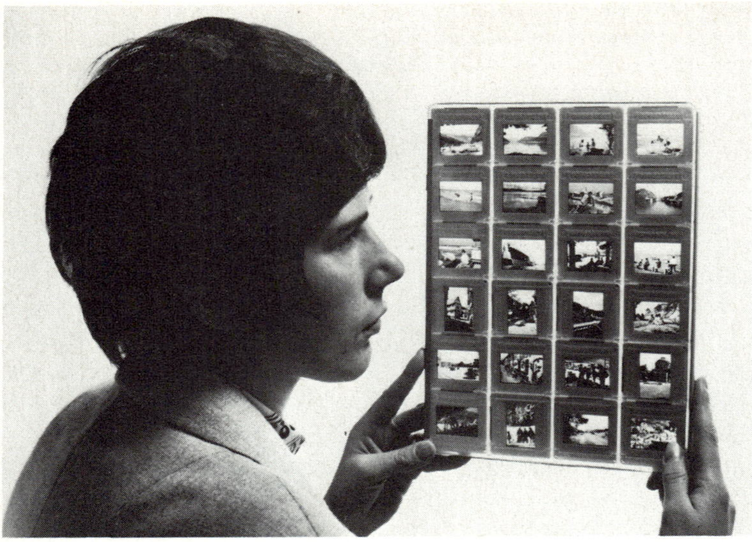

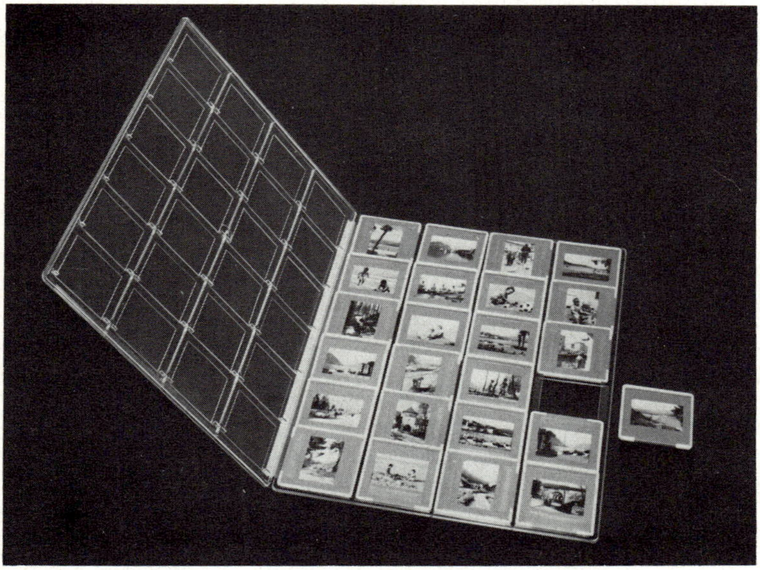

Courtesy Astado, Audio-visuele media, Zeist, The Netherlands

Fig. 42.3 - Transparent cassettes for slides

24 slides (50 × 50 mm) are visible at a glance. This sort of filing is advantageous when we need our slides in varying configurations for different occasions, e.g. lectures on various subjects.

Courtesy Astado, Audio-visuele media, Zeist, The Netherlands

Fig. 42.4 - Slides in special cassettes can be arranged as books on shelves

special *files for microfiches* with overlapping pockets (the identification lines of all the fiches are visible) make rapid selection of a fiche easy. *Slides* may be stored in the familiar cartridges if their sequence is fixed (collections of slides used always in the same sequence), but if they must be selected and recombined time and again (e.g. for a lecture requiring a special selection of slides from a large collection), they are better stored in transparent cassettes that enable 24 slides 50 x 50 mm to be seen at a glance (fig. 42.3 - 42.4). *Floppy disks* for a word processor or personal computer can be stored either in boxes or in special pockets or trays enabling the required disk to be picked out without searching (fig. 42.5).

Attention should be devoted not only to the storage devices, but also to their labelling. A clear, logical and legible system should be used; many files, cartridges, racks, boxes etc. are equipped with pockets for interchangeable labels, or they can be marked by self-adhesive *letters*. The latter are available in many sizes, colours and shapes; they significantly improve orientation in personal files. Also, self-adhesive *tape* printed by a special tang is an invaluable device for improving orderliness. Pre-numbered adhesive *labels* are used for sequential numbering of slides, disks, cassettes, tapes, files, boxes etc. Considerable improvement can be

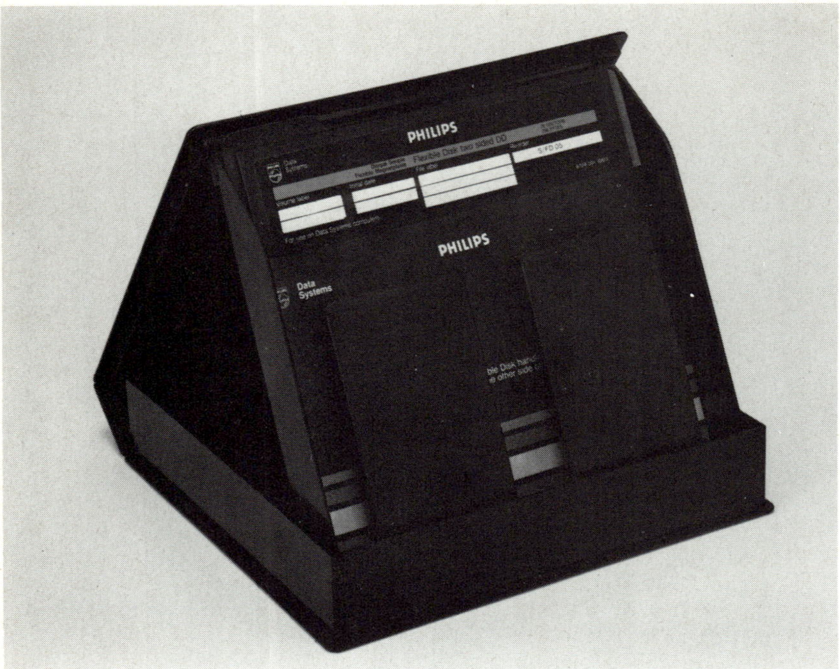

Courtesy Philips Data Systems, Apeldoorn, The Netherlands

Fig. 42.5 - Storage of floppy disks

Floppy disks for word processors and personal computers can be stored in desk stands, rotary files or in trays.

0	WHITE		
1	RED		
2	ORANGE	or	RED + YELLOW
3	YELLOW		
4	GREEN	or	YELLOW + BLUE
5	BLUE		
6	VIOLET	or	BLUE + RED
7	BROWN	or	RED + YELLOW + BLUE
8	GREY	or	WHITE + BLACK
9	BLACK		

Fig. 42.6 - Colour symbolism

Do not forget that colour is informational ! Colours improve order, overview and search in card indexes, files, book shelves, slide boxes etc. Coloured adhesive tapes or stickers can be used if files, boxes, cassettes, etc. are not available in the required colours. A fixed sequence of colours is an aid to ordering and sorting. The number/colour system begins with white and ends with black. The rainbow sequence 1/6 is mnemonic.

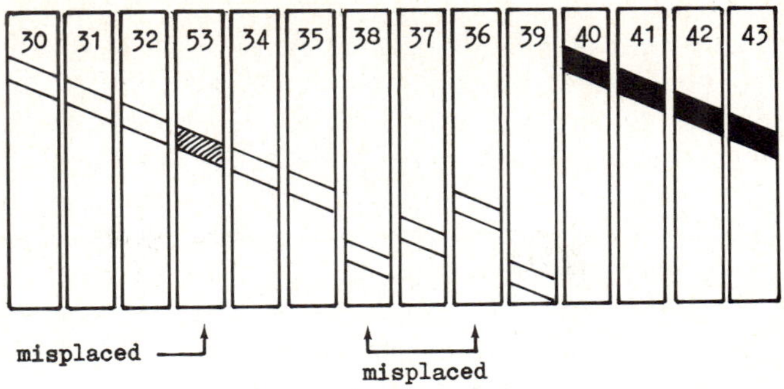

Fig. 42.7 - Visual check of order in physical document collections

Positional marking by means of self-adhesive plastic strips ensures perfect order and overview. Misplaced documents (books, files, boxes, cartridges, cassettes etc.) are identified at a glance. Different colours extend the capacity of the marking system: class is signalled by colour, place is marked positionally. Fascinated by computers, many people forget to use quite simple and cheap devices that might be very effective and could improve the organization at any workplace.

achieved by systematic use of colours - it is striking how little use is made of colours in practice. Coloured files, boxes and other archive devices, or simply coloured plastic strips, are an immense help and they have the side-effect that they brighten up the monotonous (why are nearly all files black ??) work environment.

Microfilm

Despite its advantages, *microfilm* has not yet become a technique in daily use by the majority of professionals. The reasons are that only a fraction of the literature is available in microform, only some professionals have an easy access to equipment for microfilming their own documents and to microfilm readers, and microfilm has some imponderable disadvantages: it is readable only by means of a reader i.e. only at a certain place, it has no facility for underlining and marginal notes, it is usually black and white, and reading it is more tiring than reading paper documents. It is an exception for a professional to have a microfilm reader at his work place; the necessity to have to use a reader in another room (e.g. in the library) is a further inconvenience.

It can be expected that the use of microfilm will increase: more and more primary publications and even complete abstracting journals are becoming available in microfiche form for a price equal to, and often considerably lower than, hardcopies. Many reports are also available in microfiche form (example: the NTIS - The National Technical Information Service - issues all reports on American government-sponsored projects and research activities in microfiche form at very low prices), dissertations are often published in microfiche form as well as directories, lists of zip codes, proceedings of congresses and symposia, museum collections and many other data and document files. Particularly important is the advent of the new technique of *updatable microfiches* that makes it possible to record new pages successively on a microfiche, to add headings, or to record changes (e.g. SEE, INVALID, CHANGED etc.). Recording new pages is as easy and as fast as making copies of documents by means of modern photocopying equipment; a machine of this type can be used in a large organization in a do-it-yourself manner like the photocopying machines that are in common use. Everybody can then create and update his own microfiche file consisting of bought as well as self-made fiches.

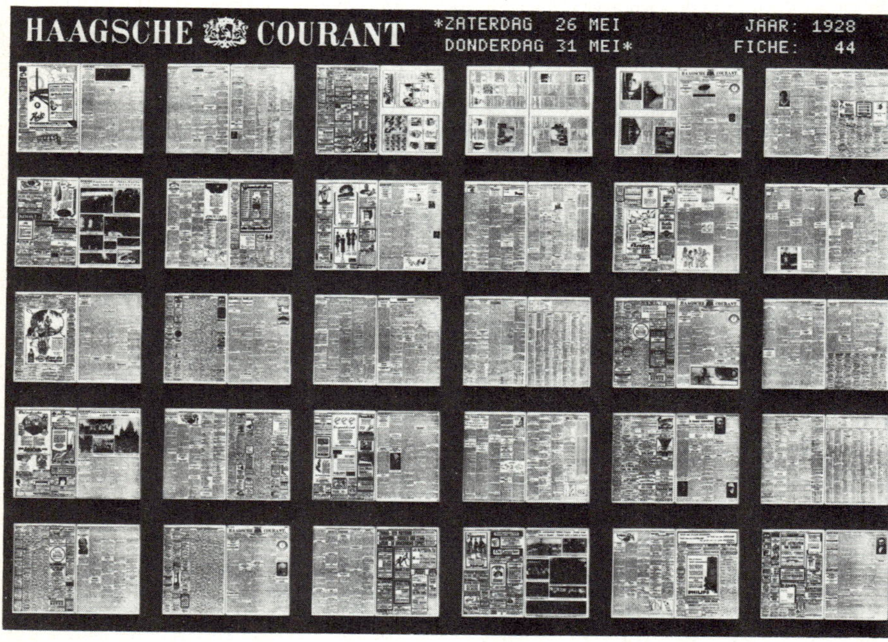

Courtesy Microformat Systems, Hillegom, The Netherlands

Fig. 42.8 - Microfiche in standard A6 (105 × 148 mm) format

Specialist journals, abstracting journals, bibliographies, reports, dissertations, directories, museum collections etc. are now available in microfiche form. Here a microfiche of a Dutch newspaper, volume 1928.

Courtesy AGFA-GEVAERT B.V., Rijswijk, The Netherlands

Fig. 42.9 - A microfiche reader

A relatively inexpensive microfiche reader with 250 × 310 mm green, blue or grey screen and 18:1, 36:1 or 42:1 objectives, suitable for personal use.

43 - Information recording and storage in a retrieval system

Some information encountered is considered irrelevant and not worth remembering or recording (sometimes, we may be wrong and regret it later). Some information considered relevant we might try to keep in our memory, hoping that we shall be able to recall it later when it is required (again, we might overestimate our memory). Otherwise, we must keep the original document and/or record and store the information in such a manner that it will be easily retrievable at any time later.

Marginal notes, abstracting, excerpting

Studying a document requires time and effort. Recalling at any future moment the information gained but partly forgotten is made easier by the following simple methods: underlining significant words or passages in the text being studied, attaching personal marginal notes, making a short abstract and/or compiling an excerpt from the document being read.

Underlining in the text and attaching short personal remarks and marginal notes is the oldest, simplest, fastest and effective means. We should not hesitate to employ it in documents or copies we are studying - provided that they are our own. To take the place of underlining, a rather more advanced technique is now available: the emphasized words or parts of text can be highlighted by means of a *fluorescent marker*; a light yellow colour is the most practical, as black on yellow is the most legible combination, and a yellow field becomes invisible in photocopies and microfilm; markers in light green, red or other colours are also available.

Marginal notes are concise, limited to short sentences, sometimes just one or two words. It is very practical to develop one's own system of signs and symbols (fig. 43.1). They save recording time, they are less disturbing and more striking than words.

An *abstract* is a concise representation of the content of a document. An abstract destined for publication must be written according to certain

<table>
<tr><th>handwritten</th><th>m e a n i n g</th><th>machine readable</th></tr>
<tr><td>|</td><td>important, interesting</td><td>!!</td></tr>
<tr><td>||</td><td>very important, very interesting</td><td>!!!</td></tr>
<tr><td>+</td><td>yes, right, correct, to-the-point</td><td>++</td></tr>
<tr><td>++</td><td>excellent, original, new,</td><td>+++</td></tr>
<tr><td>?</td><td>dubious, inaccurate, fallacious</td><td>??</td></tr>
<tr><td>×</td><td>no, wrong, mistake, error</td><td>xx</td></tr>
<tr><td>××</td><td>essentially wrong</td><td>xxx</td></tr>
<tr><td>∼</td><td>unclear, obscure, fuzzy, wordy</td><td>##</td></tr>
<tr><td>+/</td><td>incomplete, facts or data missing</td><td>&&</td></tr>
<tr><td>*</td><td>important as citation</td><td>**</td></tr>
</table>

Fig. 43.1 - A 'shorthand' system of personal remarks

A system of symbols makes it easy to add personal remarks in the margin when reading (one's own!) book or other documents. It can be used also in personal documentation. Machine-readable data must be unique to be retrievable; therefore single symbols (that also appear within the normal text) are unusable.

generally accepted rules [ref. 43-ANSI, Borko, UNESCO]. It should contain a concise but informative summary of the main ideas and conclusions of the document, no information or claims that are not present in the document, no added interpretation, no evaluation or criticism, and it must be written in complete sentences, not as a list of keywords. In a personal documentation system we need not stick to these rules. The abstract is written for our own use; it may be limited simply to facts and ideas that we have found relevant for ourselves (sometimes we even omit the core of the paper, if we found some peripheral ideas pertinent from our personal point of view); there is also no reason not to use personal remarks, comments, evaluation, criticism, abbreviations, telegraphic style or short keywords instead of complete sentences. The only condition is that the writer of the abstract will be able to understand

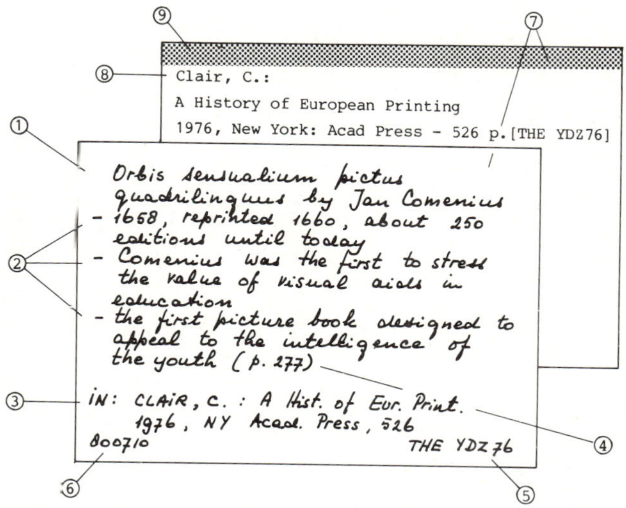

Fig. 43.2 - Example of two documentation cards

The user found some relevant data about the famous work 'Orbis pictus' by Comenius. He has written down the most pertinent facts on the spot in a library. As he also found the source (the book by Clair) important, he noted its bibliographic data on another card.

1. *This card has been filled-in on the spot in the library;*
2. *selected important facts have been documented in concise form;*
3. *short data on the source;*
4. *page must not be forgotten (for later citation and re-reading);*
5. *information about the owner (THE = Technische Hogeschool, Eindhoven) and catalogue number make it easy to find the document again later;*
6. *date of recording;*
7. *in contradistinction to the practice in libraries and documentation centres the user does not record classifiers or keywords on cards;*
8. *bibliographic data on the book;*
9. *red strip drawn by a fluorescent marker = book, not owned by the user.*

it later (sometimes we use abstracts as 'memory triggers', expecting a short remark or keyword to conjure up more details from our memory).

Abstracts in abstracting journals normally contain about 200-250 words. In personal documentation, because of the above peculiarities of a personal system, they are usually shorter. If the title is descriptive enough, the abstract may be omitted altogether.

From large, thoroughly studied documents, we often make *excerpts*. An excerpt is longer and more detailed than an abstract. It refers to the relevant ideas of a document in the original sequence, and selected passages are often reproduced verbatim. In personal documentation we are allowed to excerpt selectively. An excerpt must contain cross-references to the respective pages of the original; exact bibliographical data must also be attached, including the identification of the edition (paginations in different editions might differ). Reproduced or re-drawn figures, schemes, or graphs are often attached.

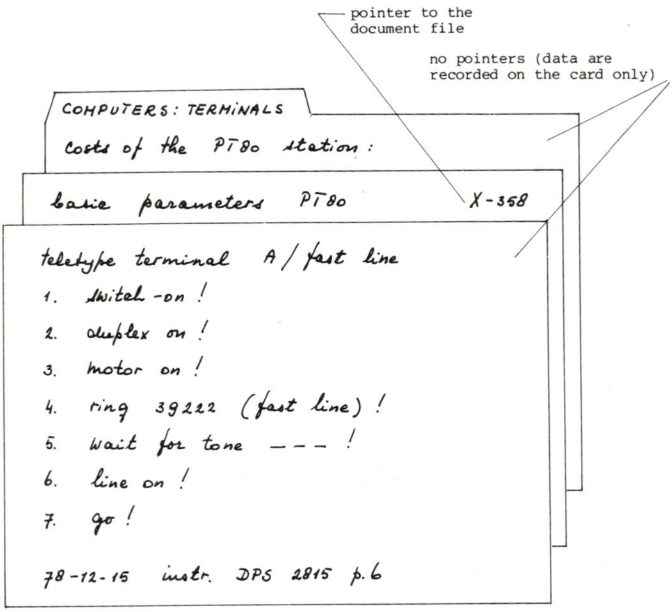

Fig. 43.3 - Cards with informal notes and remarks

Notes, remarks, excerpts, definitions, formulae etc. recorded on loose randomly stored sheets of paper can never be found when required. They are better written down on cards and stored systematically (in this case under COMPUTER : TERMINALS) in a card index or in the computer storage. Concise data on the source of the data are added. The classifiers or keywords need not be noted on the card: it is just stored in the respective part of the card index; this saves time and makes reorganization easier. Longer notes are recorded on A4 sheets and stored separately. A card with a pointer (see document number X358) serves as a cross-reference.

Recording ideas, facts and other similar data

If an idea, fact, definition, statement, formula, scheme, citation or event seems worth recording, it should be noted and stored in such a manner that it will be easily retrievable later. Some data are recorded primarily in a special form, for instance in a *diary* where they are later retrievable by date of the event. Notes and remarks recorded during a trip are usually kept in a special diary, journal or report; the chronological log commonly used in laboratories has been mentioned in section 35. Chronological recording has the advantage of being a continuous, uninterrupted record; its authenticity and completeness is formally assured if the record is kept in the form of a bound book. The weakness is the difficulty of finding specific information, if the date is not known. Then, an *index* (see fig. 46.1) or a retrieval system is necessary.

Instead of chronological recording, the *notes* can be recorded in a manner allowing them to be sorted and organized. They can be recorded on cards in a card index documentation system (see specimen in fig. 43.3) or stored as records in a computerized personal documentation system.

Retrieval system

If the personal document collection is small and the search criteria simple, then a plain arrangement of the original documents in a chosen order is sufficient and no special retrieval tools are necessary. However, when the collection is large and when we would like to find a document by more than one criterion, then such a simple system becomes inconvenient: if books are arranged by authors, then books on a certain subject are scattered; on the other hand, arrangement by subjects makes it difficult to search by author or another point of view. The physical document collection allows only one path of access. A second problem arises from the fact that the original documents must always be stored in separate groups according to their physical properties: we cannot mix books with microfiches, copies of articles, correspondence and slides. Similarly, in a music archive, we have to store gramophone records as one group, tapes as another group, cassettes as a third group. Consequently, if we wish to find a certain subject, we have to search in more than one subcollection of documents. A third problem is that some documents are polythematic so that we cannot sort them by subject.

All the above problems can be mastered if, in addition to the physical document collection, we also employ a *retrieval system*. In such a system - either manual or computerized - documents are replaced by short *records*; either they have the traditional form of a card in a card index, or they are kept in computer storage. Records are always structured: they consist of a number of fields containing specific data: author, title, date, publisher, journal, volume, abstract etc.

Then, the original documents can be arranged in any desired order (perhaps in a plain chronological sequence), and the retrieval system makes it possible to find any of the documents by subject, by author, by publisher or by any other criteria. It is obvious that there must be some *cross-references* between the retrieval system and the document collection to enable the document to be picked out when it has been identified by means of the retrieval system. The simplest form of such a 'pointer' is a catalogue number, sometimes a plain sequential number of the document.

As one is dealing often with several subcollections of documents, a pointer best consists of a one-letter code of the subcollection (B = books, S = slides, X = xerocopies, F = microfiches etc.) and a sequential number. If the subcollection is arranged systematically, then the structure of the pointer has to be adapted, for example B-33-105 is a book 105 in group 33 - national economy. Sometimes, the pointer might be omitted, for example, if the books are arranged in alphabetical order by author; the author's name found by the retrieval system functions as the pointer.

In practice, the user will probably opt for a compromise solution: some of his documents he will simply store in a chosen order without recording them in his personal retrieval system; for example, he might handle his correspondence in this manner, if he finds that its arrangement in alphabetical sequence of addressees is sufficient. On the other hand, documents that he considers important and that must be retrievable in many different ways he will make accessible via his personal retrieval system. His retrieval system, however, stores some records that do not correspond to physical documents, for example factographical data, remarks, notes etc. While there are documents without a record in the retrieval system, there are also records in the retrieval system without a corresponding document in the collection. It is also possible that several records in the system point to one polythematic document in the collection, e.g. proceedings consisting of many papers that are documented separately and stored under various headings in the system.

Input data of a personal documentation system

The *input* for various systems differs owing to specific needs for standardization and formalization. While in manual systems a less consistent form, for example, of authors' names (inconsistent sequence of surname/forenames, inconsistent use of full or initialized forenames etc.) is not disturbing because of the small volume of the document collection and the use of manual search, in mechanized systems any imperfection causes errors in sorting and in retrieval. We make below some comments on the contents and form of recording.

The *author's surname* is recorded in the form in which it appears on the publication; surnames in other than Roman characters have to be transliterated (international standards should be respected). *Forenames* are usually abbreviated to initials, titles are omitted, but identifiers Jr., Sr., and abbreviations such as 'ed.' (editor) may be attached. Co-author names are separated by a separator, preferably a semicolon (see examples in fig. 43.4). Author's *affiliation* (company, university, institute...) is attached if considered significant.

The *title* of the publication is always used in its original version (transliterated, if not in Roman characters), and a translation may be added, if necessary. If some important characteristic is missing from the title, it may be added in brackets; such an 'amended' or 'enriched' title describes the publication better and helps to retrieve it in title indexes or in online retrieval based on titles. Whimsical titles should be replaced by pseudo-titles added by the documentalist. Other *bibliographic data*, in abbreviated form in a personal documentation system, help to identify the document. International standards are used in the field of bibliography and documentation [ref. 43-ISO]. We should follow them, particularly if we intend to use the records in references in a future publication. An *imprint line* consists of the date of issue (books: year; newspaper: year/month/day), place of issue and publisher in the case of books, or abbreviation of the journal name (preferably according to the interna-

```
UDC 655                                     B-1037

Hartley, J.; Burnhill, P.:
Fifty guide-lines for improving instructional
text
1977, Program Learn Edu
Prose and grammatical f
graphs. Typographical d
45 references.
```

```
DOC: B-1037
AUT: Hartley, J.; Burnhill, P.:
TIT: Fifty guide-lines for improving
     instructional text
DAT: 1977
JRN: Program Learn Educ Technol
BIB: 14(1)65-75
UDC: 655
DES: PUBLISHING; LAYOUT; GRAPHS
ABS: Prose and grammatical features.
     Tables and graphs. Typographical
     design. 45 ref.
```

Fig. 43.4 - Example of record structure in personal documentation

Records in the form of a card (left) and of computer input data (right). The fields in a card could be pre-printed, but if standard layout and sequence of data elements are followed, blank cards can be used. Computer input is structured by means of tags, i.e. abbreviated names of record fields.

tional standard ISO-833), volume, number of issue, and pagination. In a personal documentation system it is practical also to attach a remark about the owner of the original (person or library, in the latter case we add also the catalogue number as this makes it easier to find the document again later). Finally, an abstract is usually added. Examples of records in a personal documentation system in the forms of cards and computer input are shown in fig. 43.4 and 46.2.

Practical habits

Careful primary recording of information is important for its further storage and retrieval. Anything forgotten or omitted at this phase can never, or not easily, be added later. The first rule is: record wherever possible *on the spot.* Two things must always be at hand, even when we are travelling: a set of standardized *cards* in a plastic envelope that are ready to be filled in at any moment (at a congress, in the library, in a meeting or during a discussion), and a *pocket dictating machine.*

Indeed, we recommend both because in some situations recording in written form is more advantageous (recording bibliographic data, recording during a lecture), but in other situations writing is impossible or too slow (dictating text or recording ideas while walking, when visiting an exhibition; recording important notes during a short pause at a congress etc.).

The second rule is: record wherever possible in the *final form.* Avoid notes on bits of paper, in an ad hoc, incomplete or illegible form. Get used to some fixed form, sequence, layout and punctuation, even when you are not using pre-printed cards (see examples in fig. 43.3 and 45.1). Information recorded via a dictating machine is transcribed (by the secretary or by the user himself), or (less frequently) it is stored as it is; then a note in the personal retrieval system must make it retrievable later by means of keywords, date etc. Longer excerpts, texts, drawings, graphs etc. should also be written or drawn in a form directly suitable for storage: each subject on a separate sheet of paper, preferably of A4 format. Again, we should not forget the formal data: description, title, date, author's name, source, version, comments, explanatory notes etc.

How often we encounter important drafts, schemes, sketches etc. on bits of paper without identification, without date (it is then difficult to distinguish between older and newer versions of the same draft) or without the name of the author. It is true that a clever idea does not lose its value if sketched by pencil on a scrap of paper, but a good external form improves the legibility, creates a sense of order, makes the document retrievable, and improves the general level of the system of knowledge organization. The form must not be underestimated.

44 - Classification and indexing

We have mentioned above and shown in fig. 43.2 and 43.4 that a record consists of bibliographic data (author, title, date of publication etc.), an abstract, and a pointer to the collection of original documents. For retrieval purposes, some content characteristics must also be added that make it possible to find documents about a certain subject. There are two traditional manual methods of labelling a document in this way for retrieval purposes: classification and indexing.

Classification is based on a preconceived plan: the whole field of interest is a priori divided into a number of classes. Nearly all classification systems are hierarchical, i.e. the whole field is divided into a few main classes, each of these is subdivided into subclasses, and this process of splitting-up can be repeated down to the required detail. All classes together cover the field of interest completely, and without overlapping. The creation of the system proceeds from generic to specific and also the classification of documents follows the same philosophy. It resembles the familiar classification of animals and plants: we descend from the top (vertebrata) to more and more detailed subclasses (mammals - carnivora - dogs - dachshunds).

The classes and subclasses are labelled by *classifiers*; alphabetical, alphanumerical or numerical codes can be used. The typical, most popular and practical form is *decimal classification* (fig. 44.1).

```
0 GENERALITIES
1 PHILOSOPHY
2 THEOLOGY
3 SOCIAL SCIENCES
4 VACANT
5 MATHEMATICS. NATURAL SCIENCES
  51 GENERALITIES
  52 ASTRONOMY. GEODESY
     521 THEORETICAL ASTRONOMY
     522 PRACTICAL ASTRONOMY
     523 DESCRIPTIVE ASTRONOMY
         523.1 UNIVERSE. SPACE
         523.2 SOLAR SYSTEM
         523.3 THE MOON
         523.4 PLANETS
               523.41 MERCURY
               523.42 VENUS
               523.43 MARS
               523.44 ASTEROIDS

 6 APPLIED SCIENCES. TECHNOLOGY
 7 THE ARTS. RECREATION. SPORT
 8 LANGUAGES. LIGUISTICS. LITERATURE
 9 GEOGRAPHY. BIOGRAPHY. HISTORY
```

Fig. 44.1 - Scheme of hierarchical decimal classification

Specimen of the structure of UDC (Universal Decimal Classification).

The main advantage of classification is its logical structure, being based on the stepwise approach from generic to specific. The related concepts are close together, and orientation is easier for the user; thus, a hierarchical classification system can be easily learned and employed. The principal disadvantage of a hierarchical classification system is its rigidity. It is difficult to adapt the existing divisions, and it is practically impossible to change its basic structure.

A professional will prefer hierarchical classification in his personal retrieval system if his field of interest can easily and logically be dissected according to one point of view, and if he does not expect radical changes in his system later. If he decides to employ classification, he should first consider if he could use some of the existing systems in their original or abbreviated form. In particular, abstracting journals covering specific fields of science, technology or economics use their own systems of classification that can easily be taken over or adapted by somebody whose field of interest is identical with the discipline(s) covered by the respective service.

For example, a specialist engaged in the field of bacteriology should consider applying in his own documentation the classification subsystem of the bacteriology section of the Excerpta Medica; a specialist in operations research should consider employing the subject classification that he finds in the journal Operations Research, consisting of 60 main classes and about 300 subclasses. In each case he will either take over the classification in its original form, or merely select its main classes, and the detailed subclassification only in the subclasses that are relevant to his narrow specialization.

Professionals whose interest is multi-disciplinary should consider using selected parts of one of the existing *universal classification systems.*

More than a hundred years ago (1876) the American librarian Melvil Dewey designed his universal system of decimal classification. He divided the whole field of human knowledge into ten main classes numbered from 0 to 9 (0 - general works, 1 - philosophy... 9 - history), and he subdivided each class by adding digits to the right the asummed decimal point. His classification schedule has been widely used in American libraries. At the end of the 19th century two Belgians, Otlet and LaFontaine, adapted the Dewey classification into the UDC - Universal Decimal Classification, which found widespread application in European libraries and documentation centres. Another general-purpose scheme is the classification system of the Library of Congress that uses alphanumerical, hierarchically designed codes.

Obviously, it would not be wise to take over for personal application a large, universal classification system intended for vast collections, in all its details. When adapting such a system (say, UDC), we must first adopt all its ten main classes; we are thus certain that we shall be able to store now and in the future information on any subject from philosophy to history and from mathematics to economics or photography. Some of the classes will probably remain largely unoccupied, and we shall not

UDC	INSPEC
001 theoretical aspect	A applications
002 practical aspect	B bibliography/literature survey
003 economical, financial aspect	E economic aspect, market survey
004 application aspect	G general or review aspect
005 equipment aspect	N new developments
006 space and place aspect	P practical aspects
007 personnel aspect	T theoretical or mathematical aspect
008 organizational aspect	X experimental aspect
009 realization or service aspect	

Fig. 44.2 - Documents may also be classified by aspect

subdivide them. On the other hand, classes where a large number of documents might be expected have to be subdivided. We should always go into the depth practical for our own purposes; later, when the number of documents in a subclass grows, we can split it again into more detailed subdivisions. Sometimes, not only classification by subject, but also by a specific point of view - by time, country, language, form of document, aspect etc. - might be relevant (fig. 44.2).

If the user finds hierarchical classification the best solution, but none of the existing systems - specialized or general-purpose - can meet his

0 00 01 02 03 04 05 06 07 08 09	5 50 51 52 53 54 55 56 57 58 59
1 10	6 60

Fig. 44.3 - Pre-printed scheme of decimal classification

Pre-printed form with 10 classes and 10 × 10 subclasses helps to design the structure of decimal classification. It can be used at any hierarchical level, e.g. a sheet of the subclass 49 contains 100 subdivisions from 4900 to 4999. Instead of a pre-printed sheet, the form can be stored in the memory of a word processor or a computer, displayed on the screen, filled in, edited (empty subclasses can be deleted) and printed out in the final version. Classification schemes in figures 37.1 and 38.1 were edited and printed out in this manner by means of a word processor.

requirements, then he has to develop his *own system.* Again, he must first define his field of interest (not too narrowly - he has to take account of the peripheral fields, and probable future changes, expansions and shifts in his field of activity), then try to divide it into main classes, and further into increasingly detailed subclasses. A practical help is a pre-printed form for the drafting and final editing of a decimal classification system (fig. 44.3).

A *special classification scheme* might be used if the professional designs a special-purpose, ad hoc documentation system. This is often the case when a writer is preparing a publication and gathering the material; the classification of such an ad hoc system should conform to the structure of the prepared publication (chapters, sections).

Indexing

Whilst classification is (should be !) a strictly logical, closed, hierarchical system, *indexing* gives the user more freedom. Classification, in principle, is an attempt to 'insert' a document into one of the existing, pre-defined categories ('pigeon holes') of a fixed system. On the contrary, indexing is, in principle, an attempt to 'label' a document using either a freely selected word or phrase of the natural language (often under the influence of the text of the document) or one or more keywords (descriptors) authorized by a special list (thesaurus).

Free indexing

Free indexing by means of an 'open indexing language' means the freedom to use any word or phrase of the natural language as keyword. In practice, the freedom of choice is not unlimited: the user tries to restrict the number of different keywords (he avoids synonyms, replaces rare terms by more generic terms, avoids slang or unusual words, prefers standardized orthography).

The main advantage of free indexing is that it is easy to adapt and to expand. Its disadvantage is the danger of confusion (use of synonyms, overlapping terms), increased by the fact that the alphabetical arrangement of lists of keywords brings heterogeneous terms together, while related concepts are scattered through the file. The problem of synonyms makes the system rather difficult, and the user needs to be supported by cross-references (DIALOGUE see CONVERSATION, PASS-BOOK see BANK-BOOK, LABOR see LABOUR).

In spite of the (nearly) unlimited freedom to choose keywords, the creation of a personal indexing system should not be started without a plan. At least, a rough draft should be designed in advance. An alphabetical index from a good handbook covering our field of interest or a special dictionary can be consulted, the most important keywords selected and an initial list of keywords drafted.

Controlled indexing languages

The rigidity and inflexibility of hierarchical classification, on the one hand, and the lack of system in free indexing on the other hand, led in the sixties to the creation of a new generation of indexing languages: *controlled indexing languages* consisting of descriptors organized within a structured thesaurus appeared, and they became typical instruments of the computerized retrieval systems.

A controlled indexing language consists of a limited number of previously selected and defined indexing terms, descriptors. *Descriptor* is generally understood to mean a term, word or phrase selected from the natural language and permitted for use in a particular indexing system. The essential difference from the natural language is that a descriptor is semantically defined, and free from synonymy and homonymy. It unambiguously represents one and only one concept; one concept is always represented by one and only one descriptor.

A *thesaurus* is a list of all authorized descriptors. Usually, it is structured. For every term, the synonyms (not allowed as indexing terms) are enumerated under the reference USE FOR (bank-book USE FOR pass-book). Also generic terms, specific terms and related terms are attached in most thesauri (fig. 44.4). All in all, a thesaurus is much freer, and easier to change and adapt than rigid hierarchical classification, but

FISSION REACTOR MATERIALS	descriptor
UF -nuclear reactor materials	use for (synonym that must not be used
NT -fission reactor fuel -moderators	narrower terms
BT -materials	broader term
TT -materials	top term in the hierarchy
RT -claddings -fission reactors -fussion reactor materials -heavy water -materials handling -radioactive waste	related terms

Fig. 44.4 - Example of one item in a large structured thesaurus (NASA)

it is also unambiguous and more systematic than any system of free indexing.

Thesauri have found wide application in computerized information retrieval systems, and there now exist several hundred thesauri in nearly all fields of science, technology and other disciplines. Some of them are very special, others cover broad and diversified areas (such as the Excerpta Medica thesaurus, NASA thesaurus, INSPEC thesaurus etc.).

A thesaurus can also be used in a personal documentation system. Then, either one of the existing thesauri can be employed, or a personal extract from it is used to index only the specific field(s) of interest of the user. If none of the existing thesauri is found to be suitable, then the user has to design his *own thesaurus.* In many a personal documentation, a *faceted thesaurus* is the best solution. Such a thesaurus consists of a few facets, each of them representing a certain point of view of indexing, and each of which has a separate list of descriptors.

In the book Personal Documentation for Professionals [ref. 40-Stibic] the principles of the design of one's own thesaurus are explained, and three examples of personal thesauri (the thesauri of an entomologist, an architect and a computer scientist) are given. In fig. 44.5 we present another case, the thesaurus of a musician, the owner of a large collection of gramophone records, tapes and cassettes, books and sheet-music.

The thesaurus, as mentioned above, is a typical tool of mechanized systems based on manual indexing. These systems, in contrast to traditional manual retrieval systems, permit documents to be retrieved by means of any combination of keywords, defined at the moment of inquiry.

FACETS	*	EXAMPLES
COMPOSER	G	Brahms, Debussy, Smetana...
GENRE	G	oratorio, opera, madrigal, jazz, folklore..
INSTRUMENT(S)	G	piano, organ, string quartet, orchestra ..
STYLE	A	baroque, romantic, modern ...
CONDUCTOR	A	Boskowski, Kubelík, Karajan..
ARTIST(S)	A	Oistrach, Wiener Knabenchor..
KEY	A	C major, D minor ..
TIME	X	1890/1900, 18th century..
COUNTRY	X	Austria, France, Italy..

Fig. 44.5 - Example of the facets in the personal thesaurus of a musician

Remarks: G - used generally; A - auxiliary, used if significant; X - used only in combination with some genres (e.g. country if genre = folklore).

Indexing a document by a number of descriptors (particularly if they are taken from different facets) allows the thesaurus to be relatively small, but still the number of combinations is immense. A small number of easily combinable descriptors makes deeper indexing and retrieval possible than a large thesaurus of terms that cannot be combined.

Automatic indexing

Advanced computerized retrieval systems make it possible to mechanize the indexing. The original text of documents or of abstracts is used as input, and the computer selects, according to a program, words or phrases from it that are considered as significant for characterizing the subject of the document. There exist many programs for automatic indexing, simple and also quite sophisticated. They all begin by identifying words in the text, ignoring some frequently occurring 'non-significant words' such as THE, IN, HAVE, AFTER etc., and they submit the remaining words to a number of operations: sometimes, word-endings are truncated so that a number of inflected word forms are changed into one root form (TRANSFORMED, TRANSFORMING, TRANSFORMS = TRANSFORM); compound terms are recognized and handled as one concept (DATA PROCESSING, NITRIC ACID, GREAT BRITAIN). In some systems, synonyms or orthographical synonyms can also be automatically handled by means of stored synonym relations (RAY = BEAM, LABOUR = LABOR, UNITED STATES = USA).

Many different features of automatic indexing are built into the existing systems. A description of them can be found in the vast literature on automatic indexing and on retrieval systems. A short overview, sufficient to orientate the user of a personal documentation system, with a case study of a personal information retrieval system based on automatic indexing was presented in the book Personal Documentation for Professionals [ref. 40-Stibic].

Combination of indexing languages

In many mechanized retrieval systems, a document can be indexed by several different indexing languages in parallel; e.g. it can be classified by means of a hierarchical system, *and* indexed by a few descriptors, *and* its text can be automatically indexed. In such a case the inquirer can request documents of a certain class, and/or indexed by a certain combination of descriptors, and/or containing certain word(s) in the title or abstract. Free choice of combinations of different indexing languages allows a very flexible retrieval strategy. The choice and possibilities of a classification or indexing method are strongly influenced by the technique employed: what is easily possible using a large computer can be prohibitive on a personal computer and impossible in a card index system.

45 - Card index technique

Some people may feel that the simple *card index technique* is obsolete in this age of computers. This is certainly not yet true, as regards the field of personal documentation. Not only are there many professionals who at the moment have no access to a terminal and who do not intend to buy a personal computer of a higher price class simply for documentation purpose but, in small-scale applications, cards also have some advantages over a computer. The card index technique is cheap, it allows on-the-spot input, handling and rearranging the cards is efficient, and the search time (we are thinking here of small personal collections !) is not prohibitively long. Though mechanized systems have their strengths, a card index can, for some time to come, render a good service to many persons with small files and modest technical equipment; later, a mechanized system can take over the data base accumulated in the form of card records.

The card index

Only three simple devices are needed: cards, leading cards, and a card box. The *cards* must be precisely cut; any variation, particularly in the card height, makes handling difficult. In continental Europe, the standard documentation card format is A6, i.e. 105 × 148 mm. In America, the popular formats for cards are 3 × 5 and 4 × 6 inches. The card material should be of good quality; in public libraries where heavy-duty cards must be used, paper of ca 190 g (one square meter weighs 190 g) is recommended in the current standards, but for personal documentation paper of about 80 g (the quality of good letter writing paper) should be preferred as it saves space in the card index, and it can easily be handled in a typewriter and word processor. Cards of different colours can help to distinguish between various types of documents (books, reports, articles...); a simpler solution is to use cards of one colour only (white) and to have different-coloured strips along the upper edge of the cards made by a fluorescent marker (fig. 43.2).

It is possible to use cards with pre-printed fields (author, title etc.), but *blank cards* are sufficient if we adhere to a few rules of layout; for example, if we always write the classifiers or descriptors on the first line, author(s) on the second, title beginning on the third line, and then the imprint line in a standard sequence (e.g. year, month, journal, volume, number, pages). Then, not only are the costs of printing special cards saved, but the available space is also better utilized.

Leading cards are made of stronger material; adhesive, metal or plastic labels can be used for headings or codes; they can be written by hand or typed, or self-adhesive letters and numbers can be employed.

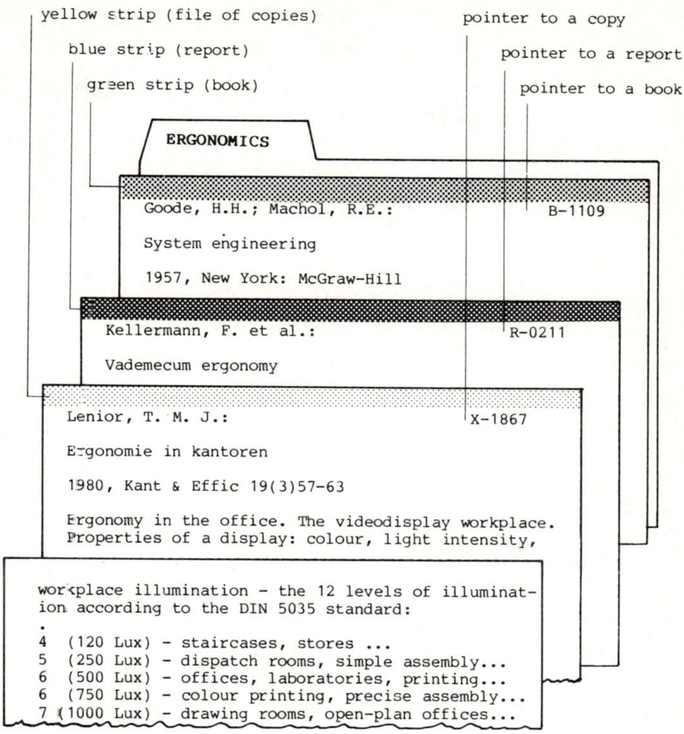

Fig. 45.1 - Example of cards in a personal card index

On every leading card the classifier(s) or keyword(s) identify the subject. Documentation cards are stored in front of (not behind) the leading card. Pointers to the original documents enable the original document to be found in the respective subcollection.

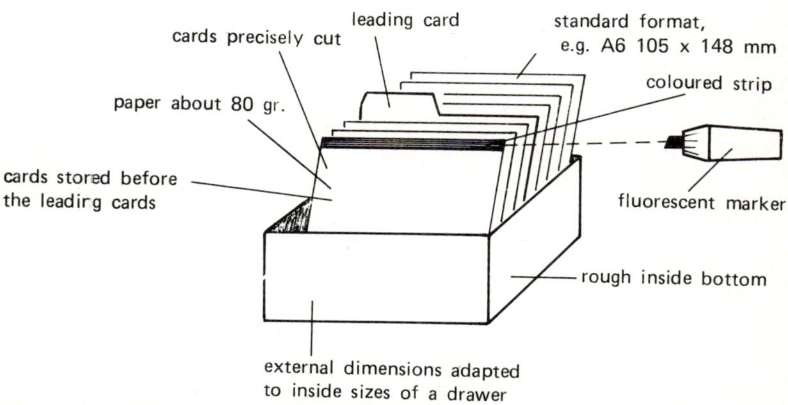

Fig. 45.2 - A card index - a few practical rules

There are plenty of good (and not so good) *card index boxes* made of wood, plastic or metal available. The simplest, and often the best, solution is to insert the card index into one of the drawers of one's writing desk; then it is always at one's elbow, and occupies no place on top of the desk.

In principle, any of the manual classification or indexing methods can be used for arranging the cards in a card index, but hierarchical classification or a system of subject headings consisting of free keywords and their combinations are the preferable solutions.

Coincidence card system

Coincidence cards, also known by the name 'peek-a-boo' cards, are a marvellous retrieval instrument. Their principle is quite simple: In this system, a card does not represent one document, but one keyword. Each card has a pre-printed lattice consisting of small windows numbered sequentially, in our example in fig. 45.3 from 0 to 1999. Also the documents are numbered sequentially. All documents indexed by a keyword (say, FINANCE) are indicated in the respective card by punching holes in the windows of the document numbers. If we are searching for documents indexed by any keyword, we simply take and inspect the respective card and we find immediately the numbers of all documents indexed by that keyword. If we want to find documents indexed by two keywords, say FINANCE and INDUSTRY, we take two cards and placing one over the other we see at a glance those documents that are indexed by both terms. The retrieval procedure is extremely fast: select a few cards, place one over the other and look against the light - indeed, the retrieval procedure is often faster than search by means of a large computer.

This technique has its limitations: the number of documents must not be too large, the number of keywords (though theoretically unlimited) must be reasonable, combinations of keywords by OR's (FINANCE or BANKS or MONEY) are rather cumbersome, changes are impossible. Consequently, the typical field of application for this technique is relatively small, but frequently used collections of a few thousand documents, indexed by a limited number (say, a few hundreds) of keywords that are easy to combine.

The book Personal Documentation for Professionals [ref. 40-Stibic] contains an example of an industrial archeologist who owns a collection of slides and who employs a peek-a-boo system for retrieval. He classifies his slides by subjects (steam engines, mills, locomotives...), by branch of industry (mines, iron industry, transport...), by countries and by time. If he is searching for German locomotives of the decade 1840/49, he takes three cards: LOCOMOTIVES, GERMANY and 1840/49, places one over the other, and within a second he finds the respective slides: holes occurring in all three cards signal their numbers. In fig. 45.3 we present the case of an owner of a musical collection (we have mentioned the creation of his own small thesaurus in section 44 and fig. 44.5) who uses a peek-a-boo system. He can retrieve a composition by genre (opera, madrigal...), by instrument (piano, string quartet...), by style (baroque, modern...), by composer, by conductor or artist, by country or time.

Terse documentation

A simplified card index (or loose-leaf) system consists of cards indexed by subject headings or classifiers. On each card or page are noted concise data on documents about the respective subject; the note is usually limited

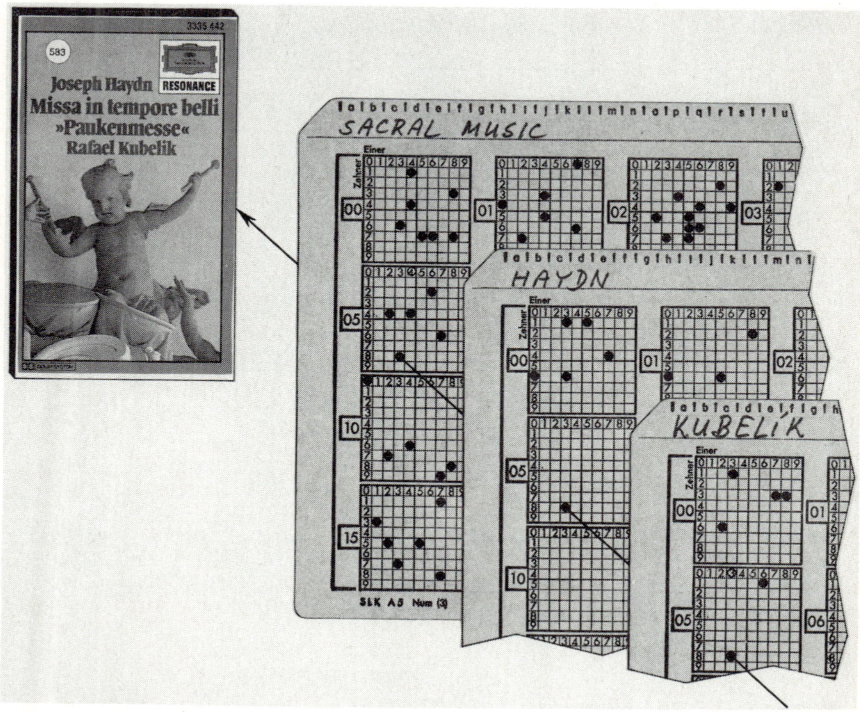

Fig. 45.3 - Peek-a-boo card system of a musician

A musician owns a collection of gramophone records, tapes and cassettes and also a number of music and books about music. He employes a simple peek-a-boo system for retrieval; his faceted thesaurus was shown in fig. 44.5. If he is searching for sacred music by Joseph Haydn conducted by Rafael Kubelík, he takes the cards HAYDN, SACRED MUSIC and KUBELÍK and places one over the other. At a glance he finds the number 0583 - Haydn's 'Paukenmesse' - Missa in tempore belli. A hole for this number occurs in all three cards.

to one line only, and it contains merely a pointer to the original document and a very short comment (fig. 45.4).

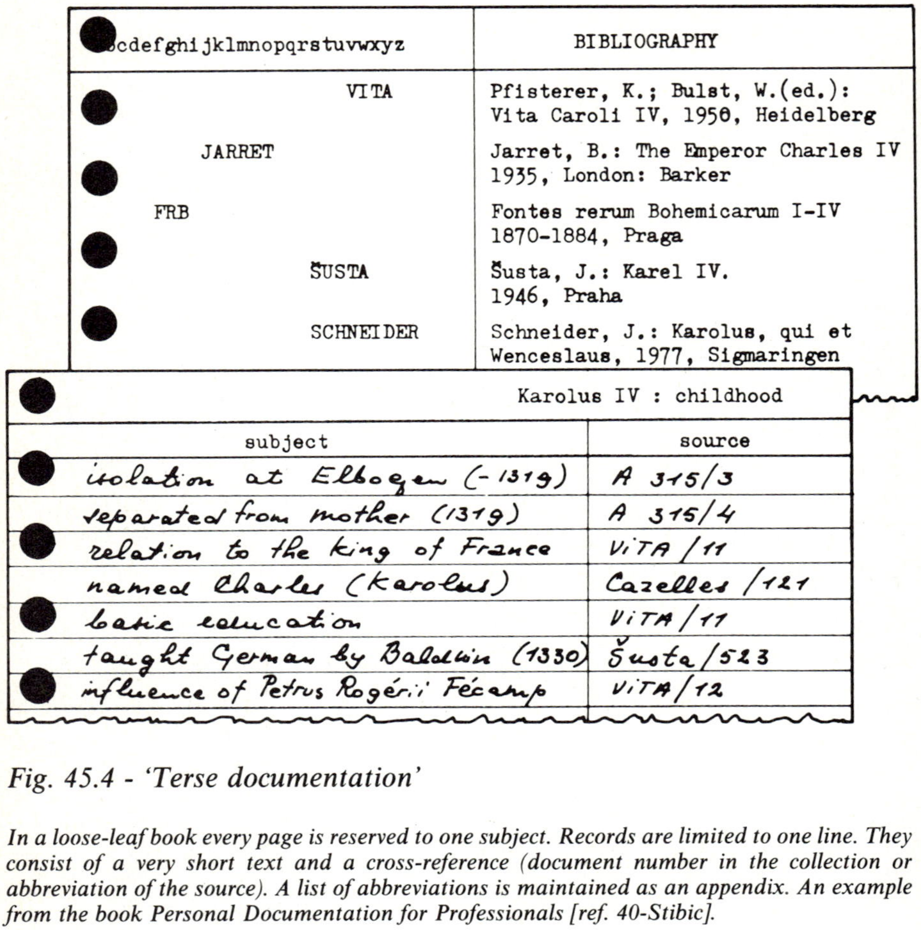

Fig. 45.4 - 'Terse documentation'

In a loose-leaf book every page is reserved to one subject. Records are limited to one line. They consist of a very short text and a cross-reference (document number in the collection or abbreviation of the source). A list of abbreviations is maintained as an appendix. An example from the book Personal Documentation for Professionals [ref. 40-Stibic].

46 - Computerized indexes

Indexes are ordered reference lists of the contents of a file or of a document with references for identification of the location of these contents. They are one of the oldest retrieval tools in libraries where they have been used for hundreds of years. They make it possible to find documents in a collection by document numbers, by author names, by titles or by keywords or classifiers characterizing their content. For centuries they have been compiled manually. Manual indexes could also be used in small files in a personal documentation system - an alphabetical index to make it possible to find a note or remark in a diary was mentioned in section 35. A simple device enabling easy manual updating of small-sized alphabetical lists is shown in fig. 46.1.

In the first half of this century alphabetical and subject indexes were pushed into the background by the more flexible and easier to update card index systems. Computers, due to their enormous ability to sort and print brought about a comeback of printed indexes, which again found wide application. Moreover, the computer made it possible to design quite new forms of indexes that had not been feasible manually: in particular the KWIC, KWOC and other permutated indexes.

A plain *alphabetical* or *numerical index* is processed by sorting and printing out a set of records according to the content of a selected record field (say, author or catalogue number) that has been chosen as the source for the index headings. Specimens of two indexes are given in figures 46.2 and 46.3. One of them is sorted alphanumerically by document numbers, the other alphabetically by authors' names. In the first case the document numbers are also pointers making it possible to find the original in the collection. In the author index, the document numbers are also printed out and they serve as pointers.

An interesting form of computerized index is the *KWIC - Key-Word-In-Context index.* Designed in 1959 by Luhn [ref. 45], it has found wide

subject	see date	N
abcdefghijklmnopqrstuvwxyz	month/day (1981)	
NTIS	0201	
Nordman	0306,13	
Naarden	0310,0421,28,0505	
NCC	0423	
NSTT	0513,14,15	
networks CDF	0515	
Norton	0522	
NAC project	0603	
Nolthen	0604,08	

Fig. 46.1 - A simple device for alphabetical sorting and updating

An index of chronological records in a diary can be kept and updated in a simple form. One page per letter (or letter group) is used. The keyword is shifted according to the second (third) letter. The index is updated chronologically and a pointer to page or date in the diary is added. This simple technique can be used for manual updating of lists of names, indexes, vocabularies, terminological lists etc. by those who have not (yet) a word processor, personal computer or terminal that make updating of lists quite easy.

```
X0748  HARTLEY, J.; BURNHILL, P.                              A; E; 7702
       FIFTY GUIDELINES FOR IMPROVING INSTRUCTIONAL TEXT
       RULES FOR EDITING, TYPOGRAPHICAL FORM AND LAYOUT OF PUBLICATIONS.
       TITLES, ABSTRACTS, SUMMARIES, HEADINGS, STYLE. TABLES AND GRAPHS.
       LAYOUT OF TABLES. TYPES OF GRAPHS. TYPOGRAPHICAL FORM: PARAGRAPHS,
       SPACING, LINES, COLUMNS, JUSTIFYING, HYPHENATION. SPECIAL RULES FOR
       TYPING THIS ARTICLE. DETAILED LITERATURE REFERENCES [***].
       PROGRAM LEARN EDUC TECHNOL 14(1)65-75

X0749  PREISS, H.F.                                           A; G; 7806
       UNIDAS/1100 - DAS INFORMATIONSYSTEM VON SPERRY RAND
       NACHR DOK 29(3)115-120

X0750  TÄUBER, D.:                                            A; G; 7806
       CONDOR: EIN INTEGRIERTES DATENBANK- UND INFORMATIONSSYSTEM
       AN ONLINE NATURAL-LANGUAGE INFORMATION RETRIEVAL SYSTEM DEVELOPED
       BY SIEMENS, PARTLY GRANTED BY THE GERMAN MINISTRY OF SCIENCE.

X0751  TEITELBAUM, H.H.; HAWKINS, D.T.                        A; E; 7804
       DATABASE SUBJECT INDEX
       FIELDS OF SCIENCE AND TECHNOLOGY COVERED BY 86 DATABASES AVAILABLE
       VIA % MAJOR ONLINE SYSTEMS (LOCKHEAD, SDC, BRS, MEDLINE, NYT) IN
       OCTOBER, 1977. ALPHABETIC SUBJECT INDEX.
       ONLINE 2(2)16-21
```

```
AARON, G.          PICTURE PROCESSING FOR DIGITAL FACSIMILE#          X0288
ABRAMSON, H.D.     PARTIAL ORDERING OF THE SYNTAX ELEMENTS OF A LAN   X0732
                   GUAGE#
ABRIAL, J.R.       DESCRIPTION SEMANTIQUE DES BASES DES DONNÉES#      X1029
ACM                3RD DATA COMMUNICATION SYMPOSIUM#                  B0213
ADAM, A.           KYBERNETISCHE MODELLE UND METHODEN#                X1027
ADRIAANSE, P.      KOSTENASPEKTEN EN NETWERKEN#                       N0060
ALBRECHT, H.R.     THE VIRTUAL TERMINAL ACCESS METHOD#                X0872
ALLARD, J.F.       GESTION EN TEMPS REEL ET BASES DE DONNEES DISTRI   R0135
                   BUEES#
```

Fig. 46.2/3 - A catalogue and an author index

The first index is sorted by catalogue numbers; it contains the essential bibliographical data and an abstract. The second index is arranged alphabetically by author. It contains further only the title and the catalogue number that serves as a pointer to the catalogue (above) where more detailed information can be found, as well as to the collection of original documents.

application and great popularity in the last twenty years. The specimen in fig. 46.4 is perhaps more instructive than a long narration. First, the user defines which record field is to be used for indexing. Typical is the title KWIC index. If the selected index field contains text in natural language (like the title field), then a small vocabulary of 'non-significant words' (THE, OF, IN, WHICH, ABOUT...) stored in the computer memory ensures that these words are ignored in the indexing procedure. All the remaining words are taken as keywords. Each record appears in the index as many times as there are keywords in the index field; all records are sorted alphanumerically by keyword and printed out in a special layout: the keywords are situated in the central column, and the text that precedes and follows is added at either side as space permits. Again, a pointer to the document is added, making it possible to find the original in the collection.

Another version is the *KWOC - Key-Word-Out-of-Context index.* Its basic design is similar, but the keywords are placed in a separate column and the content of the index field (e.g. the title) is printed in its original form, without shifting to the left or right (fig. 46.5).

Programs for the processing of indexes are (or should be !!) available in every computer centre; they are also part of the software of some personal computers in so far as these are equipped with sufficient disk capacity for sorting (sorting is a voluminous operation in processing indexes of any type). The programs are much the same as regards their basic functions, but they can differ substantially as concerns their flexibility and volume limits.

A flexible program allows the user to choose freely the index field (i.e. to produce an index by author, catalogue number, title, publisher, descriptor etc.), and to define the separators between the keywords: if, for example, space is defined as the only separator, then a term DATA-BASE is processed as one keyword and it appears only under D; if the hyphen is also considered as a separator, then the term will occur as two keywords (under D and B) in the output. If you wish to use a personal computer for producing indexes, you should survey the available programs, check what types of indexes they can produce, if they are flexible enough, and what are their quantitative limits (how large are the volumes of input data that can be processed, what is the maximum number and length of keywords etc.).

K W I C - keywords-in-context index

```
     [e]                  [d]       [b]  [a]     [c]                  [b]              [f]              [g]
                                     AN ADAPTIVE        CONTROL METHOD FOR A TEACHING SYSTEM#             N0541
                                     AN ADAPTIVE        DICTIONARY IN A FEEDBACK ENVIRONMENT#             X0257
                        THE MODELLING OF ADAPTIVE       ROUTING IN DATA COMMUNICATION NETWORKS#           X0300
PORTANCE OF LOAD SPLITTING#             ADAPTIVE        ROUTING IN STORE-AND-FORWARD NETWORKS AND THE IM  X0255
   ONLINE TERMINAL: A REVOLUTION, OR AN ADDITIONAL      INFORMATION TOOL#                                 X1088
                                MESSAGE ADDRESSING      MODES FOR COMPUTER NETWORKS#                      F0019
F THE CHANGING METHOD FOR RANDOM ACCESS ADDRESSING#                            PERFORMANCE ANALYSIS O     X0399
    GENERAL RECORD STRUCTURE FOR PATENT ADMINISTRATION AND DOCUMENTATION#                                 R0122
ERPRISE#   APPLICATION OF COMPUTERS FOR ADMINISTRATIVE TASKS IN PATENT DEPARTMENT OF AN INDUSTRIAL ENT    X0648
                               THE DATA ADMINISTRATOR FUNCTION#                                           X0973
ING SYSTEMS#                            ADVANCES        IN CIRCUIT TECHNOLOGY AND THEIR IMPACT ON COMPUT  R0166
                                    THE ADVENT OF PERSONAL COMPUTERS#                                     X0854
                      DECOMPOSITION AND AGGREGATION     IN NETWORKS AND QUEUES#                           X1136
PARTMENT OF AN INDUSTRIAL ENTERPRISE#   APPLICATION OF COMPUTERS FOR ADMINISTRATIVE TASKS IN PATENT DE    X0648
```

K W O C - keywords-out-of-context index

```
ADAPTIVE        AN ADAPTIVE CONTROL METHOD FOR A TEACHING SYSTEM#                                  N0541
                AN ADAPTIVE DICTIONARY IN A FEEDBACK ENVIRONMENT#                                  X0257
                THE MODELLING OF ADAPTIVE ROUTING IN DATA COMMUNICATION NETWORKS#                  X0300
                ADAPTIVE ROUTING IN STORE-AND-FORWARD NETWORKS AND THE IMPORTANCE OF LOAD SPLITTING# X0255
ADDITIONAL      ONLINE TERMINAL: A REVOLUTION, OR AN ADDITIONAL INFORMATION TOOL#                  X1088
ADDRESSING      MESSAGE ADDRESSING MODES FOR COMPUTER NETWORKS#                                    F0019
                PERFORMANCE ANALYSIS OF THE CHANGING METHOD FOR RANDOM ACCESS ADDRESSING#          X0399
ADMINISTRATION  GENERAL RECORD STRUCTURE FOR PATENT ADMINISTRATION AND DOCUMENTATION#              R0122
ADMINISTRATIVE  APPLICATION OF COMPUTERS FOR ADMINISTRATIVE TASKS IN PATENT DEPARTMENT OF AN INDUSTRIA X0648
                L ENTERPRISE#
ADMINISTRATOR   THE DATA ADMINISTRATOR FUNCTION#                                                   X0973
ADVANCES        ADVANCES IN CIRCUIT TECHNOLOGY AND THEIR IMPACT ON COMPUTING SYSTEMS#              R0166
ADVENT          THE ADVENT OF PERSONAL COMPUTERS                                                   X0854
AGGREGATION     DECOMPOSITION AND AGGREGATION IN NETWORKS AND QUEUES#                              X1136
APPLICATION     APPLICATION OF COMPUTERS FOR ADMINISTRATIVE TASKS IN PATENT DEPARTMENT OF AN INDUSTRIA X0648
                L ENTERPRISE#
```

Fig. 46.4/5 - Examples of the KWIC and KWOC indexes

[a] keywords are printed out in the central column and sorted alphabetically
[b] non-significant words such as AN, FOR, A, THE etc. are omitted;
[c] spaces after short keywords improve legibility;
[d] text is shifted to the left or to the right as necessary;
[e] rest of text is printed on the other side of the line if space permits;
[f] end-of-text sign;
[g] pointer (catalogue number) enables to find the original document.

The processing of indexes does not need a terminal or personal computer; it can be done periodically off-line in an in-house or service computer centre. Simple searching in a relatively small document collection by means of indexes is easy and fast, sometimes even faster than online retrieval. Indexes are also portable, they can be used at any place and at any time. If the number of documents grows, then indexes become voluminous, and too many documents appear under some generic terms (e.g. in a collection on the subject of finance, the keyword BANK or MONEY occupies many pages and the search is as difficult as the search for Mr. SMITH in a telephone directory). Search by combined keywords (e.g. BANKS and FRANCE) is impossible or arduous and special types of indexes must be produced that allow this type of retrieval. A *permutated index* is the solution: in such an index, each record can be found also by pairs of keywords, for example, under BANKS:FRANCE, BANKS:INDUSTRY, BANKS:LOMBARD. Their disadvantage is their large volume.

When the number of documents in a personal collection has grown to a few thousands, the indexes become too voluminous, and the search arduous. Consequently, online search by means of a terminal and mainframe or by a - sufficiently powerful - personal computer is the best solution.

47 - Online retrieval

As early as the end of the fifties, computers were able to produce indexes; in 1959, the popular KWIC index was born. The next step was to employ computers to search for documents. The first systems worked with data stored on magnetic tapes, that were searched sequentially; manual indexing was the only method. The computer compared record by record the keywords of the inquiry with the keywords of the documents; logical operators AND, OR and NOT were allowed between the inquiry keywords in most systems so that inquiries of the type LIBRARIES *or* DOCUMENTATION *or* INFORMATION SYSTEMS *and* UNIVERSITIES *and* USA *or* CANADA (or rather more sophisticated) could be put. Records matching the inquiry (in this case, containing the keywords UNIVERSITIES and either USA or CANADA or both, and at least one of the terms of the first three) are then displayed or printed out.

Systems based on sequential search of the data base can easily be programmed, their data structure is quite simple, they need no pre-processing of the stored records, but the search procedure is slow (all the records in the file must be consecutively compared with the inquiry) and the response time of the system grows proportionally with the file volume. This method is therefore prohibitive in large files, and sequential search was almost forgotten in the seventies. It has now returned with the advent of personal computers; what is intolerable in large information systems can be feasible in small personal data bases consisting, typically, of hundreds or a few thousands of short records.

Typical properties of systems based on sequential search that are now operational on many a personal computer are a short record, a simple record structure (author, title, abstract...) and indexing by manually attached keywords (either free keywords or descriptors chosen from a controlled thesaurus). The inquiry consists of keywords or descriptors connected by Boolean operators as mentioned above (see also the example in fig. 47.1).

There is a number of such simple systems available as part of the software of personal computers. A potential user should carefully check their functions, their capacity (maximum number and maximum length of records), their flexibility (is the record structure fixed or adaptable by the user ?), and response time (this is often the bottleneck of the system). A few retrieval systems of this sort are referred to in chapter 9 [ref. 45-Barker, Bivins, Leggate, Parker etc.]. An example of the design, structure, functions and practical application of such a small-scale system based on sequential search is described as case 3 in the book Personal Documentation for Professionals [ref. 40-Stibic].

A typical input procedure in a small-scale personal retrieval system can

```
TYPE YOUR INQUIRY:
? PERSONAL COMPUTERS : ( TANDY + APPLE + PET ) : PROGRAMMING : BASIC#
DEFINE LAYOUT:
? HELP #
YOU HAVE TO DEFINE ONE OR MORE RECORD FIELDS THAT SHOULD BE DISPLAYED
OR PRINTED-OUT:
CAT = CATALOGUE NUMBER
AUT = AUTHOR(S)
TIT = TITLE
BIB = BIBLIOGRAPHICAL DATA (DATE, JOURNAL OR PUBLISHER, VOL/NO/PAGE ETC.)
ABS = ABSTRACT
LIN = PRINT THE FOLLOWING FIELD ON A NEW LINE
USE COLONS BETWEEN THE TAGS (EXAMPLE: LIN.CAT.AUT.LIN.TIT.ABS)
IF MORE COMMENTS NEEDED, TYPE HELP AGAIN, OTHERWISE DEFINE LAYOUT
? AUT.LIN.TIT.LIN.BIB.LIN#
IF OK THEN TYPE GO OTHERWISE TYPE A SPECIFIC COMMAND OR HELP
? GO#

SEARCH STARTED 82-01-14 / 14.05 :

1
LARRECHE, J.C.:
BASIC - UNE INTRODUCTION A LA PROGRAMMATION
1981 PARIS: EDIT. EYROLLES (7TH ED.) - 120 P.

2
WEBER, K.:
BASIC FUER ANFAENGER
1979, BERN: HAUPT

3
RUGG, T.; FELDMAN, P.:
BASIC PROGRAMS FOR THE TRS-80 (LEVEL II) COMPUTER
DILITHIUM PRESS - 270 P.
```

Fig. 47.1 - Example of inquiry and output in a simple sequential search

Bold = typed in by the user; normal print = computer output

be characterized by the following steps: The input data are typed in via a keyboard of the computer, they are displayed for visual checking, the input program screens them and signals formal errors found (e.g. non-numerical date, missing title, wrong language code), and the records are finally stored in their chronological sequence on the tape or disk. Input is easier if we have available an intelligent online input program that helps the user: such a program automatically prompts for the data elements (date, author, title...), so that the user can fill in the data in the proper sequence and form; it helps to code or abbreviate data (e.g. journal names), it inserts some data automatically (e.g. date of input, record number).

The inquiry is also typed in via the keyboard, it is submitted to automatic screening for formal consistency, and then the search is performed by means of the retrieval program. The records matching the inquiry are displayed and/or printed out - an example of an inquiry and of the output is given in fig. 47.1. The search time is rather long. However, if there are several documents in the file that match the inquiry, they appear on the screen immediately they are found so that the waiting time need not always be annoying.

Terminal and mainframe

Some professionals have access to a computer ('mainframe') in the computer centre of their organization via a *terminal* situated at their workplace. They can then interrogate the company files via an in-house retrieval system, and often they are allowed to create and use their own personal files. They gain some advantages: they are no longer limited by the inadequate parameters of a small personal computer, and they have at their disposal a powerful system characterized by a number of advanced functions that often include the automatic indexing of documents. It is necessary to contact the computing centre and to discuss the possibilities of creating your own files and using the available retrieval system. Its functions and requirements must be thoroughly studied and the organization of your personal documentation, in particular the record structure and the system of classification or indexing, must be adapted.

External online information systems

In the sixties a number of *commercial online information systems* appeared. Many of them were founded by large abstracting and reference services with a long tradition (Excerpta Medica, Chemical Abstracts, INSPEC etc.). The large volume of scanned literature and hundreds of thousands of abstracts produced were an excellent base for mechanization. Many of the existing systems now contain more than one million abstracts. They are invaluable information sources for every professional. Nearly all these systems are based primarily on indexing by descriptors according to their own thesauri; many of them apply also some form of hierarchical classification, and/or permit search by words present in the titles and abstracts; they offer the user a choice of more than one retrieval strategy. They all employ a rather simple Boolean inquiry formulation.

The retrieval technique and strategy of the large systems is rather conservative. To understand their somewhat primitive technique (in comparison with the present state-of-the-art in research and development of online retrieval), we must not forget that the immense volume of information stored (think of the millions of abstracts !) requires compact data and fast procedures that do not allow sophisticated search algorithms; furthermore, it is not economically justifiable to reorganize huge volumes of data accumulated over the last ten or more years. What is easy in small and medium-size in-house data bases of, say, tens of thousands of abstracts, is not possible (at present) in data bases of hundreds of thousands or millions of records.

A typical search in a large online system starts with the user's call. When the connection is established, the user identifies himself for control and accounting purposes by typing his account number and his password. If there is more than one data base available, he must decide which of them he will access, and he can then start with the formulation of his inquiry. He defines the terms characterizing his problem. After selecting one term, he receives a reply of the system informing how many records in the data base are indexed by this term - this gives an idea how many documents might be retrieved later; if the user expects a term to occur in several inflected or orthographical forms, he gives a command to display a part of an alphabetical vocabulary, and he can select a group of words, or he makes use of automatic truncation (BANK∗ = BANK, BANKS, BANKING...). After selecting the terms of his inquiry, the user can connect them by Boolean operators OR, AND or NOT. Once again, information about the number of records in the data base matching his inquiry appears on the screen. If the number of 'candidate records' is too large, the user reformulates his inquiry by choosing more specific terms, or by narrowing the inquiry by adding terms connected by logical AND. When, on the other hand, the number of records is too small or if nothing has been found, the inquiry must be made more generic. If, finally, the user considers the number of records found to be reasonable, he gives the command for them to be displayed on the screen and/or printed on his printer, or he can order print out on a line printer in the remote computer centre; the output is then delivered by post.

Most existing large commercial online systems are certainly not user-friendly. They require a knowledge of special operations and commands, the handling of special codes and abbreviations, a very good knowledge of their classification and indexing system as well as experience in retrieval strategy; they mostly render little help to a beginner. Such systems are usually accessed by trained operators who act as intermediaries between the inquirer and the system. They help to formulate the inquiry, they can advise which data base should best be accessed, they operate the system (often in the presence of the inquirer), they adjust the inquiry strategy according to the interim results obtained, and they sometimes also edit the output.

Integration of personal, in-house and external information systems

Until recently, all the three levels of retrieval systems were isolated. If the user found some relevant information in an external system worth storing in his own system, he had to transcribe it. The same inquiry had sometimes to be placed three times (search in one's own system, then in an in-house system, then in an external system), using different commands, different indexing languages and different search strategies. All the three systems were accessible via different hardware devices: via a stand-alone personal computer, via a terminal, and via a special terminal of a commercial system. Recent technical developments have gradually brought these three levels of information systems closer together. At present it is possible to access some of the large commercial information retrieval systems by means of a standard terminal or by means of some types of personal computers via a telephone line. In-house systems are beginning to be accessible also via personal computers that can be then used both in stand-alone mode or as terminals; also word processors can be used for interrogating in-house data bases. The final stage is the total merger into the universal work station of the future. This will make it possible to communicate with the retrieval systems of all the three levels. It will be possible to accept selected records from external databases and to copy selected pertinent data into one's own personal documentation by a single command. Similarly, it could be possible to take over data from company files into one's own file or, vice versa, to send data into the company's file. Relevant records from any source will be copied and sent to colleagues and peers in the form of an individual SDI. The boundaries between systems (let us hope that the difficult problems of standardization of hardware and data as well as copyright questions will be solved) will then disappear, and the handling of information will be much easier than it is today.

48 - Viewdata

Viewdata is a new information source able to deliver selected information into every home and to every workplace. It makes use of a standard television set with a small hand-held keyboard, connected via a

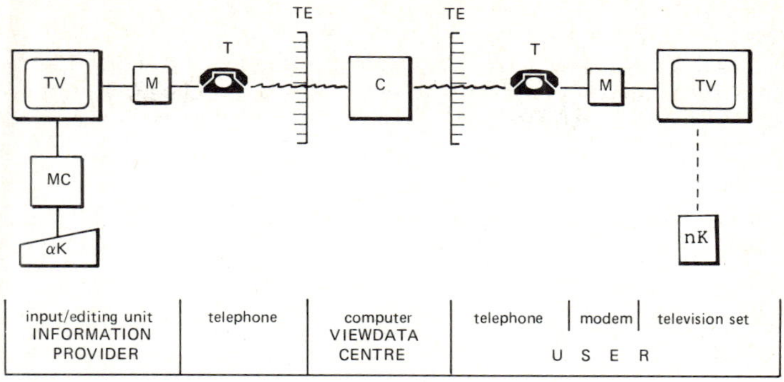

Fig. 48.1 - Scheme of the viewdata network

TV - *television set*
M - *modem*
C - *computer*
MC - *microcomputer*
nK - *numerical keyboard*
aK - *alphanumerical keyboard*
T - *telephone*
TE - *telephone exchange*

modem and standard telephone line to a computer or computer network. This combination of three commonly used technical means (television set + telephone + computer) results in a relatively cheap information service for everybody. To learn to use the system takes only a few minutes; the ease of access is surely one of the main attractions of the system and the reason for the enthusiasm of people who meet it for the first time.

A terminological note is necessary here: According to a CCITT (Comité Consultatif International Télégrafique et Téléfonique - an international representative body of PTT's) recommendation, the term *videotex* is used as the generic name for two-way low cost systems of displaying information by means of adapted television sets and telephone lines. In Britain, the term *viewdata* was originally used by the British Post Office as the name of its own system until 1978 when the name was replaced by PRESTEL. The term viewdata is still in common use so that the two terms videotex and viewdata are often used as synonyms. According to EEC, videotex is preserved as the generic name used for 'electronic systems that use a modified television set to display computer-based information' while interactive systems are called *viewdata*, and the broadcast services are called *teletext*. For the latter system sometimes also terms *broadcast videotex* or *one-way videotex* or (e.g. in Germany) *videotext* are used. The terminological problems were further increased by the introduction of the term *teletex*, meaning a system making it possible to exchange messages between individual users (not to be confused with the above-mentioned *teletext*). The confusion was completed by introduction of specific names for national viewdata (videotex) and teletext (videotext) systems. The British system, as mentioned, has been introduced under the name PRESTEL; in other countries, TELETEL (France), VIDITEL (Holland), TELIDON (Canada), TELSET (Finland), DATAVISION (Sweden), BILDSCHIRMTEXT alias BTX (Germany), CAPTAINS (Japan) and other names are used. Similarly, national teletext (videotext) systems have been introduced under individual names in various countries. How unimaginative the 19th-century people were when they introduced telegraph and telephone to the whole world under one name !

The public viewdata systems concentrate on popular, frequently required information such as news, weather, sport, commerce, finance, transport, coming events etc. The organizer (PTT) does not provide information, but leases pages in the system to the information providers (business enterprises, advertisers, newspapers etc.) for fixed amounts; on the other hand, the users pay per page displayed (the rate differs, some pages are gratis). The capacity of public viewdata systems is large: several hundred thousand pages.

The information stored in viewdata is split into *pages*. There are routing pages and information pages. When searching for information, the user proceeds from generic to specific according to the traditional rules of decimal classification. The first top page gives him the overview of the main (up to ten) subjects that he can select by depressing one of the numerical keys 0 to 9. The user selects, say, 2-NEWS; on the displayed NEWS page he selects the theme POLITICS; on this page he chooses USA and finally he comes to the required information page with the latest news from the White House.

The hierarchical decimal classification used in viewdata systems shows some peculiarities that differ from the traditional decimal systems used for more than a hundred years in libraries and documentation. First of all, the system no longer has the disadvantage of rigidity; the structure can

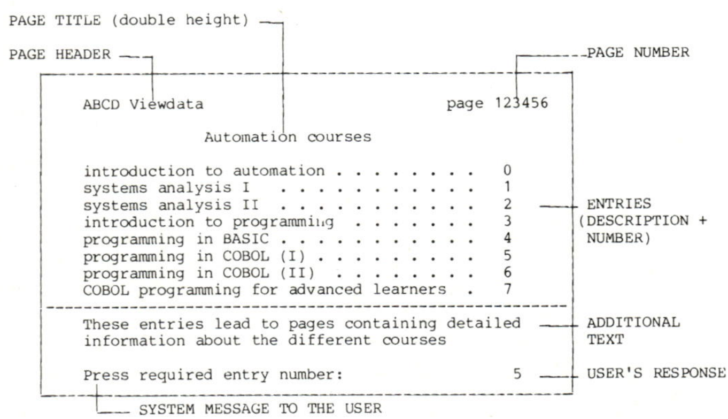

Fig. 48.2 - Scheme of a routing page in an in-house viewdata system

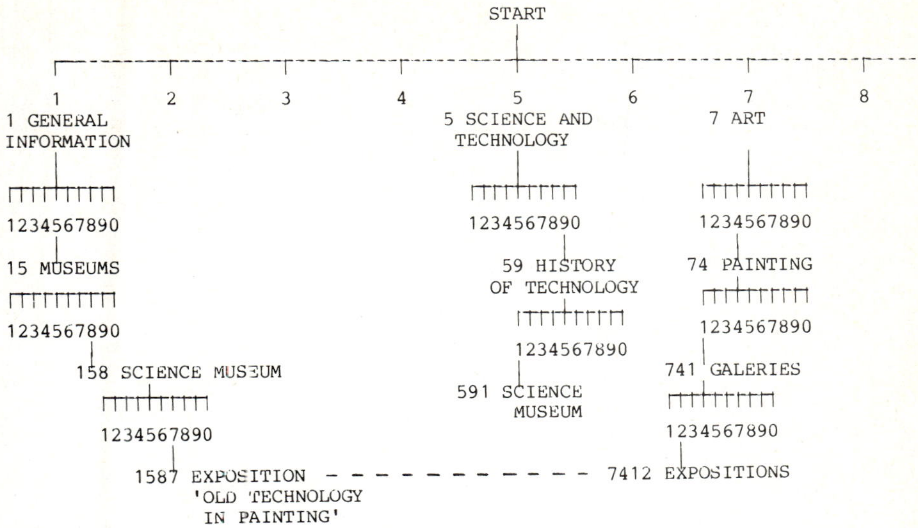

Fig. 48.3 - Hierarchical classification in the viewdata system

Viewdata is based on the hierarchical decimal classification. This old principle with a new technology receives a new dimension: the possibility of using more than one tree and of searching via any of them.

be easily changed as both the classification system and data are online. Secondly, there is a new feature available that could be called 'multiple tree'. Indeed, it is possible to design several independent tree structures, each of them branching according to another point of view, but connected by cross-references so that any piece of information can be found via two or more different ways leading finally to the same end point.

An example can be found in fig. 48.3. Here information about an exposition 'Industrial history in art' held in the Science Museum can be found by descending via the tree GENERAL INFORMATION - MUSEUMS - EXPOSITIONS, as well as via the tree SCIENCE AND TECHNOLOGY, or via the tree ARTS. Cross-references at various points in various trees make such an approach to pertinent information possible. This original feature of the viewdata system, giving a new dimension to the old system of hierarchical decimal classification, has until now achieved little attention both in theory and in the practice. On the other hand, with some embarrassment we encounter precarious discrepancies in the classification scheme in public viewdata systems. You start with the branch TECHNOLOGY and come finally to EXHIBITION OF INDIAN ART. Often, we have to try again and again to find out under which keyword and via which generic terms we can arrive at the detailed information required. Subclassification by changing and not quite logical points of view when descending from the top to bottom is often encountered. The cause is certainly lack of experience, the leasing of blocks of pages to various information providers without exact knowledge of the information content, as well as the variability and unpredictability of the detailed information.

FUNCTION TREE access via departments (=inf. providers) and their functions	SUBJECT TREE systematical access via hierarchically classified subjects	ALPHABETICAL INDEX helps to find the information by keyword
BOARD OF DIRECTORS	ADMINISTRATION	ACCOUNTING
-	- ACCOUNTING	ACCOUNTING SCHEME
-	-ACCOUNTING SCHEME	ADMINISTRATION
GENERAL MANAGEMENT	-FINANCIAL ACCTG	BOARD OF DIRECTORS
-	-COST ACCOUNTING	CALCULATION
-	-COST CENTRES	CORRESPONDENCE
STAFF DEPARTMENTS	-COST TYPES	COST ACCOUNTING
- ORGANIZATION DEPT.	-CALCULATION	COST CENTRES
- ORGANIGRAM	-	COST TYPES
- DEPT.CODES	- CORRESPONDENCE	DEPARTMENT CODES
- COST CENTRES	- IN-HOUSE LAYOUT	FIN. ACCOUNTING
- ORG. MANUAL	- CORR.STANDARDS	GENERAL MANAGEMENT

Fig. 48.4 - Scheme of a multiple-tree structure of an in-house viewdata system

In our case, the basic tree is the 'function tree' of departments (as they are the information providers); the systematic subject tree and the alphabetical keyword index make it possible to find the required information in another ways also.

Nonetheless, there are open chances of future developments in the viewdata systems. One of them is improving the rather primitive hierarchical search by retrieval via keywords. This possibility does exist at present, but in a limited form: the keyword required has to be selected rather arduously in a number of steps via a standard numerical keyboard, or a special alphabetical keyboard must be attached, help from the system is minimal and combinations of keywords (a *conditio sine qua non* in non-trivial search) are impossible. Improvement of another sort - that has been achieved in the Canadian system TELIDON - is the extension of text by image (photo). In this system it covers about a quarter of the screen. The paths for future development and extensions to this system are open in various directions.

It can be expected that public viewdata systems will become an important, though merely an extra source of information to a professional, providing him particularly with general information. His specific professional information he will take also in future from the large specialized online information systems

Shortly after the advent of the first public viewdata systems, *private viewdata systems* also appeared in large companies. They, undoubtedly, have a good chance of becoming an important source of in-house information. They can replace printed information, which is expensive, difficult to distribute to all places where it is needed, must be carefully stored and updated by each potential user, and is difficult to retrieve when needed. All internal memos, instructions, hot news, pricelists, directories, manuals etc. can now be stored in one place where they can be found at any moment; they are always up-to-date. There is also no reason why a professional could not be responsible for some pages in the company's viewdata system. He and his team or department could announce here information that is available to anyone interested. Standards of classification and a uniform layout will be supervised by an editor-in-chief, but we summarize in fig. 48.5 a few general rules for editing pages in a viewdata system.

```
PAGE       * one page - one subject
           * not overloaded with information
           * good graphical structure
           * heading preferrably at the bottom
           * heading not centred
           * not more than three colours

TEXT       * limited use of upper case
           * no or limited hyphenating
           * free line between paragraphs
           * or indent 2 characters except the
               the first line
           * space after interpunction
           * 'italics' = colour close to the
               basic text

COLOURS    * only white, yellow, cyan and green
               for information
           * green is the best 'information' colour
               (sharp, legible)
           * magenta, red and blue only as additional
               or decorative
           * use logically - don't misuse !
           * hierarchy: white-yellow-cyan-green

TABLES     * keep simple
           * self-explanatory
           * no abbreviations
           * comments on the same page
           * alternative lines in similar colours
```

Fig. 48.5 - Basic rules for graphic design of a viewdata page

5 - WORD PROCESSING

For many centuries pen and paper were the main technical means used in text creating. The *typewriter* changed the basic technique at the beginning of the present century, and in the fifties the Friden Flexowriter (an electric typewriter with punched tape input and output) made it possible to store text on punched tape, to correct, copy, amend and edit the stored data and to print the text again in edited form. Mechanical devices for handling text, however, were rather complicated, and their functions were limited. The *computer* brought about quite new possibilities; in the seventies - due to achievements in microelectronics - a special type of microcomputer was born, enabling text to be handled in a very flexible manner: this was the *word processor* that is now beginning to support the professional in creating, correcting, editing and printing texts of any sort.

51 - The traditional means

The oldest techniques of text-creating are still being widely used even in the present age of dictating machines, typewriters and word processors. The use of longhand is a long way from disappearing.

Longhand is the least effective way of creating longer texts (see fig. 51.1), but it does have certain advantages: for short notes and records it can be effective, it is always easy, it requires no special technical means, it can be used anywhere, and document handling (e.g. jumpings from one page to another, from document to document) is fast and easy. For many persons the main argument in its favour is that no additional learning is necessary - everybody learns longhand at the age of six, while the skill of typing or of operating a word processor or terminal must be learned later. There may therefore be some aversion to the typewriter and to the newer technical means.

It is not surprising to find that Emperor Franz Josef consistently refused to accept typewritten documents, similarly as he resolutely had refused to use an automobile; he did appreciate only one modern technical mean, namely the telegraph that he used fervently, even sending telegrams within the buildings of the Hofburg in Vienna (a sort of electronic mail of the *fin de siècle* !). On the other hand, it is rather unexpected to learn of General MacArthur's preference for writing large reports in longhand; but it is ridiculous to come in the eighties across handwritten internal technical documents or minutes of meetings (reproduced, paradoxically, by modern photocopying machines) in a large research institute, or to receive letters from the editors of specialist (information science !) journals or from the British Ministry of Trade, all written by hand. These are incidental observations; however, surveys in large organizations reveal that an unexpectedly high proportion of correspondence or other texts is created by the least effective techniques: one of the surveys found that 75 % of texts originated by longhand and transcribing, 17 % by shorthand dictation, and only 8 % by means of dictating machines [ref. 54-Hogben]. Similar results have been found by other studies.

M E T H O D	perf. *	minutes		time minutes (5, 10, 15, 20)	costs
	(a)	(b)	(c)		(d)
A TYPING (+ RETYPING)					
typing	180	10	-	==========	30
(retyping)	(180)(e)	(10)	-	==========	(60)
B LONGHAND + TRANSCRIBING					
longhand draft	150 (f)	12	-	============	
transcribing	250	-	7	-------	43
C DICTATE TO TYPIST					
dictating	300 (g)	6	-	======	
typing	300	-	6	------	24
D DICTATE TO SHORTHAND TYP.					
dictating + shorthand	360	5	5	===== -----	
transcribing	250 (h)		7	-------	27
E DICTATING MACHINE					
dictating	480 (j)	3.75	-	====	
transcribing	300	-	6	------	17

====== minutes boss
------ minutes secretary

Fig. 51.1 - Comparison of time and cost of five traditional techniques of text creation

The time and cost depend on several individual conditions: the boss's ability and skill at typing [A] and dictating [C,D,E], and the secretary's skill at shorthand [D] and typing [B/E]. The total cost is influenced also by the ratio between the boss's and secretary's salaries (here 3:1 has been considered). Also some side-effects have to be taken into account: the simultaneous work in cases C and D limits the freedom of work scheduling on both sides, and disturbances (telephone calls, visits) waste the secretary's time.

[a] performance - number of characters incl. spaces per minute (6 characters = 1 word)
[b] boss's time in minutes
[c] secretary's time in minutes
[d] relative cost (if boss : secretary salaries = 3:1)
[e] double time, if retyping of a draft is necessary
[f] 25 words/minute considered
[g] 50 words/minute - speed of dictating is limited by the speed of typing
[h] speed of typing reduced by 15% due to reading shorthand
[j] dictating 80 words/minute

In fig. 51.1, five methods of creating a text of one typewritten page (1800 characters including spaces, i.e. about 300 words) are compared in terms of boss's and secretary's time. The table suggests no dramatic differences in costs, but considerable differences in the productivity of a professional: dictating saves about 70 % of the author's time. Often a professional uses more than one method: he dictates simple texts, but prepares drafts of difficult texts on his typewriter or word processor.

format	
A4	210 x 297 mm
A5	148 x 210 mm
A6	105 x 148 mm

typewritten A4 page	lines	char/line	char's	words
double spacing	30	60	1800	300
$1\frac{1}{2}$ spacing	40	60	2400	400
single spacing	60	60	3600	600

typewriter letter 'pica'	pitch 10 =	2.54 mm
'elite'	pitch 12 =	2.11 mm
typewriter line, single		4.25 mm
typographical point		0.3759 mm
- - metric		0.375 mm

Fig. 52.1 - A few important formats and dimensions of typewritten and printed documents

52 - Typewriter

The *mechanical typewriter* achieved its definitive form and functions in the thirties and has changed little in the last few decades. The only differences are its modernized appearance and greater writing comfort brought about by a tabulator that is now built also into many portable machines, easier paper handling, half-pitch spacing and other small improvements.

Those who are considering buying a conventional typewriter for their personal use will find a large number of products on the market. The mechanical machines differ little in their functions, but considerably in quality and price. Any consumer's guide publishes, from time to time, comparisons and evaluation tables on portable and office typewriters, and gives recommendations that are objective, helpful and up-to-date. The user should select a machine according to his specific requirements choosing either a small and cheap *portable* or a heavy-duty *office machine.* He should also carefully choose the letter size and pitch; commonly available is the letter size 'pica' pitch 1/10 inch, i.e. 2.54 mm (2.6 mm in some machines of continental production), or 'elite' pitch 1/12 inch, i.e. 2.11 mm. The user should also carefully select a suitable character set (keyboard); every large producer of typewriters offers a set of keyboards adapted to various national alphabets and to the special requirements of some professions. There are special keyboards for mathematicians, chemists, electrical engineers, and even for such special users as dental surgeons. The buyer can also ask the dealer to replace some letters that are less practical by others, provided they are present in one of the manufacturer's keyboards. The re-tooling is not expensive (many a dealer is willing, when selling a machine, to undertake it at his own expense).

After World War II the *electric typewriter*, which had been manufactured since 1921, found general acceptance in offices, and in recent years also inexpensive electric portable typewriters for personal use have been on the market. A significant improvement was the advent of the *golf-ball* element, an exchangeable typing element enabling the size and type of letters to be varied (normal, bold, italics in various forms and sizes); also provided were balls with special symbols (mathematical, chemical, etc.) and various non-Roman alphabets, including Greek and Russian. This feature, which makes the typewriter into a very flexible instrument, is now available in typewriters of the price class that can be afforded by a private person. Another new printing element is the *daisy wheel* (fig. 52.2) that is often found in the printers of word processors and personal computers. Compared with the golf-ball unit, it is lighter and cheaper. A light plastic daisy wheel that has a life expectancy of about 10 million impressions allows speeds of up to about 55 characters/sec; a metal wheel (life-

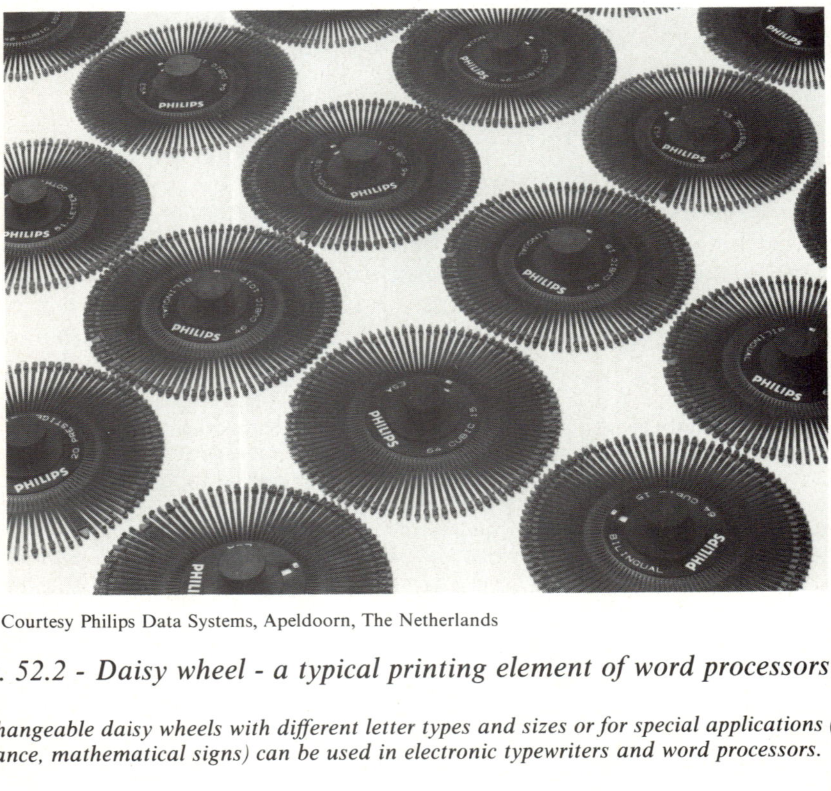

Courtesy Philips Data Systems, Apeldoorn, The Netherlands

Fig. 52.2 - Daisy wheel - a typical printing element of word processors

Exchangeable daisy wheels with different letter types and sizes or for special applications (for instance, mathematical signs) can be used in electronic typewriters and word processors.

expectancy about 50 million impressions) is rather slower, permitting about 30-40 characters/sec. Daisy wheels are inexpensive; their prices vary from $ 3 to $ 30 (1981).

The quality of print has improved due to finer fabric ribbons (nylon) and single-strike paper ribbons. Some typewriters facilitate corrections of typist's errors by means of a 'correct' key. It effects a step one letter backwards, and switches to the white half of a special ribbon; the erroneous letter is then overtyped, and the proper letter can be typed in its place.

The most advanced typewriters make it possible to exchange the letter-types, but also to change the pitch (e.g. to type alternately 10 or 12 letters per inch), to use proportional spacing (letter spacing depending on the breadth of the letter - larger breadth of *m*, smaller of *i*), right-hand justification, decimal tabulating, easy exchange of ribbon in cartridge form, etc.

A revolutionary change in typewriting has been brought about by the application of microelectronics and memory elements. The first step in a long range of existing machine types is the *'electronic typewriter'*. It has a limited memory 'buffer' (sometimes, it is called 'buffered typewriter') and a 'narrow window display', usually of one line. The typed line is visible in the window, and it can be corrected before it is printed out. An electronic typewriter usually performs many other interesting operations, for example, automatic right-hand justification of text, centration of some lines (e.g. headings), indentation of parts of text, end-of-page signalling (remaining number of lines available). It also offers a rich character set including bold letters, automatic underlining, and sometimes (Olivetti)

Courtesy Olivetti Nederland, Den Haag

Fig. 52.3 - Electronic typewriter Olivetti ET-221

also negative print (white letters on black background). A limited 'fixed memory' of some types of electronic typewriters makes it possible to store frequently used names, addresses, phrases etc., and to place them in the text by means of a simple command.

A '*memory typewriter*' (sometimes called 'small-revision typewriter') is equipped with a larger memory than the 'buffered typewriter'; it can store, usually in its internal memory, one page (sometimes perhaps a few pages) of text. A one- or two-line window display is a typical feature. Corrections of typist's errors can be made immediately by visual monitoring of the line displayed; further corrections are made from the hard copy: a page is printed out, proof-read, the stored text is then corrected line by line, and printed again in the corrected version. Then, the memory is cleared and

Courtesy SONY Corporation, Tokyo

Fig. 52.4 - Portable Typerecorder

A small, briefcase-sized (22 × 28 × 4 cm, 1.5 kg) 'typerecorder' announced recently by Sony is a combined electronic typewriter, dictating machine, transcriber and communicator by a telephone acoustic coupler transmitter. It makes it possible to record and reproduce dictation as well as to store key-typed text on the same 3" microcassette - a single microcassette can hold up to 100 pages text or 60 minutes dictation. One line of the typed text is visible in a 'thin window'. The text can be corrected, edited and transmitted. A portable printer, also briefcase-sized, can be attached.

is ready again to store temporarily a new page. Machines of this type can be equipped with an external memory - a cassette or magnetic cards.

The last-mentioned type, particularly if it is equipped with two external memory units, is sometimes called a '*blind text editor*'; it makes it possible to store, correct, edit and print-out also long documents consisting of many pages (reports, articles etc.). Its functions are similar to the functions of a word processor, but as the machine has no display screen of larger capacity, all corrections (with the exception of correcting typist's errors at the moment of typing the particular line) must be done by means of hard-copy.

53 - Dictating machines

Dictating machines are well known but little used. They are, of course, installed and employed in a large number of places, but the ratio of actual users to potential users is rather low, and the majority of actual users regard dictating machines as suitable only for dictating business letters; however, they can offer invaluable services in many non-traditional applications.

The equipment

The basic functions of dictating machines need not be explained. The comforts of dictating as well as of reproduction have increased considerably in the last few decades, and the machines now fall into a range of categories adapted to special requirements: from *office dictating machines*

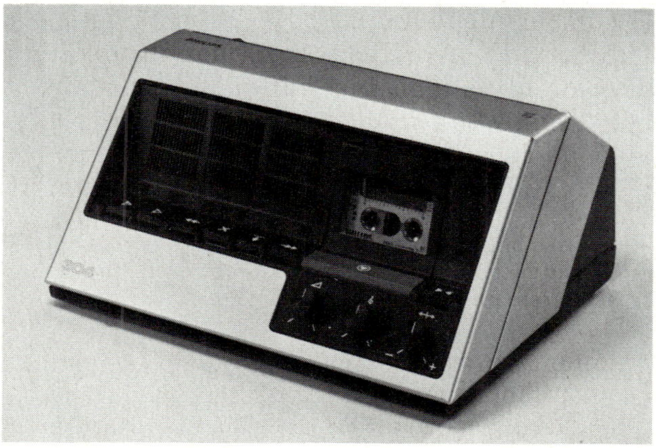

Courtesy Philips Data Systems, Apeldoorn, The Netherlands

Fig. 53.1 - The Philips office dictating machine using mini-cassettes

with many special functions and accessories to the miniaturized battery-driven *pocket dictating machines.*

The various information carriers of earlier days (magnetic cards, foils or belts, special tapes and cartridges) have been replaced by cassettes - either standard cassettes as used in tape recorders or special mini-cassettes. Standardization improved compatibility and has made it possible, for example, to dictate by means of a pocket machine, and have it transcribed in a typist's office by standard office equipment, or to send cassettes by post as 'spoken letters'.

Also the basic features of all dictating equipment have improved and many of them have become practically standard: a *hand-held microphone*

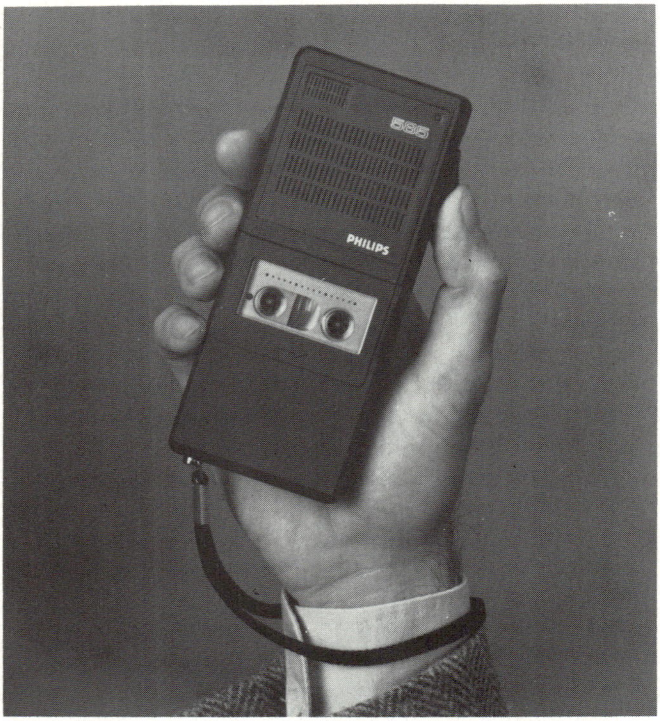

Courtesy Philips Data Systems, Apeldoorn, The Netherlands

Fig. 53.2 - 'Pocket memo'

A pocket-sized, battery-driven dictating machine is an indispensable device for every professional and manager. The Philips Pocket Memo 585 is ergonomically designed with all the controls positioned for single-hand operation. A four-position thumb control permits record and playback, fast forward and rewind. In the fast forward position, an audible scan facility is engaged, enabling easy scanning of dictated items and a rapid search for blank tape. The apparatus accepts either standard or rechargeable 9V batteries or a power supply unit. A mini-cassette (55 × 34 × 7 mm) has capacity of 2 × 15 minutes dictation time.

offering easy remote control of the machine by start-stop, rewind and playback commands; optical signalling of the operation (recording or playback); easy orientation with regard to position on tape by a simple scale, by digital counter or (in some machines) by a visual mark/find feature allowing the secretary to see at a glance where letters begin, how many letters are recorded and which of them have to be typed first. There are also a number of special accessories available: *telephone adaptors* for recording of telephone calls, *conference microphones* for recording discussions in a room, large *loudspeakers* to enable playback to a number of participants, and of special features for the secretary: *stethoscopic headphones* and a *foot-pedal* for controlling the machine thus leaving the hands free.

Pocket dictating machines (sometimes called 'pocket memos') have somewhat limited functions (but still all required in practice); their essential advantage is that they are easy to use at any place and at any time. They are battery-driven, their weight and volume are minimal. They are indispensable tools of any professional and manager.

Except for the situation when the user employs a dictating machine only as a notebook and transcribes the notes himself, one dictating machine is insufficient. Typically, three units are needed: one of them permanently on 'stand-by' at the workplace, the second one at the workplace of the secretary. Both these machines should be 'heavy-duty' office types. The third machine should be portable, best a 'pocket-memo' using cassettes compatible with the above-mentioned two machines. It is employed during travelling, or at home. If home use is intensive, then a fourth machine of the office type should be installed at home.

Principles of use of dictating equipment

Speaking is the most convenient and fastest form of expressing ideas in the natural language. As shown in scheme 51.1, dictating by means of a dictating machine is nearly twice as fast as dictating to a typist, and about three times faster than writing in longhand. It is also faster than dictating to a shorthand typist (unless the secretary is an excellent stenographer, the boss must adapt his dictation to her shorthand speed). Another advantage of using a dictating machine is that the presence of the secretary is not needed (dictating can be done at any time and at any place), and, as opposed to the cases of longhand, shorthand or typing, the user's eyes and hands are free for other things (see below the examples of the use of dictating equipment in a laboratory).

There are also significant barriers to the practical use of dictating machines. First of all, there is the invisibility of the dictated text, and - consequently - the difficulty of orientation and uneasy search in a recorded text. This is a particular drawback to people with no great ability to formulate ideas, and in the case of fairly long and difficult texts. Another inhibition is the need for strict self-discipline; the boss must not forget at the beginning of his dictation to give all instructions (what form to use, layout required etc.), he must be careful in his pronunciation, not forget to spell all less familiar proper names, acronyms or difficult terms; he should also help the typist by inserting instructions regarding punctuation (comma, full-stop etc.), case (upper case, lower case), layout (paragraph, indentation, free lines, new page etc.). He should also carefully distinguish such instructions from the dictated text (to prevent the typist from starting to type these notes !) either by changing the modulation of his voice, or by a short hiss, or simply by addressing the typist by name ('Mary, the following text must be indented'). If the instructions are omitted, then the whole work might be spoiled and have to be re-typed.

It is not easy to formulate a text without visual control, to think of all the necessary instructions and to dictate the text quite distinctly. A surprisingly large number of professionals are not willing or unable to accept such a style of work. Clumsy stylists who can never write a sentence without corrections even if the draft is visible in front of them will apparently never be able to dictate by means of a dictating machine. The author of the present book remembers someone - no incompetent person in other respects - who misused his dictating machine in quite an original manner: he first drafted his text in a rather abbreviated form in longhand, then dictated it into the machine and sent the cassette to the typing pool. He had the reputation of a man capable of dictating in a perfect manner.

Applications of dictating equipment

A common application of dictating equipment is the dictating of letters. It is a very suitable field for dictating machines, as the texts are mostly short and simple. Nonetheless, effective use of a dictating machine requires good preparation and the right style of dictation. First of all, the necessary documents must be prepared (letters received that have to be answered, copies of preceding correspondence and other documents containing relevant facts), and they should be sorted in the sequence of dictating. Secondly, the content of every letter must be considered; we should not begin to dictate before we are sure what we would like to say. If the subject is complicated, then a few written notes (points) will help us to follow a logical line. Data that can be found in the correspondence or other documents need not be dictated in full (addresses, quotations etc.); the secretary should receive all the relevant documents in the sequence of the dictated letters.

At the beginning of the dictation, the name of the dictating person (if the text is being typed in a typing pool) and the date must be recorded. Then, the instructions mentioned earlier must not be forgotten: what form to use (standard business letter, private letter, blank paper, special form), layout, number of copies etc. Finally, the user should also say explicitly that the dictation is at an end, perhaps with a word of thanks. He will sometimes add directions regarding the dispatching or handling of the typed copy and the documents enclosed.

Simple and repetitive letters are easy to dictate; dictating and typing of these can further be rationalized by using standard text elements (initial and closing phrases, standard paragraphs) that are recorded in a list of text elements and referred to only by numbers - a simple form of 'modular correspondence' mentioned in section 55.

Special use of dictating machines

Dictating equipment can help in many other situations when written recording is too slow or inconvenient. Here are a few examples:

A dictating machine is an excellent means for *messages* to the secretary or colleagues when personal contact is impossible, for example messages dictated after working hours in the office or in the evening at home, particularly if the boss will be busy the next morning and not able to give the instructions personally.

Recording of important *telephone calls* is another well known application; it requires only a simple telephone adaptor. The records are either transcribed or are stored without retyping (a good index is then necessary). Also *meetings* and conferences can be recorded; a complete record is required only in exceptional cases, and a dictating machine can be used more frequently for recording conclusions: after a subject has been discussed and a conclusion accepted, a summary of the discussion and the decisions taken are dictated by the chairman or by a secretary; the advantage is that the summary is dictated in the presence of all participants, it can be immediately approved or corrected, and the minutes of the meeting are ready for transcribing at the moment the session ends.

Another application is the *inventory* of technical equipment, stores etc., particularly if it requires going through a number of rooms and places. Similarly, the gathering of *notes* during an inspection of technical equipment in a factory or on the grounds, is an opportunity to use dictating equipment. Also the recording of comments and *notes* at a pause in a congress if you need to record important ideas when they are fresh in your memory, or at an exhibition where you have no time or opportunity to make written remarks (as there is no place to sit down and write) are excellent applications for a pocket dictating machine.

A very interesting use of dictating machines in many professions is the recording of *observations*. For instance, a biologist can dictate his notes when sitting at his microscope - dictating is faster than writing in longhand, and allows him to keep his eyes on the object being observed, and both hands free for manipulations. The dictating machine can also help in time measuring if no great precision is required: the beginnings and ends of observed events are simply dictated (in non-stop record mode) and the times are measured later from the record. To take an example from a quite different field of activities - a coach of a sports team can dictate his notes while observing the play or training of his team; again, a detailed record is obtained without one's close attention being distracted. When *browsing* through information sources - in a library or at a computer terminal during an online search - we can also employ a dictating machine to record notes and our own ideas, criticism, associations, tasks and other remarks that emerge at the moment of browsing and that might otherwise be forgotten. Finally, a dictating machine in a portable pocket form is a unique instrument for recording ideas and drafts when *travelling* or *walking*. Peripatetic thinking is no rarity, and too many ideas and formulations that appear at an unexpected moment are lost if we cannot record them immediately. A 'pocket memo' should always accompany the creative man.

Dictating centres

In some large companies the typing service is performed by centralized typing pools. Cassettes are then sent to this centre, and the typed texts are sent back to the authors. Good organization (labelling of the cassettes, handling the enclosures, respecting priorities, messenger service or tubular post) are a *conditio sine qua non.* The originator must respect the fact that it is no longer his personal secretary, but an anonymous typist transcribing his dictation and having no detailed knowledge of the special terms, addresses, individual layout requirements etc. He must be extremely careful in his instructions.

The most progressive solution is *remote dictation* by means of a normal telephone. The user simply dials the number of the centre, is connected to one of the free dictating machines and - after identifying himself, giving his address and other instructions - dictates the text. Commands to the dictating machine are given by dialling (e.g. dialling 1 = record, 2 = stop, 3 = rewind etc.).

54 - Word processor

For centuries, paper was practically the only information carrier for textual information, and its dominance was not affected when punched

Courtesy ICL Nederland, Amsterdam

Fig. 54.1 - Flexowriter - the predecessor of word processors

An electric typewriter making it possible to produce punched tape, as well as to type automatically data from a tape; also copying of punched tapes and combination of manual and automatic typing was possible. This marvellous automatic typewriter of the fifties was a mechanical forerunner of the word processor.

cards appeared as the oldest machine-readable medium. They were used mainly for formatted numerical data and very short text comments. Punched tape was the first medium able to accept reasonable volumes of text, and it also had been used in the predecessors of our modern word processors - in the electromechanical automatic typewriters of the fifties (fig. 54.1).

Computers began also to process data in the natural language; typical tasks were initially the automatic compilation of indexes, vocabularies, concordances, information storage and retrieval, and various special applications in the field of mathematical linguistics. In the seventies, '*text processing*' or '*word processing*' appeared.

The terminology in this young field has not yet been stabilized. The terms 'word processing' and 'text processing' are used sometimes as synonyms; some authors and standards distinguish between them but, unfortunately, use varying definitions. Though the term 'text processing' is logical (it is *text* of course that is processed, not the *words* !), the less appropriate term is winning, in particular because of the general acceptance of the term 'word processor'.

Some of the elementary functions of word processing can be realized by means of an electronic typewriter with memory, which has been mentioned in section 52. However, 'full-fledged' word processing is performed by devices that consist of five elements (see fig. 54.2): the operation unit with internal storage, keyboard, display unit, external storage and printer. A *word processor* is a special-purpose microcomputer. A general-purpose microcomputer can also be used for word processing, if it has sufficient internal and external storage capacity and special word processing software. Similarly, the mainframe in a computing centre can serve for word processing, provided the necessary software is available.

The text is originated via a keyboard, and simultaneously displayed on a screen. It can be changed or corrected immediately (typist's errors), then

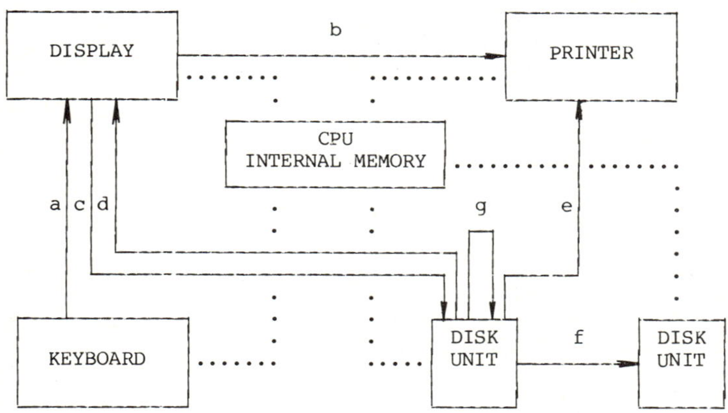

Fig. 54.2 - The basic units and modes of work of a word processor

This is a scheme of a stand-alone word processor. Several modes of work are possible:
[a] key-type and display
[b] print-out the displayed text
[c] store the displayed text on the disk
[d] recall the text from disk to display
[e] print text from disk
[f] copy text from disk to disk
[g] special operations, e.g sorting of stored files.
The interconnections between the units are, of course, not direct. All operations are performed via the central processing unit and internal memory.

printed and/or stored. Today, a floppy disk is a common storage medium. One to four (typically two) read/write disk units can be attached. The printer is a separate unit.

Keyboard

The *keyboard* of a word processor has a layout similar to that of the keyboard of a typewriter, but a number of functional keys have been added. First of all, arrow-marked keys to control the *cursor* - an optical signal in the form of a flashing underline or of an inverted letter (dark on white if white on dark is normal), identifying the position on the page where an action is to be performed, started or ended (typed or corrected letter, start of copying, end of copying etc.). Instead of keys for moving the cursor, some machines have a control stick or pad that can be handled in four directions to move the cursor to the left, right, up or down. Special keys are often available for fast moving of the cursor to certain places ('home' position in the left-hand upper corner, beginning of the next word, next sentence, next line, next paragraph). A set of keys controlling the various functions (store, recall, print, insert, delete etc.) is also added (fig. 54.4).

Advanced word processors have a larger character set than a standard typewriter: for example, the Philips P-5002 word processor on which this book has been typed, has a keyboard with 48 keys; each is normally used in two positions (as on a typewriter), but many keys also allow to print

Courtesy Philips Data Systems, Apeldoorn, The Netherlands

Fig. 54.3 - The Philips P-5002 word processor

and to display special characters and symbols in the third and fourth position. Secondly, all machines with a golf-ball print element or with a daisy wheel permit a standard element to be exchanged for a special one (say, Greek or Cyrillic alphabet, special mathematical character set, or for another letter size or type). If the word processor is used for preparation of text that will be set by means of a phototypesetting machine that has many various types and sizes of letters and a few hundred special characters and symbols, then the characters not available on the keyboard and on the ball or daisy-wheel element must be coded as we show in section 56. Some advanced word processing systems make it possible to display *virtual keyboard(s)* and to type special symbols by means of a light pen or by a touch technique - the screen being simply touched by a finger. Similarly, a few *virtual functional keys* can be displayed and operated in some systems; their functions are variable and can be appointed by the user.

Typing comfort is increased if the keyboard is designed as a separate element connected only by a cable; it can then be moved into the position the typist finds most comfortable.

Courtesy Philips Data Systems, Apeldoorn, The Netherlands

Fig. 54.4 - Detail of the keyboard of a word processor

The keyboard of the Philips P-5002 word processor consists of three parts. The central block of (dark) keys is similar to a normal typewriter (only a part of it is shown here). While the keys of a typewriter can be used only in two (upper and lower case) levels, the word processor enables four levels to be used by employing the CODE key to type special characters. The function keys to the right (not shown here) are for handling the cursor, controlling the display and correcting the text. The function keys to the left (the eight light keys) are used to control the commumication with the floppy disks (store and recall page) and to control the printer.

The display

Instead of the small 'window' of an electronic typewriter, a word processor is equipped with a *display screen* of larger capacity. A minimum, that is typical of personal computers, is display of 24 lines of 40 characters each. For standard word processing this is insufficient, and a display of 24 or more lines and 80 characters per line is more typical. An ideal display shows a whole A4 page, that is (including margins) 70 lines and 100 characters per line at pitch 12. An A4 page format (210 × 297 mm) is in fact a natural unit of typed text, and it should be visible without scrolling (shifting the text of one page vertically or horizontally on the screen). Recently, the first word processor with a display of 2 × A4 capacity appeared.

Reading a text that exceeds the format of the screen is done by means of the above-mentioned *scrolling*; this is necessary also if large formats (e.g. statistical tables, forms) are being processed.

The letters displayed should be large enough, sharp and have sufficient contrast. Until now it has not been proven whether a positive picture (dark letters on light background) is better than the usual negative display. Some word processors offer a choice. Also the *screen colour* (typically green) has been found less important, if the letters have sufficient contrast. Light intensity should always be under the control of the user. The *cursor* must be easy to see; a negative cursor is easier to recognize than a blinking underlining. A screen with a non-reflective surface, placed in a separate casing that can be tilted and swivelled, can improve user's comfort and performance.

There are some special features available in advanced word processors, for example, shadowing of a part of text that is to be submitted to a special operation (deleted, copied, moved etc.), visible signalling of the tabulator setting, visible margin setting, highlighting of selected parts of the text (having a similar function to italics in the printed text), blinking of selected characters or words (that must be carefully used) or displaying commands when operative. In many word processors, a special command line is displayed. Colours are not usual on the screens of word processors; on the other hand, some personal computers using a standard colour television set as the display unit take advantage of the use of colour output; it can identify various types of print, as mentioned in section 56.

Drafting texts on the screen often requires one to see the draft and, simultaneously, other documents; the possibility to split the screen and to display two or more documents or parts of them is invaluable. At present, this feature is an exception, but it is a must for a work station of the future.

Storage

Data that have been typed on the keyboard and displayed on the screen are temporarily held in the internal storage of the processor, and they can be stored after the user's command. The *floppy disk* is a typical storage medium for word processors. Its capacity depends on its size (diameter 5¼ or 8 inches), single or double density and one- or double-sided recording. Capacities between 70,000 and 250,000 characters per disk are typical. Large word processing systems offer hard disk(s) with a capacity of one up to several million characters per disk.

The user can hold on a disk a number of separate data sets consisting of one or more pages. Every set must have a unique name. The system automatically keeps a directory of stored data sets; this directory can be displayed after the user's command.

The user can retrieve any page of any data set; it appears on the screen, can be corrected, amended, edited, copied, printed out, stored again or it

Courtesy Philips Data Systems, Apeldoorn, The Netherlands

Fig. 54.5 - DOR - digital optical recording

Digital optical recording is a new technology permitting the storage of large volumes of information with a very high density. An optical disk (diameter of 30 cm) has a capacity of 10^{10} bits, which is equal to about 500,000 pages of text. One disk can store information equal to a large encyclopedia or a set of handbooks and a large volume of specialist literature.

	DOR	magnetic disk	magnetic tape	micro fiche	paper
capacity	+++	++	+	++	+
random access	++	+++	–	+	–
erasable	–	+++	++	–	+
archivability	++	+	+	+++	+++
volume	+++	+	+	++	–
machine-readability	+++	+++	+++	–	–

Fig. 54.6 - The typical properties of external storages

can be deleted. The disk can be protected from rewriting or deletion of the stored data. Voluminous or important files should be stored in duplicate form on back-up disks; they should be always kept separate from the originals.

Printer

Cheap personal computers used as word processors are mostly equipped with *dot matrix printers* sometimes even limited to upper or lower case letters only. They are inexpensive, relatively fast, but the quality of print is poor, and cannot be used for external correspondence. Word processors mostly have a *daisy-wheel printer*, mentioned in section 52. Less usual is an electric typewriter with a golf-ball element attached as a printer.

Producing documents for external use (letters, reports, originals for camera-ready print) requires not only a good quality of print, but also a sufficiently rich character set, a line length of at least 80 characters, and variable line spacing. A universal printer allows printing on single sheets of paper or on endless forms. The printers use mostly standard typewriter pitch (typically either 10 or 12 characters per inch); printers of higher quality (and price) allow the user to choose the pitch, either only 10 or 12, or a larger number of variants (the word processor Philips P-5002 makes it possible to select pitches from 3 to 13, and also 15, 17, 20, 24, 30 and 40). Some printers allow proportional spacing, and the printing of semibold types. A very important feature available on all higher-price printers is optional right-margin justification and optional automatic centering of text. Also, automatic line numbering is practical; it offers an excellent opportunity to improve cross-referencing (drafts sent to

MINI	MIDI	MAXI	SPEC	KEYBOARD
+	+	+		abc keyboard
1	2	4		key levels
48	92	92	92	number of different characters
	+	+		upper and lower case
		+		numerals both in upper and lower case
			+	special numerical keyboard
	+	+		functional (control) keys
			+	programmable functional keys
			+	virtual keyboard(s)
	+	+		detachable (free) keyboard
				DISPLAY
	+	+		tiltable/swivable display unit
24	40	70		number of lines displayable
24	70	100		maxi number of lines per page
40	80	100		number of characters displayable per line
40	140	200		maximum number of characters per line
1	1	1	7	number of colours available
		+		highlighting
		+		blinking
+	+	+		light intensity control
	+	+		shadowing of parts of text
	+	+		scrolling
			+	proportional fonts on the screen
			+	justification on the screen
	+	+		diacritical signs
	+	+		sub- and superscripts ($\pm\frac{1}{4}$, $\pm\frac{1}{2}$ line)
	+	+		true ascenders and descenders
			+	marker line or point
+	+	+		cursor moved by keys
		+		cursor moved by stick/pad
	+	+		fast cursor move to left upper, begin line,...
			+	cursor moved by touch or voice
	+	+		margin and tabs
	+	+		visible tab and margin setting
	+	+		special command and information line(s)
			+	splittable screen
				EDITING
+	+	+		wrap-around feature
	+	+		flexible line spacing (from - step - until)
		+		optional line numbering
		+		page reformatting (length, lines, spacing)
	+	+		underlining on the screen
				(justification - see printer and display)
	+	+		centration
		+		automatic page numbering and re-numbering
		+		semi-automatic hyphenation
			+	automatic hyphenation

Fig. 54.7 - Word processor features (cont.)

MINI = *usable only for drafts and internal documents; personal computer with elementary word processing functions*
MIDI = *typical correspondence applications;*
MAXI = *advanced functions for long complicated texts, also compatible with automatic typesetting*
SPEC = *additional features of sophisticated systems; special requirements*

MINI	midi	maxi	spec	SEARCH
+	+	+		string search
+	+	+		universal search (ABC=Abc=abc)
		+		specific search (ABC or Abc or abc only)
		+		rejoining of hyphenated words in search
		+		global search (through the whole document)
		+		dot-feature search (MA.ER = MAYER, MAIER, MAJER..
	+	+		search/replace function
		+		global search/replace function
		+		search for headings (chapters, sections..)
		+		search for first lines in sections or paragraphs
				STORAGE
1	2	2		standard number of ext. storage units
2	4	4		maximum number of units
40K	100K	> 100K	> 1M	storage capacity of one unit
40K	200K	> 400K	> 1M	total storage capacity
	+	+		system software loaded from disk
	+	+		disk protection
		+		protection of parts of the storage
+	+	+		automatic directory of stored documents
	+	+		file name duplicate protection
				SPECIAL OPERATIONS
		+		alphanumerical sorting
		+		multiple field sorting
			+	automatic compiling of indexes
			+	calculating facilities
		+		automatic editing of a list of contents
			+	automatic compiling of a glossary
				PRINT
48	92	92	92	character set
	+	+		upper and lower case
		+		interchangeable types
	+	+		diacritical signs
	+	+		subscripts and upperscripts
	+	+		'correspondence' quality of print
150	210	300	420	minimum width of paper mm
40	80	120	160	minimum characters per line
	+	+		variable pitch (from - step - to)
	+	+		variable line spacing (from - step - to)
		+		bold print
	+			right-hand justification (word spacing)
		+		right-hand justification (letter spacing)
		+		right/left hand justification
			+	negative print (white on black)
		+		'clean' and 'dirty' print
		+		automatic endless form feeding
		+		simultaneous print

Fig. 54.7 - Word processor features (end)

This is a maximalistic list of possible word processor features; at present, there is no word processor having all the above functions and these are also not necessary for every user. He must consider his specific needs, use this table as a check-list, fill in his own requirements and then verify whether the type of a word processor he intends to buy copes with them. Data in this table are intended as examples of typical features.

consultants, texts to be corrected etc.). Pages can often be automatically numbered. In some texts, sub- and superscripts are required (chemical formulae, mathematical texts); an advanced printer enables characters to be printed a half (or quarter) space above and below the line. Simultaneous printing is another feature of a good word processor: it makes it possible to give a print command, and while a page or a whole document is being printed, the keyboard and screen are free for other work.

Special functions of a word processor

There are more than 150 types of word processor on the market, produced by about fifty manufacturers. Many a personal computer is also equipped with some form of word processing software, and mainframes are also sometimes used for word processing from remote terminals. All the available systems differ in many details, functions, capacities, performance and price. A list of features in fig. 54.7 gives an overview, and a professional who intends to buy a word processor can use it as a check list; he must evaluate which of the functions is important for him and assess his wishes against the functions of the machine that he considers buying.

Many of the functions and properties of a word processor have already been described. We must now mention a few others. One of the essential features that improve ease of correcting and updating is the *wrap-around* function. This means that after inserting or deleting a word or longer part of text, the subsequent lines up to the end of a paragraph are adjusted so that their lengths accord with the required layout. Word wrap-around is also a very useful function: the typist can type a text without interruption; there is no need to listen for the bell at the end of a line, or to decide where to start a new line - the system automatically starts a new line and moves any incomplete word at the end of a line to the beginning of a new line.

The *search and replace functions* offer many important features. The user can define a string of characters (say, a word 'silicium'), and give a search command. The system then searches the text, and the cursor moves automatically to the first occurrence of this word; after a further command it proceeds to the next occurrence. If a search/replace command (say, 'silicium = silicon') is given, then all occurrences of the first string of characters can be replaced by the second one. Practical use of this function is by no means restricted to plain corrections; we can use it for systematic updating and improving of a text, and for testing consistency of terminology as described in section 56.

The buyer of a word processor, particularly a personal computer with word processing facilities, should very carefully check all the functions essential for his application.

Particularly, the wrap-around and the search/replace functions are often rather primitive in cheap systems. Sometimes the search procedure is unable to distinguish between lower and upper case, so that the system cannot differentiate among the words 'best', Best (a town in the Netherlands) and BEST (acronym). A check should also be made whether search must be commanded page by page or whether it can continue automatically through the whole text ('global search'). Omitting the check on such details may result in many a disappointment later.

Some systems are able to process semi-automatically an *index* to one or more words or phrases. The strings of characters searched are defined by the user, and the system prints them out, together with the numbers of pages or even lines where they occur (fig. 54.8). Automatic design of a *concordance* is an uncommon feature at present, yet it might be useful as a source for editing an alphabetical index, for checking consistency of terminology, and for text analysis.

Special functions, available only in sophisticated word processing systems, are *automatic hyphenation* (splitting words at the end of a line according to grammatical rules) combined with automatic de-hyphenation (after re-organizing the text of a paragraph, hyphenated words may come into the middle of a line and have to be rejoined). Hyphenation

```
KEYBOARD            HIGHLIGHT                    P=29
          P=3                 P=16               P=35
          P=13      BLINK                        P=37
          P=14                P=15               P=39
          P=15                P=16               P=42
          P=16      SHADOW              CENTRAT
          P=17                P=15               P=5
          P=37                P=41               P=17
          P=39      TABULAT                      P=27
          P=40                P=3                P=31
          P=41                P=4                P=33
LINE SPAC                     P=16               P=35
          P=17                P=35      INDEX
          P=39                P=42               P=10
PITCH               JUSTIF                       P=12
          P=3                 P=4                P=19
          P=4                 P=5                P=26
          P=15                P=15               P=27
          P=17                P=17               P=33
          P=26                P=26               P=34
                                                 P=43
```

Fig 54.8 - Automatic index by a word processor

The user defined a word or a group of words - in our example, the words or word-stems 'pitch, tabulat-, justif-, centrat-, line spa-' etc. He defined the file - in our example, the stored text of chapter 5 of the present book (in the word processor version, paging of the draft). The word processor sequentially searched the text word by word and printed out the numbers of the pages on which the mentioned words occur. The search for 10 terms in the text of about 15,000 words was performed in 9 minutes. One single term is searched at a speed of about 6000 words per minute. The stems make it possible to find all inflected forms (tabulate, tabulated, tabulating, tabulator); search for phrases consisting of two or more words (see 'line spa-') is also possible.

requires a sophisticated program, and it must be supported by a stored vocabulary of exceptions. Semi-automatic hyphenation is less intricate: the word processor looks down through the text and selects 'candidates' for hyphenation; these words are then split manually. A vocabulary is also a new device for automatic *spelling control.*

The 'display writer' of IBM is a desk-top word processor (called 'text editing machine' by the manufacturer) with a dictionary of 50,000 frequently occurring English words, with the facility for another 500 individual words (frequently used special terms and names) to be added by the operator. The OMEGA word processing system of the Compucorp makes it possible to attach a multilingual 'International Unabridged Dictionary' that enables the spelling of up to one million English and foreign language words including specialized terms to be checked. To verify spelling, the user depresses the key SPELL; the cursor then races through the text at up to 2000 words a minute, and if a word not present in the dictionary is encountered, the cursor stops and the machine gives an acoustic signal. The user either corrects a misspelled word, or gives a command to ignore it and to move on, or adds the word to the dictionary. This check, though valuable, does not, of course, prevent misspellings resulting in a word that actually exists (DAIRY instead of DIARY, OF instead of OR).

In sophisticated systems, the automatic search function can be improved by further special features, for example by automatic *search for headings* of chapters, sections or paragraphs or automatic search and display of first chapter, section or paragraph lines. Also important is automatic *content page editing* - display and printing of headings with the respective page numbers. This feature saves effort and ensures absolute consistency of the contents page with the text.

Advanced word processing systems, in particular the centralized ones, offer as a by-product a number of *statistical data* on the volume and structure per data set, frequency of use of program modules, number of corrections, connection time per data set, total on and off time of the connected terminals, etc. These data are essential for the control and management of centralized word processing services and for analysis of their use.

Use and misuse of a word processor

A word processor is a marvellous instrument that offers a professional something absolutely new: the chance to correct, change, amend and edit his text extremely quickly and easily. However, the functions of a word processor are not always exploited to their full extent. Their most popular use is for *business correspondence*; undoubtedly, it is a mass application. The word processor is very effective in this field, it can be introduced without problems, and the functions required are practically standard. The word processor helps to improve the secretary's or typist's performance, and makes her work more pleasant: corrections of typing errors are easy, and the boring task of re-typing is avoided. In this application the word processor improves the clerical work only; it does not directly help the professional in his own activities.

In the particular situation where the word processing is centralized in pools overloaded with work, most authors are discouraged from making full use of the advantages of word processing; they are deterred from returning the text and asking for changes, amendments, layout improvements (that are now so easy to do !) more than once.

However, it is not only the easy handling of text, and its iterative improvement that offers the professional new opportunities. The word processor can help him to improve his style of work. One example is easier use of a dictating machine; we have mentioned that the secretary's work can be wasted by missing instructions, indistinct pronunciation of proper names or terms etc. If the text is typed on a word processor, then corrections of misspelled words, amendments of data etc. are quite easy. One of the barriers to the widespread use of dictating equipment thus disappears.

A professional can also employ (perhaps in certain situations only) a quite new form of text creation: he can dictate by means of an intercom to his secretary who types the text onto a word processor while he simultaneously proof-reads the typed text on his display connected in parallel with the display of his secretary (fig. 26.3). The greatest problem with a dictating machine (the invisibility of the dictated text) now disappears, the author has his text before his eyes, he can check it word by word, and he can immediately correct errors or ask for changes. The time delay caused by sending a cassette to the secretary, waiting for a hard-copy, sending it back for correcting, and waiting again for the typed text has now gone. This technique cannot be recommended as a general solution (it also has its own disadvantages), but it expands the number of variants of text creating techniques, and it is up to the professional to choose the best one to suit the concrete case.

55 - Special applications of word processors

The typing of correspondence is the simplest application of a word processor. However, the word processor can even in this field be exploited to the full in more challenging manners.

Standard documents with variables

In the commercial world, it is often the case that a standard text has to be adapted to concrete individual conditions by inserting variable names, dates, addresses, prices or paragraphs: offers or individualized advertising letters are typical examples. Similarly, legal documents such as contracts, drafted and written by lawyers or public notaries, consist of a standard text in which only a few dates, the names of the two contracting parties, the object bought or the prices vary. Technical documentation on industrial products that are supplied in slightly differing versions is another example of such a semi-variable text.

In such cases the basic text is stored in the memory of a word processor; the places where variable data should be inserted are marked by special codes. In each individual case the basic text is copied from the memory, the specific names, data, numbers, prices etc. are filled in, and a final document is printed out. A number of changes can be done in a single operation, for example, in the text of a legal document where the buyer's name occurs many times, it can be inserted by a single search/change command, e.g. NAME-OF-THE-BUYER = John Smith. Similarly, any parameter in technical documentation can be replaced by another throughout the entire text by one instruction only.

This technique can be used also in the many non-commercial activities performed by a professional. Everyone from time to time has to write letters or short documents of similar though slightly varying content, say, letters asking authors to send reprints of their articles, or individualized messages to a circle of recipients.

The technique was used three times by the author of the present book. First, 38 letters asking various manufacturers of hardware for photos of their products and permission to publish them in the book; the basic text was standard, the addresses and concrete requirements were variable. Secondly, 14 letters were typed, addressed and sent to persons or teams who have been asked for data or advice on some parts (chapters, sections, selected paragraphs) of the manuscript; again, the basic text was standard, the requirements were individual. Thirdly, a set of 25 letters has been prepared that will accompany the author's copies of the book to be sent to friends, colleagues, consultants and reviewers.

Form filling

Recording information in formalized and standardized form is a common task. Form filling, writing structured reports, technical records, memos, certificates, minutes are a few examples. A word processor makes this work easier by displaying the headings in the right order, it guarantees a uniform layout and content (nothing can be forgotten), it makes it possible to store and to reproduce fixed or slightly variable data - for example, minutes of weekly reports can be typed using a stored heading that is copied, and only the date is changed, the names of absent people are deleted from the list of those regularly present, standard headings of sections are used, etc.

Advanced word processors can also work in *graphical mode.* They can draw vertical and horizontal lines quickly and precisely, add headings of columns and fields, i.e. draw *tables* or produce a *form.* The form is then stored and, when needed, is recalled from the memory to the screen, completed with the variable data, and then printed out and/or stored. Our decimal classification form in fig. 44.3 has been drawn on the Philips P-5002 word processor; it has been stored, and displayed every time when a part of a decimal classification system has been created. The form when filled in and edited is illustrated in concrete applications in figures 37.1 and 38.1. A specific property of such a form is its flexibility; whilst a pre-printed form is rigid, a stored form can be adapted to any individual case; columns or fields that are not needed can be omitted, the number of lines in any field can be extended or reduced as required, etc.

Modular correspondence

A further step is to use a word processor to type letters or other documents consisting of a number of variable elements that can be combined in a large number of variations. The modules can comprise a number of initial phrases, many typical paragraphs, and a number of closing expressions. Again, this application is appropriate to the commercial world, but it could also be used by many a professional (answering typical repetitive inquiries). The work is rationalized by compiling a list of frequently occurring modules (phrases, sentences, paragraphs) and having the modules logically sorted, numbered or coded, and stored in the word processor memory. The professional and his secretary have a list of text elements at their disposal, so that dictating is limited to the module numbers in the required sequence and a few additional remarks or variable data, and typing to the recall of the elements from the memory and adding the variable data.

Assembly of a document from other documents

A similar technique can help when a new document is to incorporate parts of existing documents, for example, if a letter is to quote passages from previous correspondence, or an article contains lengthy quotations from other documents. Often, basic information has to be published in various forms for various recipients. The word processing technique can be used to transfer paragraphs or whole pages in the original or slightly adapted form from one document to another.

Lists, catalogues, and directories

Creating, updating and publishing lists (of people, addresses, telephone numbers, companies, products, parts, etc.) is a quite common activity. A word processor is an excellent device for keeping such lists and directories up to date; it enables them to be changed continuously, and their most up-to-date version to be kept in its memory; the list can be displayed or printed out at minimum cost and at any moment. As the list as a whole does not have to be re-typed, it is free of typing errors.

In our personal environment there are, of course, a number of practical situations where our word processor or personal computer can be used for this purpose: a personal directory of addresses and telephone numbers, a list of selected terms and definitions in our specific field of interest, lists of assets (see fig. 38.5), lists of pending tasks (figures 32.5 and 32.6), lists of the participants at special meetings, etc.

Layout editing

A word processor is an ideal instrument in all situations where a document is to be published in several forms and layouts. The number of lines per page, length of lines, spacing between lines, pitch of print, types and size of letters, justification or indenting, and many other layout parameters can easily be changed and new versions of the same document produced without re-typing, proof-reading and correcting. A common case is the printing of a first copy of a new text for proof-reading or for consultation. The best way is to print in double spacing and with line numbers; also any internal notes (that will later be deleted) are attached, usually in distinctive layout. The proof-readers and consultants are better able to insert their remarks and proposed changes, and cross-referencing to specific parts of the text is easy. When the text is finally edited, the format is changed, double spacing is replaced by the required final spacing, internal notes and line numbers are deleted. Also, 'dirty' or 'clean' printed version should be optionally available: in the former case, we receive a copy with all the technical codes, separators, special signs etc. needed for the control of the word processor or computer, or for later conversion by photoelectric typesetting (see example in fig. 56.2); in a 'clean' version, all these codes are suppressed (though they are latently present), and the text is printed out without them.

56 - The word processor helps the author

Of all the various applications of word processing, perhaps the preparation of a large text for publication is the most interesting. It offers the author much more than an easy facility to correct and to change his text. The word processing technique increases the author's overview of the whole text, it relieves him of the burden of many trivial, time-consuming operations, helps him to manage a large number of cross-references, to administer all citations and references, to control the placing of the figures and to check the progress of their creation, it gives him a unique instrument for checking the consistency of his terminology and language, helps him to compile a good alphabetical index, and finally it permits efficient camera-ready publication or automatic typesetting. Intelligent use of the word processing technique fundamentally changes the author's style of work, it improves his productivity as well as the formal quality of the publication.

The author and the computer

In this section we concentrate our attention solely on the use of the word processing technique. However, an author may also be supported by other available techniques. Chapter 4 described the modern style of working with information: the systematic acquisition, selection, sorting, organizing, storage and retrieval of information are essential for an author. The author sometimes organizes a separate file only for the purpose of the publication to be prepared. During the preparation phase and during writing he makes regular use of his personal information system, and of in-house as well as external systems. He also makes use of his computer facilities (his personal computer or terminal) for the planning and scheduling of a large number of activities (see figures 33.1 and 33.2) relating to all phases of the writing of his publication.

The book 'Personal Documentation for Professionals' as well as the present book were written with computer and word processor support: the computer terminal was used for personal documentation, and for online search in in-house and external data bases, for planning and scheduling of running activities; a synopsis was created and updated in online form, the text was written, corrected and edited on a word processor, testing for consistency of terminology and bibliographical data was performed online, the list of figures and the stages in their processing was kept in online form and regularly updated. The text was finally converted to magnetic tape that was used as input for the automatic phototypesetting system. Also the alphabetical index and bibliography were compiled in online form. The techniques used, and practical experience gained, have been published in ref. 50-Stibic.

List of contents and synopsis

The final structure of a large publication is never designed in one step. The author tries to sort and arrange the large number of gathered ideas and facts, data and text elements as systematically and logically as possible. The many interconnections of the subjects do not make this easy: a text is, in principle, linear, but any complicated subject is a network of ideas with many cross-connections and interrelationships. Numerous trials, changes, shifts, text reorganizations, deletions, amendments and updatings are needed before the publication structure can be accepted as satisfactory.

A *list of contents* is a very brief overview of the whole work and its structure. It defines the numbers and headings of chapters and sections, and usually contains data on the estimated (later actual) volume of text and on the number of figures per chapter and section. It can be kept in the memory of a word processor and updated throughout the work.

The *synopsis* is an outline of the contents, typically a few lines per section, and a few dozen lines per chapter of the prepared publication. It gives a total overview of the main ideas and their sequence. The time and effort spent on synopsis compilation pays off later. The more intensive and careful the preparation of the synopsis, the easier the writing and the better the structure of the publication.

The word processing technique that makes changes, updating, deletions, insertions and shifts easy is an excellent help in this phase of the author's work. It makes it possible to improve the structure of the publication step by step; the new version can be printed out, re-edited time and again until the final form has been found and accepted. It remains

```
MEMBER=PDOC      (NEW):WERKLIB              JOBNAME=TEXT-SC     DATE=25 JUN 79

        <26> CONTROLLED LANGUAGES AND THESAURI
        --------------------------------------

        * PRINCIPLES OF CONTROLLED LANGUAGES AND THESAURI
        * BASIC TYPES OF CONTROLLED LANGUAGES AND THESAURI
                   |------------------------------------------|
                   |      ONE ITEM FROM THE NASA THESAURUS    |
                   |------------------------------------------|
                   |------------------------------------------|
                   |  ONE PAGE FROM THE EXCERPTA MEDICA THES. |
                   |------------------------------------------|
        * USE OF EXISTING THESAURI OR EXTRACTS FROM THEM
        * OWN DESCRIPTOR SYSTEMS
                   |------------------------------------------|
                   |     FACETED THESAURUS OF AN ARCHITECT    |
                   |------------------------------------------|
                   |------------------------------------------|
                   |    FACETED THESAURUS OF AN ENTOMOLOGIST  |
                   |------------------------------------------|

        <27> AUTOMATIC INDEXING
        -----------------------

        * PRINCIPLES OF AUTOMATIC INDEXING
        * BASIC VARIANTS: THEIR ADVANTAGES AND DISADVANTAGES
        * FEATURES OF AUTOMATIC INDEXING (NON-SIGNIFICANT WORDS,
          TRUNCATION OF WORD-ENDINGS, COUMPOUNDS, SYNONYMS..)
        * THESAURUS AND SEMANTIC TERM RELATIONS
                   |------------------------------------------|
                   |     SCHEME OF THE AUTOMATIC INDEXING     |
                   |------------------------------------------|
```

Fig. 56.1 - Synopsis of a publication created and updated in online form

The synopsis was, in this case, created and updated by means of a terminal and mainframe computer. Editing was done online, the successive versions were printed by the remote line printer in the computing centre [ref. 50-Stibic].

stored in the memory during the writing of the text when smaller changes and shifts are made; the synopsis is kept up-to-date continuously.

The *placing of figures* can also be indicated in the synopsis (fig. 56.1); it is the source of the future list of figures.

Text creation

If the author is guided by a well-structured global plan of his publication and a well designed synopsis, he can write the text without the

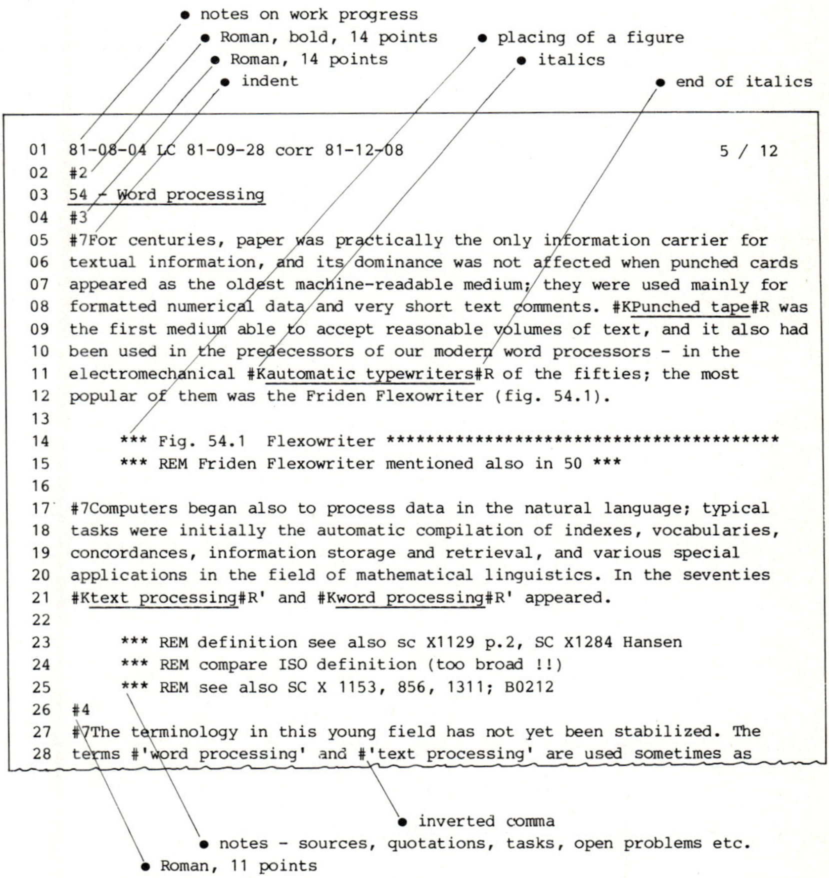


```
81-08-04 LC 81-09-28 corr 81-12-08                                5 / 12
#2
54 - Word processing
#3
#7For centuries, paper was practically the only information carrier for
textual information, and its dominance was not affected when punched cards
appeared as the oldest machine-readable medium; they were used mainly for
formatted numerical data and very short text comments. #KPunched tape#R was
the first medium able to accept reasonable volumes of text, and it also had
been used in the predecessors of our modern word processors - in the
electromechanical #Kautomatic typewriters#R of the fifties; the most
popular of them was the Friden Flexowriter (fig. 54.1).

     *** Fig. 54.1  Flexowriter ****************************************
     *** REM Friden Flexowriter mentioned also in 50 ***

#7Computers began also to process data in the natural language; typical
tasks were initially the automatic compilation of indexes, vocabularies,
concordances, information storage and retrieval, and various special
applications in the field of mathematical linguistics. In the seventies
#Ktext processing#R' and #Kword processing#R' appeared.

     *** REM definition see also sc X1129 p.2, SC X1284 Hansen
     *** REM compare ISO definition (too broad !!)
     *** REM see also SC X 1153, 856, 1311; B0212
#4
#7The terminology in this young field has not yet been stabilized. The
terms #'word processing' and #'text processing' are used sometimes as
```

Fig. 56.2 - Draft text typed on a word processor

Special codes for controlling the automatic typesetting machine have been added. The author also attached notes about the progress of the work, the placing of the figures and cross-references to his personal documentation or other sources of information. These notes will be deleted in later phases.

danger of losing his way. A word processor makes it easy to type the first version in draft form and layout, e.g. in double spacing and with numbered lines, with many technical notes, cross-references etc.

Proof-reading, corrections and *editing* can be done online, on the display unit, yet most authors prefer hard-copy editing. Compared with the screen that displays only a part of a page, or at best one page at a time, printed pages are easier to overview, they can be laid side by side, compared, sorted, merged and handled, and correcting by pen is generally preferred. Also if we wish to do our editing work outside the workplace, or if we send drafts to reviewers and consultants, then hard-copies are necessary.

After all corrections, changes, amendments and editing modifications have been made and the text is considered to be final, the last version can be printed out. It is then either sent to the publisher for setting in the traditional way, or delivered as a *camera-ready text* in the required layout - usually, the length of lines, the spacing between lines etc. are changed, the text can be right-hand justified etc. In the case of *phototypesetting*, the commands necessary for controlling the setting procedure must be inserted and very carefully checked as mentioned in the next section (see also fig. 56.2).

Notes and remarks

The word processing technique makes it easy to attach any notes important to the author and his consultants during the writing and editing phases. When the author is writing his first draft, he often encounters situations when he feels the need to consult or verify quotations, data, examples, references etc. It would be a waste of time and distracting to stop writing time and again merely to insert a minute fact or number that still needs to be found. It is more effective to leave the respective space in the text free to be filled in later.

All the *missing data* must be unambiguously flagged so as to be retrievable by the search or search/change function of the word processor: one inserts as flags special unique codes so that one can always recall all the places requiring correction or amendment. In the final text one will test whether all the details have been inserted i.e. that no flags indicating 'blank' places or places that need checking remain.

The author notes all temporary notes directly in his text: he inserts signals to indicate missing data, data that have to be verified, the need to search in the literature, inquiries to peers or colleagues, library requirements etc. The notes are best placed directly in the text, not as footnotes or at the end of a chapter; a separate line initialized by a unique code that makes retrieval possible is recommended. The codes chosen must not be signs or groups of signs that appear in the normal text or are used as codes for the phototypesetting procedure. For example, double signs $$ or ** can be employed (single signs might well occur in the text, double signs are unique and easy to type). Also, the main categories of remarks and notes should be distinguished by short but unique codes, for example *** BIBL could initiate all remarks that mean 'find and check in the library', the sign *** ONL might signal all reminders to make some time later an online search on a specific problem, etc.

When we have found and inserted the missing information or have verified dubious data, we delete the signals in the text; often it is practical to add a new internal note on the source of information or verification; this is important for the later compilation of the list of references and as an aid to memory - we are also later able to find the sources of our information again.

It is practical that all the references that we shall later concentrate in a separate chapter or section are noted primarily in the places of the text where they are used or to which they belong thematically. If data, definitions, citations etc. from a large work are used, then we also note the respective page. The *list of references* can be updated stepwise during the writing; thus, we keep the text of our work, and also a separate 'references' file online.

We can store every reference immediately; we are certain then not to forget it later. The purpose of marking references (also) in the text is self-evident; we gain not only an overview of the sources cited, but also an idea of the places *where* a certain source has been used or cited. The reference numbers can be blocked in the early phases and replaced by final numbers later. Also all other data that cannot be properly filled in during the draft phase must be blocked by special codes. For example, numbering of figures can be done in a later phase; again, the missing numbers of figures are preliminarily marked by a sign (e.g. ***). A check on the presence of *** before editing the final version gives the writer absolute assurance that he did not forget to fill in any of the missing numbers.

FIND	REPLACE BY
documet	document
documne	documen
sytem	system
abovemention	above-mention
isation	ization
databas	data bas
indices	indexes
classificator	classifier
Internat Classif	Int Classif
Int Class	Int Classif
Int Classificat	Int Classif

Fig. 56.3 - Consistency test by means of a word processor

The first four corrections are 'chronic' typist's errors that have been found at many places in the text; the text is systematically scanned and also the errors not found are corrected automatically. The following changes eliminate the author's inconsistency in his use or spelling of some words, and the last three lines correct some non-standard abbreviations of a journal name to the standard form [ref. 50-Stibic].

Testing for consistency of terminology

The word processing technique enables all occurrences of any word or phrase in a large text to be found quickly. The author can make practical use of this feature in several ways; one of them is to check the *consistency of terminology.*

Sometimes the author is not quite sure whether he has been consistent in his spelling or abbreviating of a term or name; perhaps, he has used the alternatives data base, data-base and database, or he has been inconsistent in the use of word-endings -isation and -ization etc. Similarly, he can check that he has always used the same form of a proper name or abbreviation. He can quickly find all unwanted variants by the search command.

References

The word processor enables a list of references to be built up stepwise and every new reference to be put into its proper place according to a systematic or alphabetic sequence or a combination of both. Also, the

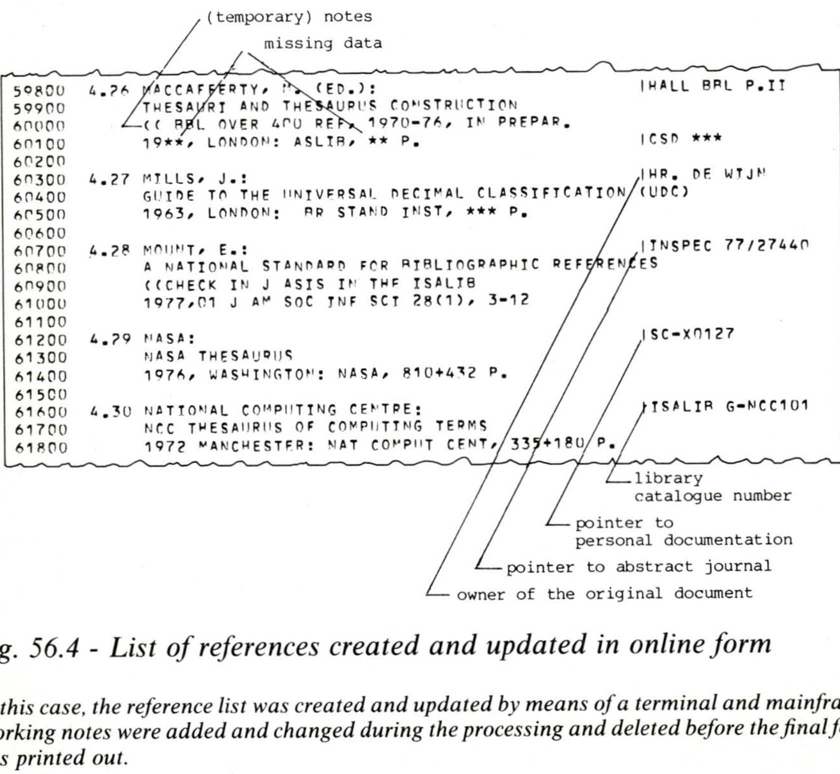

Fig. 56.4 - List of references created and updated in online form

In this case, the reference list was created and updated by means of a terminal and mainframe. Working notes were added and changed during the processing and deleted before the final form was printed out.

numbering of references can easily be updated and changed. It is important to check the consistency of the bibliographic data, in particular of standard abbreviations of journal names through the reference section (check, for example, whether the journal International Classification has been abbreviated according to the ISO standard, that it is always Int Classif not Internat Classificat or any other variant). Any wrong variant can be identified by means of the search command, and it can automatically be altered to the standard form by means of the search/replace command.

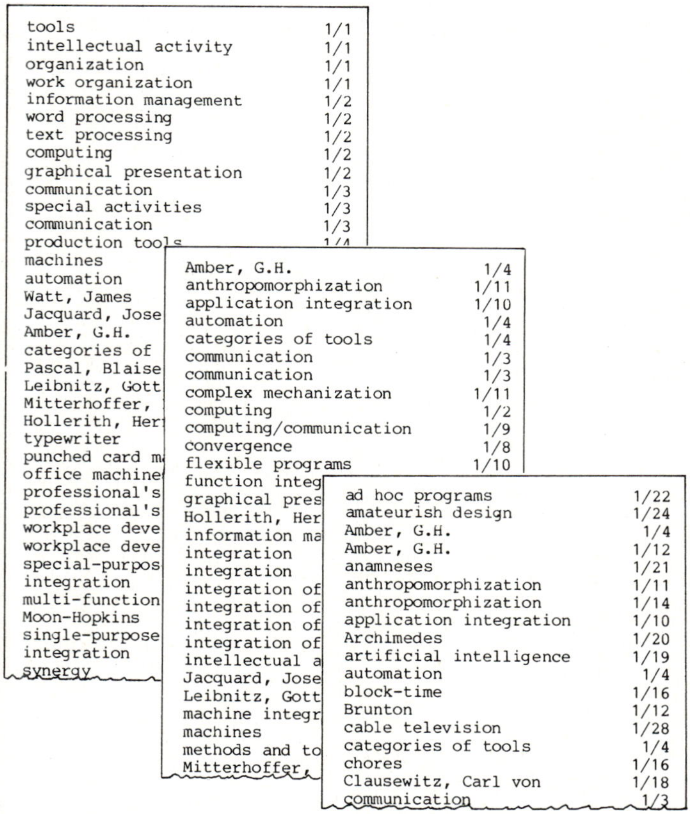

tools 1/1
intellectual activity 1/1
organization 1/1
work organization 1/1
information management 1/2
word processing 1/2
text processing 1/2
computing 1/2
graphical presentation 1/2
communication 1/3
special activities 1/3
communication 1/3
production tools 1/4
machines
automation
Watt, James
Jacquard, Jose
Amber, G.H.
categories of
Pascal, Blaise
Leibnitz, Gott
Mitterhoffer,
Hollerith, Her
typewriter
punched card m
office machine
professional's
professional's
workplace deve
workplace deve
special-purpos
integration
multi-function
Moon-Hopkins
single-purpose
integration
synergy

Amber, G.H. 1/4
anthropomorphization 1/11
application integration 1/10
automation 1/4
categories of tools 1/4
communication 1/3
communication 1/3
complex mechanization 1/11
computing 1/2
computing/communication 1/9
convergence 1/8
flexible programs 1/10
function integ
graphical pres
Hollerith, Her
information ma
integration
integration
integration of
integration of
integration of
integration of
intellectual a
Jacquard, Jose
Leibnitz, Gott
machine integr
machines
methods and to
Mitterhoffer,

ad hoc programs 1/22
amateurish design 1/24
Amber, G.H. 1/4
Amber, G.H. 1/12
anamneses 1/21
anthropomorphization 1/11
anthropomorphization 1/14
application integration 1/10
Archimedes 1/20
artificial intelligence 1/19
automation 1/4
block-time 1/16
Brunton 1/12
cable television 1/28
categories of tools 1/4
chores 1/16
Clausewitz, Carl von 1/18
communication 1/3

Fig. 56.5 - An alphabetical book index produced by a word processor

[a] The author made a note of index items page by page - here the pages of the draft (chapter/page).

[b] Every index page containing 60 items is sorted alphabetically by the Philips P-5002 word processor in two seconds.

[c] All sorted pages are merged into an alphabetical index of the book (here the first chapter only - this index was used by the author during the text editing); the final index contained the numbers of the printed pages (after the photoelectric typesetting).

Alphabetical index (register)

A detailed alphabetical *index* (alphabetical register) is an important help to the reader. Unfortunately, it is underestimated by some authors and editors; too often we encounter technical or scientific publications with an insufficient index or even - sad to say - without an index at all. Index compilation is an intellectual task. Fully automatic methods of index compilation are not yet available, but the indexer's job can be made easier by proper use of technical means.

A simple method is to flag in the text all the terms that are subjectively felt to be suitable index entries, re-type them with the respective page

```
                                                                                  W O R K C O P Y
     PERSONAL DOCUMENTATION - LIST OF FIGURES                                         79-11-08
     ========================================
           TYPE OF THE FIGURE                                ===
                                         SCHEME      =       SCH
                                         GRAPH       =       GRA
                                         COPY        =       COP
                                         PHOTO       =       FOT
                                         TABLE       =       TAB
                                         TEXT        =       TEX
           FORM OF THE FIGURE                                     ===
                                          BLACK&WHITE             B&W
                                          AUTOTYPE                AUT
           NETTO ORIGINAL HEIGHT IN MM; ESTIMATE ()                    ===
           ACTION REQUIRED                                                      ====
     ====            FINAL NUMBER
          ====       WORK NUMBERING (NUMBERS IN THE WORK COPY OF OCT, 1979)
     0  - TECHNIQUE OF THE INTELLECTUAL WORK
     ----------------------------------------
    0.01 0/1  FIELD OF INTELLECTUAL WORK           TAB  B&W  228        AMEND
    0.02 0/2  COMPUTER APPLICATIONS 1940/1980      SCH  B&W  120        DRAW
                                       CHAPTER 0   --------  348 ------
    1  - INFORMATION SOURCES AND NEEDS
    -----------------------------------
    1.01 11/1 GROWTH OF LITERATURE PER DECADE      TAB  B&W   55        OK
    1.02 11/2 GROWTH OF NO JOURNALS/ABSTRACTS      GRA  B&W  135        DRAW
    1.03 11/3 VOLUME OF LIT ON INF SCIENCE         TAB  B$W   60        OK
    1.04 12/1 INTEREST SPECTRA                     SCH  B&W  140        CORRECT
    1.05 12/2 INF NEEDS, SOURCES AND CHANNELS      TAB  B&W   95        DRAW
    1.06 12/3 CASE STUDY ON INF NEEDS              GRA  B&W  108        CHECK
    1.07 13/1 DOCUMENT CATEGORIES                  TAB  B&W  155        OK
    1.08 13/2 BRADFORD'S LAW                       TEX  B&W   40        OK
```

Fig. 56.6 - List of figures with data for planning purposes

This list was created and updated online by means of the terminal and mainframe in the computing centre. Type of figure, dimensions and stage of the processing were added for planning purposes. Such an updatable list is an invaluable tool helping the author to overview tens (sometimes hundreds) of figures of different types and the work already done and still to be done.

numbers, sort mechanically and print out in alphabetic sequence as shown in fig. 56.5; finally, entries have to be concentrated (a word occurring ten times must appear in the index only once and must be followed by ten page numbers).

List of figures

If the numbers and titles of figures in the text are flagged by unique codes, then they can easily be found and copied into a separate list of figures; the advantage is that none of the figures is forgotten and the titles in the text and in the list are consistent. A simpler way is to re-type such a list from the text. During the work phase the list of figures is used also as an invaluable means of work scheduling (see fig. 56.6). The processing stage that each figure (draft, drawing etc.) has reached is noted so that the author gains a perfect overview of the work that has to be done even if the number of figures is large and if various sorts (photographs, drawings, tables, specimens of computer output, copies of documents) have to be edited and prepared in the camera-ready form.

57 - Camera-ready print and phototypesetting

The increasing quality of text typed by means of modern typewriters and word processors, the increased flexibility of output form and layout, as well as improvements in printing techniques have made it possible for traditional typesetting to be replaced by so-called *camera-ready publishing.*

The text must be typed in a consistent *layout* - the rules for margins, spacing, indenting, placing of headings, underlining, free lines between paragraphs, footnotes, page numbering etc. must be exactly defined before typing starts, and they must be adhered to later. In many companies, institutes and publishing houses, detailed ‘house-style manuals’ stipulate the uniform layout of all publications. Similarly, organizers of conferences and congresses ask the authors to follow their layout standards when publishing proceedings in camera-ready form. Even when preparing a larger publication that does not need to conform to a compulsory standard, we should define in advance our own layout rules. Indeed, it pays off if they are defined in writing and in the form of a specimen page before typing starts.

A standardized layout is much easier to follow by a typist if he types on pre-printed forms (fig. 57.1) on which the margins, indenting, centering lines, placing of page numbers, end-of-page warnings are pre-printed so as to be visible to the typist but ‘invisible’ to the photocopying or offset machine (pre-print in light blue). This method relates, of course, only to typing by means of a typewriter. A word processor assists the layout standardization with a number of its own features: the margins are pre-set, the automatic tabulator can be set to required positions, the number of lines per page is automatically checked and displayed, the positions of page-numbers and page headings are pre-defined, headings can be centered automatically, text can be right-hand justified, etc.; moreover, it is always possible to change layout later.

Text intended for reproduction has to meet rather high quality-requirements: single-strike carbon paper ribbon gives a sharp imprint and unvarying contrast; it is to be preferred to a normal textile ribbon. The appearance of the text is improved if the titles of the chapters and sections are accentuated graphically. This is possible in many ways. For one, in typewriters and printers with exchangeable typing elements (golf-ball or daisy wheel) an element with another letter type (bold letters) can be set

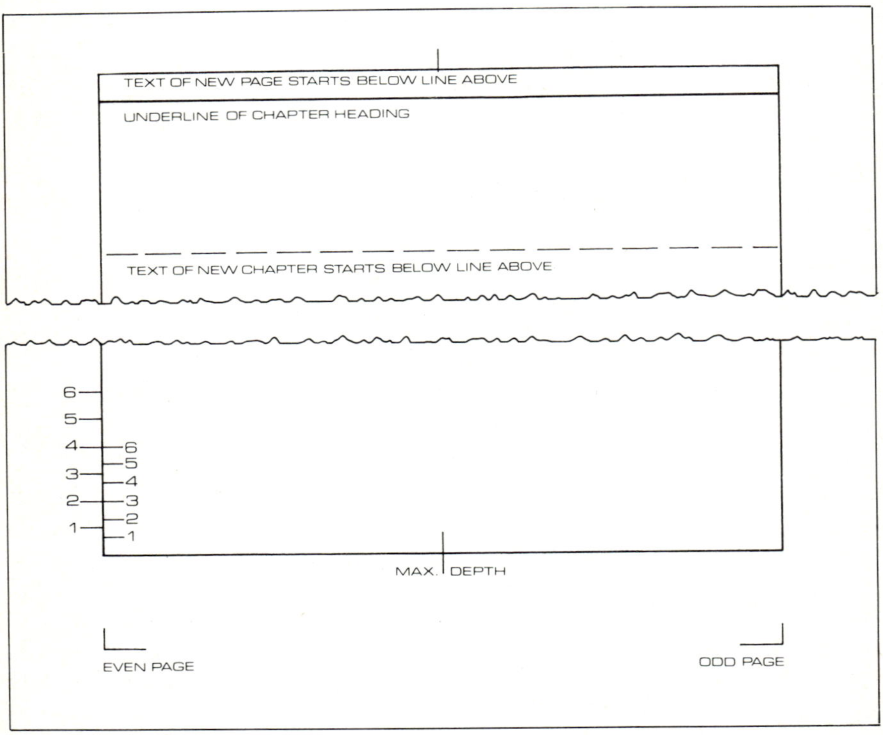

Fig. 57.1 - Typing format sheet

The typing format sheet defines the typing area for internal papers such as reports, minutes, memos, manuals etc. within a company or publishing house. It is printed on art paper, in light blue ink which is not reproduced if photocopied or printed.

up for typing headings. The disadvantage is that automatic printing must be stopped and the element exchanged manually. The letter size cannot differ too much from the basic one. Many word processors make bold typing possible using a normal daisy wheel: the text is printed a second time in a slightly shifted position (see fig. 32.5, 37.1, 38.1, 41.1 etc.). Another solution is to leave space free in the copy, and to insert text set on a *lettering device* (fig. 84.4). The titles can be set in various sizes, and a large number of letter types is available. The film is cut and pasted on the respective places. The typist must not forget to keep sufficient space free for the heading and for the free lines above and below it. Free space must also be reserved in the text for placing figures, photographs, tables and other graphical extras that are not typed by means of a typewriter or word processor.

Phototypesetting

Electronic and computer technology has also penetrated into the field of book printing. The revolutionary event was the transition from traditional typesetting to *phototypesetting.* It changed printing technology fundamentally. Instead of the physical composition from metal letters, resulting in heavy typeset forms, an electronic beam creates letters of any size and font at electronic speed, and the result is a photographic page - light, easy-to-handle and portable.

The output of the word processor stored in machine-readable form on a floppy disk can be used as input for a phototypesetting machine - usually some interim operations are necessary to create a bridge between the output of the word processor and the input of a phototypesetting machine. Indeed, linking the two techniques is not always simple. First of all, not every word processor is compatible with each type of phototypesetting machine. The incompatibility is caused by different information carriers, different codes and commands.

An author who intends to prepare his manuscript on a word processor and to use the output data as input for automatic typesetting should first consult his publisher or printing house, check the compatibility between his word processor and the available typesetting machines, and ask for information on the necessary conversion techniques. Often, the data from a floppy disk of a word processor have first to be converted to a magnetic tape by means of a special conversion program, and then this tape (sometimes after another conversion) can be used as input for the setting procedure. The compatibilities between 13 word processing systems and 25 types of phototypesetting machine are given in tabular form in ref. 50-Fritz. Nonetheless, consultation with a specialist is still needed.

The second problem is the *special commands* for controlling the typesetting procedure. First, general commands must be inserted controlling the selection of font, size, line length, justification, spacing, page format etc. Within the text, control commands must be inserted to initiate a change of font (begin italics, end of italics, bold and normal fonts, large font in headings etc.). Another problem is the *special characters* that are available in the phototypesetting machine (its character set is extremely rich, consists of several hundred special characters - letter-forms of national alphabets, Greek letters, mathematical signs and symbols, chemical, meteorological, astronomical symbols, symbols used in railway timetables, symbols of chess diagrams etc.) but which are, of course, missing from the keyboard of a word processor and from its printer. Again, a special combination of letters must be used in the word-processor text that will later be automatically converted into the special letter or symbol in the phototypesetting. A list of codes used and their translation into the machine code of the typesetting machine must be attached to the beginning of the text.

Many commands are rather complicated, and it would be boring for the operator of the word processor to have to type them time and again; they are replaced by short *macro-commands* - for example, in the

TYPESET INSTRUCTIONS
V. Stibic: Personal Documentation for Professionals

Basic text:	#3	Times 14/15 points, Roman, 426 points blocktext hyphenated, first line in paragraph indented except after a free line
Subtext:	#4	Times 11/12 points, Roman, 426 points blocktext hyphenated, no indenting
Chapter headings:	#1	Times 18 points bold, Roman, non-hyphenated, 2 free lines (30 points) following
Section headings:	#2	Times 14/15 points, Roman, non-hyphenated, one free line preceding, one following
Italics:	#K	beginning italics
	#R	end of italics (beginning Roman)
Index:	#9	Times 11/12, 17 aug., blocktext

Fig. 57.2 - Layout parameters for phototypesetting

The layout of a publication (character type and sizes, length of lines, indenting etc.) is specified first in the form of general rules. Short macrocommands are defined, which are used to signal beginning of chapter headings, beginning of the main text and subscripts, beginning of italics, end of italics etc.

specimen in fig. 56.2 the symbol #3 is a macro-command meaning 'begin of text font Times, Roman, 14 points, spacing 15 points, length of line 426 points etc.' as shown in fig. 57.2. Before the output from the word processor is used as input for phototypesetting, all the inserted macro-commands must first be compiled by means of a special compilation program; this translates all short macro-commands into the detailed commands in the machine language of the phototypesetter.

In fig. 56.2 we can see a small part of the text of the present book typed on the word processor Philips P-5002 with the codes inserted for the phototypesetting machine. Their meanings are self-evident when compared with the printed text. The list of macro-commands must be prepared by a specialist. He first discusses with the author his wishes concerning layout: format of the publication (number of lines per page, spacing betwen the lines, length of lines), fonts (Bodoni, Helvetia, Times...), size of letters, use of italics, semibold and bold letters etc. He then has to know which special characters are needed, and he prepares the coding. Then, the author or his secretary only needs to know the short macro-commands and codes. In large publishing houses or in companies where a number of publications are printed in this way, standard commands are established and the author will receive help and advice on how to prepare his manuscript to meet the in-house layout standard.

All in all, with the help and advice of a specialist, the preparation of a text for automatic typesetting is not as difficult as might be expected. After typing a few pages, the operator knows by heart the limited number of frequently occurring commands (such as 'begin paragraph', 'end of italics', 'indent' etc.); codes of rare occurrence (such as a Greek letter, an uncommon special character) can be found in an auxiliary table. In future, the virtual keyboard will make the typing of text for phototypesetting much more user-friendly.

The text, before being sent for phototypesetting, must be carefully proof-read; a single erroneous code could be disastrous; for example, a missing command 'end of italics' would cause a long part of the text, perhaps a whole page, to be printed out in italics. Similarly, a small omission in the definitions of macro-commands could spoil the output.

Automatic typesetting has essential advantages: it saves the costs of manual typesetting, it eliminates repetitive proof-reading, corrections and corrections of corrections, and it is fast - a complete book can be set in one day. On the other hand, for the author and/or his secretary it is an additional burden. In the past, the author sent his manuscript in typewritten form to a printing house, and a qualified, intelligent typesetter and corrector in the printing house took care of the consequent layout and of error-less typesetting. Now, the author and/or his secretary also work as typesetters. They must bear in mind that each typist's error and each erroneous or omitted code inevitably spoil the final product. The automatic setting machine works fast but it does not think and it never corrects errors as a human would probably do.

What we need are more intelligent programs for input preparation. First of all, automatic screening of codes would be helpful; the machine should be able to check the consistency of inserted commands and to warn automatically if, say, the command 'begin bold' is not followed at a reasonable distance by the command 'end bold'. Secondly, commandless conversions should be used wherever possible, e.g. all text that has been underlined in the word processor output could be, according to one initial command, converted automatically to italics without the arduous typing of special codes at the beginning and end of such a part of the text. Thirdly, the initial instructions could be filled in in a 'menu' form allowing the author to define his layout by answering a number of questions (number of lines per page? font? letter size? line space ? etc.). Also, developments in hardware may improve the path from text writing to automatic typesetting: the virtual keyboards already mentioned, as well as a screen and printer that permit any character to be reproduced, automatic right-hand justification on the screen etc. will be helpful. Also a colour screen could enable colours to be used to distinguish various fonts, sizes and sorts of print (e.g. normal text = green, italics = yellow, bold = red...).

58 - Shared word processing, terminal and mainframe

In the preceding sections we have presumed that the user is working with a stand-alone word processor. At the moment, this is the most common style of work. Another possibility is to use a *shared system.*

Shared word processing

Several users can share one or more printers, also the external memory and logic of a word processing system. In the former case, two or more word processors are connected to a common printer (or a larger number of processors to a battery of centralized printers). Printing is much faster than key-typing, so that several keyboard/display units can be served by one printer, and considerable costs can be saved. The user must then allow for a certain inconvenience in waiting for his output that is no longer produced on the spot and immediately after the print command has been given. A compromise solution is to centralize the expensive high-quality printers and to equip the decentralized units with cheap types, e.g. with dot-matrix printers. Centralized memory-units, e.g. hard disks with capacities of some million characters, make it possible to store large volumes of individually owned data sets. Every user has access only to his own files that he can create, update, correct, edit or print out in remote mode. If the system logic is also shared (which means that the software is stored in a central processor and shared by all users) then the decentralized units consist merely of a keyboard and display, and perhaps a cheap printer.

It is largely an economic decision as to whether to prefer a *stand-alone system* or a partly or fully *shared word processing system.* From the point of view of the user there are no essential differences except in the handling of his files (physical handling of his floppy disks compared with remote recall) and his printed output (on-the-spot printing in contrast to remote printing), provided the access-time is short, the internal post is not too slow, and the speed of the centralized system is not hampered due to overloading at peak times.

Terminal and mainframe

The user encounters more differences if he uses a *terminal* of a large remote computer, mainframe, in the computer centre. In principle, every mainframe computer can be employed on word processing jobs, if it is equipped with the appropriate software. In this case the user meets many differences from the use of a word processor. First, he no longer has the special keyboard of a word processor with its many functional keys (recall page, update page, print, store, insert...) and he must use key-typed commands in all situations. Secondly, the screen-capacity is usually smaller, and some of the excellent display features typical of a modern word processor (such as shadowing of the text being handled) are not always available. Thirdly, the quality of printed output depends on the printer available - it can be rather poor if a standard impact line-printer is used.

On the other hand, the use of a fast computer with its huge external memory capacity offers many interesting opportunities that are prohibitive in small-scale word processing systems. First of all - because of the high operating speed and large memory - the word processing software can be much more sophisticated. Not only may all advanced functions of a high-level word processing system be available, but also sophisticated linguistic help can be given based on intricate algorithms and large stored vocabularies: for example, intelligent hyphenization of words based both on algorithms and on a stored vocabulary of exceptions, intelligent spelling check based on voluminous vocabulary.

By way of example, the TEXED system of the software house Wootton, Jeffreys & Co [ref. 50-TEXED] may be mentioned: It was developed as a system capable of servicing up to 64 terminals simultaneously by means of a mainframe with an internal memory of one half a megabyte and an external memory of 32 million characters. It can solve simple word-processing jobs (letters, short memos) as well as handling large documents of practically unlimited size. It is user-friendly, menu-driven, comprises all the sophisticated word-processing functions including phrase-inserting, automatic hyphenization, formatting of text both by stored default values as well as by individual commands, intelligent search function including search for paragraphs and section titles or for first lines of paragraphs or top lines of pages, automatic numbering of chapters and sections in six levels by numerical or alphabetic codes, display of output in justified form, tabulation to any of 20 pre-selected positions, and many other features that are only rarely available in traditional word processing systems.

Utilities and data processing

Word processing via a terminal and mainframe differs essentially from the use of a single-purpose, stand-alone word processor, because the user has direct access to a large library of programs on the mainframe. He can integrate his word-processing jobs in many ways with other types of work. A simple case is using the sorting program of a mainframe (though sorting programs are now available also in some advanced word processors): data created by the word processing technique (addresses, directories, lists, vocabularies, documentation records) can be sorted alphabetically or numerically, or two or more sets of data can be merged via existing mainframe software. Similarly, the output of word processing can be directly submitted to processing by means of indexing programs: traditional alphabetical indexes, indexes of the KWIC or KWOC type or special permutated indexes can be produced from data created by a word-processing program. Also, automatic compilation of concordances, mentioned several times above, is possible by means of a mainframe and its large memory capacity. Another way open to the user is information storage and retrieval: First, the word-processing technique can be used for preparing the input data for retrieval systems. Secondly, a retrieval system may be used for interrogation of various files during the creation of a text. Finally, word processing and data processing can be merged and integrated in many interesting ways.

Word processing then is no longer an isolated job, but is converging with the many existing programs and routines of data processing, and with the processing of graphical data. The integration of these wide fields of computer applications is bringing about an enormous synergic effect in terms of both economy and quality.

6 - PERSONAL COMPUTING

It is not easy to define the subject of *personal computing*. In this chapter we consider computations that are on the fringe of the professional's activities and have largely an auxiliary nature, including computations in the private sphere such as those relating to personal finance, housekeeping or hobbies. Until a few years ago, the slide rule, logarithmic tables and mechanical calculating machines were the only technical means used by a professional. Now the pocket calculator, the personal computer or the terminal are available to anybody and the possibility of using powerful means even for auxiliary computations has increased immensely.

61 - Pocket calculators

No other technical means has come so rapidly into common use as the *pocket calculator*. It appeared on the market in the last decade and during a few years proliferated so rapidly that it is now used by everybody from a school boy or housewife to a scientist. The *slide rule*, the traditional tool used by generations of technicians, disappeared without a trace within the short time of a few years, as no other tool has done in history.

The rapid and wide acceptance of the pocket calculator contrasts sharply with the hesitant acceptance of other devices - for instance microfilm (after more than a hundred years of existence) or dictating machines (after a half century of practical use). The reasons are obvious: a low price affordable by everybody and the small dimensions are important, as also are the high performance (fig. 61.2), precision (8, 10 or more digits) and enormous versatility. The decisive factor however is the ease of use: the users need to learn nothing, no special skill is required. A pocket calculator could never have found such mass usage if the designers had not adopted the algebraic entry: the user enters data and operates the functional keys in the same sequence as they are stated algebraically, e.g. $9.15 \times 2.11 = 19.3065$ is entered in the traditional sequence (input 9.15, press multiplication key, input 2.11, press key =). Had the designers chosen mathematical or even Polish notation, the pocket calculator would never have attained mass popularity.

Indeed, the pocket calculator needs no recommendation, but a few remarks on its use and misuse ought to be mentioned.

Types of pocket calculators

There are many types of pocket calculators on the market from the cheap and simple, capable of performing merely the four basic arithmetical operations, to sophisticated machines with more than one internal memory and with a large number of mathematical, goniometrical, statistical and other functions; the prices range from about $ 5 to about $ 300. Besides general-purpose calculators *special machines* are also available that make it possible to perform both general and specialized calculations such as are needed in the field of finance, statistics, technics etc. The number of types and of manufacturers in the lower price class is boundless, the number of manufacturers of sophisticated and specialized machines is more limited.

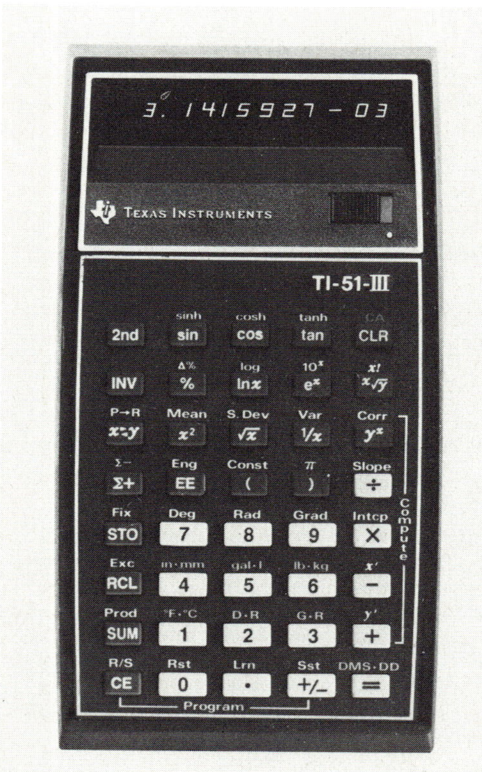

Courtesy Texas Instruments Holland, Amstelveen

Fig 61.1 - A general-purpose pocket calculator with a number of special statistical functions

SKEWNESS FORMULA

$$C = \frac{Z}{d_a} \left(1 - \left(1 - t_a / T \right)^{T / Z} \right)$$

where

C = coefficient of skewness of the word a
T = total number of words ('tokens') in the file
Z = total number of documents (abstracts) in the file
t_a = occurrence of the word a in the file
d_a = number of documents (abstracts) containing the word a

examples
T = 2 496 246 Z = 26 203

word	occurrence t_a	documents d_a	skewness C
EMPHASIS-	279	272	1.020
FILM	578	286	1.999

COMPUTATION OF THE FORMULA	time in seconds	performance factor
manual + logarithmical tables	600	1
pocket calculator	60	10
ditto, repetitive calculation, values T, Z and T/Z stored as constants	30	20
programmable calculator	15	40
ditto, T and Z constant	8	80

Fig 61.2 - Comparison of the calculation of a formula by means of a pocket calculator

A simple calculation of word skewness: a mathematical linguist uses the skewness coefficient to measure the specific and common use of words. Commonly used words (such as EMPHAZISE) are randomly distributed in the file, specific words (such as FILM) are concentrated in a lower number of documents than could be statistically expected. Computation by means of a slide rule is impossible (its precision is insufficient), computation by means of logarithmical tables is arduous.

The user should carefully analyse his own need for computations (simple as well as special calculations, need for several memories, types of special functions needed) and compare them with the types of calculators available on the market. However, a word of warning must be given here: when analysing your need for computation, do not think only of the computations you have been in the habit of performing until now. Think also of functions and calculations that you never used in the past because they were too arduous to do by means of the traditional tools.

By way of example: many a professional works with statistical data and curves; he has also some knowledge of methods of linear interpolation and extrapolation of curves. The computation is not intricate, albeit very arduous, if done by means of paper, pencil and a mechanical calculating machine: interpolation of only 12 monthly data requires 22 additions, 2 subtractions, 13 multiplications and 3 divisions. The result is that many professionals (with the exception of statisticians) never use these methods in practice, and have totally forgotten that they exist. A pocket calculator with statistical functions (fig. 62.1) makes it possible to calculate linear interpolation quite simply: enter 12 items and press two functional keys ! A stimulus therefore to use a method that was learnt at school but is negleted in everyday practice by so many.

Misuse of pocket calculators

There are no objective data available on the extent and style in which pocket calculators are used. Thus, it is merely a suspicion based on incidental observations, stimulated by the knowledge of the general users' aversion to the sophisticated use of technical means, that only a minority of users takes full advantage of their pocket calculators. It appears, that many owners of calculators limit themselves to the basic functions, and even ignore the memory function that enables them to multiply or divide by a constant factor. A calculator then becomes degraded to nothing more than a substitute for an old mechanical calculating machine capable only of plain addition, subtraction, multiplication and division. The reason is twofold: firstly, the user is unaccustomed, as mentioned above, to using special operations and functions, secondly, he dislikes learning and acquiring the skill to perform non-common operations that require him to master certain new rules for input and use of functional keys in the proper sequence.

The future of the pocket calculator

One would expect the market to be saturated the moment every potential user owns his calculator. This stage has practically been reached. However, the market is still growing, as the growth of the market for radio receivers continued even after the moment when practically every household was equipped with a set.

In the same way as the radio receivers diversified into many specialized categories, and many persons own more than one set, calculators are also diversifying, and many a professional now owns more than one machine - for instance a 'heavy-duty' calculator at his workplace (a machine with special functions, perhaps a programmable type, or a desk-top calculator with large keyboard and large display), a similar type at home, a pocket-size calculator with simple functions (often in the popular form of a mini-card, or in wristwatch form) and/or a calculator with time, calendar, stopwatch and alarm-clock functions.

The low price, portability and versatility of pocket calculators guarantee that this marvellous device will not disappear even when personal computers and terminals are available to everybody. Further developments in microelectronics in the next few years will bring about new types of pocket calculators with ever larger memory capacities and stored programs permitting ever more complicated calculations. The user's task is to buy the proper type and to use it intelligently, not only to do the old tasks faster, but also to perform tasks that he did not do hitherto, as they were too arduous or impossible using the old technique.

Courtesy Texas Instruments Holland, Amstelveen

Fig. 62.1 - A programmable calculator with external memories

Texas Instruments TI-59 programmable calculator is capable of performing 177 computational and logical functions, its memory can be used for storing 100 items in addressable registers and 160 program steps, or 960 program steps. The user can store his program or data on small magnetic cards and create his own program library or data base. Standard programs are also available in the form of 'Solid State Software' plug-in modules. The 'master library module' contains 25 mathematics, statistics, and finance programs. Special modules containing programs for marine navigation, geodesy, aeronautics and applied statistics are also available, others can be expected in the future.

62 - Programmable calculators

In the mid-seventies a typical pocket calculator had only one memory, but at the beginning of the eighties calculators with internal storage capacities of ten or even a hundred memories were available at reasonable prices. This made it possible to design calculators with a large number of memories addressable by the user and, furthermore, *programmable calculators.*

The user of a programmable calculator either can buy standard and application programs, or can write his own programs. A program supplied by the manufacturer is stored in some type of external memory: this can be a magnetic card of miniature dimensions or a plug-in unit (see fig. 62.1) containing the programs on a chip. The programs are either general-purpose, or designed for specific groups of users - such as sets of programs solving specific problems of geodesy, electrotechnics, mechanical engineering, the building industry, statistics, finance, navigation and many other special fields.

A professional, who has repetitively to solve non-trivial computations that are too arduous to be done step by step using a standard pocket calculator, but still within the range of capacity of a programmable calculator, should always check if his problem could be solved by means of available program packages. A visit to a specialized shop, careful study of the manuals of various types of machines, or advice from colleagues and peers can help him make the right choice.

Those who do not find a program to solve their problem have to write their own program. The programming of a pocket calculator is not difficult, though it does have certain inconveniences. The *programming language* is rather simple and rudimentary. Commands usually consist of a symbolic operation code (e.g. ADD = add, MOV = move, SUB = subtract, DIS = display etc.) and an numerical address of an operand or (in the case of jumps) number of a program line.

Controlled by a program, a calculator is then able to process a string of operations in sequence or in loops. It can help solve many computational problems in various fields of professional activity.

Despite its marvellous functions and flexibility, the pocket calculator has rather narrow limits of use. Firstly, its restricted memory capacity is a threshold that excludes a number of tasks. Another obstacle is the inconvenience of programming in a primitive symbolic language together with the small display usually limited to 12-14 digits; the user can never see more than one line of his program. Another weakness, the lack of printed output, also makes checking programs more difficult, but this disadvantage can be overcome by attaching a small (usually thermic) printer; this means, of course, a considerable increase in price.

To conclude, a programmable calculator can offer excellent help to a rather limited class of users whose needs are for repetitive *and* complicated calculations with a limited volume of input data and programs *not* exceeding the capacity of the calculator, *when* they do not have a personal computer or terminal available (that would allow such problems to be solved more comfortably) *or* who need to perform such operations in the field (geodetical calculation, navigation calculations).

However, progress is fast. New types of programmable calculators are appearing with new functions and improved features. Fig. 62.2 shows a calculator with alphanumerical keyboard, a memory of 1900 characters and a 24-character alphanumerical LCD display, that can be programmed in the BASIC programming language, and fig. 62.3 a calculator (not

Courtesy ORMAS B.V., Bilthoven, The Netherlands

Fig. 62.2 - A programmable calculator with 24-character LCD display and BASIC programming

A TRS-80 pocket calculator can be used for simple calculations, but also programmed in the BASIC programming language. Prompting in English, program commands, data and results are displayed in a one-line, 24-character LCD display. The calculator has an internal memory of 1900 bytes. Programs and data can be stored in and loaded from a magnetic tape cassette that can be attached as an auxiliary unit. Program tapes on different topics including real estate, civil engineering, personal finances, aviation etc. are available. The calculator weighs about 170 g and is about 180 mm long.

Courtesy Hewlett-Packard Nederland B.V., Amstelveen

Fig. 62.3 - A programmable calculator with an integrated printer

The Hewlett-Packard 97 programmable calculator is distinguished by having separate functional and numerical keyboards, a display of 15 digits and an integrated thermic printer. It has 26 addressable registers, a capacity of up to 224 program lines and input/output on magnetic cards. The borderline between the programmable calculator and a personal computer becomes rather vague.

more a pocket-sized) with a 16-digit display, separate functional and numerical keyboards and an integrated printer. The difference between a programmable calculator and a personal computer has become rather blurred.

63 - Personal computers

In the last thirty years, computer performance and the capacity of memories have increased immensely, computer dimensions have diminished rapidly, and the price per performance unit has fallen accordingly.

It is extremely instructive to study the comparison (fig. 63.1) of a computer of 1956 (the IBM-650, the most successful machine at the time), with a programmable pocket calculator of 1980 (Texas Instruments 59, see fig. 62.1) - as published by Isaacson and Juliussen in Computer [ref. 60]. The hand-held calculator of today is more than ten times as fast at addition and five times as fast at multiplication; its internal memory is 2.5 times as large, it weighs 8,400 times less, it is 15,000 times smaller, and it consumes 10,000 times less energy. The 1956 computer was installed in a large, air-conditioned room, and its price was $ 200,000 (1956-dollars); the calculator can be held in the hand, and it costs $ 300 (1980-dollars).

The applications of computers have shifted in keeping with these dramatic changes of parameters. The initial applications of computers were for large scientifical and technical computations and, later, data processing jobs in large companies, banks and governmental bodies, but they have moved into medium-size and finally small enterprises: the *office computer* within the price range of small companies made its appearance and proliferated during the late seventies.

In the mid-seventies, a new category of computer appeared: the *hobby computer*. Originally in a minimum configuration, often delivered as a kit and assembled by the hobbyist himself, it consisted of an operational unit with a modest internal storage (4K was typical), a keyboard, and a screen display that was often replaced by a standard home television set. It was bought exclusively by individuals with a background knowledge of electronics and computers who employed it as a new form of hobby and entertainment. The hobby computer is able, of course, to perform many technical and scientific computations, and some very limited tasks in the field of personal data processing (such as storage and updating of short lists and directories, simple personal accounting), but the main goal was

	1955 (IBM-650)	1980 (TI-59)	factor
components	2000 tubes	166500 t.e. *	84 : 1
power	17.7 kVA	0.0018 kVA	9830 : 1
volume	7700 dm^3	0.5 dm^3	15400 : 1
weight	2550 kg	0.3 kg	8500 : 1
air-conditioning	5-10 tons	none	
intenal memory	3000 bits	7680 bits	1 : 2.5
external memory	100K bits	40K bits	2.5 : 1
execution time			
addition	0.75 msec	0.07 msec	1 : 11
multiplication	20.0 msec	4.0 msec	1 : 5
price	$200000 (1955-$)	$300 (1980-$)	

* transistor equivalents

Fig. 63.1 - Comparison of computer parameters 1955/1980

entertainment and education. From the beginning of their existence, a new type of leisure-activity also appeared and gained enormous popularity: the computer game.

Growing internal storage, the attachment of a number of peripheral units - in particular a magnetic tape unit (using a standard tape cassette), a printer and disk units - as well as the increasing availability of software, enabled this computer to be used for the practical small-scale jobs of an individual. The *personal computer* was born.

It is difficult to give a precise definition of a personal computer. In principle, a personal computer is generally considered to be a stand-alone general-purpose microcomputer that is purchased and/or operated by an individual, or a small group (small team, family), and is affordable by an individual.

The smallest configuration consists simply of a central processing unit and an internal memory of 4K (4096 bytes), an alphanumerical keyboard, a screen display, and a magnetic tape unit. Such a configuration can be used for learning and teaching programming, for technical and scientific computations, for some small personal data-processing tasks, and for games. Though it might be used as an excellent means of mastering the problems of programming and as a practical aid in some limited areas, it cannot be used for the majority of jobs that are typical of the personal applications of a professional. This configuration must then be extended with regard both to internal storage and to periphery.

Some practical advice to the prospective buyer of a personal computer should be added: before deciding to buy a personal computer, carefully analyse your present and probable future requirements. Many prospective users have some certain application(s) in their minds but forget that, after a short time, they will discover a number of further tasks worth mechanizing, sometimes tasks they have not thought of at the moment of purchase. The history of computers installed in computing centres now repeats itself in the field of personal computers: generally, the capacity of every computer installed has in a short time been found to be insufficient because new jobs have proved to be ripe for mechanization, and the jobs originally planned have been expanded. The user should also not forget that the effectiveness of his applications will grow if other applications are added: the synergic effect so often mentioned stimulates expansion of the applications of a personal computer. Consult, therefore, tables 67.1 and 67.2 characterizing typical fields of personal computing, consider their usefulness in your situation, add your own specific requirements, try to define priorities of jobs and carefully plan your initial hardware as well as its future extensions. Conclusion: do not take too narrow a view of the functions of your personal computer, do not be afraid to buy a machine of a somewhat larger class, or choose a system that can be expanded in the future as regards internal memory and periphery.

Operation unit and internal memory

The central *operation unit* (in practice, a microprocessor) and the *internal memory* of the computer are both integrated circuits. In some

Courtesy COMPU 2000 B.V., Amsterdam

Fig. 63.2 - Personal computer APPLE II

types they are physically housed as one unit with the keyboard. In most personal computers the internal memory is modular, and can be extended by steps of, for example, 4K bytes, or is supplied in capacities of 4/8/16/32K or more bytes. The largest main memories of personal computers do not at present exceed 64K bytes, but predictions of main memories of one megabyte in the mid-eighties do not seem unrealistic. The capacity of the internal memory limits the volume of programs that can be processed and the volume of data that can be stored internally.

A prospective user should, if he is aware of the tasks he would like to solve, carefully check the requirements of his own programs or of programs that form part of the chosen software; for instance, if he considers using a word-processing program, he must be sure that sufficient internal memory capacity is available, and the capacity of external storage is sufficient for his typical documents.

Many computers also have a *ROM - read-only-memory* attached in which special programs, subroutines or operating systems are stored. Expanding this part of the internal memory will make it possible in the future to keep the compilers of higher-level programming languages (say, COBOL, PASCAL etc.) and the interpreters in the internal memory - then, it will no longer be necessary to store them in external memories (disks) and to load them into the main memory for execution time and again. In the future, the complete user's manual in conversational form and with many 'help' functions (warnings, messages, comments, explanations) could also be stored in a ROM memory.

Screen display and acoustic output

The *screen display* (sometimes replaced by a standard home television set, even a colour one), is a standard part of any personal computer. For the practical user several properties are important. Firstly, the capacity - a minimum would be about 24 lines of 40 characters each, but about 40 lines of 80 characters are usual in the computers of a rather higher class; such a capacity is convenient for word processing; a full A4-page capacity (at present found rarely even in advanced word processors) would be the best for word processing. Numbers, special characters and letters (for the user it is crucial whether only lower or upper case, or both) can be displayed. The resolution of the screen is important for everybody who intends to use his personal computer for graphical work (display of schemes, graphs, charts); a resolution of about 1000 × 1000 dots is required for graphical pictures of good quality.

Another important factor is the use of *colour.* This is crucial in graphical output, but it can be useful also for data and word processing. Colours can improve the legibility of large tables of numerical data (change of colour per group of lines or columns), colour can distinguish certain parts of a text (headings, comments) and overcome the inability to display various letter sizes and fonts (e.g. we can use coloured words and phrases within a displayed text in the way we use italics or bold letters in a printed text).

Acoustic output is affordable now; for example, for a price of only $ 20 it is possible to extend the PET Commodore personal computer by an output unit that acoustically announces the depression of each mumerical or functional key. A more advanced speech generator is also available. In the future we can expect optional acoustic messages and warnings to be a common feature of the personal computer.

Magnetic tape unit

A *magnetic tape unit* with a standard tape cassette is the cheapest unit for external storage; it is a common accessory also of the quite modest configurations of personal computers. Its primary function is to keep stored programs and to transfer them to the internal memory of the computer before they are to be executed. It can also store input data, but

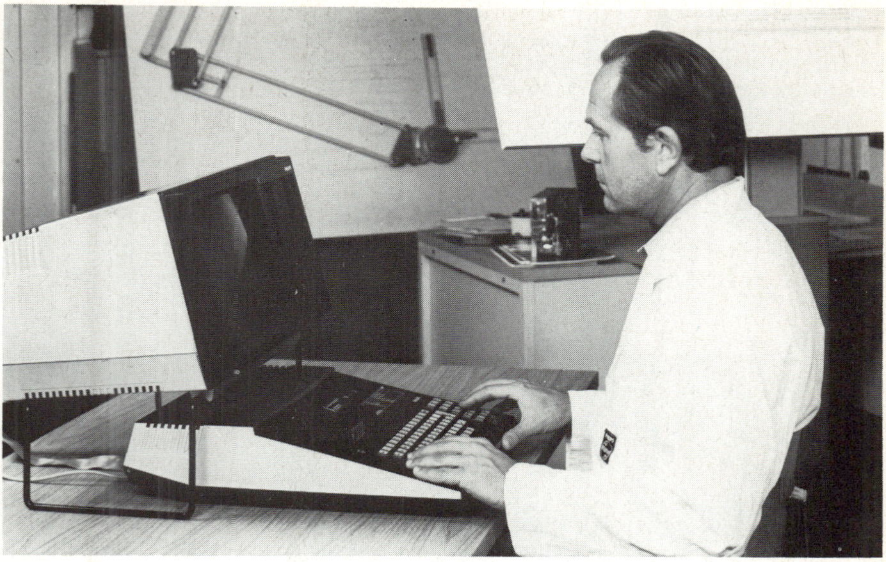

Courtesy Philips Data Systems, Apeldoorn, The Netherlands

Fig. 63.3 - Personal computer becomes an indispensable tool of the technician and scientist

it is unsuitable for random access to them. For fast access to data, disk units are necessary.

Disk units

While the cheap and simple magnetic tape units serve merely as an auxiliary external storage suitable for one-time loading of programs or data sets, disk units make it possible to store relatively large volumes of data and to access them randomly. Most personal computers make use of *floppy disks* (diameter 5¼ or 8 inches), which were mentioned in section 54 on word processors. Capacities between 70K and 1M characters (depending on the disk dimension, on one- or double-sided recording and on single or double density of record) are common. Some producers supply also *hard disks* (for a substantially higher price) with capacities from 1 to 10 million characters.

For some personal applications - such as word processing or personal documentation - the capacity of floppy disks is the bottleneck. The user should carefully calculate his need for external storage considering the types and volumes of his files, also taking into account the fact that some files must be used simultaneously (compare fig. 67.2). For the majority of users two disk units are the minimum - they make it possible to copy the files, to make back-up copies of disks, to update files (keeping the preceding generation as a back-up copy), or to permit easy interaction between two or more files.

Printer

The cheapest printer type available at present is a *thermic printer.* It can be found as a peripheral unit of many machines used mainly as hobby computers or for technical and scientific computations in which the

Courtesy Hewlett-Packard Nederland B.V., Amstelveen

Fig. 63.4 - Larger configuration of a microcomputer

The Hewlett-Packard HP-125 microcomputer is an example of a configuration at the upper end of the range of microcomputers; it is intended to be used primarily for small-business applications. Nonetheless, the development of computer parameters, their peripherals and falling price will soon make computers in a similar configuration available for personal purposes.

volume and quality of print are not crucial. Typically, it prints short lines of about 20 characters on a strip of special paper. Another cheap type is a *dot matrix impact printer.* In both cases, the quality of print is poor; the printing speed is reasonable.

Higher quality ('correspondence quality') is achieved by an attached electric typewriter (however, this is an exceptional solution), or by a *daisy-wheel printer* similar to the printer of many word processors.

Plotter

Also a typewriter and line printer can serve as plotters producing rather crude graphs - their resolution depends on minimum line space and pitch. Rather more detailed graphs can be plotted by a dot matrix printer. Precise graphs and figures can be drawn by special *plotters,* attached as peripheral units. They plot by means of a pen movable in a coordinate system; precision is about 0.1 mm (see section 77).

Trends of development

The personal computer is only a few years old and is still in the early phase of its development. Significant improvements in hardware can be expected in the next few years: the continuous developments of very large scale integration (VLSI) will allow an operating unit and internal memory of a large computer of today to be stored in one or a few chips in the future. Also, the capacity of external memories, floppy disks and hard disks, will grow and perhaps the technology of bubble memories (no moving parts, therefore reliable, but too expensive at present) will be economically feasible. A new high capacity external storage appeared recently and might also be usable in some personal computer configurations of the future: the *optical disk.*

The optical disk that uses digital information storage by means of diode laser recording opens up new prospects: the capacity of one disk is 10^{10} bits of information which is equivalent to about 500,000 pages of text. One disk can store a large encyclopedia, a number of handbooks or a whole special library in certain fields of science and technology. As an amendable but nonvolatile memory, it will be used mainly for storage of vast volumes of static information accessible also by means of a personal computer.

Likewise, *display units* will also develop, will enlarge their capacities, improve their resolution, and colour output will become standard. New types of displays (plasma display) are beginning to be used in practice. High-quality *printers* will fall in price and will also be affordable in cheaper configurations. Dot-matrix printers with improved quality of print will permit the printing of a practically unlimited character set - as each character is designed as a matrix of points, any special character, symbol or the letters of non-Latin alphabets (e.g. Greek, Arabic, Japanese) could be printed out.

Personal computers will increasingly be used as *terminals* of in-house mainframes able to interrogate in-house databases and to participate in the company's data processing, etc., or of external computers, also making use of external information systems including public viewdata systems. Personal computers will also be used as a means of communication, i.e. as stations for internal or external electronic mail and instruments of electronic conferencing. The trend of development is towards a *universal work station.*

64 - Programming personal computers

The first hobby computers were programmable only in their *machine language* - the commands consisting of a numerical operational code (say, 01 = add, 02 = subtract, 16 = print, 07 = move...), and an absolute address of the respective operand. The programming was arduous; the program was difficult to read, and usable only by the computer in the machine code of which it had been written. Programming was restricted to a small class of enthusiast hobbyists from the field of computer science. A slight improvement towards making programming a little easier came with symbolic programming languages in which instead of numerical codes and addresses of operands mnemonic codes were used.

Personal computers can be programmed by a *higher-level programming language.* Its main characteristics are: the operation codes are mnemonic and expressed in words or abbreviations of words from the natural language (such as ADD, DIVIDE, MOVE, PRINT, IF... ,THEN... ELSE), the operands may be called by names or abbreviations given by the user (RATE, SUM, WAGE, DOCUMENT-NUMBER, DATE-OF-ISSUE etc.), and one command may represent a large group of simple commands in machine language. For example, a formula can be written as one command, and a group of logical and arithmetical operations can be defined by one command (say, IF TYPE = 'BOOK' THEN PRINT PUBLISHER OTHERWISE PRINT JOURNAL). A specimen of a short and simple program in the BASIC programming language is shown in fig. 64.2.

The computer cannot execute a program written in a higher-level language directly. It must first translate each command into its machine language, and then the program in machine language can be executed. The translation may be done in a separate run in which the program written by the user in the higher-level language is used as input, and it is translated ('compiled') by means of a translating program, called *compiler*, into the machine language of the respective computer. A compiler is produced and supplied by the computer manufacturer; a special compiler is necessary for each higher-level language/ computer pair (for example, compiler COBOL/TANDY-II computer). The output of the compilation run is the program in the machine code language of the computer.

Instead of a special compiling run, the program written in a higher-level language can be used directly, but each command is translated (interpreted) just before it is executed. In this case, a special program called *interpreter* is employed.

The point is that a new program can be written and immediately executed without a special compiling run and without loading the compiled program in machine language. On the other hand, a substantial disadvantage of an interpreting program is that it is slow - each command has first to be interpreted ('translated') and then executed. This is not a nuisance if we execute short ad hoc calculations: a few seconds or so are negligible. On the other hand, if the program

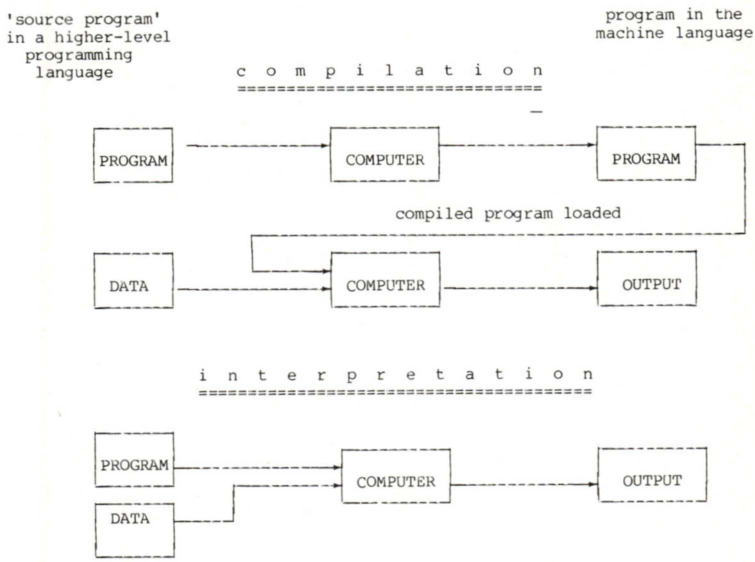

Fig. 64.1 - Compiling and interpreting

A compiler is usually designed and supplied by the computer manufacturer. It translates a program ('source program') written in a higher-level language (e.g. BASIC, COBOL, FORTRAN, PASCAL etc.) into the machine language of the respective computer (e.g. Philips 2000, Apple II etc.). The source program is used as input, the compiled program is produced as output. This program is loaded into the internal memory before execution. An interpreter translates every command of a source program into the machine language immediately, enabling the command to be executed before translating the next command.

is long and run repetitively, then compiling is the only way to effective processing, as it is done only once, and for any later execution the compiled program is simply loaded.

There is a large number of *higher-level programming languages*, some of them universal, others more or less application-oriented. The oldest widely used programming languages for scientific and technical computations are ALGOL and FORTRAN - the compilers for these languages are also available for some personal computers. A widely used language in the field of data processing is COBOL, which has also become available in the last few years in some personal computers of a rather higher class. Similarly, compilers for PASCAL or other languages are available for some personal computers. However, by far the most popular programming language, available for nearly all personal computers, is BASIC. It is simple, and therefore easy to learn. One can learn enough within a few days to be able to write simple programs to solve problems in the field of scientific and technical computations; full mastery of all the possibilities of programming in BASIC and gaining the necessary practice and skill require a rather longer time. However, the threshold for a beginner is low.

Programs written in higher-level languages have an essential advantage that they are machine-independent: they can be executed on any personal computer provided it is equipped with a compiler of the respective language, and the memory capacity and the available peripheral units of the computer satisfy the requirements of the respective program. Unfortunately, there are limits in practice: some languages, in particular BASIC, exist in many incompatible variants ('dialects'). The user must check very carefully the variant available in his (intended) personal computer.

Programming is no problem for users of personal computers who come from the computer science field - until recently they were the majority of the owners. Programming a personal computer is also no problem for youngsters who acquire a sound knowledge of computers and programming at school; fortunately, nowadays, university and also many high-school students are taught to use computers. There are problems however for other potential users of personal computers. If they need to solve specific problems in their field for which no usable software exists, they have to learn programming so as to be able to manage at least (in the beginning) simple computational tasks of their profession. There are plenty of good textbooks and courses to help them.

In a few years many of the present problems will have disappeared. More and more persons will learn programming at school, a less experienced user will be greatly helped by the system when writing his own program, e.g. in the form of 'menu-programming', the number of available programs will grow and many will be manageable even by 'computer-illiterate' users.

The proliferation of terminals and the ever-increasing number of naïve users will stimulate the creation of *user-friendly* online conversational systems. Instead of requiring specific commands that must be learnt and well understood, such a system helps the user by prompting him into actions, by presenting him, at any step, with a 'menu' of possible actions, helping him to decide, giving more detailed comments and recommendations on demand or spontaneously if the user apparently needs help.

PROGRAM

```
  1  Rem  *****   MORTGAGE   *****
 10  Rem  MORTGAGE COMPUTATION
 20  Rem  INPUT:  SUM, % INTEREST, ANNUITY
 30  Rem  OUTPUT: YEAR, REST OF MORTGAGE
 40  Y=0
 50  Input"SUM ",S
 60  Input"INTEREST RATE % ",R
 70  Input"ANNUITY ",A
 80  I=S*R/100
 90  If A>I Then Goto 120
100  Print"INSUFFICIENT ANNUITY"
110  Goto 190
120  Y=Y+1
130  I=S*R/100
140  S=S+I-A
150  If S>0 Then Goto 170
160  S=0
170  Print Using "-------#",Y,S
180  If S>0 Then Goto 120
190  End
```

COMMENTS

```
-name of the program;
-Rem = remarks;

-set year equal zero;
-print out the text in
  between the "" marks and
  accept input from keyboard;
-check if annuity is greater
  than interest;
-if not so, print out warning
  and go to the end;
-count years;
-compute the interest;
-compute the rest;
-check if paid off;
-avoid negative rest;
-print out year and rest;
-paid off ?
-if so, end.
```

COMPUTATION

```
   Run "MORTGAGE"

SUM 80000
INTEREST RATE 10
ANNUITY 13500
1                 74500
2                 68450
3                 61795
4                 54475
5                 46422
6                 37564
7                 27821
8                 17103
9                 5313
10                0
***190 End***
```

COMMENTS

```
-command to start computing;

-keytyped 80000;
-keytyped 10 (%);
-keytyped 13500;
-computer output;

-end message.
```

Fig. 64.2 - Specimen of a program in BASIC

65 - Personal software

Most owners of a personal computer do not intend to use their machine for only one purpose. Even if they start with limited jobs (say, technical computations), they soon discover the wide possibilities of their machine, they will make use of more and more programs and build up their own personal program library step by step.

There are three main sources of *personal software:*
- programs supplied by the computer manufacturer,
- programs written by the user himself,
- programs bought on the software market from various sources.

The first group always includes the compilers and interpreters for one or more higher-level programming languages mentioned above, operating system(s) controlling all the computer functions, sorting and merging programs etc. Besides these commonly needed programs, the manufacturer offers a varied assortment of *application programs* for solving various practical tasks, e.g. for special technical computations, statistical analyses, business data processing of small enterprises (invoicing, bookkeeping) etc.

It is essential for the prospective user of a personal computer to know what software and of which quality he can expect from the manufacturer or from other sources. A less expensive computer with poor software is not the best choice, unless we intend to build our own library of individual programs. Comparative tables and lists of software are published from time to time in specialist journals. Computer manufacturers or dealers publish lists of their software with some functional description (unfortunately, not always detailed and exact enough), and they are able to demonstrate the programs in their demonstration rooms - this is one of the best ways to check the facilities offered provided the buyer knows precisely what he wants and comes to such a demonstration with concrete requirements and questions. Advice from colleagues or members of a computer club owning the computer type in question is a valuable source of objective information.

A professional's *own programs*, unless they are of ephemeral value, are named, dated and stored. They should be provided with clear comments and remarks - many an author of a program forgets after a time his own intentions and algorithms, and it costs him considerable effort to study, analyse and understand his own program. If one's program library is fairly large, then a good index should be created and maintained.

A beginner will design his program in an inflexible form; he will adapt it precisely to his ad hoc needs. If certain conditions change in the future, he must change or re-write it. After gaining some experience, he should always consider the possible future applications of his program and try to write it in a *modular* and *flexible* form. Then, a new combination of modules, or changing a few parameters will enable a program to be used for various tasks. Another aspect that should never be forgotten is *compatibility* of programs. It is a fault if our program for maintaining a personal address directory is incompatible with the sort program, or with the program for the creation of alphabetical indexes. A general plan for personal software and a standard data structure are therefore recommended.

In view of the vigorously growing number of hobby and personal computers, the number of programs available on the market is increasing rapidly, and the number of sources (manufacturers, software companies, organizations, hobby clubs, individuals) is enormous and growing all the time. Indeed, a *mass software market* is opening up.

The present state and prospects of this mass market for a new type of merchandise - programs for personal computers - are described by Isaacson and Juliussen [ref. 60] and compared with the present gramophone-record or book market. Programs representing one or more man-years work are being sold, typically, for prices between $ 20 and $ 200, large data-processing packages (e.g. for invoicing) or word-processing programs may cost a few hundred dollars. If someone succeeds in writing a 'best-seller' that sells in many thousands of copies, he can become rich - the above authors give an example of a program requiring one man-year's effort plus some advertising costs which, if sold in 50,000 copies for, say, $ 50, would return 2.5 million dollars. Indeed, one successful program, VisiCalc, has been sold in 100,000 copies for $ 200 apiece; it has returned 20 million dollars to its authors [ref. 60-Uttal]. Nobody knows how many thousands of programs for personal and hobby computers there are now available. Programs exist for nearly every activity from personal bookkeeping or mortgage calculation, to statistical and mathematical programs, and even to programs for such specific and sometimes curious calculations as weight control and diet kitchen, for car-pooling, for compiling genealogical trees, for learning touch typing, for timing functions in a darkroom, and many others.

The main problem facing a user who would like to avoid writing his own program is to find out whether and where a program solving his particular problem is available. At the moment, this is quite a difficult task. There is as yet no complete documentation on available programs.

The user must try various strategies: place an inquiry with his dealer, read specialist journals that publish articles and advertisements on new software, scan abstracting journals (e.g. section 78.30 - personal computing in the INSPEC Computer & Control Abstracts), consult colleagues and members of computer hobby clubs, particularly those owning the same computer type; all these can help find a needle in a haystack.

Unfortunately, even when we encounter information on an existing program that may seem usable, we are not always able to decide whether it meets our requirements. For example, we find announcements of a dozen or more programs called 'personal accounting', or 'private bookkeeping' or 'check-book control' etc., but are unable to ascertain what their functions are, whether they are adaptable to individual use, how they cope with the requirements of the tax regulations, and whether they will be useful to us.

What we badly need is a *database* of personal (and not only personal !) software in structured form, if possible online-accessible via one or more host online information retrieval systems, that will make it possible to find a suitable program for a given task. Each program would be characterized by an abstract describing its functions, parameters, hardware required, performance, programming language, author, distributor and price.

Then, on demand, a more detailed description of possible ‘candidate’ programs could be acquired before the final decision is made.

Interesting prospects for the creation and use of personal software have arrived with the advent of viewdata systems: these systems could help the user to find via his personal computer (functioning also as a viewdata terminal) a suitable program from a vast volume of stored software when he needs it, to retrieve it from the memory of the central computer, to load it for a small fee into his own personal computer and to perform the job. It might also be possible to execute the selected program remotely in the computer of the viewdata system, and to have the results on the screen of his terminal. Such *tele-software* could make an immense volume of software available from anywhere, at any time and without delay. Part of the fee would be repaid to the author of the program as a royalty.

The development and organization of the personal software market is at present hampered by a number of circumstances: the market is *in statu nascendi*, and the traditional hobbyist approach of users and program authors has its specific influence on the software produced. The manufacturers are not too fervent about the systematic building up of personal software for the use of a professional: it is easier to make and sell computer games for hobbyists, and software packages for small businesses (invoicing, ledgers, debtors accounting, etc.). Professionals who use their personal computers to support their intellectual activities are not (yet) mass customers.

66 - Terminal and mainframe

The typical personal computer for many years has been a *stand-alone unit*. For communication with a large computer in the computing centre (‘mainframe’), *terminals* have been used that allow access to a large computer in remote mode, and simultaneously with other users. In principle, any personal computer could be used as an intelligent terminal of a mainframe. Its user might choose between two modes of work: either working with his personal computer as an isolated machine, in stand-alone mode, or employing it as a terminal connected with the mainframe.

When does a professional prefer the use of a mainframe ? First, if the job exceeds the capacity of his personal computer; secondly, if the respective program is available only on the mainframe; thirdly, if a special peripheral is needed. Indeed, the advantage of a mainframe is the high speed of operation and its almost unlimited (if compared with the modest parameters of a personal computer) internal and external storage capacity (internal storages of millions of bytes, and disks of 30, 300 or 600 million characters compared with the 70 to 500 thousand characters of a floppy disk). A further advantage is the rich software that includes many sophisticated programs and program packages, rich peripherals, and the availability of higher-level programming languages of various types. One disadvantage can sometimes be the rather slow access, particularly in the peak hours when too many users are sharing the computer simultaneously.

The present author remembers the situation at a university where one of the fastest computers in the world was accessible via terminals after a wait-time of three to ten minutes - the computation was as fast as lightning, yet the wait-time meant that the system was unusable for interrupted operative jobs. Also, the speed of operations might be influenced by the momentary machine occupation, and priority job scheduling. Participants at courses and demonstrations laughed when they were told that an in-house online retrieval system is extremely fast on sunny afternoons, and rather slower on rainy days. In fact, due to variable working hours, the occupation of the computer was more intensive in the afternoons when the most people prefer to work longer hours than in fine days when many tend to leave earlier.

67 - Personal applications and files

Decades ago, punched card machines and, later, computers were used in simple, isolated jobs, and after a long period of experience the general conviction prevailed that complex mechanization (a term belonging to the punch card technique era) brings about resounding success due to the synergy effect mentioned earlier. Similarly, personal computers were employed first for small and isolated jobs. The proud new owner of a personal computer finds it a pleasant experience to manage his small directory of addresses and telephone numbers by means of a computer, and does not think too much about the time and cost of such a miniature job. However, as (perhaps later) he begins to consider the effectiveness of his personal computer, he will find it better not to use it in such a manner. An *integrated system* solving a number of tasks should be his goal.

Before deciding to buy a personal computer or to use a terminal and mainframe for personal purposes, the prospective user should make a *long-term plan* containing

- list of activities that he intends to mechanize,
- characteristics of the programs required,
- definition of the priorities of the activities and programs,
- a rough time schedule for completion,
- list of types of personal files,
- estimate of their volume and rate of growth.

The result of such considerations is a plan that defines the steps in the successive mechanization of a professional's jobs in a logical sequence, the growth of his files, and the stepwise extension of his hardware.

SOFTWARE FOR PERSONAL USE

1 TIME AND DATE	time & date display/print (printing stopwatch) alarm clock wih acoustic & displayed messages calendar function & date computations elapsed time computation
2 SIMPLE CALCULATIONS	functions (log, sin, a^x, x! etc.) simple calculations (formulae) standard programs, one's own programs
3 ADVANCED COMPUTATIONS	library and one's own programs computations via mainframe library computations via mainframe, one's own programs
4 DATA PROCESSING	planning and scheduling appointment scheduling network planning (CPM) personal accounting time accounting DP library programs and one's own programs DP by means of mainframe
5 TEXT PROCESSING	'mini' word processing (one-page level) 'midi' word processing (simple wp software) 'maxi' word processing ('fully-fledged' software) concordance, alphabetical index (register)
6 INFORMATION MANAGEMENT	flexible index program (alpha,KWIC,KWOC) simple sequential search program online retrieval program input and search in company files interface to external online information systems
7 GRAPHICAL WORK	simple graphs (bar, pie, Gantt etc.) line graphs (simple, advanced) chart and scheme design advanced graphical work (creation, animation etc.)
8 COMMUNICATION	in-house electronic mail teletex facility
9 UTILITIES	compilers & interpreters (BASIC, COBOL, PASCAL..) sort, merge, copy, edit, screen etc. hashing, text compression etc.

Fig. 67.1 - Software for personal use

A general overview is shown - the content of the personal software depends on the specific requirements of the professional concerned.

Time/date functions

Only a minority of personal computers is equipped at present with an automatic *time and date* function; some manufacturers offer it as an additional feature (for an additional price). The feature is battery-driven, thus independent of the computer on/off. This function does more than merely to replace a clock and calendar: *automatic dating* of output offers practical advantages (distinguishing between newer and older versions of texts, data or programs); also, precise time in hours, minutes and seconds that can be automatically recalled and displayed and/or printed is a practical feature that can be effectively used for automatic time measurement, and it offers an excellent facility for a personal computer to be used as a '*printing stopwatch*': measured times (in a laboratory etc.) are registered by one stroke on the keyboard, they are displayed and printed out, and the observer can type in his notes. The output is a written record with exact and objective times and all the necessary comments. Also, a *calendar* function and computations with dates (number of days elapsed between two dates) is useful. Dating and timing are both important features for the *automatic alerting* mentioned in chapter 3.

Simple calculations

Any personal computer can be used for simple calculations; for many a technician or scientist this is the most important and sometimes the only application of his machine. The calculations range from simple functions (log, sin, etc.) to ad hoc or repetitive calculations of formulae, iterative calculations etc. To the technician and scientist a personal computer has become a modern version of his old slide rule, working with high precision and enabling him to do much more.

Advanced computations

The type and volume of the computations depend on the professional's field of activity. Personal computers can be used for a wide range of the technical calculations of engineers and technologists, scientific calculations in various fields of science, and many types of business and financial calculations. The user has to define his needs and then to start his search for suitable programs, as mentioned earlier. This process may be short and easy if he encounters programs to meet his requirements exactly, but it may also be slow and arduous. Sometimes the end result will be that the user has to sit down and write his own program. Let us hope that in the near future software for personal computers will be not only more extensive but also better accessible. Sometimes the conclusion will be that the personal computer is not capable of processing the desired computations either due to the lack of software or due to the limited hardware parameters. Then the use of a mainframe in an in-house computer centre or in a service centre is the only answer.

Personal data processing

Everybody needs to *plan, schedule* and *manage* his work. We mentioned some methods of personal planning and accounting in chapter 3. The user should try to find programs to meet his requirements. He should prefer those that are compatible with his other application programs - remember the compatibility recommended between the various parts of personal software.

Updating of *directories* and *lists* is of use to everybody. Every professional needs his personal list of addresses, but also various lists of terms, definitions, formulae, acronyms, projects, program modules etc.; all must be easily updatable. We should try to use one program for various tasks; then, only the data will differ per application, but the program functions and commands will be uniform. The *data processing* jobs of a professional (administration of doctor's list of patients, cost and fees accounting of a free-lance journalist etc.) need special programs; some of these are available on the market.

Word processing

Many professionals require from their personal computers support also in the field of word processing. We mentioned these applications in chapter 5.

Information management

The goals of computerized *information management* have been discussed in chapter 4. A professional should evaluate his own needs for personal documentation, keeping in mind the ambitious aim of the organization of knowledge. He must choose between offline (indexes) or online retrieval, and he must select his system of classification or indexing; further, he must consider the type and form of his records, their optimum structure, and estimate the volumes of his files and their possible rate of growth. The personal documentation file is the most voluminous of all the personal files of a typical user; unfortunately, it is also prohibitively large for many a personal computer. The decision has then to be made whether to use existing software (programs for producing indexes, offline or online retrieval) or to make use of a mainframe. Whilst most professionals can write their programs for technical or scientifical calculations without difficulties, only a few hobbyists are willing to create their own retrieval programs; a simple program would hardly meet serious demands, and a more sophisticated program is too difficult to be designed purely for personal purposes.

Graphical work

For many a professional, hardware and software facilities offering graphical output are extremely important. The ease with which charts, graphs and diagrams can be created, changed, and actively adapted stimulates the use of graphical presentation. Specialized intelligent graphical terminals offer excellent features including sophisticated methods of CAD - computer-aided design. Also, many a personal computer offers some facility for graphical work. The resolution of the screen, the type of hardcopy output, availability of colours, and level and friendliness of software determine the extent and scope of the graphical output from primitive bar charts to sophisticated methods of drawing intricate figures and graphs, and to computer-aided design or animation.

Utilities

For every user of a personal computer the availability and quality of general-purpose *utility programs* are essential. The availability, capacity,

		unit	number of units	bytes per unit	file volume
WORK PLANNING AND CONTROL					
alerting file	*	message	50	40	2K
diary graph	*	day	365	32	12K
diary items/year	*	item	1 800	40	72K
log	*	item	400	40	16K
time accounting	*	account	40	24	1K
pending tasks	*	task	60	40	2K
PERSONAL ACCOUNTING					
accounting		account	60	20	1K
journal - instant	*	item	300	20	6K
- history		item	3 000	20	60K
selected items		item	150	20	3K
asset accounting		item	120	80	10K
INFORMATION MANAGEMENT					
directory of addresses	*	name	300	90	27K
vocabulary; terminology		term	400	200	80K
user's own bibliography		record	60	150	9K
personal documentation		record	3 000	300	900K
recipes		recipe	120	800	96K
TEMPORARY FILES					
CPM		activity	60	30	2K
text processing					
- texts in processing	*	page	40	2 400	96K
- text file		page	300	2 400	720K
ephemeral notes	*	note	50	40	2K

* files kept continuously online

Fig 67.2 - Example of the personal files of a professional

The type and volume of personal files are quite individual; our table must be interpreted as an example only. Think of the type and volume of your own files. A teacher's file might include a list of his students and his roster of lectures, a doctor's file a directory of his patients, chemist's file special documentation on laboratory experiments and measurements, linguist's file an organized collection of etymological and phraseological notes and examples etc.

performance and limits of sort, merge, copy, and other programs offered by the manufacturer must be taken into consideration. The importance of programming languages, interpreters and compilers has been emphasized in section 64.

Files

The intended field of applications and its peculiarities also influence the type and volume of *personal files.* As an illustration we present in fig. 67.2 an example of personal files of a professional who intends to employ his personal computer for a number of activities.

68 - Personal work station

In his wide variety of activities, the professional has been increasingly supported by a continuously growing number of more and more specialized technical means. The telephone and typewriter have been extended by an interphone for local communication, telex for remote written communication. In the last few years, the pocket calculator, word processor, personal computer, plotter or graphical display, terminal of a mainframe and special terminals of external online information systems, as well as a television set connected to public teletext and viewdata systems have also made their appearance.

If a professional wanted to be supported in all his various activities by technical means, he would be obliged to install in his workroom a telephone, intercom, dictating machine, word processor, personal computer, graphical display, terminal of the in-house mainframe, special terminal to commercial online information system(s), a television set with a viewdata modem, perhaps also a videophone, a scribophone or other devices. This would be rather ridiculous: a dozen technical means, each with its own keyboard, switches and push-buttons, each operated according to its own rules and its specific commands, while the output of one system could not easily, or at all, be used as input for another. Each of the devices would be used for a fraction of the time, the rest being idle. The total price would be exorbitant, the space requirements enormous, and the aesthetic effect would be bad: an ugly conglomerate of devices of various dimensions, shapes, colours and designs.

The *integration* of specialized machines and devices into universal units has been explained in section 13 as one of the most important development trends of the last few years. Indeed, at present it is possible to use a personal computer also as a terminal of an in-house mainframe or to connect it as a terminal to some commercial online information systems; a word processor can be used as a station for electronic mail, many a personal computer permits some sort of graphical work etc. This development is continuing, single-purpose machines are being replaced by multi-purpose units, the number of machine types is diminishing as their functions widen.

The ultimate goal has been described in section 13 (see also fig. 13.2): a *universal work station* able to support its owner in the majority of his activities, and also using the output of some operations as the input for subsequent processing. A personal work station will become the central point of the professional's workplace.

The work station will perform all the word processing functions, will help prepare, correct, edit, store and print out texts and tables. It will also perform the functions of a personal computer with a large internal memory, a friendly operating system, compilers and interpreters of higher-level programming languages and a rich library of programs, together with the facility of easy access to large external program libraries. External storage will no longer be the bottleneck of personal applications: the capacity of floppy disks will be extended and hard disk or new types of external memories with large capacities will be available. Graphical display and graphical output of good quality in colour will be available and supported by intelligent software and will be capable of designing graphs, charts and drawings of many types. Another essential feature will be the *communication function:* the work station will be usable either in stand-alone mode, or as a terminal both of the in-house mainframe and of external and public information systems including viewdata. It will also serve as a station for electronic mail and a means of computer conferencing. The *interaction* between the user and the station will be smooth owing to a friendly conversational system enabling both communication in menu-form with maximum help and advice for a beginner or incidental user, and fast communication by means of concise commands and macro-commands in the hands of an experienced user. Communication will be made easier by means of acoustic output (signals, warnings and messages in voice form), by voice input (limited number of frequently used voice commands), and by fast input of some commands and data by means of light-pen and touch techniques.

Besides its use for word processing, computations, graphical work and communication, the station will be able to support the professional in managing his own work, in particular in the planning and control of his activities: it will be able to serve as a telephone answering unit, it will alert its owner to dates and times when actions have to be taken, it will inform him about waiting messages, signal urgent messages, register activities and maintain his diary and log.

A work station therefore has the opportunity to become a highly efficient, flexible, general-purpose helpmate. No new inventions are necessary to bring it about; all the elements necessary are already available. Only the price of some of them is rather high at the moment, and there are still some problems of standardization and compatibility of various techniques. Another question is whether users are willing and prepared to use this new tool.

Are we prepared to use a work station effectively ?

Once again: History repeats itself. The new techniques are developing faster than methods, and our habits are changing even more slowly. We cannot expect a work station to be used perfectly from the first moment by every professional. It will offer us support in many ways, but it will require a little more systematic work and some formalization and standardization, though it will be helpful and tolerant to some deviations from the strict formal rules. We have many times emphasized the uneffectiveness of small, isolated ad hoc jobs, and the need for a complex, *integrated approach.* Activities, programs, and data must be organized from a common point of view, the implementation of a personal work station must be carefully planned and thoroughly prepared. Although work with the station will be friendly, and to some extent even less formal due to the intelligent man/machine interface, the preparatory phases are not so straightforward.

Bearing this in mind, what should we do *now* before the advent of the perfect universal personal work station equipped with modular, flexible software for personal use ? There is only one answer: Let us use the existing means, and let us use them intelligently; we should not only make use of the trivial functions of the new equipment, but employ it where possible in a complex manner. We must also use the meantime to create some basic personal files that cannot be built-up later overnight - personal documentation takes years to grow; a file of formulae, terms or definitions is built up step by step. The prospective user of a personal work station needs some time to learn and to comprehend the special requirements of personal computing and word processing, to recognize their strong and weak points, to acquire some habits of order and formalization, to master conversation with a computerized system, to develop his system of classification and indexing of files and records, to improve it by trial-and-error, and to develop new skills that seem perhaps inhibiting at first sight but that open the way to new, effective styles of personal work. A tiger's leap from the primitive paper-and-pencil technique to a personal work station has little chance of success.

7 - GRAPHICAL PRESENTATION

Graphical presentation is a work technique widely used by professionals. In what follows we shall not try to describe in detail all the methods and techniques of graphical presentation, nor shall we try to explain all the rules of how to design and use different types of graphs, charts and schemes.

There are many instructive books on this subject - from the classical, such as the literature on Gantt, Hymans or 'Z' charts, to modern textbooks and handbooks [ref. 70]. They can help a professional to improve his style of working with graphs. This short chapter is not intended to take their place; its aim is to show that new technical means make graphical methods easily accessible. The design and drawing of graphs, charts and schemes need no longer be as arduous as it was in the days of the paper-and-pencil technique. New graphical methods are appearing, but - and we should like to emphasize this - some old methods, known for decades but little used in practice, can now be revived.

71 - Aims and basic forms of graphical presentation

The power of graphical presentation results from the fact that quantities are presented by quantities (lengths, surfaces), not by numbers, and relations are presented as relations in space, not described by sentences. This makes the data and relations easier and quicker to comprehed.

Even a plain *table* is a form of graphical presentation *sui generis*. Its advantage is in its two-dimensionality that makes orientation easier. The reader can use a table for quick selective information; he can follow one line or one column only or look at an intersection of both. Think of the table in figures 12.1 or 54.6 and imagine the amount of text that would be needed to replace it !

The curves in a graph show at a glance the development and also the relation between the events. A more advanced 'Z' graph in fig. 73.3 tells us in seconds what was the development in the recent periods, how it increased or decreased from month to month, but it also depicts the general trend (the cumulative curve) as well as the long-time development by means of the curve of sliding sums. Presentation of the same data in the form of three columns, each consisting of 12 figures could never be as informative. Similarly, the graphical presentation of intricate relationships helps us to grasp them: think of an enormous help provided by a chessboard - it is possible, indeed, to play chess without a chessboard and pieces, but what a difference it makes using one ! Compare the scheme in fig. 75.1, that presents a logical problem in graphical form, with the traditional word description in the form of long sentences bristling with 'if... then... else... provided...' - sentences that you have to read three times to comprehend and sometimes even then are not quite sure whether you are interpreting the point correctly.

72 - Basic types of graphs

Typically, a graph makes it possible to:

- *compare* a number of independent *data* - such as the population of two or more countries, the turnover in different commodities;
- illustrate the *division of a whole* into its components (e.g. total costs split into cost types, total power production by its sources);
- show the *development* of a variable in time (e.g. the development of fees in the last ten years);
- demonstrate the *correlation* between variables (e.g. between the revenues and expenses).

Graphical elements that can be employed are *points*, *lines*, *bars* (these are a special form of lines) or *surfaces* (circles, squares, oblongs); sometimes also *symbols* are used. In fig. 72.1 examples of four elementary graphical presentations of quantitative data are given and the graphical elements are shown.

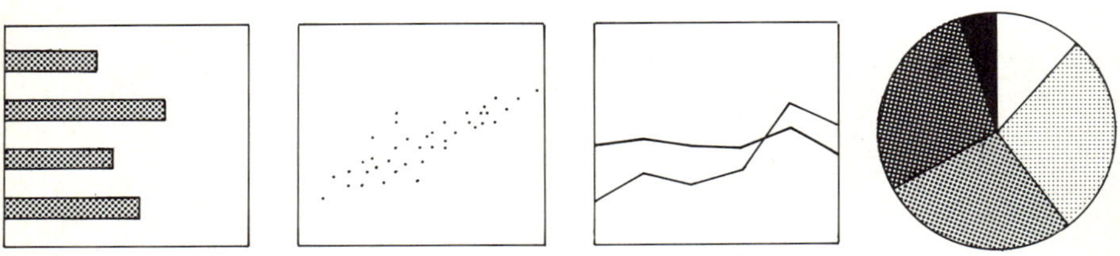

Fig. 72.1 - Basic types of graphs

The bar, plot, line and pie graphs are the most commonly used elementary forms of graphical presentation. They can be combined or adapted in a number of variants.

Basic rules for designing a graph

The purpose of a graph must always be kept in mind: what it is to present, which facts or relations are to be emphasized, which unimportant facts are to be suppressed, for whom the graph is intended, and by which technique it will be presented. The designer must check that his graph is instructive and comprehensible; he should adhere to the following points:

- The *title* of the graph must identify its subject; it can be included in the graph, or attached as a subscript.
- *Definition of data* - the data are unambiguous to the designer of the graph at the time of drawing (but perhaps not so some time later) but not to the reader; they must be exactly defined (e.g. turnover = net turnover without reductions and allowances, excluding goods returned, including tax...).
- *Sources of data* - these enable the original data to be found and checked by the reader, and even by the designer some time later.
- *Units* - how often we encounter graphs and tables where curves and numbers are presented with no explanation given as to the monetary or physical units used.
- *Scale* - clear scaling on both axes of a graph must never be forgotten; the scale should always be drawn from zero (with the exception of the

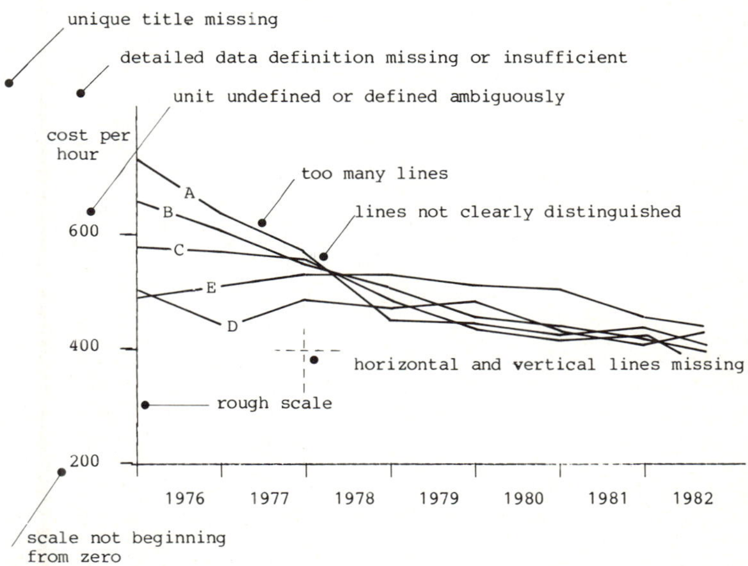

Fig. 72.2 - The most frequently occurring inadequacies of graphs

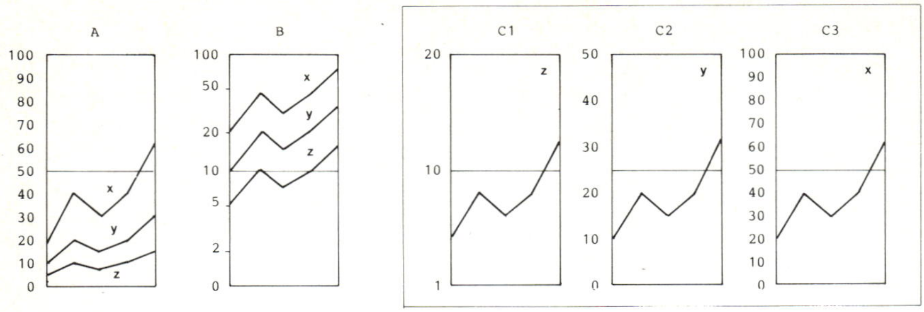

Fig. 72.3 - Importance of scales in linear graphs

It is difficult to compare curves that are drawn in the same scale if the values differ substantially. In the case A, the relative changes of all the events x, y and z are equal, but the fluctuations of the event x are seemingly much larger than of the event z. Logarithmic presentation (B) shows the relative changes of values without distortion, but the absolute values are difficult to compare. A good solution is to draw and store each graph separately and to use individual scales. The graphs can be compared in any combination in overlay.

time scale) and it should be continuous; time must always be drawn on the horizontal axis from the left to the right.

- *Combination* of graphical presentation with the original numerical data is often advantageous (fig. 73.3).

Improvements and combinations of the basic forms of graphs

The basic forms schematically shown in fig. 72.1 can be improved and combined in several ways. First, it is always possible to present more than one event in one graph. We can then confront two or more events and analyse their relations by simple visual comparison. Colours, different types of lines, shadowing or symbols help us to identify and distinguish specific curves, bars or points.

The presentation of several events in one graph has its advantages, and it is to be preferred if we intend to emphasize certain relationships between events, e.g. in a publication or at a presentation. Otherwise we must refer to section 73 where one of the basic rules of 'Z' charts is explained: never draw more than one event in one graph; if a comparison is required, prefer the overlay technique, as it makes it possible to compare any pair of (or more) graphs in a modular way according to ad hoc requirements. Thus: combine several events in one graph only if it is required for a specific purpose, but in general stick to the principle 'one event = one graph'. Also, never overload a graph with too much information. It becomes difficult to decipher and it defeats its own purpose. When selecting a graphical display, check that the overlay facility is available. This would give you an excellent chance to design your graphs as isolated units, and to display, at any moment, two or more graphs (distinguished by colour or other graphical means) on the screen simultaneously.

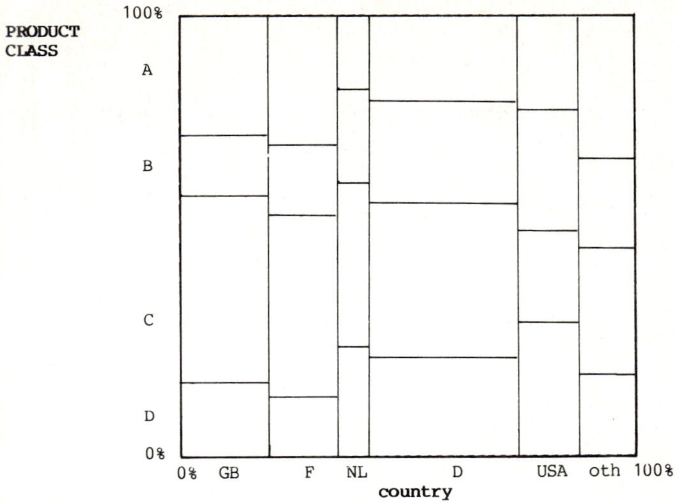

Fig. 72.4 - The square graph compares the structure from two points of view

The traditional pie chart compares the structure of a whole. The square graph permits to compare two values, in our case the sales by country and by products.

Another interesting possibility is to extend the traditional two-dimensional presentation into three-dimensional. While the drawing of three-dimensional graphs (typically: histograms) using three axes x, y and z is very laborious by means of the pencil-rule-paper technique, and is therefore rarely used, an intelligent graphical terminal makes it fast and easy. Again, we encounter a method that has been known for a long time but is hardly ever used because, without the help of advanced techniques, it is arduous.

Another well known technique is *interpolation* and *extrapolation* of curves. Everyone learns this at university or high school, but only professional statisticians, mathematicians and a few other scientists use it regularly, as we have mentioned in connection with the pocket calculator that now makes it easy to calculate linear trends by simply keying-in the numbers and by operating two functional keys. Automatic linear interpolation and extrapolation is, or should be, a common feature of an intelligent graphical display. Check the availability of this feature when choosing 'your' type.

73 - Special graphs

The basic elements of graphs - points, lines, bars, geometric figures and symbols - can be combined in endless forms into a large number of special graphs. We shall discuss only two of them, excellent for use in the personal sphere, the *Gantt chart* and the *'Z' chart.* Both are more than fifty years old, were used in planning and control some decades ago, and both can serve as examples of the renaissance of old methods in a new technical environment.

The Gantt chart

The *Gantt chart* is a special graph employed in planning and control. Its horizontal axis is a time axis. The columns represent time units (days, weeks or months). Each line in the graph is for one task only, e.g. action, item, product (fig. 73.1). The width of each column is considered to be equal to 100% of the task planned in the time unit. The actual performance is then expressed by a horizontal line; its length is proportional to the work actually performed.

In fig. 73.1 the widths of the columns represent monthly tasks: if the January task was 50 units, then 20 mm width of the column represents 50 units, and the 45 units actually finished are drawn as a horizontal line of 18 mm; if the February task was 60 units, and if 70 units were actually finished, then the horizontal line is drawn across the full field width (20 mm = 60 units) and a short additional line of 3.3 mm (= 10 units) is attached.

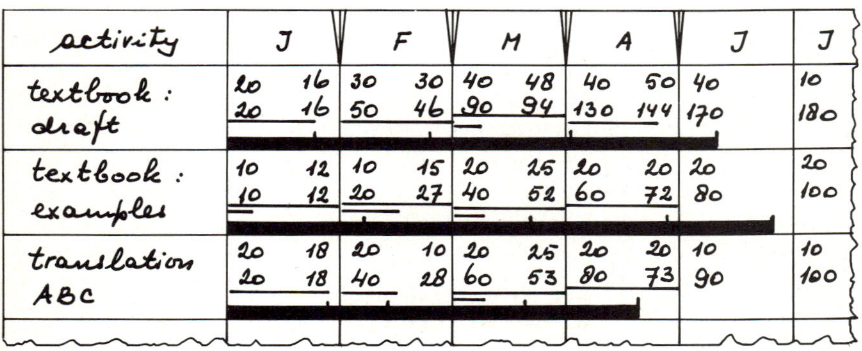

Fig. 73.1 - Gantt chart - a forgotten device ?

The Gantt chart compares the work planned and actually done. One line per activity, one column per period (month in our example) are used. Planned work is recorded at the left-hand side, actual at the right-hand side. In the second line the cumulative data, both planned and actual, are recorded. Horizontal lines depict the plan/actual ratio per month and in total (the thick line). The V sign marks the latest period recorded.

In such a way the fulfilling of each task (on lines) in each period (columns) is signalled and easy to read-off. Besides the detailed one-period comparison, a bold summary line is drawn. This compares the cumulated task (sum of the tasks of all periods up to date) and the cumulative actual performance.

The chart was invented and patented by Henry Lawrence Gantt, a well known American industrial engineer who developed this graphical control system during his work in artillery workshops in the USA during World War I. Used in drawn form as well as displayed on planning boards, these charts were one of the most popular planning devices before World War II. The use of computerized online planning and scheduling of industrial production reduced the need for visual control of details; they were monitored by the computer, and new methods of network planning came into use, but the Gantt chart remains a useful planning tool that can be employed also in personal planning and control.

The essential advantage of the Gantt chart is its comprehensibility and compactness: the progress of each task (one line) is represented in a one-dimensional form. This makes it possible to draw on one page of A4 format or on one screen about 20 different tasks, each of them split into a number of time periods. This could never be done in the form of a two-dimensional graph; 20 curves are difficult to survey. Moreover, detailed control (per task and period) as well as total control (cumulative plan/actual comparison) are both possible at a glance.

'Z' charts

Another excellent graphical technique is also more than a half century old; it was well known before World War II, and slowly fell into oblivion. This chart is two-dimensional, and it presents one event by three curves: first, by the 'basic curve' characterizing the development from period to period (e.g. monthly expenses); secondly, by the curve of cumulative sums (from the beginning of the year up to date); thirdly, by a curve of sliding sums, i.e. sums of a fixed number of recent periods up to date (e.g. sum of the last 12 months or last 52 weeks).
The principle of the 'Z' chart is shown in fig. 73.2. While the basic curve characterizes the actual running of things from period to period (from month to month in our example), the cumulative curve gives an overview of the development trend during the year and allows it to be extrapolated into the future; the third curve is the sum of the last 12 months, in our case its value in August '81 is the sum of the monthly values from September 1980 to August 1981. This curve eliminates seasonal irregularities, and it shows the long-time trend in development. A little experience is all that is needed to extract from a 'Z' diagram a great deal about the events presented.

month 1981	units	cumulative from 1.1.81	month 1980	sliding sum
1	4	4	4	50
2	3	7	3	50
3	3	10	2	51
4	5	15	3	53
5	7	22	7	53
6	7	29	5	55
7	8	37	7	56
8	6	43	5	57
9	7	50	5	59
10	5	55	4	60
11	3	58	3	60
12	4	62	2	62

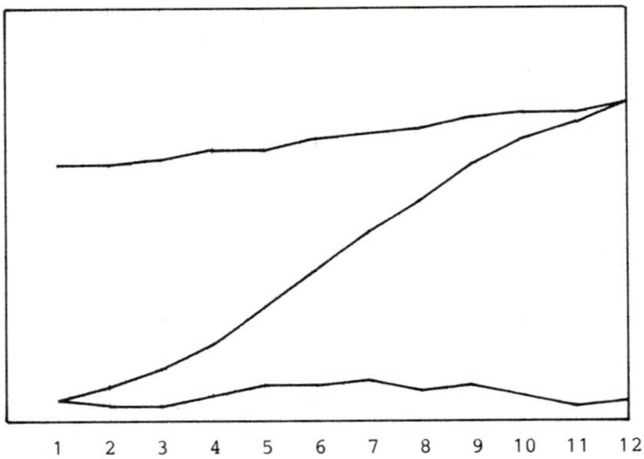

Fig. 73.2 - Principle of the 'Z' chart

The basic curve describes the development of an event from period to period. The cumulative curve characterizes the tendency within a longer period (usually, a year), the curve of sliding sums eliminates seasonal influence and emphasizes the general trend.

It goes without saying that the curves of cumulative data and sliding sums must meet at the end-point of the whole period (usually, a year), and that the starting point of the curve of cumulative data is the same as the point of the basic curve in the first period. This gives the graph the shape of the letter 'Z'; hence, the name 'Z' chart. In practice, this form of drawing is not the best: the values of the basic curve are too low down in comparison with the two summary curves: the basic curve would display too small differences and the comparison would not be a true one (see also fig. 73.2). It is a common practice to use two different scales in the 'Z' chart, namely a more detailed scale for the basic curve, and a larger scale for the curves of cumulative values and sliding sums.

In a month/year graph (the most popular form of 'Z' chart) the ratio of scales is usually 1:5, i.e. if the year sum is estimated, say, to be $ 1 mil., then the scale for the both cumulative curves

INCOME

TITLE (abbr.): INCOME

TITLE:
gross income

DEFINITION:
gross income excl. expense compensat., excl. interest and dividend

SOURCE OF DATA:
accounts 81+82+84

CHANGES:
since 1979 without interest & dividend

COMPARE WITH:
expenses

NOTES:

basic data	cumulated	sliding sums
10 026	10 026	117 238
8 741	18 767	119 216
10 625	29 392	118 332
9 104	38 496	119 274
14 414	52 910	123 071
10 896	63 806	126 515
9 542	73 348	127 226
5 221	78 569	123 020
11 480	90 049	127 714
14 655	104 704	129 992
11 297	116 001	127 477
13 713	129 714	129 714

SCALES:

DM 40 000 DM 200 000

DM 30 000 DM 150 000

DM 20 000 DM 100 000

DM 10 000 DM 50 000

0 0

1981

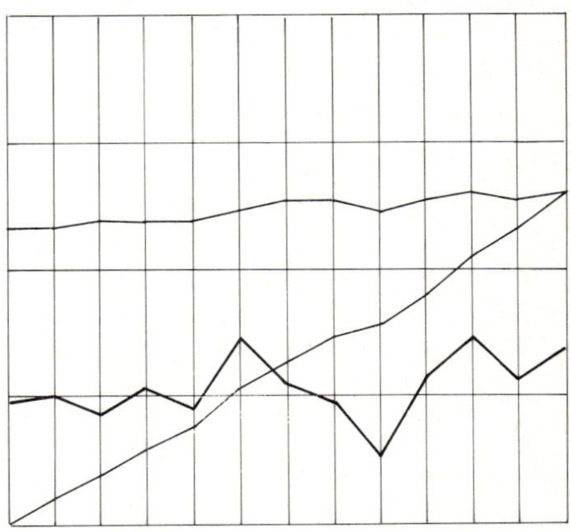

12 1 2 3 4 5 6 7 8 9 10 11 12

Fig. 73.3 - The 'Z' diagram form for month periods

The form designed by Prof. K. Žlábek combines the original numerical data with graphical presentation, contains fields for title and comments, and situates the 100 × 100 mm graphical field in the right-hand lower corner to make comparison of graphs easier.

is set at 100 mm = \$ 2 mil.; the top of the curves of cumulative data and sliding sums is then situated approximately half way in the graphical field. For the basic curve we choose a scale five times greater, i.e. 100 mm = \$ 200,000; the average monthly values are then slightly below half way in the graphical field (see fig. 73.3).

Adapting the scale individually for each graph, and using two different scales ensures that the curves run roughly in the middle of the graphical field; they are then easier to compare than if some are in the region near the X axis and others in higher regions (see also fig. 72.3-A).

The 'Z' chart was invented and patented by Willard C. Brinton in 1917; in the following years the technique was improved. The first standardization of special forms of 'Z' chart was done by Arthur R. Burnet in 1921. The principles mentioned below require that the graphs are comparable in a modular manner; a standardized form is then necessary. The greatest perfection was achieved in the version of a standard 'Z'chart sheet designed by Prof. K. Žlábek [ref. 70]. The form was printed on a semi-transparent high-quality paper in a light green-grey colour, in A4 format (297 × 210 mm) in variants for 12 (month), 13 (4-week), 26 (2-week), and 52 (week) periods. The 100 × 100 mm graphical network in the bottom righthand corner of the sheet makes comparison by overlay or linear arrangement easy. The numerical data are filled in so that they relate directly to the respective points of the curves. Space is reserved for the title of the graph, the date, for comments and the two scales (fig. 73.3).

One of the basic principles of the 'Z' chart technique is to restrict one graph to one event and one period (year) only. The graphical field is limited to a relatively small part of a sheet of A4 format and is situated so that mechanical comparison of several graphs is easy; graphs can be laid abreast to create a longer chronological sequence of curves, or placed on top of one another and observed against the light; two sets of curves (say, expenses and revenues) can be compared and the relations between them analyzed. The principle of modularity (one event - one period - one graph) offers an enormous flexibility for analysis of data.

Indeed, this form of graphical presentation has enormous descriptive power and - like the Gantt charts - it should not be neglected in our computer age. As so many other techniques of the past, it is now more convenient than it ever was in the past. Think of the calculations needed to draw the curves in the pre-computer age ! It was necessary to use 2 × 12 monthly data as input, to calculate 2 × 12 values for both cumulative curves, to recalculate positions of 36 points in the graph; now, the historical data are stored in the computer memory, only the 12 numbers are entered, and all the rest is calculated and displayed automatically; also the linear trends of all three curves (recommended by the authors but scarcely used in practice half a century ago) can now be drawn by the computer with no hardship to the user.

Other special graphs

For special purposes, there is a large number of specialized graphical methods. We mention briefly here the well known *Sankey graph* (fig. 73.4) that is employed typically to illustrate structure of input and output of

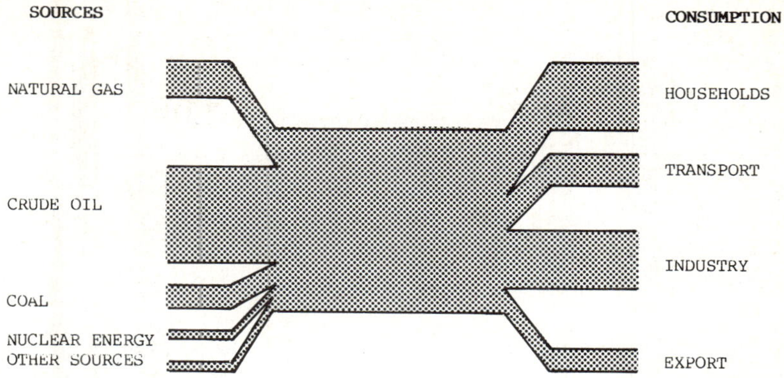

Fig. 73.4 - Sankey graph

processes (say, sources and consumers of energy, sources of financial funds and the use of them etc.).

Histograms are frequently used by statisticians, sometimes in specially adapted forms; the 'age pyramid' used in demography is one of the most popular. We also mentioned before intelligent graphical terminals that are able to draw three-dimensional histograms.

Combinations of graphical elements and various forms of graphical presentation are numerous. We have mentioned only a few of the graphs that are general-purpose and may find wide acceptance. We have not described, of course, the many special types of graphs used in specific fields of science and technology (meteorological synoptic maps, polar diagrams used in some branches of technology, triangle graphs used typically in metallurgy, etc.). We again refer the reader to the abundant literature on this subject. For example, the fine book by Herdeg [ref. 70] presents 354 excellent examples of various forms of graphical presentation in systematical arrangement. Also a well edited statistical yearbook or other similar publication might serve as a source of examples and inspiration on how to use graphical presentation.

74 - Organizational charts

The title of this section is somewhat narrow. The aim is to characterize all the graphs and charts that do not depict quantities, but structures and/or relations of ideas, things, concepts, activities, people, or organizational bodies.

Spatial relations, descendence relations (broader/narrower, older/newer, ascendent/descendent), hierarchy relations (generic/specific), logical relations (similarity, associations, logical AND/OR/NOT relations of Boolean logic) can be included in this category. The graphical presentation of the sequence of actions or activities also falls under this heading, but because of their specific importance in the field of organization and mechanization (e.g. flowcharts, Hymans charts, arrow charts etc.) we discuss them in a separate section 75.

Descendence graphs illustrate the development, succession and relation of units - genealogical charts (family trees), with a tradition of hundreds of years, are well known. Similar trees can depict the history of the development of animals and plants, the sequence of synthetic and analytical chemical processes, the process of diversification of natural languages, the development of an industrial concern, and many other subjects.

Hierarchy schemes depict the specification from generic to specific. They are employed to illustrate the structure of hierarchical classification

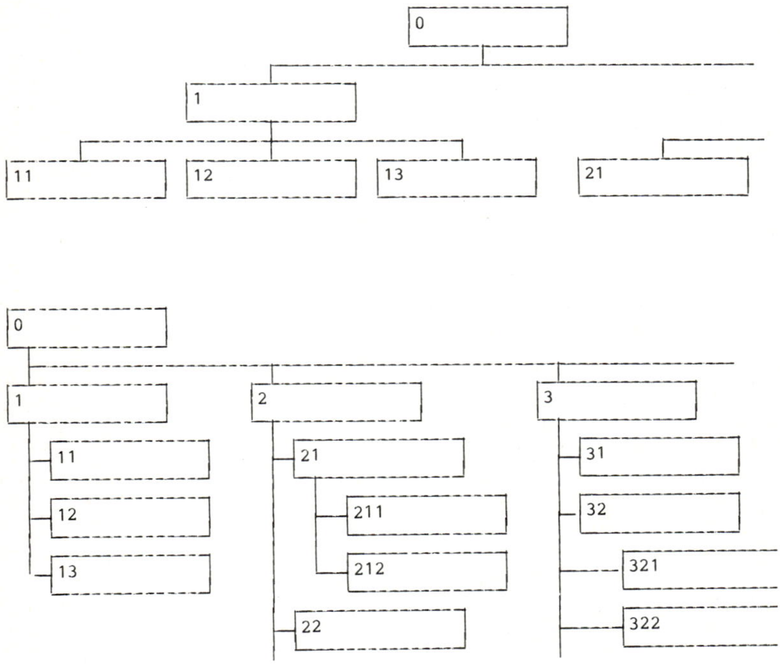

Fig - 74.1 - The organization scheme

The traditional layout (above) can be redesigned in the form that saves space and is at least equally easy to survey. The word processor makes it possible to draw an organization scheme very efficiently - it draws the vertical and horizontal lines, makes layout editing and later also updating very easy. Horizontal and vertical scrolling permits to draw in formats larger than A4. Both specimens in this figure were drawn by a word processor.

systems - the reader of the present book will have encountered examples in figures 37.1, 38.1 and 44.1. In the field of organization the *organization scheme* is the most popular and commonly known form of this scheme (fig. 74.1). The simplest and most compact form of a hierarchical scheme is a simple print-out of the items in indented form - each hierarchical level has its own indented position hierarchically shifted from left to right (see the example of the UDC hierarchy in fig. 44.1).

Logical relations between concepts, ideas or physical objects can be graphically presented in a large number of ways; one of many possible examples is the graphical presentation of concepts in a thesaurus (see fig. 74.2).

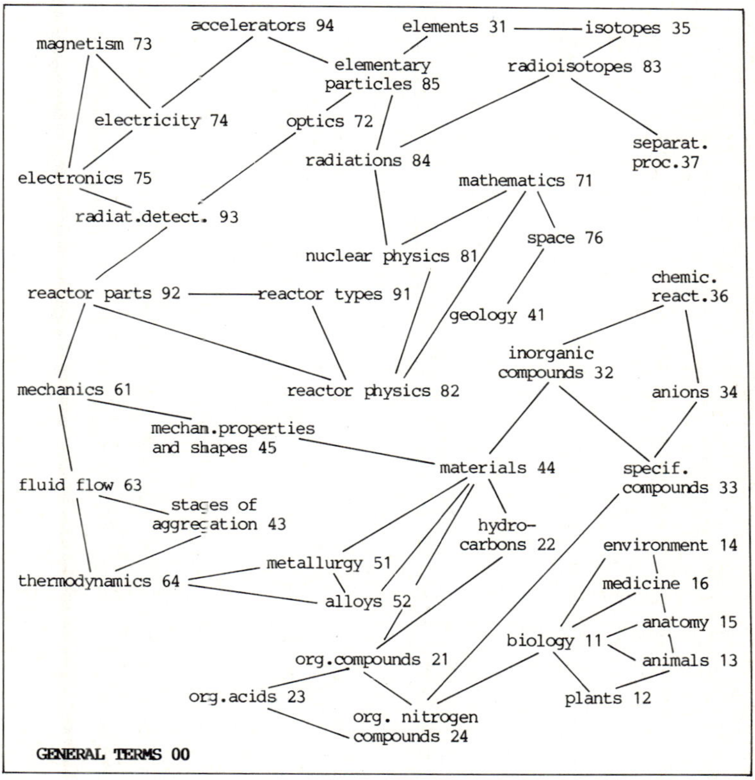

Fig. 74.2 - Informal graphical presentation of descriptor relations

Complicated relations between a large number of concepts, terms or descriptors are better presented in graphical form than in the form of lists. This is a specimen of one descriptor category from the Euratom thesaurus [ref. 70-Rolling].

A special form of graphical presentation of logical relations are the *Venn graphs* presenting concepts as graphical figures (usually circles) and characterizing their relations by overlaps (fig. 74.3).

Rosters are lists of duties arranged (usually in tabular form) by person, time and type of activity - a common form of this is a school roster. The compilation of the roster is a special problem, as several variables have to be allowed for: class / subject / teacher / room. In the past, graphical methods were generally used, but now a large number of programs exist to help solve this intricate problem. The output is presented in graphical form.

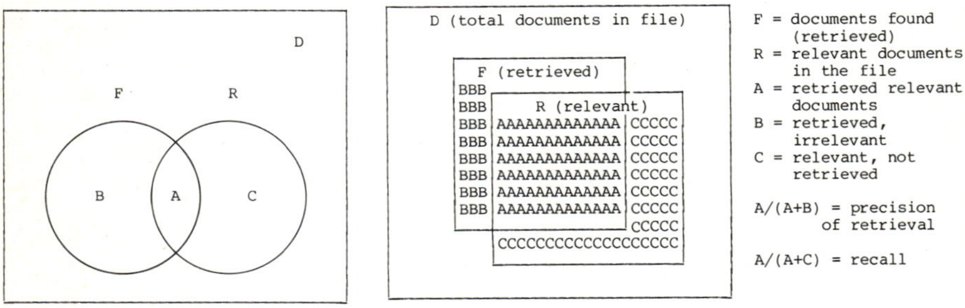

Fig. 74.3 - Venn graph

The Venn graph depicts the logical relations of concepts in terms of the Boolean AND's, OR's and NOT's. Traditionally, it has been drawn in the form of circles. Using squares or oblongs instead, we can draw this graph easily also by standard printers of personal computers or by word processors (the square Venn graph in this figure has been drawn by the P-5002 word processor).

The graphical presentation of *space relations* is also generally known and used in numerous fields: maps and plans are a form of this graphical presentation, and specific variants of them are used in many disciplines: meteorology, geodesy, agriculture, transport, statistics etc. All these applications use their own special symbolics and forms of presentation. Other widely used applications are technical drawings and schemes that also use their own forms of drawing and a specific language of symbols in mechanical engineering, electrotechnics, electronics, chemistry, architecture etc. CAD - computer-aided design - is now an important field of application of an intelligent graphical display making it possible to create points, straight lines, curves, to draw geometrical figures, to shift, turn, enlarge or reduce figures or their parts, to make perspective drawings, and to insert special symbols, texts and comments.

75 - Decision tables, flowcharts and CPM charts

One important type of chart illustrates a sequence of operations, activities or events that depends on variable conditions. A chain of logical decisions can be made more comprehensible if drawn instead of described in a narrative form (fig. 75.1).

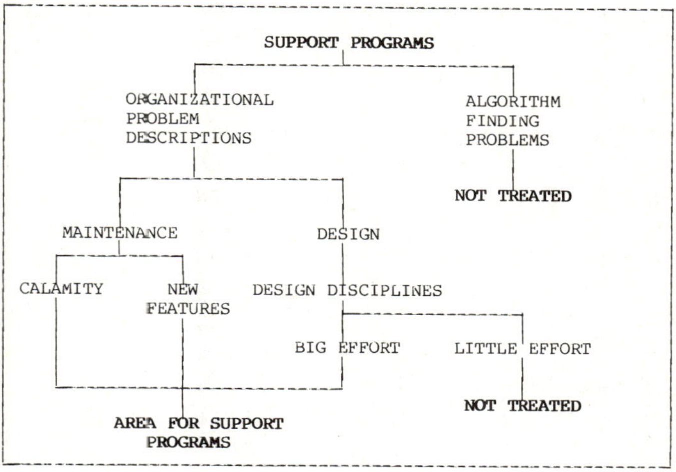

Fig. 75.1 - An informal graphical scheme of concept relations

A quite informal scheme helps both the author and the reader or listeners. Instead of traditional means (blackboard, paper and pencil) the word processor or computer display, printer or plotter can be used. They offer the avantages of easy layout changing, re-editing, updating and print out [example from the publication ref. 70-Kommeren].

A nice little book published by HMSO (Her Majesty's Stationery Office) in London presents many excellent examples of how to make difficult conditions stipulated by law and regulations, or described in manuals, easier to understand by using graphical presentation [ref. 70-Lewis]. This publication can be recommended to everybody who wants to present complicated logical problems to his readers or listeners in the most comprehensible form.

Another form of presentation of complicated chains of logical decisions is *decision tables.* In principle, they are tables of true/untrue values of statement logic. Their purpose is to display, in concise form, the results of decisions in accordance with a number of interrelated conditions. The nature of the decision table reduces the danger of a combination of conditions, even an unexpected one, being overlooked. The table consists of intersections of two zones, the zone of conditions,

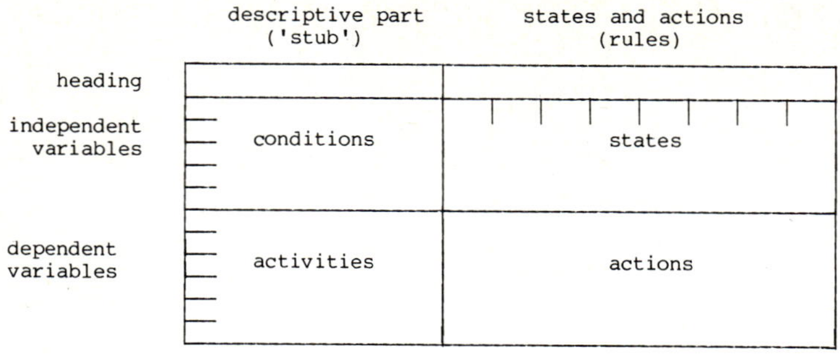

Fig. 75.2 - The basic structure of a decision table

EMPLOYEE'S LEAVE

	1	2	3	4	5	6	7	8	9	10	11	12	13	14	15	16
employed longer than 5 years ?	1	1	1	1	1	1	1	1	0	0	0	0	0	0	0	0
employed longer than 15 years ?	1	1	1	1	0	0	0	0	1	1	1	1	0	0	0	0
younger than 18 years ?	1	1	0	0	1	1	0	0	1	1	0	0	1	1	0	0
older than 50 years ?	1	0	1	0	1	0	1	0	1	0	1	0	1	0	1	0
2 weeks	i	i	-	-	i	i	-	-	i	i	i	i	i	-	-	Y
3 weeks			-	-			Y	Y						Y	Y	-
4 weeks			Y	Y												

EMPLOYEE'S LEAVE

	1	2	3	4	5
employed longer than 5 years ?	0	1	0	0	1
employed longer than 15 years ?	0	0	0	0	1
younger than 18 years ?	0	0	1	0	0
older than 50 years ?	0	-	0	1	-
2 weeks	Y				
3 weeks		Y	Y	Y	
4 weeks					Y

Fig. 75.3 - Full-scale and abbreviated decision tables

The length of an employee's leave (2, 3 or 4 weeks) depends on the employee's age and length of employment. The above table covers all possible combinations of these conditions, including those that are unrealistic (younger than 18 years and employed more than 15 years etc.). The table below considers only the significant variants.

and the zone of actions, and two columns: the description column ('stub'), and the rules column resulting in four quadrants: a quadrant of condition definitions (top left), a quadrant of states (top right), of activities description (bottom left) and of actions (bottom right). The conditions are independently, the actions dependently variable. Decision tables are more condensed than graphical presentation according to fig. 75.1, but they are rather difficult to interpret by a layman. They are sometimes used by systems analysts and programmers instead of the traditional flowcharts mentioned below

Flowcharts

Flowcharts can be used as instruments for graphical presentation of any procedure comprising a number of steps that depend on logical conditions, but their greatest popularity has been as a typical instrument for graphical presentation of algorithms in systems analysis and programming.

Flowcharts consist of *blocks*, connecting *lines*, and *auxiliary symbols*. There are two main sorts of block: *Operation blocks* represent one operation or a group of operations; each has one input and one output. They are generally symbolized by oblongs. *Decision blocks* symbolize a condition. They also have only one input each, but two (rarely three) outputs. Fulfilment of the condition (YES/NO or LOWER/EQUAL/GREATER) is decisive for the way in which the processing follows. The standard form of a decision block is a rhombus.

As has happened so often in the history of standardization, it is not always the most practical solution that has been chosen as the standard. The graphical symbols of flowcharts, standardized 'de jure' by valid standards and 'de facto' by the available stencils, are far from being practical. The most standardized symbols are too high and too short; they require too much vertical space, thus reducing the capacity of a standard sheet of paper, and they make filling-in a text difficult. In particular, the rhombus is extremely unsuitable - the horizontal oval used in the fifties in the UNIVAC stencil and later in some national standards (fig. 75.5) was more practical.

The operations defined by operation blocks can be described by words ('compute maximum temperature' or 'subtract income tax'), and the conditions in the decision blocks can be formulated in natural language ('Is temperature higher than 20°C ?' or 'Income lower than $ 10,000 ?'). Instead of using narrative descriptions, the operations and decisions can be described in symbolical form, e.g. 'N = S-T' expressing an operation 'subtract tax from salary and store result as net-salary', or 'TEMP > 20'; in this case, symbols for operands and arithmetical and logical operators between them replace description in the natural language. The narrative

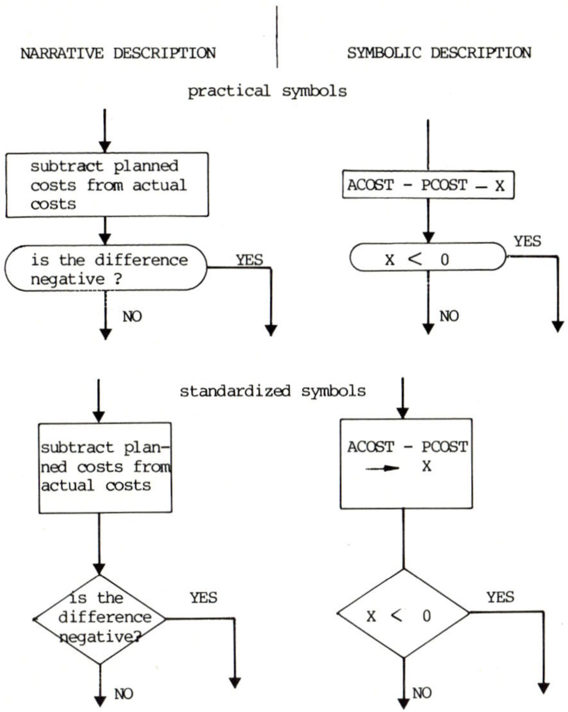

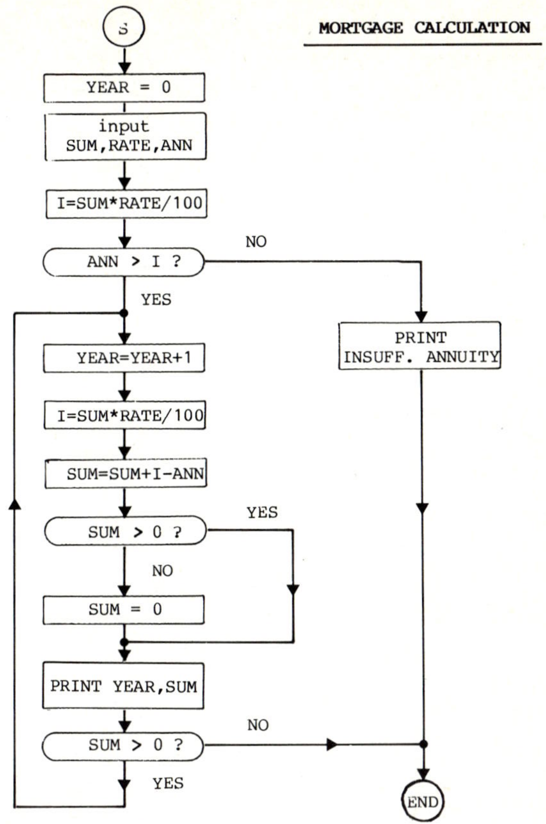

Fig. 75.4 - The basic symbolics of flowcharts

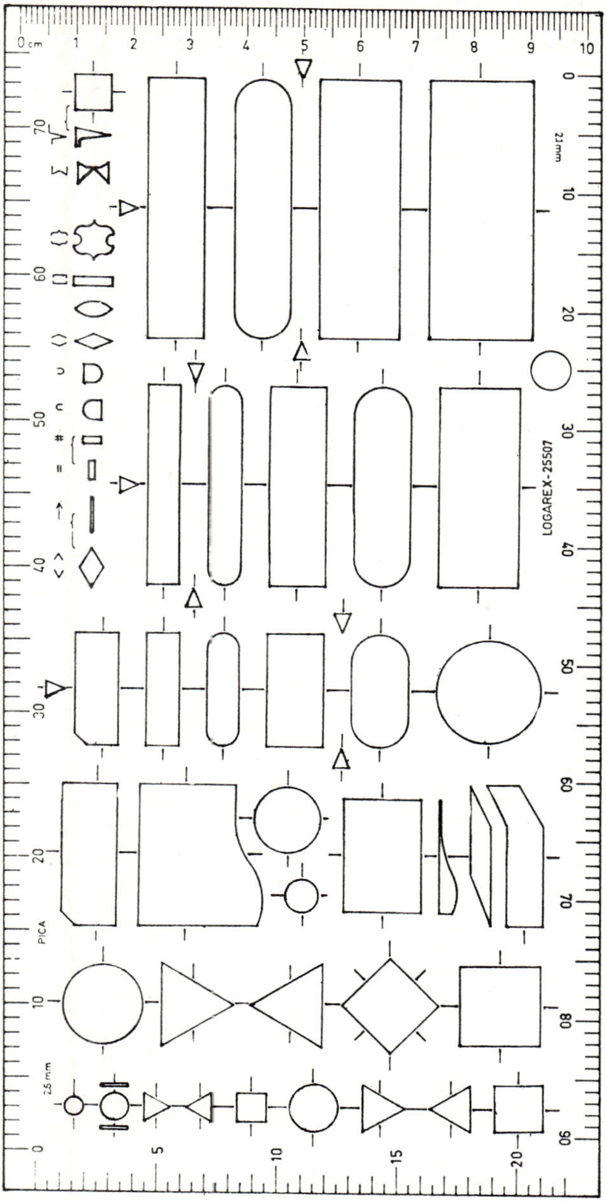

Fig. 75.5 - A universal stencil for organizational charts, Hymans diagrams and flowcharts

The lefthand column gives the symbols used in Hymans diagrams, the next column some general-purpose symbols. The righthand half of the first line contains auxiliary and mathematical symbols, the rest are symbols of flowcharts in three sizes.

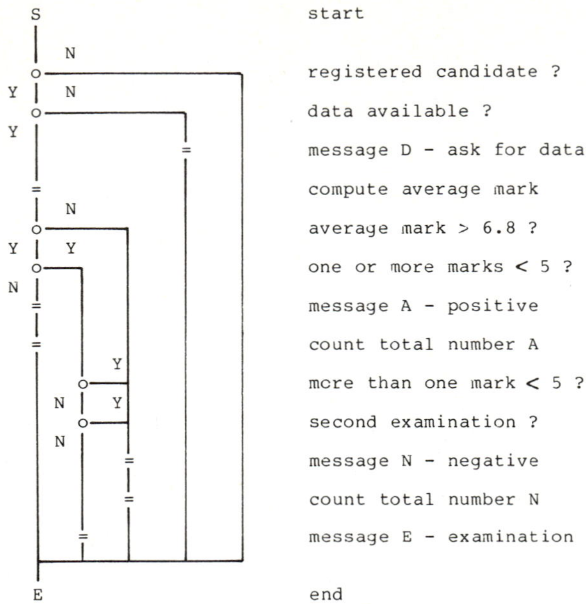

Fig. 75.6 - Simplified flowchart

form is preferred in popular presentations, the symbolic form in professional flowcharts, particularly if they are intended to be used as sources for writing a program. An explanatory list of symbolic names must be attached.

The direction of the flow of operations is symbolized by *arrows.* As additional symbols are used *connectors* of broken lines, symbols for *start* and *end* of operations, for input, output and storage media, for subroutines and other items. The 'classical' form of a flowchart such as that shown in fig. 75.4 is sometimes varied, and a simplified graphical presentation is used. One such variant in which the sequence of operations and decision points is drawn in the form of simple branching lines with textual comments in a separated column is shown in fig. 75.6.

The skill to express logical problems in the form of flowcharts (like the use of decision tables) should become part of general education, should be learnt at an early age, be a regular working instrument of every professional and not just used only when he is preparing a program for his computer.

Hymans charts

A *Hymans chart* is a special form of a flowchart. Invented by the

Belgian engineer Ernst Hymans in the twenties, it was popular in the pre-computer age as it made it easy to follow the paths and successive processing of business forms (orders, invoices, shipping and accounting documents etc.) through different departments, to indicate operations, parallel processing, transmitting of data from one form to another, etc., and to draw the whole picture of complicated document circulation and processing. Overview is improved by drawing the flow of work in a network of columns and rows; one column is usually for one sort of document, the rows represent departments, workers and operations. A system of special symbols is used to mark the various types of operations (fig. 75.7).

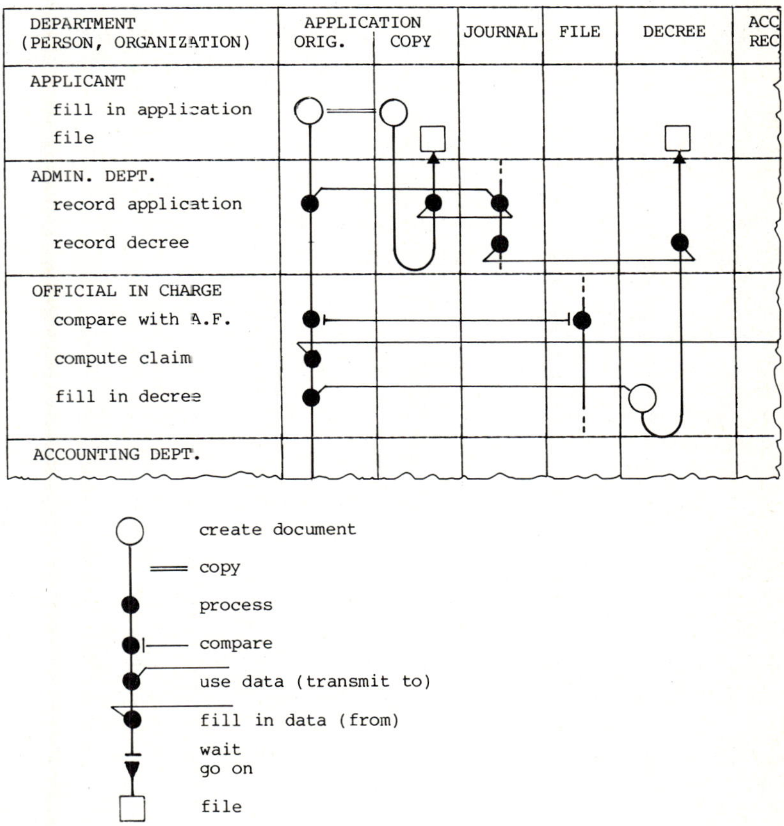

Fig. 75.7 - The symbols and principle of a Hymans diagram

Processing of documents or other information media by different subjects, and the existing interconnections are graphically presented in the Hymans diagram.

This interesting graphical method has lost its popularity in the computer age when documents no longer flow through departments and are no longer processed manually step by step. The processing is centralized, data processing is integrated, and computer programming developed its own graphical methods. Nonetheless, the Hymans charts need not be entirely forgotten; even today they can be an excellent aid in describing complex non-computerized activities in which several organization units are involved.

CPM charts

The Critical Path Method is, in principle, not a graphical method; it is a computational method that makes use of a special graphical presentation - network planning graph - as an auxiliary tool that enables an overview of the logical relations between the many various activities planned. We gave a brief description of the CPM in chapter 3 and gave some examples of network plans in graphical form in figures 33.1 and 33.2.

76 - Traditional drawing tools

For centuries, pen and paper were the principal tools used for drawing. They are still employed by many individuals, though in modernized form.

The old-fashion drawing pen has been replaced by a set of tubular pens of standardized thicknesses. For drawing graphs and charts, dimensions of 0.25, 0.35, 0.5, 0.7 and 1 mm can be recommended. Tubular pens maintain standard thickness of line without difficult adjustment, do not need to be refilled every minute, and are ready for use at any moment. A transparent ink reservoir and semi-automatic cleaning by slight shaking make them convenient to use.

It is practical to standardize the lines in graphs with regard to thickness, colour and type. This is important if we occasionally have to combine different graphs into sets for comparison, publication, demonstration, making slides etc. A standardized style makes them compatible and improves the appearance of the collection. For example, for basic lines in all graphs we use lines of 0.5 mm, for cumulative and sliding sums lines of 0.35 mm, for trend lines 0.25 mm in black & white graphs; or black for basic lines, red for cumulative and sliding sums, and green for trends. Then, even graphs produced at different times keep the same form and can be always presented as a uniform set.

There are also many different *graphical papers* with preprinted grid on the market. From standard graph paper with millimeter grid, to paper with semi- or double-logarithmic scales of various modules, to polar graph paper and special preprints. They are available in two versions: with reproducible scale (mostly in a red-brown colour) or with preprint in a light blue colour that is visible to man, but not to a camera.

These remarks may seem trivial, but practice has shown us that many professionals (with the exception of architects, designers or draughtsmen) do not know what excellent technical means (and not just those mentioned above) are available to help them improve the ease of their drawing and the appearance of the graphs, charts and schemes that are drawn. A visit to a specialist shop or a brief stay at an appropriate stand at a large special exhibition or fair, or the advice of designers and draughtsmen in a drawing office can give the professional an idea of the modern techniques available.

Stencils are very useful for drawing symbols of various types. There are many stencils on the market; a specialist will know the stencils of his profession but is often not aware of the existence of many types of stencils employed by other professions that might also be useful to him. Scanning the catalogue of a specialist manufacturer can offer valuable suggestions.

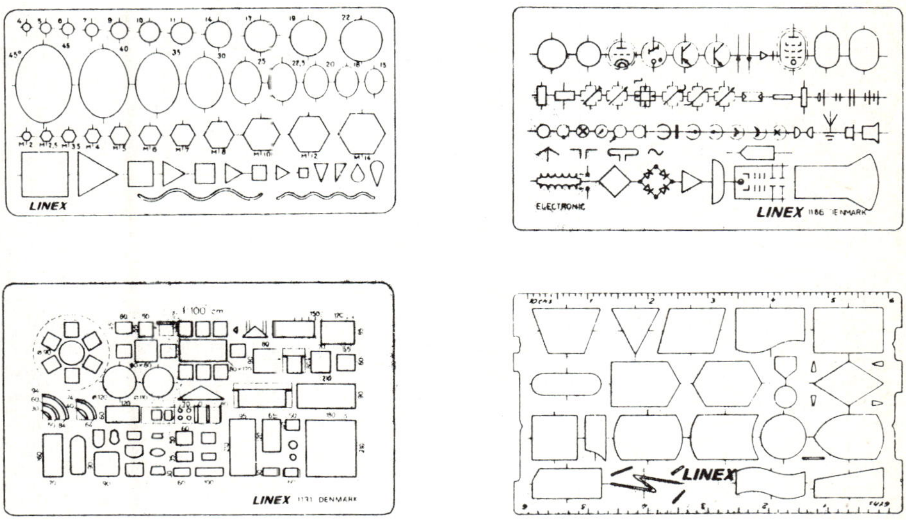

Fig. 76.1 - Examples of a few general-purpose and special stencils

There are many different stencils available both for general use (geometrical figures, common symbols, curves) and for special drawings (in the field of architecture, chemistry, electrical engineering, electronics, meteorology, programming etc.). Every professional knows 'his' own special stencils, but scanning a manufacturer's catalogue could give an idea of how to make use of other types.

Instead of drawing by means of stencils, symbols can also be stuck on the graphs, charts and schemes as *self-adhesive stickers.* A large assortment of sheets with self-adhesive letters, digits, lines, arrows, special symbols and shading is available. A small specimen is shown in fig. 76.2.

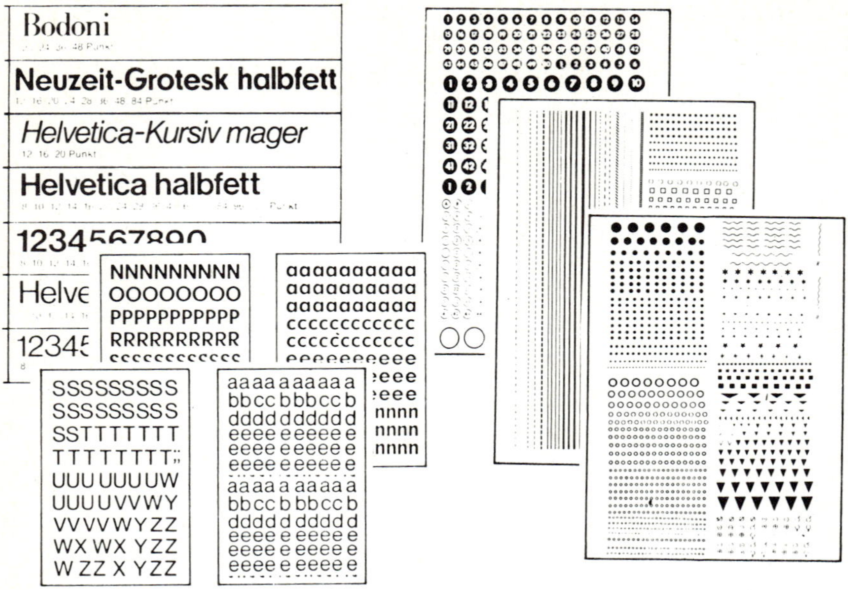

Fig. 76.2 - Self-adhesive letters, numerals, symbols, and lines

These simple and cheap devices are easy to use and they considerably improve the appearance of drawings, schemes, charts and slides. Letters and numerals are available in more than a hundred fonts (Univers, Times, Bodoni, Futura...) and types (normal, semi-bold, bold, italics...) and in many dimensions from 8 points (ca 2 mm) to 84 points (ca 24 mm) or more. Hundreds of graphical symbols and special symbols are available. Border tapes and lines in many forms are useful graphical elements in drawings, charts and schemes.

Comments (titles, text, scale, remarks etc.) can be typed onto the graphs, charts and schemes by means of a *typewriter;* a machine with variable letters (exchangeable golf-ball element, daisy wheel) or a special typewriter (for example the well known IBM composer) offers letters of various sizes and types. Some standardization is recommended also in this case. The self-adhesive letters mentioned can also be used for this purpose. Another technical means is the *lettering device* (mentioned later in section 84 - see fig. 84.5) that enables a very wide assortment of letter sizes and types to be set.

Photocopying and *reproduction techniques* help to create, edit and update graphs, charts and schemes. Not only simple reproduction but also size reduction or montage can be used effectively.

77 - Plotters and digitizers

A *plotter* - a special device for transforming digital data into drawings - is a device that has been in common use by designers and some scientists (physicists, meteorologists, geologists etc.) for many years. It has been used as a special peripheral unit of computers enabling graphs, technical drawings, maps etc. to be produced. A plotter can be programmed to produce drawings in required form and scale, and with texts and comments. Special plotters for technical drawings of mechanical parts or electronic circuits are able to produce also large-size drawings of A1 format or larger with a precision of 0.1 mm. Some plotters draw in more than one colour, employing more than one drawing pen.

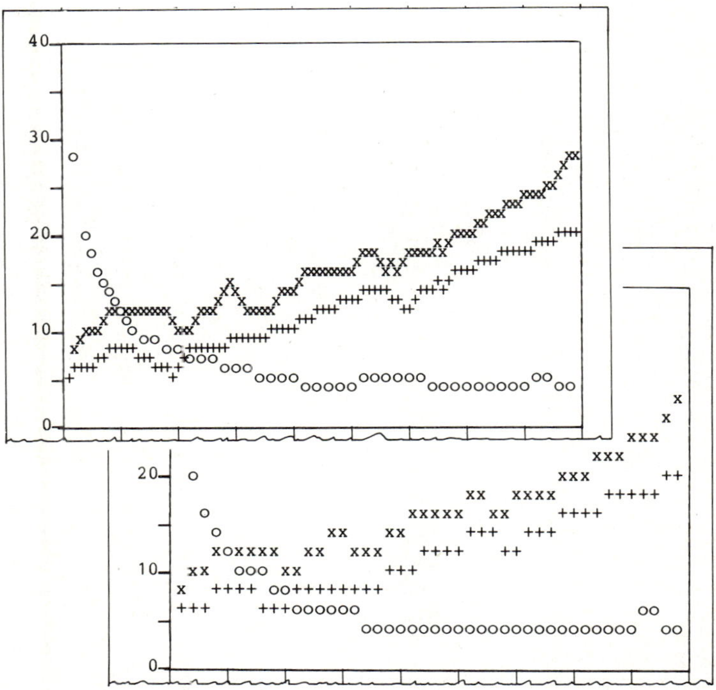

Fig. 77.1 - Data plot drawn by a printer

A standard printer may be used for drawing graphs, in this case for plotting curves. The graphs are rough, but the technique may be useful in situations where a general picture, not high precision, is required. Bottom: Standard pitch 10 and single-line spacing. Top: a high-quality printer allows half-line spacing and pitch 20.

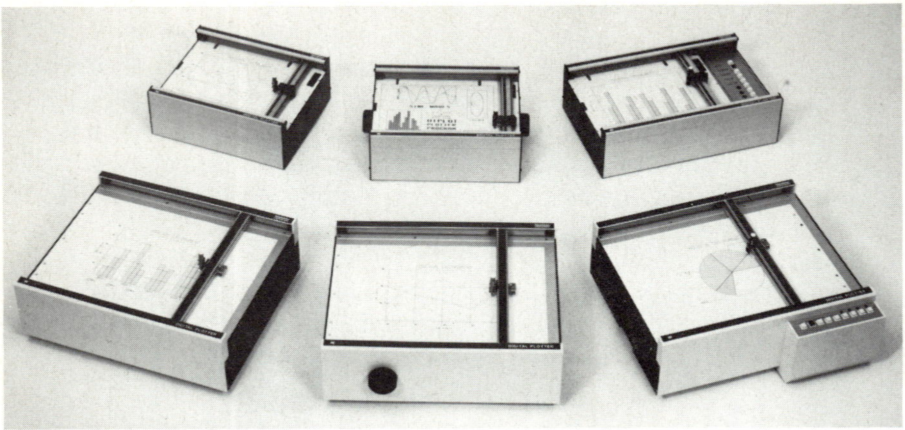

Courtesy Houston Instruments, European Office, Gistel, Belgium

Fig. 77.2 - The plotter converts digital data into a graph.

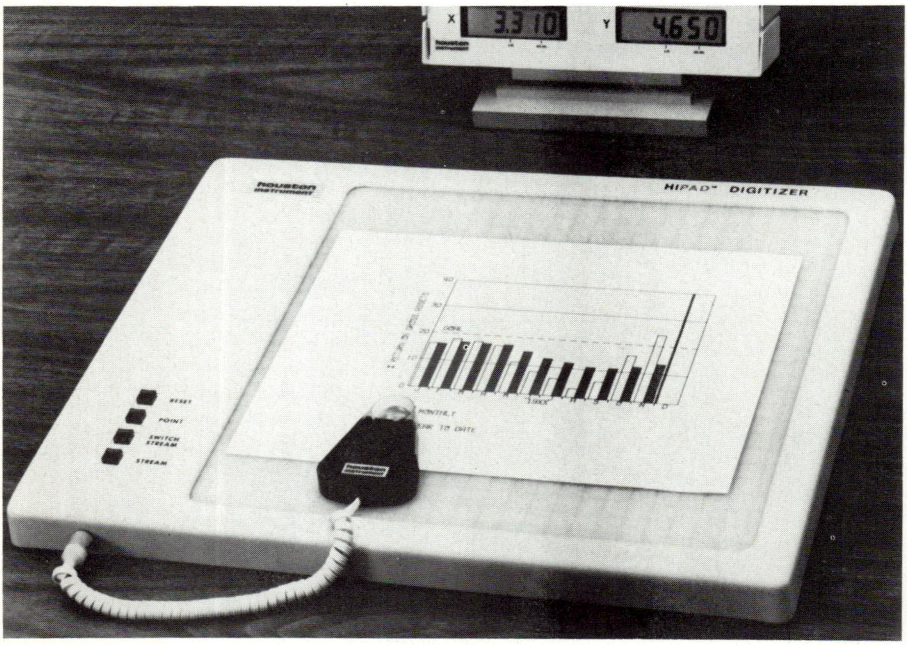

Courtesy Houston Instruments, European Office, Gistel, Belgium

Fig. 77.3 - The digitizer

The digitizer converts graphical information into digital data. A scanner moved by hand to required points of a graph records the two coordinates x and y. Both values are also displayed on an attached liquid-crystal display.

Courtesy COMPU 2000 B.V., Amsterdam

Fig. 77.4 - The 'Graphics Table' of an Apple personal computer

The 'Graphic Table' makes it possible to draw schemes, graphs or pictures on the screen. A menu enables to select the required mode (create, update, store etc.), the background colour, the colours of lines or surfaces (six colours are available: black, white, magenta, green, orange and blue) and the functions such as draw, frame, box, line, dot, window, calibrate, reduce etc. The user also can define his own menu functions. Images can be moved about on the screen and they can be scaled up and down. They are stored on a floppy disk for subsequent recall. The provided software will even calculate the area of any closed figure.

With the advent of microcomputers, plotters became available to a larger population of professionals. Some personal computers are equipped with printers that can be used as (rather modest) plotters. Plotters of higher quality are now available for reasonable prices and can be attached as special peripheral units also to personal computers (fig. 77.2).

A reverse function is performed by a *digitizer:* whilst a plotter converts numerical data into drawings, a digitizer converts analog data available in the form of a graph into digital data that can be printed out and/or processed by a computer. A digitizer consists of a small movable head that can be situated at any point on a drawing or a graph, a device that registers the coordinates of the precise positions of the head, and a microcomputer that computes both x and y coordinates in numerical form. The two values are sometimes also displayed on a small attached display unit (see fig. 77.3). Digitizer is an excellent aid for evaluating data in graphical form, e.g. curves drawn by measuring devices (records of automatic thermographs, seismograms, cardiograms etc.) for further processing. Also digitizers are now available for very reasonable prices as peripherals to personal computers.

78 - Graphical display

A *graphical display* is a powerful instrument in the hands of a professional who can now use graphical presentation in a quite new style. Within a matter of seconds it is possible to create, change, update, modify, shift, compare and analyse graphs, to evaluate curves of basic as well as of cumulative data, to calculate and display trends of development, to compute correlations, etc. It is possible to observe complicated data from many different points of view, and to analyse their development, interrelations and structure. A knowledge of graphical methods and the skill to use a graphical display in an interactive way should now be a task of general education and a valuable tool for use by every manager, scientist, technician or researcher.

Hardware requirements

The potential of a graphical display is influenced basically by the format, resolution and availability of colour. The *format* requirements are similar to those in the case of word processing: the full A4 format (at least) is also badly needed for a graphical display.

It is, of course, possible and often necessary to use scrolling in both the horizontal and the vertical directions to create a drawing larger than the limited screen capacity, but this makes the job more difficult, as one can at any time see only a part of the drawing through a 'window', and one has to shift it constantly to the right and left and up and down; also the crucial advantage of graphical presentation - fast overview - is then destroyed. Graphs limited to a small-capacity screen cannot be detailed enough, it is difficult to display more than one curve at a time and it is not easy to attach scales, titles,comments and other descriptive data. Future developments will surely bring about enlarged screen dimensions.

The *resolution* of the screen is another important factor. For drawing simple graphs (the primitive bar charts) in which only horizontal and vertical lines are needed, a standard screen can also be used. It is able to display crude figures. A resolution of about 1000 × 1000 points is needed for all applications in which line graphs (requiring drawing lines in all directions) and other charts or schemes are to be drawn in a reasonable

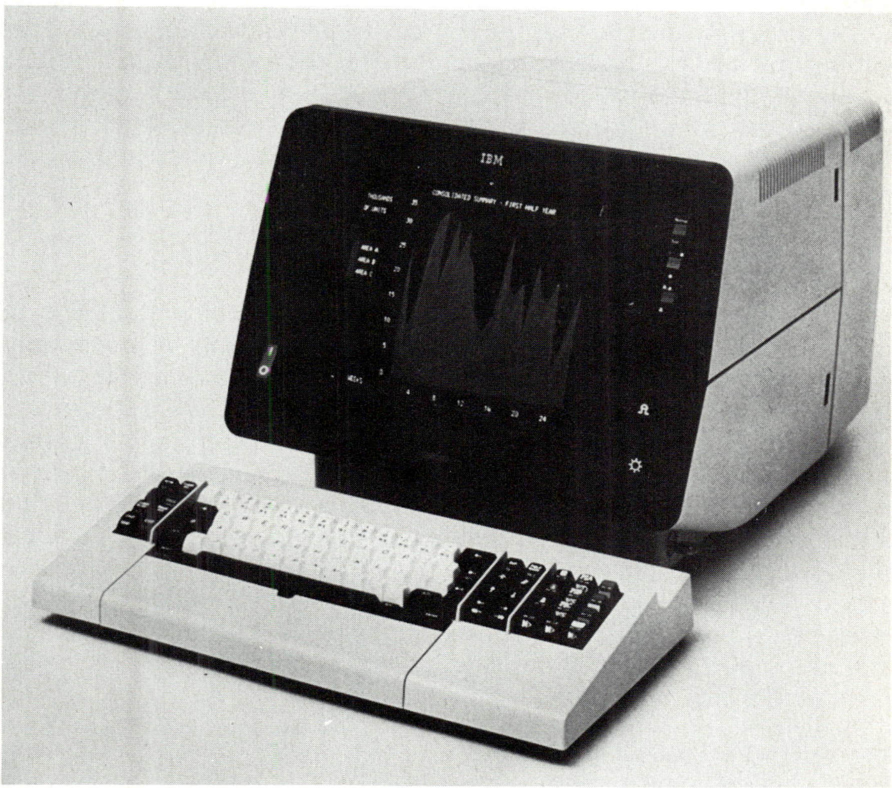

Courtesy IBM Nederland, Zoetemeer, The Netherlands

Fig. 78.1 - Graphical colour display IBM 3279

quality; on a screen of typical dimensions this resolution is equal to about 0.3 mm.

Colours are also essential as they increase the power of discrimination and the informational value of the graphical presentation. They make it possible to distinguish and to compare different curves and figures. Four to seven colours are typically available in colour displays. Four of them are recommended as the main colours (preferably white, green, yellow and cyan as the most easily legible); the others (usually blue, magenta and red) should be used cautiously as auxiliary colours for comments etc. (see also the remarks on the use of colours in section 48). We also mentioned above that the use of colours in graphs should be standardized.

Another interesting hardware feature in advanced systems is the possibility of calling up *special symbols* and placing them in any position in a drawing. In plots, simple symbols such as points, circles (solid or open, of any size), triangles, asterisks, crosses etc. help to distinguish various points; in special graphs (Hymans charts, flowcharts etc.), other symbols are needed: symbols of operations, connectors, start and end marks etc. In technical drawings, large sets of special symbols are necessary (say, in electronics the symbols for transistors, resistors, diodes; the special symbols for meteorology, architecture etc.). Such symbols can best be recalled by means of the *virtual keyboard.*

Software requirements and system friendliness

Easy commanding of a graphical display is essential for every user, in particular for a beginner or for an occasional user. Simply, all commands can be given by means of the *keyboard.* The coordinates of the points, straight lines and curves must be defined, the coordinates of the beginning and end points of a line and its type have to be typed-in before the line can be created and displayed; similarly the coordinates of the central point, type of the figure (circle) and the diameter must be given before a drawing of a circle appears on the screen. In some systems the cursor is employed to define the respective points. Finally, a *light pen* can be used in some machines to define manually on the surface of the screen the respective points, or a special writing pad is attached. Intelligent terminals have special commands or command keys for enlarging, reducing, shifting or rotating a drawing or part(s) of it.

In the future, *voice commands* will also make some operations easier - indeed, it is annoying to have to use hands to give simple repetitive commands again and again. The vision of a man sitting in his easy chair, commanding his terminal by voice and observing the drawing on a large projection screen on the wall, as he creatively changes and edits it, is no longer in the realms of phantasy. Nonetheless, a combination of a few frequently occurring types of commands given by voice and other commands given in the traditional manner, via the keyboard, drawing pad or light pen, is a realistic vision for the next few years.

Not only must the command technique be easy (keyboard, light pen, voice), but the *command language* must also be simple and friendly so as to make graphical display accessible to everyone and for any purpose. An easy-to-use conversational system (this is present in a few modern systems) will generally be preferred.

Such a system helps graphical figures to be drawn in a number of query/answer steps. The system prompts the user to take his decisions and helps him define his wishes; the creation of a graph is then initiated in the form of a controlled dialogue such as Query: 'What type of graph ?' Answer: 'Gantt', Q: 'How many time units ?' A: '12', Q: 'How many activities ?' A: '20', Q: 'Scale ?' etc., or in the form of a menu-driven dialogue, or the filling in of a displayed table. Of course, a good system will also offer a fast conversation in 'telegraphese' that will be preferred by more experienced users who find an inquiry/answer or a menu-driven system too tedious.

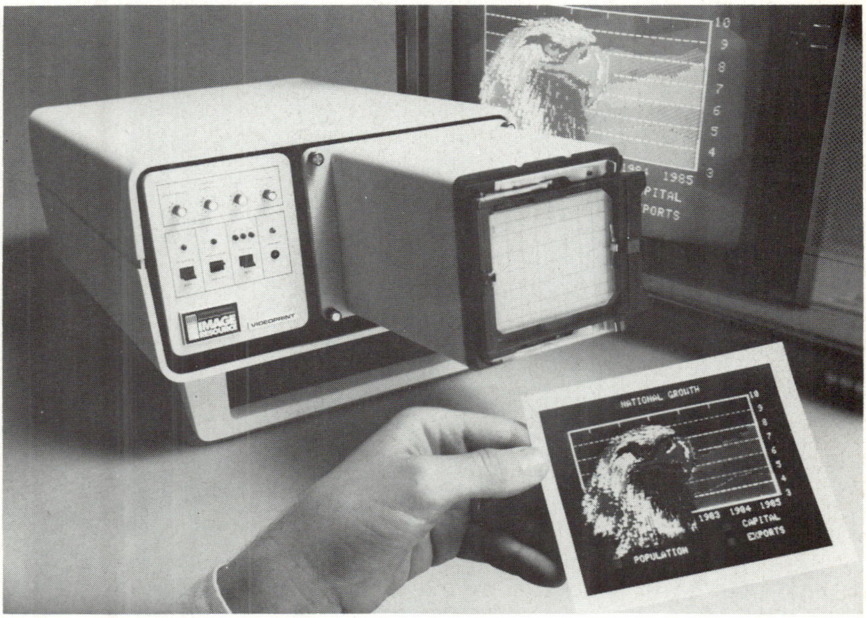

Courtesy Image Resource Corp., Westlake Village, CA, USA

Fig. 78.2 - Computer graphics can be converted to colour photo or slides

The 'Videoprint' technique produces distortion-free line and continuous tone hardcopy from raster line computer graphics display. It eliminates such off-the-screen photography problems as barrel distortion or loss of colour fidelity. The prints are instantly produced with Polaroid SX-70 or Polacolor 4" × 5" films as well as with conventional colour negative on 35 mm slide transparency film.

Hardcopy output

If the image created on the display is to be produced in the form of a hardcopy, then either the plotter or a dot-matrix printer with sufficient resolution must be used as the output unit, or the image photographed from the screen. Some graphical terminals contain a built-in unit for *hard-copy output;* some of them are even able to produce colour slides for a slide or overhead projector (fig. 78.2). They offer a new opportunity to create one's own slides for lectures and demonstrations in a creative way.

A simple technique of making hardcopies of graphical output is to take a photographic picture from the screen. Any amateur photographer can take pictures from the screen of his personal computer (see fig. 78.3). It

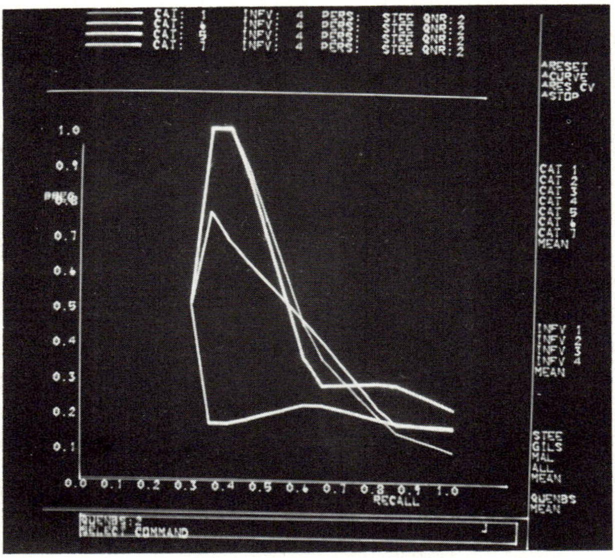

Fig. 78.3 - Graphical output photographed from the screen

The picture was taken by an instant Polaroid camera from the screen of a graphical terminal. This figure also serves to illustrate the flexible use of a graphical display. In the case shown, the performance of specific retrieval strategies was measured by a number of controlled experiments involving 30 inquiries, three inquirers, four ranking formulae and seven parts of text of patents, or combinations of these factors. In total, 1580 retrieval runs were processed and the detailed results stored on disk. The analyst used the graphical display to select by means of a light pen any variant (inquiry / inquirer / data base / formula, or summary data for all inquiries, all inquirers etc.) and to see the curve of recall/precision; up to four curves were displayed simultaneously to permit comparison of selected search strategies. Important variants were photographed [ref. 70-Gerzon].

is the cheapest form of recording graphical output - without a plotter or special equipment. The most suitable is an automatic single-lens reflex camera, or a Polaroid camera.

From a simple graphical display to the work station of the future

Many existing personal computers also offer graphical display, but in many of them this is only in a modest form (one colour, low resolution, primitive graphs, arduous commands). On the other hand, there are in existence intelligent graphical terminals that produce every required variant of graphical output. They are used intensively by specialists (designers, engineers, scientists in special fields). However, such special equipment is rather expensive for use by a professional for whom graphical presentation remains at the fringe of his activities and who would use his graphical display only for a fraction of his working time and for simple drawings. For these persons the solution is the integration of graphical presentation into his standard hardware and software: in the universal work station high resolution display, use of colours, advanced software and friendly conversational design of graphs, charts and schemes will be a subset of its functions. This will bring about a new age of graphical presentation: designing and editing of graphs in a creative style will become a tool in daily use by any professional. It will then also be possible to employ in new dimensions and new forms the old ideas of the pioneers of graphical methods in planning, control and management - the industrial engineers and economists like Brinton, Gantt, Burton, Nordsieck, Žlábek, Hymans, Sankey and others. We should make intelligent use of graphical methods, develop them into new forms, employ them creatively and never again have resort to primitive bar and pie charts.

8 - COMMUNICATION

The explosive growth of *communications* in many forms and over any distance by means of various technical devices is one of the signs of the time. The volume of messages sent by the traditional communication techniques - post, telex, and telephone - has expanded enormously, and a wide spectrum of new communication media is appearing. Videophone combines voice and image transmission, facsimile transmits copies of documents including drawings and figures, online systems make vast information resources accessible from many places, teletext distributes limited information by means of slightly adapted television sets, viewdata enables the required information to be selected from large files via an adapted television set and telephone, teletex is a new means of fast communication between many stations that can receive and store messages even when the addressee is absent, and computer conferencing enables communication in both written and spoken form between two or more persons.

Undoubtedly, the various forms and techniques of communication will be in competition. For a long time, the traditional and new techniques will operate in parallel, and the user will show a preference for one or other depending on the type and volume of information, the required speed of delivery, the quality and reliability of transmission, the distance, the need for two-way communication, the need for written form, and the price. As ever in the history of technology, not only the technical and economical parameters, but also certain imponderable factors will be decisive.

The convergence of telecommunication techniques with data processing techniques is offering new opportunities, as it enables us to combine transmitting and storing and processing of information in the form of voice, text, data or image, or in all these forms simultaneously.

81 - The traditional means of communication

The wonderful prospects offered by the new techniques of communication must not restrict human relations, replace personal contacts or prevent us from making effective use of the traditional means.

The remains of human and personalized contact that are still found in business letters and in the majority of telephone calls (greetings, a few friendly words, some personal questions and answers) will probably disappear with the use of electronic mail - it will be more like a telegram than a letter - or electronic conferencing. This mass communication in a cold, rigid, dehumanized form will have to be deliberately compensated for by more personal contacts, where possible of an informal nature. Working at home will underscore the necessity. One recent study [ref. 80-The new office look] revealed that about half the time taken up by telephone calls is spent on greetings, courtesies and informal dialogue; a substantial cost factor, indeed, but is it always really time lost ? Similarly, someone once compared a photocopying machine standing in a hall or corridor and used by everybody in a do-it-yourself manner, to a water fountain in ancient cities. It is a place of chance meetings, a place to have a chat and maintain contacts. Again, a loss in terms of time and money - but is it really always time lost when looked at from the point of view of the work climate and human relations in a large organization ?

Attracted by the prospects of the new means of communication, we should also not forget to rationalize the traditional techniques that continue to play a significant role in the next few decades.

Much has been published on preparing discussions, meetings, and the rationalization of correspondence or telephone calls. Careful preparation for a discussion, meeting, consultation or an important telephone call, i.e. defining the points of a speech, gathering together all necessary documents, making short notes, focussing the discussion on important points, summarizing the decisions and conclusions - all these are old principles, well explained and recommended in the literature but often ignored in practice. How can we expect the rational use of advanced means of communication from someone who is not in the habit of having paper and pencil by the side of his telephone (not to mention a dictating machine on stand-by) ?

Correspondence in the traditional letter form can now be substantially rationalized by intelligent use of a *word processor*, as mentioned in chapter 5. Modular letters, semi-automatic addresssing, or writing individualized letters consisting of a common body and variable parts of text, are new methods that can be employed by everyone in his professional as well as private correspondence.

Photocopying equipment can also be effectively used in less formal written contacts (in internal memos, in correspondence between peers and colleagues): instead of sending a letter in reply, a copy of the letter received with short answers and notes in telegraphese often saves time and effort.

Interphone is a well known device for voice communication over short distances, mostly between the boss and his secretary or among the members of a team or department (fig. 81.1). However, interphones are also practical for use in a private house. There are relatively cheap but high-quality devices on the market that make it possible to communicate, say, between the workroom, hobby room, garage and the living room. 'Wireless' devices are the most advantageous; strictly speaking, they are

Courtesy Philips Data Systems, Apeldoorn, The Netherlands

Fig. 81.1 - Intercom for easy voice communication

A space microphone and loudspeaker make it possible to speak and listen at a distance and with hands free. It is used for fast contact between the boss and secretary or between the members of a team, also during a telephone call with other people.

not wireless, they just send their signal via the normal electric network so that they can be plugged-in at any place in the house via any socket in the mains power supply (fig. 81.2).

Courtesy Tandy Corp., Amsterdam

Fig. 81.2 - An inexpensive intercom can also be used at home

This apparatus operates on two separate frequency channels via existing electric AC power lines over a distance of up to one kilometer as long as the AC line is connected to the same side of the power distribution transformer. The apparatus is simply plugged-in in the nearest AC power socket in the house. Intercommunication is possible between the work room, living room, garage, hobby room or kitchen.

82 - Facsimile, teletex and electronic mail

Facsimile alias *fax* - transmission of figures by telecommunication means - is no new invention. As long ago as 1924 a picture was transmitted from Cleveland to New York and printed in the New York Times. Today, in a modernized version, it is becoming a widely used means of communication. It enables a copy of an original document (text including signatures, drawings, statistical tables, pictures) to be sent by telephone line or by wireless communication, even by satellite. Either public services offered by the PTT, or private connections can be used.

Since June 1980, about 600 post offices in West Germany (including West-Berlin) have been equipped with compatible facsimile machines transmitting a text or drawing of A4 format in about 3 minutes to any other office. This service - which at present costs DM 10 for the first page and DM 4 for any following page - fills a gap between the telegram or telex and the express-letter. The message is delivered by a special messenger on the day of dispatch. The owner of a facsimile apparatus can receive the message from his post office at a lower price and without delay. Similarly, the US postal service Intelpost (International Electronic Post) provides such a service on an international scale (from the USA to Argentina, Belgium, Canada, France, Germany, Holland, Switzerland and United Kingdom) by means of digital facsimile using land lines and satellite communication across the ocean, promising same-day or next-day service to the customers, mainly banks, government agencies, multinationals, legal firms and businessmen. It is mostly signed documents, legal documents, statistical tables and graphs or drawings that are transmitted. The price is at present about $ 5 per page.

There are now also on the market relatively cheap devices of the size of a portable typewriter that can be connected to any telephone apparatus (without special connectors, simply by inserting the microtelephone into

Courtesy Olympia Kantoormachine Import B.V., Den Haag, The Netherlands

Fig. 82.1 - The facsimile ('fax') transmits an A4-format letter or drawing via any standard telephone

the right position in the machine) and can send an original of A4 format over any distance.

Teletex (not to be confused with Teletext - a one-way information service via an adapted television set) could be called a 'second generation telex'. Using the existing telephone network, it transmits text but, in contrast to traditional telex, the transmission is performed from the memory of one station to the memory of another station. This enormously improves the transmission speed which is no longer limited by the slow mechanical parts of the sending and printing mechanisms; another advantage is the fact that the user of a teletex terminal is not hampered by the incoming messages. A further essential improvement is the full typewriter character set (both lower and upper case) and the traditional format (A4) and layout of the messages. Another advantage is the fact that it offers direct communication from workplace to workplace. While a telex is a specialized machine installed usually in a telex department,

Courtesy Philips Data Systems, Apeldoorn, The Netherlands

Fig. 82.2 - The teletex terminal

The Philips teletex P-5900 has both a word processing function and a communication function. It can be connected to a public telex network.

teletex can be decentralized: a word processor or personal computer can serve as teletex stations at any workplace in the company.

Teletex is about 40 times faster than telex. While the telex transmission of one A4 page containing 1500 characters requires about 3 minutes, by teletex it is transmitted within 10 seconds; this means an essential saving of time and costs.

Transmitting of written messages from workplace to workplace within an organization or to external addressees is generally called *electronic mail.* A station for electronic mail may be a terminal, personal computer, word processor or universal work station of the future, i.e. technical means that are multifunctional and that are not employed only for sending messages. Connection within an organization is accomplished by means of an in-house network and controlled by a computer or special switching exchange (fig. 82.3). Messages can be sent to one addressee, to a group of addressees, or to all stations ('electronic circular'); received messages are temporarily stored in a memory performing the function of an 'electronic post box', and are presented to the addressee (displayed or printed out) at the moment he wishes to accept them. After reading the message, the addressee can either delete it from the temporary file, or store it in his own file.

Each message is automatically dated and timed (date, hour, minute, second), it is identified by automatic recording of the sending and receiving station, and other data can be automatically added (e.g.

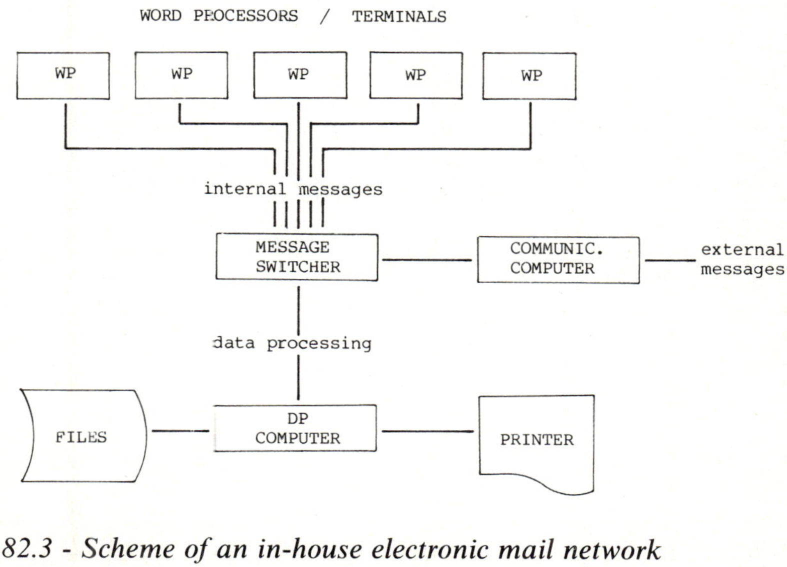

Fig. 82.3 - Scheme of an in-house electronic mail network

department, name of the sender), while still others can be attached by the sender (urgency code, security code, classification or indexing, sender's identification code replacing signature etc.).

Properties and advantages of electronic mail

The basic advantages can be summarized as four points: the availability at any workplace, the full character set, the temporary storage of messages and, finally, the recording of the messages in machine language.

Many people think of electronic mail in terms of the traditional post. They see it simply as the replacement for a letter, that is typed and then transmitted by wire instead of physical transport and delivery by a postman. In this case the fast delivery is assumed to be the main or perhaps the only advantage. However, the other features of electronic mail mentioned are at least as important.

The advantage of easy accessibility is self-evident. The path from sender to receiver can be direct without intermediaries and without loss of time. The advantage of a technique that is similar to traditional typewriting is obvious. What is more interesting and new is the sending of a message into a temporary storage of the receiving station, from where, as stated above, it can be called up at any moment by the addressee. Electronic mail is - like traditional mail, and in contrast to the telephone - *asynchronous means of communication.* It combines the (increased) quickness of the telex and telephone with the advantage of traditional mail: the received message need not be accepted immediately, and the simultaneous presence of both sender and receiver is not required. The 'electronic post box' compensates for any time disparity.

In reality, it is difficult to reach a busy person by telephone. Statistics reveal that about 25% of telephone conversations in a large company are achieved at the first attempt (in military terminology, the FRHP - 'first-round-hit-probability' is about 0.25). The head of the Philips internal telephone service estimates that about 50% of telephone attempts are unsuccessful because the line is engaged or there is no answer; in the remaining 50% of cases the call is answered, but the required person is not always present. However, we all know without statistical analyses how many times we may have to try to call a person and to leave a message asking him to call back, then to wait, try again etc. Variable working hours, so advantageous in other respects, make the communication more difficult than ever. Our present style of work is deeply disturbed by telephone calls that occur randomly throughout the day and split working time into short slices of a few minutes (remember Mintzberg's data mentioned in section 37 which indicate that a manager was able to work for 30 minutes or longer without interruption only once in two days).

Electronic mail is one of the most important instruments capable of improving our work style. It makes it possible to send any message at any moment regardless of whether the addressee is present or not; we do not need to remember to call him later, or try again and again. We can read incoming messages at the moment we find most convenient, e.g. once in the morning, then before the lunch break, then in the afternoon, and finally before the end of the working day. We read them all in one batch, send our replies and can then concentrate on our work again without being disturbed by the telephone ringing every few minutes. Another significant advantage of electronic mail is the fact that all the operations are done *in one place*, by means of one device, and in one operation.

When writing a letter or internal memo, we must first find a letter head, type the message on a typewriter, correct it, sign it, go to the photocopying machine to make a copy, wait if it is busy, then find an envelope, address it, go to the internal mail box, then punch holes in our copy, and store it in the file. Many operations to be performed at many, sometimes distant, places ! An electronic message is typed, corrected, addressed, sent, copied and stored in one operation and in one place.

Another essential difference between electronic mail and the traditional letter is its *conciseness*. Though it is certainly technically possible to write and send a wordy message in the traditional letter style, most users will probably prefer short messages. Electronic mail will resemble a

traditional correspondence	telegraphese
out of the question	impossible
up to the present	hitherto
by the end of October at the latest	31.10. latest
meeting will be held on the 15th November at 2 p.m.	meeting begins 15 Nov 14h
with reference to your letter of 23rd November	your letter 23/11
the conference cannot be postponed any further	any postponement impossible
delivery within 14 days	fortnight delivery
please advise us by cable when you expect delivery of the order X1234	cable date dispatch X1234
type A987 ordered by you is unfortunately not in full quantity on stock	ordered A987 not fully stocked

Fig. 82.4 - Examples of telegraphese

Over the years enormous practical experience has been gathered on how to avoid wordy messages in telegrams and cables. We can learn a lot from the rich literature on this subject; our examples are taken from D. Závada's New Commercial Dictionary [ref. 82]. Electronic mail will certainly find its own style and form.

telegram more than a letter. This will change our style of communication: what would be unacceptable in a letter (rigid, concise wording in telegraphese without polite initial and closing phrases and greetings) might become standard in electronic mail. Of course: while most traditional correspondence is typed by a secretary or typist from the dictation or notes of her boss, many of the electronic messages will be sent directly by the professionals themselves; typing is slower and more tiresome than speaking. Conciseness is the result.

We can learn much from the long experience gained with telegrams and cable messages. High fees per word, particularly in overseas communication, led to the creation of a special concise style, and to the use of cable codes. It will be practical to read something about the basic rules of styling telegrams and cables - a few typical examples of the compression of the natural language are presented in fig. 82.4. The tendency to conciseness can also have a negative influence on our style: oversimplification of style and grammar can bring about some linguistic distortions - such terrible words as 'interestinger' instead of 'more interesting' or 'difficultest' instead of 'most difficult' are sometimes encountered in cable messages.

Finally, one significant property of electronic mail is the fact that an incoming message is received and stored in the *machine language.* This does not matter in the case of ephemeral messages, but is essential if we decide to store the message or to submit it for further processing: electronic mail allows us to use the incoming messages directly and without re-typing as input to our personal documentation or to copy them into other messages or documents.

Until now the main problem of correspondence storage in computerized retrieval systems was the fact that incoming letters in typed form had to be re-typed in full or in the form of abstracts, the necessary formal and descriptive items had to be added (date, sender, form, subject, security code, classifiers...) before they could be used as input to the system. Electronic mail solves this problem: the incoming message can be directly transferred into a personal information storage and retrieval system without re-typing.

Organizational problems of electronic mail

There will be no problem with the ephemeral type of message that simply replaces telephone calls, and which neither the addressee nor the sender considers worth committing to storage. Their content, language, style and structure will be informal and free.

All other messages, which replace traditional correspondence and which the sender as well as the addressee must store, should be formalized and standardized; otherwise the procedure for their storage and retrieval would be arduous. The messages must be *structured* so that the system is able to recognize data elements such as date, sender, addressee, document number, subject etc.; the types and identification of data elements must be defined, and their content standardized. Internal *standardization*, and in the case of electronic mail between companies and organizations, national and international standards are badly needed; standardization makes the interchange of messages effective, as it makes it possible to accept messages from various senders and to store them in a common file without mechanical re-formatting or difficult manual coding and editing. An intelligent system can support the user in meeting the standards: it will prompt him to type in all the respective data in the right sequence, it will check for their completeness and formal consistency, and re-arrange them into the standard form even if the user has not followed the rules quite precisely (see fig. 14.3). Moreover, the system can fill in some data automatically (we mentioned automatic dating and timing of messages, automatic identification of sender etc.). An example of a message structure is given in fig. 82.5.

For retrieval purposes and for cross-referencing, every message must also contain its *unique identification.* It can be attached semi-automatically by an intelligent terminal of the sender as well as of the receiver (the receiver usually uses his own numbering of incoming messages).

tag (abbreviated name of the field)
content

tag	content	(comment)
NOS:	OM/AC/4234	sender's message number
STS:	54-11-02	sender's station
SEN:	**Gerzon, F.**	sender's name
DAT:	81-10-07 / 10,24	date and time
STA:	**41-61-07**	addressee's station
ADD:	**CSM dept, Mr. O. Holla**	addressee
MES:	**CSM/HA/1097**	your message number
SUB:	**ACRIM classification**	subject
TEX:	**We agree with the proposal (your report CRM-18 p. 14-18) except classes 4/5; we urgently recommend an adapted version of the structure according to standard CSD-1476-15 .**	

Fig. 82.5 - Example of the message structure

With the exception of ephemeral messages that replace telephone calls and are not filed, all messages in the electronic mail must be structured. Structuring increases uniformity and legibility, and it is necessary for mechanized storage and retrieval. Numbers, codes and formal rules for identification of departments, persons, stations, dates, subjects etc. will be standardized. Intelligent programs will help the user to cope with the standards; they will automatically fill in some of the data (station number, date, time), prompt the data key-typed by the user, screen them and transform them into standardized form even when the user has not followed the strict rules of the valid standards. Only the bold typed data are filled in by the user; the rest is displayed or filled in automatically by the system.

No great problems will occur in connection with descriptive and identification data such as calendar date, sender, type of message, urgency code, security code, addressee etc.; this is simply a task of standardization. Serious problems can be expected regarding the *classification* and *indexing* of the outgoing and incoming electronic mail. Until now most professionals have kept their own correspondence files and maintained their own system of classification or indexing. We cannot expect a standardized classification and indexing system to be introduced parallel with the advent of electronic mail; experiences with uniform systems of correspondence classification are discouraging (except for the specialized mono-thematic files in banks, insurance companies etc., stored in centralized archives); the points of view of sender and receiver differ, and individual criteria are pertinent for the storage and retrieval of correspondence. Identification of the subject of a letter is a commonly used practice. The field 'subject' in electronic mail is therefore nothing new; it must be used more consistently, and the subject description must be more strictly standardized.

In the transitional period when a part of the correspondence will arrive in the traditional paper form and the other as electronic mail, undesirable problems will occur: then, both physical and computer files will exist in parallel, or pointers to the letters (or their microfilm images) will be needed in the computer file; this would require troublesome input.

All in all, electronic mail - one of the most essential components of the office of the future - will change the style, rhythm, organization and efficiency of our daily work.

83 - Meetings and conferences

Managers have been estimated to spend between 20% and 40% of their total working time in meetings. Other professionals also have to attend work meetings and brainstormings; visits to lectures, conferences, congresses etc. are an important component of their work.

It is not the task of this book to describe the general rules of organization, preparation and management of meetings and conferences [ref. 83-Nadler, Lawry]; the following remarks concern only the questions of using technical means. Some have been discussed in the preceding chapters: for example, a word processor or terminal can be employed as an effective help in the many various phases of preparation and organization of a meeting (typing, editing and distribution of announcements and programs, mechanized compiling of lists of participants). These techniques are well known but are rarely used. Even at international congresses in the fields of computer science or information science one is given merely a plain alphabetical list of participants, sometimes sorted by country, but no overview regarding the affiliations or fields of interest of those attending. A rich index (that is now so easily available) could indirectly improve informal contacts among the participants.

The conference rooms

Special rooms regularly used for congresses and conferences are always well equipped with all technical features such as illumination, dimming and darkening controllable from the speaker's desk, sound and recording equipment, interpreters' booths and portable wireless receivers, projection facilities of all types (overhead projection, slide and film projection, closed circuit television, sometimes also television monitors for smaller groups of participants). However, the same attention should be devoted to the rooms used for meetings and lectures in companies and organizations. In most cases, these contain only simple equipment such as furniture, blackboard, projection screen and an overhead projector, and the environment is not always suitable for presentations (problems with darkening, not the best visibility of the screen etc.). Development is tending towards more comfortably equipped lecture rooms and special *decision rooms* ('strategic rooms') for the top management.

Indeed, the time for a radical change in the *technique of meetings* in which important decisions are taken has arrived. The general picture of a group sitting and discussing around a table filled with papers and files is a thing of the past. Modern techniques can support effective discussing and decision taking in many ways. In particular, it must be easily possible during the meeting to find and display any required information in the most suitable form (as data, figures or graphs and schemes); not only prepared information, but also additional information (documents, technical, statistical or factographical data) according to ad hoc requirements that emerge during the discussion must be available in seconds and presented to all participants. The data and graphs should then be able to be used in a dynamic manner: on-the-spot calculations of variants, estimates of probable impacts of possible actions should be computable in real time and without delay. Then, analyses of results, prognoses, modelling, calculations, evaluation of variants of actions can be performed during a meeting, arguments can be supported by documents, data and graphs retrieved and presented when they are needed.

Of course, the chairman cannot be expected to handle a terminal during the meeting - he or other participants will probably express their wishes for data, graphs or computation in an informal manner and either the secretary or an intermediary in his special booth (similar to the interpreter's booth) will arrange to retrieve the required information from in-house or external databases, complete and format it (say, the comparison of technical parameters of products X and Y in graphical form), and display it in the 'strategic room'. Also every participant should be able to contact his own secretariat and ask them to find certain specific information illustrating or supporting his arguments, to send it to his screen or to display it on the large screen or the monitors of all participants. The presented information, the discussions and decisions taken can be then automatically recorded in the combined form of data, graphs and voice information.

There is available at the moment little practical experience and advice on how to design and use a modern 'strategic room' - except for military purposes, and in this field only fragmentary information is published from time to time about the communications used and the large screens on which instant information, data, maps, schemes and satellite photographs on a variable scale can be projected. Indeed, the military were always (and have had to be) progressive in this field: remember Eisenhower's room equipped with microphones enabling every discussion, even an informal one, to be recorded and a written record to be available immediately at the end of it [ref. 83-Eisenhower], or the visual aids in the form of planning boards or large maps with actual and 'online' (manually) adjusted positions of ships and aircraft formations during World War II. Modern technical means enable any large company to have at its disposal the presentation of information, fast retrieval of any fact or data, instant computations, comparisons and evaluations, and creative graphical methods.

Teleconferencing and videoconferencing

In contrast to the meetings in the perfectly equipped 'strategic rooms', where personal presence is essential, there is an opposite variant: conferencing via telecommunication means without personal presence of the participants. Simultaneous connection of several telephone subscribers is easy and it has in fact been used for *telephone conferencing* for many years.

Very little is needed to achieve telephone conferencing: arrangement of a simultaneous connection according to the rules of the PTT, and some organization skill, experience plus self-discipline on the part of the chairman and the participants: the chairman has to open the conference, he has to call up all the participants who then acknowledge their presence (this is also important for the identification of voices), the chairman should announce the points of discussion, introduce the discussion, and everybody who wishes to say something must ask for the word, every time he begins to speak he should give his name (except for small meetings of people who easily recognize the voices of their colleagues), and the conclusions should be formulated by the chairman.

The lack of personal contact can be compensated to some extent, and limited visual information can be transmitted (simple drawings and schemes displayed) if a *videotelephone* is employed instead of the normal telephone.

Computer conferencing

Whilst in the case of a meeting or of telephone conferencing the main form of communication is the spoken word, in *computer conferencing* the information is exchanged primarily in written form. Text and data are simultaneously displayed on two or more remote screens of participants who can jointly work on a common text, finally producing a paper in co-authorship. Remarks, notes, proposals of changes, arguments etc. can be given also in written form, but parallel voice communication by telephone (a loudspeaker is advantageous in this case as it leaves hands free for typing or handling the light pen of the terminal) is more convenient.

We mentioned earlier a small-scale use of this technique: possible communication between the boss and his secretary who can simultaneously examine the same text on their displays and discuss correcting and editing it via interphone (fig. 26.3). This is a form of 'computer conferencing' in miniature.

Sometimes, parallel display and discussion may concern a drawing, graph or scheme. In the future it will certainly be possible to connect two

Courtesy Philips Data Systems, Apeldoorn, The Netherlands

Fig. 83.1 - Philips Scribophone

The Scribophone makes it possible to design a graph or figure on a pad, to display it on the screen and to transmit it.

or more universal personal work stations and to transmit image information from screen to screen with simultaneous voice communication. At present a limited service of this type is offered by the *videophone* already mentioned (it does not enable detailed drawings to be transmitted). Also special devices can be used - an example of these is the Philips *scribophone*; it uses a special pad on which a drawing, graph or scheme is designed, its image appears on the screen of the sender and it can be transmitted to the remote screen of the receiver (fig. 83.1).

Computer conferencing can be held in real time or as *delayed conferencing.* In this case it is combined with electronic mail - the latest version of a text with the respective notes is always stored in the 'electronic mailbox' of the recipient(s), who can read, change or comment upon it any time later and send it back again.

Meetings and conferences (both the traditional and often the computerized) are characterized by uninterrupted discussion: inquiry/answer, proposals, arguments and counter-arguments are exchanged in rapid succession, without delay and often without sufficient time to consider, find exact data, calculate etc. Not every participant is capable of instant debate and of the fast and correct reaction. Often, the study of material, the finding of data, the numerical evaluation of variants, preparation of arguments etc., require time. Real-time conferencing might save time, but it does not always achieve the best results. Sometimes the argument of the participant with the quickest (but not the best) reaction is accepted, sometimes the opinion of the participant who is able to speak more loudly and longer is the one that wins out. Delayed computer conferencing is slow, it is not feasible in all situations, but it can produce decisions of better quality.

Problems of new forms of conferencing

In this case, little practical experience is available at the moment. Use, and sometimes misuse, trial and error, thorough evaluation of results are needed to help find and establish the best solution in various practical situations. There will also be a problem of *security:* in-house cryptographic methods, coding of voice communication, in-house systems of coded names of persons, departments, projects and actions resembling military jargon ('operation Dachshund starts on D-day minus 3 in the region of Pluto') will perhaps be sometimes used. They may have a side-effect: they could bring a romantic element into the grey style of office communication. Also *verification* of documents by special codes replacing signatures, and perhaps the brief style of dialogues in telegraphese will become common.

As in so many other situations, the classical means of communication will not disappear without a trace, at least not within the next two decades. Personal meetings will continue to be held in the future (though supported more and more by technical means), and the modern form of teleconferencing will merely extend the number of options. It is the duty of a professional to be aware of the advantages and disadvantages of all the methods and to choose the most suitable of them for a given concrete situation.

84 - Presentations

There is a wealth of literature on the style and form of presentations: how to prepare a lecture and how to structure it, about language and style, form of presentation, use of graphical means, projection etc. As in the preceding section, we shall mention only the technical means that can be employed and the basic rules for their selection and use, with particular emphasis on the facilities offered by the advent of new techniques.

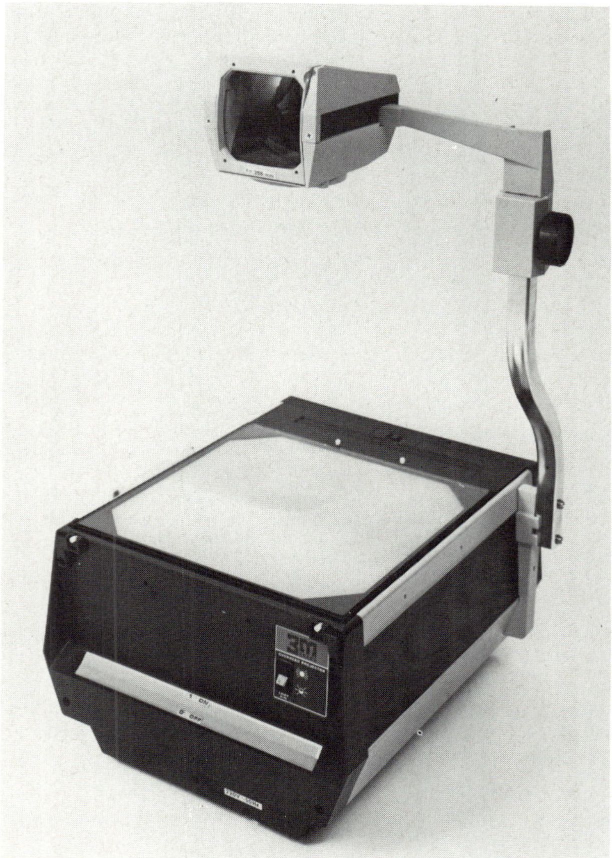

Courtesy 3M Nederland, Leiden

Fig. 84.1 - The overhead projector

The overhead projector is a commonly used device. Nonetheless, it is still possible for this well known device to be used in a rather sophisticated manner: projection of slides can be combined with drawing; the overlay technique can help to visualize phases of development, etc.

The traditional technical means of a presenter - blackboard, flip board and overhead or slide projector - will remain in practical use for a long time, sometimes as additional means employed simultaneously with more modern technical devices. A professional should master the technique of using them effectively.

Indeed, we often encounter persons who dream about the techniques of the future but are unable properly to use a tool that is hundreds of years old: a simple blackboard. They ignore the basic rules which are: write large letters; write legibly; when writing, speak the same text; otherwise, do not speak when drawing; keep blackboard clean when not actually in use; write in yellow on a black or in white on a green background; use colours if they are functional; do not overload the blackboard with information. Simple rules, indeed, but often neglected.

1 - Do not use too many slides - about 50 is usually the maximum

2 - adapt rhythm - about 2 slides per minute is a good average, but avoid regular timing

3 - present only one subject on one slide

4 - a slide should contain simple and concise information

5 - avoid disparity between the picture and spoken word as regards subject, terminology and text

6 - legibility is the supreme requirement: use large letters and graphic elements

7 - choose suitable lettertypes - recommended: half-bold, prefer lower-case letters, capitals only in short headings

8 - avoid handwriting wherever possible

9 - do not hesitate to use 'headings' at some points of the speach (short titles of the 'chapters' of the speach); distinguish them in form and colour from the other slides

10 - use colours; avoid black & white; black letters on yellow background give the best legibility; large white letters on dark blue background are excellent for short texts (headings); use more colours when they are meaningful (graphs, schemes)

11 - the use of colour must not be overdone; avoid dark colours (blue); employ colours functionally

12 - if possible, use development slides or overlay slides; the rhythm of their projection may be higher than average

13 - employ a suitable technique of slide production

14 - keep screen dark when no slide is needed; do not let the audience look at a slide when you are discussing another subject

15 - carefully check the completeness, sequence and position of slides

16 - signal the sequence of slides in your manuscript or notes

17 - check the coincidence of slides with your notes

18 - check it again

19 - use automatic projector; otherwise ensure good signalling arrangement with the operator; never interrupt speach by instructions 'next slide, please' (when necessary, say 'In the next slide, we can see..')

20 - inspect the room and equipment before the presentation; agree all actions with the operator (incl. darkening the room etc.)

Fig. 84.2 - The basic rules for use of slides in presentations

How can someone who has not yet mastered the technique of a blackboard work intelligently with a graphical display or videoprojection ?

A word of criticism must also be said with regard to the practical use of *slide projection.* Though the majority of presenters at congresses or courses use this technique properly, and many of them excellently, the number of bad visual presentations is not negligible. A short list of basic rules for a good projection is presented in fig. 84.2.

Various technical means are available for the production of *slides* in excellent quality that help improve visual presentations. Slides for an *overhead projector* are usually made by special thermographic copying machines that produce a slide from a drawing in a 1:1 scale within five

Courtesy 3M Nederland, Leiden

Fig. 84.3 - The transparency maker

The transparency maker produces transparencies on special infrared film within five seconds.

seconds (fig. 84.3). The background colour as well as the colour of the text or drawing can be chosen (avoid using black on white; the best variants are black letters or drawings on a yellow background; white letters on a dark blue background are also a good choice). Multicolour slides can be prepared by drawing every colour on a separate sheet and making separated copies in various colours; they are then assembled into a multicolour slide. A similar technique can be used to make 'dynamic' slides - two or more phases of development are drawn on separate sheets; the slides are made and are then projected successively in overlay.

The text used as the original for making slides (either for overhead projector or for a slide projector) can be significantly improved by employing *self-adhesive letters* that are available in many types, sizes and colours (fig. 76.2). Besides letters and numbers, many special symbols

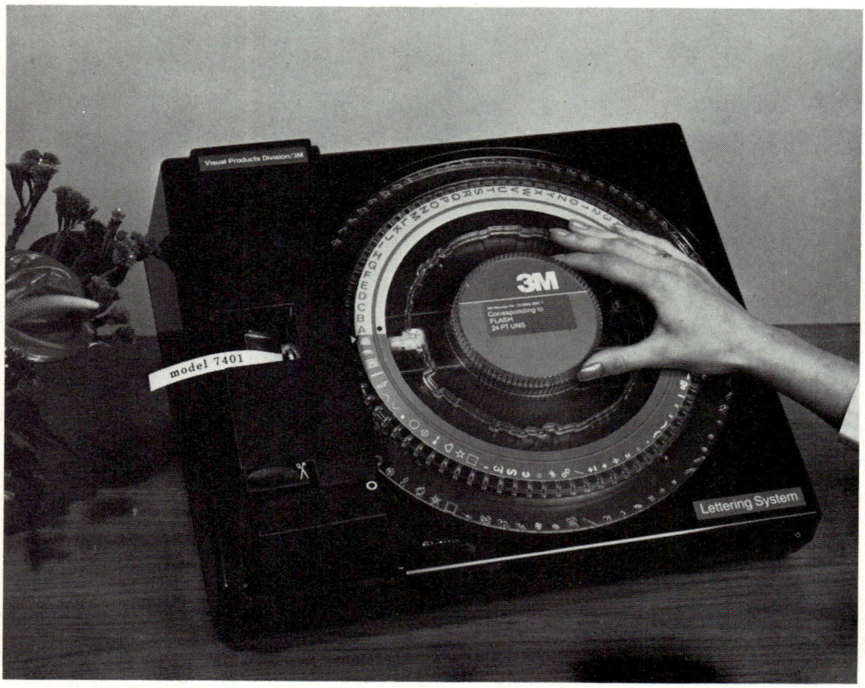

Courtesy 3M Nederland, Leiden

Fig. 84.4 - A lettering device

Exchangeable disks each containing 81 characters are available in various letter sizes, types (Helvetica, Times, Century, Gothic etc.) and forms (normal, bold, italics etc.). Also transparent texts for overhead projector slides can be produced.

(architectural, electrotechnical symbols, road signs, etc.) and graphical elements (lines of various types and thickness, arrows, hatched surfaces) are available. It is up to the inventiveness of the author to make use of this simple, cheap and very helpful aid. Another technique is a *lettering device* that produces transparent texts in a large variety of lettertypes and sizes (fig. 84.4).

The *slides* for a slide projector (mostly in the standard 24 × 36 mm format) can also be produced with an amateur's camera. The most suitable is an automatic single-lens reflex camera. It permits close-up pictures (an extension tube makes close-up work possible), the object appears in the finder with no parallactical shift, and the built-in exposure meter measures the light actually passing through the lens thereby guaranteeing the correct exposure. A tripod or (better) a special

Courtesy Bell & Howell Benelux N.V., Nieuwegein, The Netherlands

Fig. 84.5 - Automatic slide projector synchronized with a tape recorder

Up to 80 slides and spoken text or music of up to 45 minutes can be synchronized by means of magnetic pulses stored on the magnetic tape. The slides are projected onto the built-in screen or onto a large screen. Projection can be stopped at any moment - e.g. during a discussion - or it can be controlled manually.

reproduction quadripod or an even more convenient special reproduction stand makes it comfortable to take pictures at any short distance.

The originals are typed or drawn, and the above-mentioned self-adhesive letters or texts produced by a lettering device improve their appearance. The plastic letters used by film amateurs for montage of titles can also be employed. Text typed on a normal or special typewriter (composer) or word processor can be used provided the picture is taken at close-up.

A common fault is the tendency to overload a slide with information. Too much text and too many data are more disturbing than helpful. There is a simple aid: Write, draw or type the drafts of your slides on cards of A6 format (postcard format, 105 × 148 mm), not on standard A4 sheets ! Then, you will automatically keep your message concise and legible in projection.

Another effective means of presentation can be achieved by both professional and simple amateur techniques: a *sequence of slides* with comments (perhaps also with music and sound effects) reproduced by a *tape recorder.* A good script (see the concise rules in fig. 84.6), a set of slides of good quality and a recording of comments (or music) on a tape recorder can be prepared by any photo and audio hobbyist. Projection is done manually, or (better) by means of an automatic projector that coordinates the projection and sound reproduction by signals stored on the tape (fig. 84.5). *Videotechniques* are now also becoming available to the amateur author to prepare lectures and instructional material in image and sound.

1 - Short sentences; clear text; no unfamiliar words!
2 - maximum about 50 slides
3 - optimum length about 25 minutes
4 - on average fifty words per slide; maximum about 100 words
5 - variable length of text per slide (avoid monotony !)
6 - allow about 3 seconds for observation a new slide (music only, no words)!
7 - no tables!
8 - no change of slides during a sentence!
9 - from example to generic, or from generic to example!
10 - conformity between picture and word!

Fig. 84.6 - Basic principles of a slide / tape recorder show

(According to IDIS - Institut für Dokumentation un. Information über Sozialmedizin und öffentliches Gesundheitswesen, Germany)

Interesting new possibilities of improving the present technique of slide projection are offered by the in-house viewdata system. A station of this system can be used for preparation of a special sequence of frames that can be projected either in the prepared sequence or in a random sequence, as each frame can be easily retrieved. This technique can be effectively used at exhibitions and by lecturers and teachers as well as by speakers at meetings and conferences. An optical disk can be employed in a similar manner in the future.

Even the oldest technique of presentation - a lecture presented directly in person - is changing and improving. Traditional presentations at congresses and conferences given by speakers are now being amended by the new form of *poster sessions.* The authors present their short theses in the form of a concise text and a few graphs or schemes displayed on large boards (of about 1 to 3 square meters) in the hall of the congress centre. These boards can be then extended by written inquiries, comments, critical remarks and counter-theses of the participants in the form of a 'wall newspaper'. On certain days and at certain hours, announced in the programme and on the posters, the authors, standing in front of their posters, give short explanatory talks and try to defend their theses in an informal discussion with a group of people interested in the problem

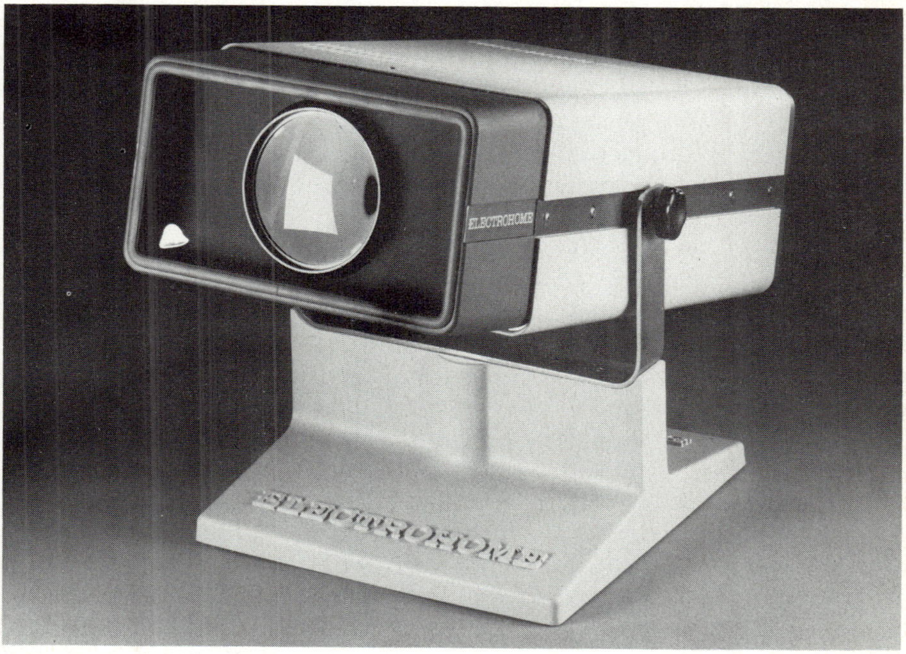

Courtesy Electrohome, Kitchener, Ont., Canada

Fig. 84.7 A special projector makes it possible to display computer output (text, data, graphics) on a large projection screen.

presented. Though simple, this form of presentation could become an excellent means of compensating for the cold, formal, rather official style of the traditional presentation of congress papers. It encourages informal exchange of ideas between a selected group and it stimulates direct personal contacts.

Poster sessions made their first appearance in Europe, and were introduced in America in 1974. This form of presentation is becoming quite popular. Short and simple theses and graphical presentation stimulate interest and discussion. Similarly, an announcement 'I am interested in the following problem...' presented on the display board can create a small community of specialists who may remain in contact long after the congress has been terminated. Interesting methods, that are able to offset the increasing danger threatened by impersonal information exchange via mechanized channels.

The new technical means available include the *videorecorder*, large screen *television projection*, and *closed-circuit television*. They offer the possibility of presenting detailed views of experiments and demonstrations to a large audience. We may use also the *computer* and *terminal*, displaying the output of computations, simulations, online retrieval, data processing and graphical data that can be followed simultaneously by many persons.

85 - Education

Most of the techniques mentioned in the preceding section can also be used by teachers and lecturers. A few additional comments should be made, however.

In this field, the traditional aids to education - blackboard, books, figures, films, slides etc., - are improving and new ones are appearing. Some of them are no longer quite so new: the *tape recorder* has been used, particularly in language teaching, for many years; *slides* and slide shows with comments recorded on tape, and *videorecording* are now widely used techniques in education.

Computers have opened up quite new opportunities in education. They enable the traditional fixed sequence of explanation to be replaced by a programmed flexible sequence, adaptable by the learner or automatically by the computer controlled by the feedback based on the man/machine conversation. *Programmed teaching* consists of small, isolated parts of an explanation (a short explanatory text, figures, graphs, data, maps, drawings, schemes) that can be followed in a basic sequence, but the selection of the next information frame depends on the knowledge and intelligence of the individual student and on his comprehension of the previous explanation. This is usually tested by multi-choice inquiries: if the student's replies are evaluated as good, then the explanation proceeds to the next subject, otherwise a more detailed narration, additional examples and more comprehensible text are displayed, followed again by new test questions. Only when the evaluation is positive does the teaching go a step further. In this way the tempo and the level of the lesson can be individualized.

There is a wealth of courses in programmed form on videocassettes, sets of slides or magnetic tapes with or without a computer-controlled programmed system. Many special devices have appeared in the last two decades and have been used in schools and training centres. The general availability of personal computers and videorecorders will probably trigger an expansion of these modern (yet not brand-new) methods of programmed learning.

Courtesy Philips Ltd., Eindhoven, The Netherlands

Fig. 85.1 - Use of the videorecorder for self-study

A videorecorder in combination with a standard colour television set is a commonly used instructional device. An optical disk that permits random access to static pictures or television records, and that is controlled by a personal computer, makes programmed learning and teaching in perfect form a feasible proposition.

A problem similar to the one mentioned in connection with personal software is encountered again: it is quite difficult for an individual to orientate himself in the enormous and ever-growing volume of available programmed courses and other instructional material produced by the many schools, institutes and organizations throughout the world. One practical aid, as regards instructional films, is the Educational film locator [ref. 83] that contains about 37,000 references to educational films on a wide range of subjects. Many of the available schemes can be found by means of the educational online database ERIC. A periodical devoted to announcing instructional and educational aids of all types is the journal PREVIES - audiovisual aids and reviews; it contains an annotated bibliography on audiovisuals, films, filmstrips, videocassettes, tapes, slides, books on tape, programmed courses and other instructional material.

New storage media such as the *videodisk* in combination with a computer search system will bring about radical changes in our technique of teaching and learning.

For example, let us mention the large electronic dictionary of the future. It would be naïve to expect that it will merely replace the traditional dictionary in book form. It could not compete in terms of low price, portability and ease of use. It will, however, possess several quite new qualities: a word will be not only displayed in its translation in the required language, but also reproduced in voice form in its proper pronounciation by the acoustic output unit, sometimes a picture will be displayed (flowers, birds, mechanical parts, geometrical bodies etc.), and a number of relations can be then retrieved as additional information: generic terms, specific terms, synonyms, antonyms, associated terms, etymological notes, and many examples of the use of the word in phrases and sentences both in the form of text and voice [ref. 83-Fox].

A significant improvement in educational methods will be brought about by the easy accessibility of large volumes of general information of the nature of *encyclopedias* and special *handbooks* in the large-capacity storages of the near future. This information will be either available in online mode through telecommunication services, or retrievable by means of a personal computer from an optical disk. One disk, as we mentioned in section 54, has a sufficient capacity to store a large encyclopedia or a whole set of voluminous handbooks. This new form of structured information storage will make it possible to retrieve and display the explanatory text as well as coloured figures, maps, photos, graphs, formulae etc., and sometimes also acoustic information (say, the pronunciation of foreign words, voices of birds, examples of the sounds of musical instruments, specimens of musical compositions, original voices of famous individuals etc.). The explanation will be available at several levels from the elementary ('child-level'), to basic ('man-in-the-street') and the more detailed ('student'), and it will make it easy to find associated or more specific information and citations of recommended sources for further study, including books, special courses, audiovisual aids, programmed teaching material etc.

A large-scale attempt to introduce new methods of teaching and learning has been started by Control Data in the USA under the name PLATO. A package based on a programmed learning system includes complete school education in the fields of mathematics, languages, social sciences, physics, chemistry, biology and astronomy. It is intended to be used in schools as an auxiliary, individualized instructional feature, as well as in companies, government agencies and in the military service for anybody who wants to augment his school education.

86 - Publishing

In the present age of the information explosion, publishing is a much more difficult task than it has ever been. The number of scientific, technical, commercial and other special publications is immense and every new publication is another drop in the ocean of accumulated information in printed form. The danger of redundancy is increasing all the time. On the other hand, redundancy is inevitable in many practical situations with the present publication techniques: every author is obliged to insert in his text many an explanation that is not new but which, if omitted, would cause loss of context. The author must take account of the fact that the level of knowledge and field of interest of his readers are far from uniform; a subject that needs to be explained to one person, might be quite familiar and trivial to another. This problem can ultimately be solved only by programmed teaching. In a book, article or report the author can help the reader by good design. Important features are: a good combination of generic and specific explanations, illustration by examples and case studies, a well structured text that provides quick orientation, easy retrieval of selected parts, the facility to skip parts of minor interest to the reader, and the recommendation of sources for further detailed study or for introductory orientation.

A publication should be properly characterized by its *title.* Modern techniques of SDI and online retrieval systems have brought about new requirements in this direction: the author should be aware that his publication will be referred to in abstract journals, in mechanically produced indexes and bibliographies, in SDI services, and that the reference will be retrieved by means of online information systems. He should choose therefore an indicative title and/or subtitle characterizing the content of his work.

It is not just whimsical titles that are bad, even traditional titles should now be chosen more carefully taking account of the question: Which term(s) would an interested reader choose if trying to find my book or article by means of KWIC indexes or online systems ? A number of bibliometric studies has been published, and the general conclusion is that titles are now on average longer and contain more significant terms than in the past.

A good *structure* of a publication (chapters, sections, paragraphs) is a traditional requirement that does not need to be emphasized; again, the titles of chapters and sections should be informative. *Numbering* makes orientation and cross-referencing easier; systematic decimal labeling is the best form in larger publications (books, longer reports). Mixed numbering (Roman numbers, Arabic numbers, letters) is out of fashion and generally worse than simple decimal numbering which clearly defines the hierarchy. Devices that help the reader to orientate himself in the text are well known: italics in the printed text, colours in the displayed text (cautiously used), bold or semi-bold words, terms, phrases or parts of text, sometimes even marginal notes - all these can improve orientation.

The various graphical means that improve structuring and legibility of printed and displayed text have been thoroughly studied in the excellent papers by Wright [ref. 86] and by Hartley and Burnhill [ref. 86]. Both studies are based on a large number of published special investigations and experiments; they therefore represent widely based experience and recommendations. They should be carefully read by every author of a scientific, technical or commercial publication; he will find a wealth of practical recommendations for improving his work. Another fine study concerned primarily with the problem of text legibility is that of Reynolds [ref. 86]. This paper is also based on a number of special investigations, experiments and measurements and is full of practical advice for every author. In all three studies the modern techniques are considered, and abundant references are attached.

One of the most effective means towards a concise, structured and acceptable form of publication is to replace the narrative text with a *table*, *scheme* or *graph*. We explained the advantages of this form in chapter 7. Another effective form is *structuring* the text by writing it at several levels that are distinguished graphically, enabling the reader to choose his own style of reading. He can either read only the main text (set in larger lettertype), or the main text with the comments, examples and case studies (set in smaller lettertype), or read the main text and descend to details only when required.

In larger reports and similar publications, summary information can be given in the structured form shown in fig. 86.1. This summary should be distinguished from the basic text either graphically or by the colour of the paper (yellow pages). The summary text (it often has the function of the 'management information') is printed in two columns, the left-hand column containing only the theses in the most concise form, and the right-hand column giving a more detailed explanation, short comments and cross-references to the main text. Such a form, though available by quite simple means, can substantially improve the perception of the main ideas and orientation in the whole publication, and can help the reader to find immediately any part that contains the required details.

Every publication must contain a *list of contents*, an *abstract* (however, how many books do contain an abstract ?), and a detailed *alphabetical index*. Modern technical means (word processors, computers) are able to compile a list of contents automatically, and they can help compile an alphabetical index (fig. 56.5).

SUMMARY INFORMATION

Document retrieval was chosen as one of the research tasks	– due to its importance and – its broad applicability in the libraries or documentation centres; in archives of special documents (patents, standards); for managing the document files in a department or work team; or for personal documentation.
The research was oriented toward retrieval methods based on the natural language of documents or abstracts.	– This is a progressive method, – the traditional methods for manually classifying or indexing documents are expensive, – the cost of manual operations is steadily increasing, while the cost of mechanized operations decreases, – classification systems are rigid, – controlled languages are orientated towards specific fields of science or technology; these languages are incompatible to one another, and – the natural language is a link between documents that come from different sources and are stored in many local files.
The idea of a future in-house information system, in the form of a network of local information centres that use compatible record formats, has been kept in mind.	– No huge, centralized super-system is expected, but a network of specialized, autonomous, local information systems – these will use compatible (i.e. exchangeable) data structures and a compatible command language; – medium-sized document collections (tens of thousands of documents) can be expected as typical.
The IREC document retrieval system was designed	– because external software packages are less useful for research and experiments, and are not adaptable, – because some particular retrieval algorithms were meant to be used.
based on the philosophy outlined in this report:	– see section 14.
usable as an experimental nstrument:	– using parameters as much as possible; – containing many switches and counters, making it possible to change, adapt, test and measure various indexing and retrieval methods;
but also economically feasible in practical applications of small and medium size:	– not only a laboratory instrument, but a practically usable and economically acceptable system – intended for small (thousands of documents) and medium-size (tens of thousands of documents) applications).

Fig. 86.1 - Example of layout of a structured 'management information'

The left-hand column contains the basic facts in the most concise form; comments, explanations or references to the detailed text can be found in the right-hand column. A report of, say, hundred pages is condensed into one to four pages for fast information and orientation of the reader, particularly of the management.

Much has been published about the kind of language to be used in technical and scientific writings, and the number of books, handbooks, guides and textbooks on this subject is large. Simple style, standardized terminology (if this exists in the particular field of science or technology), the avoidance of slang, local terms or unfamiliar acronyms and abbreviations are recommendations that are repeated time and again.

The employment of automatic indexing will sometimes influence our style and diction. At present, we must bear in mind the technique's peculiarities if we are writing abstracts that will be subjected to automatic indexing, e.g. in online systems. The author should prefer terms that will probably be used by prospective searchers, and should avoid negative statements, homographic acronyms and terms that are either too specific or too generic.

Usually we publish for anonymous readers interested in the subject treated. However, this practice could sometimes be inverted: A professional might instead of publishing answers to problems, try to publish his inquiries, in a 'who can help me ?' form.

This is not a novelty: sporadically, we find such a question in a specialist journal, but why do we not try to use it more frequently ? Maybe we could find a hidden 'grey publication' that is irretrievable via existing abstracting journals and online information systems, locate colleagues who are busy with problems similar to ours, and unearth unpublished information: some people are shy of publishing, others suffer from the lack of time to publish, many have excellent practical knowledge and experience that they do not consider suitable for publication. A published inquiry (e.g. in a special new section of a specialist journal or in an online system) could trigger new contacts between people and open up a new style of knowledge exchange.

It need not be repeated that the modern techniques from word processor and computer to photoelectric typesetting are beginning to influence the form, style and layout of publications. Printed books and other publications have a very old tradition, and their form has developed over hundreds of years. They will not change radically, nor will they disappear in the short term. One reason is their outward appearance and certain imponderable properties: a book or a journal is a physical unit, it is portable, it can easily be handled, and it can be read anywhere. A book, moreover, has its individuality, and an indefinable charm - it is possible to love books, it is scarcely possible to love magnetic disks.

87 - New forms of publication

The various forms of secondary publication produced by modern technical means - indexes, SDI services, online systems, viewdata - help us to find the required information from the mass of primary publications. However, something must be done about these primary publications. Their volume and redundancy have to be reduced dramatically.

One of the simplest proposals aimed at trying to solve the problem of the huge volume of published information and the long delays involved in publication, is *terse publication*, i.e. publishing articles and reports in concise form (not more than about two pages) containing only the basic ideas, the essential data and main conclusions. This form is similar to an extended informative abstract. It would make it possible to achieve rapid publication of new discoveries and new technical information.

Another form could be *on-demand publishing.* Instead of articles, only indicative abstracts would be published and the interested reader would be expected to ask for a copy of the full text.

Microfiche is the most suitable form of sending the required full-text versions to the interested people. It is cheaper than a paper copy, it is easier to store and to re-order, and it can be sent by air mail for the normal postage of a letter. Dissertations are frequently distributed in this manner - in Germany, a special instruction from the Ministry of Education permits dissertations to be published in this form, and microreproduction centres offer their services for reasonable prices (the price per one microfiche with capacity of 300 A4 pages is at present about 3 DM for 100 copies ordered).

The above-mentioned forms can be combined: A report or article can be published in the terse form in a specialist journal, can serve as general information for a wider readership, and those interested in details could receive on demand a microfiche of the full text from the author. Some inconvenience to the author - distribution of copies - is compensated by the fact that the people interested in his work are no longer anonymous. This form of publication can therefore stimulate contacts between peers who have hitherto been unknown to each other. Do not forget that we must try to offset the impersonal, dehumanizing influence of modern communication means with all available resources. This is one of them. Both terse and on-demand publication can be achieved by conventional methods. A more radical change can be brought about by *paperless publishing*, sometimes called *electronic publishing.* In this case, publications are directly stored in computerized information systems and then either distributed according to the stored interest profiles of subscribers, or retrieved by means of an online retrieval system when an individual user has concrete requirements.

Both scientific and technical information, as well as commercial literature and in-house information (manuals, reports, instructions and other documents), are apt to be published in this form in future. Instead of being distributed in hardcopy form, the information will be online available to everybody, and always in up-to-date form. Similarly, electronic newspapers in full or in an individually selective form may replace the traditional newspapers; they could be available on a display screen or printed out as hardcopy at the end-station of the subscriber. Experiments in this field have been performed in Japan.

Undoubtedly, paperless forms of publication have appreciable advantages over traditional publishing in printed form: information need no longer be produced, mailed and stored in physical form. This saves material, energy, space and time. These advantages, however, are offset by certain inadequacies and dangers that should be avoided if possible:

information in an automatic system is hidden and invisible unless its display is triggered by the mechanism of an automatic SDI system, or unless it is found by an mechanical retrieval system after the user has put his inquiry. Because the information need cannot always be expressed by exact criteria (the user's associations of ideas and thoughts are often rather vague and unexpected), a mechanical system can easily overlook very essential information.

Think of the difference between a traditional newspaper and an 'electronic newspaper' of the future. Nobody reads a newspaper 'cover-to-cover', but the reader normally scans the headings very quickly. Long tradition has taught journalists to use headings that best capture the reader's attention. Fast scanning of headings and the reading of only selected paragraphs according to some indefinable, subjective and often whimsical pattern enables the reader to keep himself informed on subjects over an extremely large spectrum varying from politics to culture, from economics to sport. Similarly, scanning an abstracting journal or browsing through the shelves of a library can unearth many a document that would never be found by a rigid mechanical method. There is a danger therefore that automatic selection of news or special literature will narrow our spectrum of information. The freedom to browse and randomly select, to choose by informal criteria or by vague and sometimes unconscious associations must also be provided by the new services of the future. The electronic newspaper that automatically selects only certain paragraphs may be useful for politicians, artists or sportsmen who search out everything published about themselves but the normal reader will probably appreciate the new form only if it gives him a broader view and a certain freedom of selection.

There is another threat. Uhlig et al. [ref. 80] mention the danger of the homogeneity of the information media of the future. Books, journals, reports and many other printed publications differ in form, size, colour, layout and style, but information stored in the electronic media is uniform, monotonous and sometimes even boring. It is important that we find ways of overcoming it and of bringing some individuality and variability into this grey mass of information.

For years the exciting idea of a *world encyclopedia* has been discussed [ref. 10-Kochen, 80-Kochen, 86-Sörgel etc.]. Expressed originally by H. G. Wells as early as 1932 [ref. 86], it is now taking on new forms and shapes as a result of the contemporary technology. The basic aim is to overcome the terrible redundancy of literature and the lack of structure and organization of accumulated knowledge. If there were a uniform classification system, and all the available information were organized by it, then the whole 'knowledge of mankind' could be stored in a structured form, any one piece of information would occur only once and in one place, interrelated with other elements of knowledge via a multi-access and cross-connected system. Every new item of information gained in science and technology, all new statistical data or facts could be added to the sum of knowledge, again once only and in the right place. Editorial boards in special disciplines would assess every paper submitted, examine it for originality, and accept it into the respective section of the encyclopedia so that only new information would be stored and added as an organic element to the whole system of knowledge.

Though attractive at first glance, the idea of a world encyclopedia could only with difficulty be translated into reality. The problem of structuring the wide fields of knowledge and the complicated interrelations and intersections between them, the difficulties of defining the branches of science and technology (which differ traditionally in some countries), the rapid technical development (think of the considerable difficulties that the Dewey and UDC classification systems have had in coping with this) will all present problems. Nonetheless, the idea is worth trying out in one or more fairly narrow disciplines.

Despite all the problems and the danger of losing some of the advantages of traditional techniques, new and future methods of publication, organization and dissemination of knowledge are going to have a tremendous influence. This influence comes from the performance and flexibility of computers, the enormous capacity of the new storage media, the fast and cheap communication facilities, and the convergence of written, voice and sound, and graphical forms of information that will soon be accessible in any place, at any time, and to anybody.

9 - REFERENCES

This chapter contains in section 94 a list of references arranged by subject. To facilitate specific search and search for later published papers, selective lists of specialist journals and online databases covering the subjects of the present book are added in sections 92 and 93.

91 - Reference classification and selection

The references are arranged in fifteen thematic groups that correspond to chapters, sections or groups of sections:

10	The technique of intellectual work in general
20	Workplace
30	Personal planning and accounting
40	Information management in general
41/43	Information gathering
44	Classification and indexing
45/47	Information retrieval - technical means and methods
48	Viewdata
50	Text and word processing
60	Personal computing
70	Graphical presentation
80	Communication in general
82	Electronic mail
83/85	Conferences. Presentations. Education
86/87	Publishing

Selection criteria

The references have been selected according to the following criteria: First, all papers explicitly mentioned in the text have been included without reservation (i.e., older or difficult-to-obtain documents have not been excluded). These references are mostly placed under the heading of the respective chapter or section in which they are cited. Secondly, one or more basic works giving a general overview of the subject have been added in each thematic group to give the user a general orientation in the respective field. Thirdly, references are made to documents that could be useful to readers who need more detailed information about specific subjects or technical details that cannot be explained in this book. Some sections also contain one or more classic works, e.g. the classic book on ergonomics by Goode and Machol in section 20, the 'evergreen' on business graphics by Nordsieck in section 70, etc.

It is extremely difficult to make a selection from the vast volume of publications in existence, considering the probable interests of the heterogeneous readership. It is easy to find, via abstracting journals or online search, hundreds of documents that may be probably pertinent, but only some of them are accessible without long delay and difficulties. The subject, aspect, age, availability and language of the publications have been taken into account and assessed: in general, preference is given to new papers rather than older papers, to those that are easily accessible, and to publications in English, further in German and French. The result is, undoubtedly, a compromise, influenced by a subjective point of view and also by personal preference: the papers used by the author have been preferred to those that have only been scanned or identified via secondary sources. Moreover, any reference list becomes obsolete the day after it is compiled: new literature is appearing continuously. The reader should use the attached list of references merely as a starting point. He will find here a wealth of pertinent information, but also abundant references to other interesting documents. The above-mentioned list of selected journals in section 92 and online databases in section 93 make further search easier. The reader should not forget, when searching for specific information, to make use of abstracting journals, SDI or online search. The headings of the 15 thematic groups and the titles of the literature cited may be used as a source of keywords for effective search. *Good hunting !*

92 - Selected specialist journals

Papers on specific problems of intellectual activity, its organization, tools and methods are dispersed in a large number of journals. Table 92.1 tries to make the selection easier. The added numbers of chapters of the present book help to find journals covering the specific subjects.

journal (* reference journal)	country	chapter	language
Artificial Intelligence	NL	1,8	E
BTA/BTO Bürotechnik (see Office Management)			
Bulletin of the Amer.Soc. for Inf. Sci.	USA	4,8	E
Bulletin Signalétique sect. 101 (Docum.)*	F	4	F
Bureau gestion	F	2,5,6	F
BYTE	USA	5,6,7	E
Computer	USA	6,7,8	E
Computers and People	USA	1,6,8	E
Creative Computing	USA	6,7	E
Database - the magazine of database ref.*	USA	41	E
Datamation	USA	5,6,7	E
Documentaliste, Sciences de l'Information	F	4	F
Educational Technology	USA	85	E
Electronic Publishing Review	GB	48,8	E
IEEE Transaction on Profess. Communicat.	USA	8	E
Information Science Abstracts *	USA	4,5,6,8	E
INSPEC - Computer & Control Abstracts *	GB	4/8	E
Interface Age	USA	6	E
International Classification	D	44	D
IO Management Zeitschrift	CH	2,5,6	D
Journal of Documentation	GB	4	E
Journal of Information Science	NL	4	E
Journal of the Amer.Soc.of Inf.Scientists	USA	4	E
Kantoor en Efficiency	NL	2,5,6	NL
Kilobaud Microcomputing	USA	6	E
Library and Information Science Abstr.*	GB	4,5,8	E
L'ordinateur Individuel	F	6	F
Nachrichten für Dokumentation	D	4,8	D
Office Management (former BTA/BTO Bürotech.)	D	2,5/8	D
Online	USA	4	E
Online Adi Nachrichten	D	6,8	D
Online Review	GB	4	E
Personal Computer World	GB	6	E
Personal Computing	USA	5,6	E
Practical Computing	GB	6	E
Previews - audiovisual software review *	USA	85	E
Programmed Learning Educ. Technology	GB	85	E
Referativnyj zhurnal Informatika *	UdSSR	4,8	R
Reference Services Review *	USA	4	E
Science Citation Index *	USA	41	E
Scholarly Publishing	CAN	85	E
Which Computer	GB	6	E
Which Word Processor	GB	5	E
Word Processing and Information Systems	USA	4,5	E
Words	USA	5	E

Fig. 92.1 - Selected journals covering the subjects of this book

93 - Selected online databases

The reader can try to find the literature on his special problem by online search; he can make use of a number of host systems and databases. Tables 93.1. and 93.2 help to select databases that probably may help.

DATA BASE	main subject and host online information system(s)
ABI-INFORM	business organization (ESA-IRS, LIS, SDC, DATA-STAR INFO)
ACCOUNTANTS' INDEX	accounting, auditing, taxation (SDC)
AVMARC	audiovisual aids for education in all fields (BLAISE)
COMPENDEX	technological sciences, multidisciplinary (ESA-IRS, INKA, LIS, SDC)
CONFER.PAPER INDEX	papers presented on conferences, multidisciplinary (ESA-IRS)
ECONOMIC ABSTRACTS	(LIS, BELINDIS)
ERGODATA	biometry; ergonomics
ERIC	education and research in education (SDC, LIS)
INSPEC CCA	computers & automation abstracts (ESA-IRS, INKA, LIS, SDC)
INSPEC EEA	electrical & electronic abstracts (ESA-IRS, INKA, LIS, SDC)
LISA	library and information science (SDC, LIS)
MANAGEM. CONTENTS	management, organization (LIS, SDC)
NTIS	USA government-sponsored research reports, multidisciplinary (ESA-IRS, INKA, SDC, LIS)
PASCAL	technology, multidiciplinary (ESA-IRS, TELESYSTEMS EURODIAL, INFODATA)
PSYCHOL ABSTR DATA	psychology (DATA-STAR)
PSYCHOLOGICAL ABST	psychology (LIS, SDC)
SCISEARCH	Science Citation Index, multidisciplinary (LIS)
SOC SCI SEARCH	social sciences (LIS)
TELEDOC	telecommunication, electronics (TELESYSTEMES-EURODIAL)

Fig. 93.1 - Online databases covering the subjects of this book

Chapters	databases (classes)
1 intellectual work	ERIC; PSYCH ABSTR; LISA; ERGODATA
2 workplace organization	ERGODATA; ERIC; COMPENDEX; INSPEC
3 planning, accounting	ACCOUNTANTS' INDEX, INSPEC-CCA (78.30) ECONOMIC ABSTRACTS, MANAGEMENT CONTENTS
4 information management	LISA; INSPEC CCA (71.00)
5 word processing	INSPEC-CCA (71.00); LISA (169); PASCAL
6 personal computing	INSPEC-CCA (78.30); PASCAL
7 graphical presentation	INSPEC-CCA (55.40, 61.30); PASCAL; ERIC
8 telecommunication	INSPEC-EEA; TELEDOC; LISA (181)+ PASCAL
83/85 conferences, presentation, education	ERIC; INSPEC (71.10)
86/87 publishing	INSPEC CCA (72.30); LISA (7/77)

Fig. 93.2 - Online databases covering the subjects of chapters 1/8

94 - References

10 - The technique of intellectual work in general

Intellectual activity, its methods and techniques in general. Creative work. Professional's and manager's work style and habits. Productivity of intellectual work. Mechanization and automation. Future prospects. Further general sources cited in chapter 1.

AMBER, G.H.; AMBER, P.S.:
Anatomy of Automation
1962, Englewood Cliffs: Prentice-Hall, 246 p.

ARIETI, S.:
Creativity - the magic synthesis
1976, New York: Basic Books - 448 p.

BATES, M.J.:
Idea tactics [generation new ideas or solutions in information searching]
1979, J Am Soc Inf Sci 30(5)280-289

BEER, U.:
Methoden der geistigen Arbeit [Methods of intellectual work]
1978, Tübingen: Katzmann - 104 p.

BURNS, C.:
Information storage and display [perspectives]
1981, J Am Soc Inf Sci 32(2)141-147

CLAUSEWITZ, C. VON
Vom Kriege [On war]
1832, Berlin: Dümmler

DERTOUZOS, M.L.; MOSES, J.:
The computer age: a twenty-year view
1979, Cambridge: MIT Press - 492 p.

DIEBOLD, J.:
Office information systems - productivity improvements using office automation technology
1978, Data Exchange n.v.(4)2-5

HAYES, P.; REDDY, D.R.:
An anatomy of graceful interaction in spoken and written man-machine communication
1979, Pittsburg: Carnegie-Mellon Univ., 70 p.

HÖHN, R.:
Die Technik der geistigen Arbeit [Techniques of intellectual work]
1979, Bad Harzburg: Verl WWT - 340 p.

KOCHEN, M.(ed.):
The growth of knowledge - readings on the organization and retrieval of information
1967, New York: Wiley - 394 p.

KOESTLER, A.:
The Act of Creation
1978, London: Pan Books - 492 p.

KORFF, E.; REINEKE, W.:
Arbeitstechnik für Vielbeschäftigte [Work techniques for busy people]
1980, Heidelberg: Sauer - 242 p.

KRÖBER, W.:
Kunst und Technik der geistigen Arbeit [The art and techniques of intellectual work]
1971 (7th ed.), Heidelberg: Quelle & Meyer - 202 p.

LANDAU, R.M.:
Productivity, information technology and the office
in: 2nd Int Conf Inf Storage Retr, Dallas 79
1979, ACM 14(2)59-63

LEPKOWSKI, W. et al.:
The impact of automation on people
1980, Comput & People 29(11/12)17-22

LUEHRMANN, A.:
Computer illiteracy - a national crisis and a solution for it
1980, Byte 5(7)98,101,102

MARTIN, J.:
The wired society
1978, Englewood Cliffs: Prentice-Hall - 300 p.

MASARYK, T.G.:
Jak pracovat [How to work]
1898 (4th ed. 1939), Prague: Čin - 88 p.

MOKHOFF, N.:
Office automation: a challenge
1979, IEEE Spectrum 16(10)66-69

PARKINSON, C.N.:
Parkinson's law
1958, London: Murray - 122 p.

RAPOPORT, A.(ed.):
Clausewitz on War
1968, London: Penguin - 462 p.

SHNEIDERMAN, B.:
Human factors in designing interactive systems
1979, Computer 12(12)9-19
SKOW, J.:
Games that play people
1982, Time 119(3)56-62
SLAMECKA, V.:
MARIS - A knowledge system for internal medicine
1977, Inf Process Manage 13(5)273-276
SMITH, L.C.:
Implications of artificial intelligence for end user of online systems
1980, Online Rev 4(4)383-391
STIBIC, V.:
A few practical remarks on the user-friendliness of online systems
1980, J Inf Sci 2(6)277-283
TAPSCOTT, D.; MACFARLANE, D.:
Perspectives for the office of the future
1979, Proc 7th Ann Can Conf Inf Sci, p. 148-167
TOFFLER, A.:
The third wave
1981, New York: Bantam - 540 p.
WARR, P. (ed.):
Personal goals and work design
1976, London: Wiley - 364 p.
WEIZENBAUM, J.:
Computer power and human reason - from judgment to calculation
1976, San Francisco: Freeman - 300 p.
WEIZENBAUM, J.:
The computer revolution
in: Dertouzos p. 439-458 [see ref. 10]
WIERSBA, R.K.:
The role of information retrieval in the second computer revolution
In: Proc 2nd Int Conf Inf Storage Retr, Dallas 1979 - ACM 14(2)52-58
ZIMAN, J.:
Reliable knowledge - an exploration of the grounds of belief in science
1978, London: Cambridge Univ Press - 198 p.

20 - Workplace

Workplace of a professional. Workplace organization. Work room. Work space. Work environment. Illumination. Writing desk and furniture. Auxiliary devices. Principles of ergonomics. Ergonomics and office work. Further general sources cited in chapter 2.

ALFORD, L.P.(ed.); BANGS J.R.(ed.):
Production handbook
1955, New York: Ronald Press - 1676 p.
BRIGNOLI, F.:
Office automation planning within the executive office of the president
1979, ICC 79 Int Conf Commun, New York, IEEE
CAKIR, A. et al.:
Bildschirmarbeitsplätze [Visual display workplaces]
1980, Berlin: Springer - 314 p.
CAKIR, A. et al.:
Visual display terminals
1981, London: Wiley
GOODE, H.H.; MACHOL, R.E.:
System engineering [Human engineering]
1957, New York: McGraw-Hill
GRANDJEAN, E.:
Der Bildschirmarbeitsplatz [The visual display workplace]
1980, Manage Z IO 49(4)205-209
GROB, R.:
Gestaltung von Bildschirmplätzen [Design of the video-display workplaces]
1980, Online-ADL Nachr n.v.(9)662-666
HALLER, E.:
So planen wir Arbeitsplätze mit dem Computer [Planning of computer workplaces]
1980, Manage Z IO 49(7/8)376-379
KELLERMANN, F. et al.:
Vademecum ergonomie
1963, Eindhoven: Philips, 92 p.
LENIOR T.M.J. et al.:
Ergonomie in kantoren [Ergonomy in

the office]
1981, Deventer: Kluver - 136 p.
MANCHESTER, W.:
American Caesar [Douglas MacArthur]
1978, New York: Dell - 960 p.
MOSES, J.:
The computer in the home
in: Dertouzos p. 3-20 [see ref. 10]
PETERS, T.:
Ergonomics and medical aspects of office design
1979, BTA/BTO Bürotech 27(6)694, 696, 705
SAMPLE, R.L.:
Coping with the 'Work-at-home' trend
1981, Adm Manage 42(8)24-27
SCHWARZ, E,:
Die Arbeitstättenverordnung... (III) [Workplace regulations]
1979, BTA/BTO Bürotech 27(6)707-711
VELLINGA, R.:
De functie van de ergonomie in de kantoorinrichting [Ergonomy and the office equipment]
1981, Kant Effic 20(spec.no)27-31

30 - Personal planning and accounting

Personal planning and scheduling. Critical path method. Personal budgeting. Personal accounting. Personal performance. Further general sources cited in chapter 3.

DOUSE, E.:
Computerize your day-to-day happenings...
1980, Comput today 2(26)29-32
KELLY, D.A.:
Structured programming and personal organization
1980, Pers Comput 4(3)29-31
MEDRESS, M.F. et al.:
Speech understanding system [the HARPY project]
1977, Artif Intell 9(3)307-316
MINTZBERG, H.:
The manager's job: folklore and fact
1975, Harvard Bus Rev 53(4)49-61
PHILIPS, F.:
45 Jaar met Philips [45 years with Philips]
1979, Rotterdam: Donker - 384 p.
ROEHRIG, J.:
Deeper in the heart of taxes [a program for tax calculations]
1980, Pers Comput 4(4)27-30
ROSEFSKI, R.S.:
Personal finance and money management
1978, New York: Wiley - 613 p.
SCHLESINGER, A.M. Jr.:
A thousand days - John F. Kennedy in the White house
1965, New York: Fawcet - 968 p.
SPARKS, L.:
Home inventory [incl. calculation of replacement cost]
1980, Creat Comput 6(5)84
SPARTI, J.:
The personal financial statement
1980, Interface age 5(2)56-64
WILLIAMS, B.:
Personal accounts system to keep your records straight
1980, Pract Comput 3(9)70-71,73-76,78-79...

40 - Information management in general

Principles of information management. Organization of knowledge. Information storage and retrieval in general. Personal documentation. State-of-the art and prospects of information management. Terminology. Further general sources cited in chapter 4.

ANDERLA, J.G.:
Information in 1985 - a forecasting study of information needs and resources
1973, Paris: OECD 130 p.

ATHERTON, P.:
Handbook for information systems and services
1977, Paris: UNESCO - 260 p.

CUADRA, C.A.(ed.):
Annual review of information science and technology ('ARIST')
1966-1975, New York: Wiley, vol. 1-10 [volumes 11- see 40-Williams]

DESVALS, H.:
Comment organiser sa documentation scientifique [How to organize one's own scientific documentation]
1978 (2nd ed.), Paris: Gauthier-Villars - 272 p.

GEBHARDT, F.:
Dokumentationssysteme [Documentation systems]
1981, Berlin: Springer - 336 p.

HEAPS, H.S.:
Information retrieval - computational and theoretical aspects
1978, New York: Acad Press - 368 p.

HUSBANDS, C.W.(ed.); TIGHE, R.L.(ed.):
Information revolution - proceedings of the ASIS annual meeting
1975, Washington: ASIS - 170 p.

JAHODA, G.:
Information storage and retrieval for individual researchers
1970, Wiley, 135 p.

JUDGE, A.J.A.:
Knowledge-representation in a computer-supported environment
1977, Int Classif 4(2)76-80

KOCHEN, M.:
Information for action: from knowledge to wisdom
1975, Washington, Acad Press - 248 p.

KOCHEN, M.:
The growth of knowledge - readings on organization and retrieval of information
1967, New York: Wiley - 394 p.

PAICE, C.D.:
Information retrieval and the computer
1977, London: MacDonald - 206 p.

RESCHER, N.:
The systematization of knowledge
1977, Int Classif 4(2)73-75

SAUVAIN, R.W.:
Computer-based personal retrieval systems (a bibliography)
1979, ACM-SIGIR 13(4)8-31

SOPER, M.E.:
Characteristics and use of personal collections
1976, Libr Q 46(4)397-415

STIBIC, V.:
Personal documentation for professionals - means and methods
1980, Amsterdam: North-Holland - 214 p.

TOU, J.T.:
Knowledge engineering
1980, Int J Comput & Inf Sci 9(4)275-285

TOWNLEY, H.M.; GEE, R.D.:
Thesaurus-making: grow your own word-stock
1980, London: Deutsch - 206 p.

WERSIG, G; NEVELING, U.:
Terminology of documentation
1976, Paris: Unesco Press - 274 p.

WILLIAMS, M.(ed.):
Annual review of information science and technology ('ARIST')
1976- , New York: Wiley, vol. 11- [see also 40-Cuadra]

41/42 - Information gathering

Information sources and channels. Primary, secondary and tertiary sources of information. Directories of information sources. Information systems and data bases. Information needs and habits. Storage of documents. Further general sources cited in sections 41/42.

BAYER, A.E.; JAHODA, G.:
Effects of online bibliographic searching on scientific information style
1981, Online Rev 5(4)323-333

BERNIER, C.L.:
Reading overload and cogency
1978, Inf Process Manage 14(6)445-452

BROWNSTONE, D.M.; CARRUTH, G.:
Where to find business information: a worldwide guide for everyone who needs the answers to business questions
1979, New York: Wiley - 616 p.

CARTER, C.:
Reference sources in the computer sciences
1974, New York: MacMillan - 238 p.

CODLIN, E.(ed.):
ASLIB Directory - Information sources in science, technology and commerce
1977, London: ASLIB

CRONIN, B.:
Databanks
1981, ASLIB Proc 33(6)243-250

ETTEL, W.:
Informationsvermittlung in den Vereinigten Staten [Information procurement in the United States]
1980, Nachr Dok 31(4/5)185-189

GARFIELD, E.:
Citation indexing - its theory and application in science, technology and humanities
1979, New York: Wiley - 274 p.

HUBER, W.:
Referral, a tool to increase the use of available informations resources
1977, Online Rev 1(4)289-294

LANDAU, R. et al.:
Directory of online databases
1980, Santa Monica: Cuadra Assoc - 154 p.

MAIZELL, R.E.:
How to find chemical information
1979, New York: Wiley - 262 p.

MORE DATABASES AVAILABLE
1981, Euronet-DIANE News

MOUNT, E.:
Guide to basic information sources in engineering
1976, New York: Wiley - 204 p.

NTIS:
A directory of computerized data files and related technical reports
1980, Springfield: NTIS - 404 p.

REGAZZI, J.J. et al.:
On-line systems of disciplines and specialty areas in science and technology
1980, J Am Soc Inf Sci 31(3)161-170

ROSS, N.M.:
Newspaper databases
In: Proc Nat Online Meet 1981
1981, Medford: Learn Inf - p. 415-420

SUBRAMANYAM, K.:
Scientific and technical information resources
1981, New York: Dekker - 418 p.

TEITELBAUM, H.H.; HAWKINS, D.T.:
Database subject index
1978, Online 2(2)16-21

THOMPSON, G.K.:
The use of microcomputers by secondary services and individual researchers in the social sciences
In: Inf Age in Perspect - Proc ASIS 1978, p. 341-344

URQUHART, C.:
Reading, looking and learning [reading styles and speed]
1980, J Inf Sci 1(6)333-344

WHITEHALL, T.:
Personal current awareness service: a handbook of techniques for manual SDI
1979, London: Brit Libr - 120 p.

ZIELKE, W.:
Lesetechniken für Ingenieure
1976, Düsseldorf: VDI Verl 158 p.

43/44 - Classification and indexing

Recording of information. Document description. Bibliographical data. Standards. Abstracting. Principles of classification and indexing. Decimal classification. Thesauri. Descriptors. Automatic indexing.

AITCHISON, J.; GILCHRIST, A.:
Thesaurus construction
1972, London: ASLIB - 96 p.

ANSI:
American national standard for writing abstracts Z39.14-1971
1977, IEEE Trans Prof Commun 20(4)252-254

BIBLIOGRAPHY
of UN thesauri, classifications, nomenclatures
1979, Genève: IOB - 252 p.

BORKO, H.; BERNIER, C.L.:
Abstracting concepts and methods
1975, New York: Acad Press - 250 p.

BORKO, H.; BERNIER, C.L.:
Indexing concepts and methods
1978, New York: Acad Press - 350 p.

BSI:
Guide to the Universal Decimal Classification (UDC)
1963, London: Br Stand Inst - 128 p.

CHAUMIER, J.:
Les langages documentaires [Documentation languages]
1978, Paris: Enterp Mod Ed - 148 p.

COONEY, S.:
A standard procedure for generating personal classifications and indexes
1980, J Inf Sci 2(2)81-90

DEWEY, M.:
Dewey decimal classification and relative index
1971, New York: Forest (18th ed.) - 1628 p.

FOSKETT, A.C.:
The Universal Decimal Classification: the history, present status and future prospects of a large general classification scheme
1973, London: Bingley

GARFIELD, E.:
Citation indexing - its theory and application in science, technology and humanities
1979, New York: Wiley - 274 p.

GILCHRIST, A.:
The thesaurus in retrieval
1971, London: ASLIB - 184 p.

ISO:
International standard ISO 214-1976 Documentation - abstracts for publication and documentation
1976, ISO - 6 p.

ISO:
International standard ISO 690-1975 Documentation - bibliographical references - essential and supplementary elements
1975, ISO - 8 p.

ISO:
International standard ISO 832-1975 Documentation - bibliographical references - abbreviations of typical words
1975, ISO - 38 p.

ISO:
International standard ISO 833-1974 Documentation - international list of periodical title word abbreviations
1974, ISO - 38 p.

LANCASTER, F.W.:
Vocabulary control for information retrieval
1972, Washington: Inf Resour Press - 234 p.

MCCAFFERTY, M.:
Thesauri and thesaurus construction
1977, London: ASLIB - 192 p.

MILLS, J.:
Guide to the Universal Decimal Classification (UDC)
1963, London: Br Stand Inst - 128 p.

NASA:
NASA thesaurus
1976, Washington: NASA, 810 + 432 p.

NATIONAL COMPUTING CENTRE:
NCC thesaurus of computing terms
1972, Manchester: Nat Comput Cent - 335 + 180 p.

ROBINSON, G.:
UDC - A brief introduction
1979, Den Haag: FID - 8 p.

SOERGEL, D.:
Indexing languages and thesauri: construction and maintenance
1974, Los Angeles: Melville - 632 p.
TOWNLEY, H.M.; GEE, R.D.:
Thesaurus-making: grow your own word-stock
1980, London: Deutsch - 206 p.
UNESCO:
Guide for the presentation of author abstracts for publication
n.d., Paris: UNESCO - 2p.
UNIVERSAL
Decimal Classification - abbridged English edition
1961, (2nd ed.), London: Br Stand Inst
VAN DER AA:
Thesaurus bibliography
1977, Amsterdam: NOVI - 88 p.
VICKERY, B.C.:
Information systems
1973, London: Butterworth - 350 p.
WÄHLIN, E.:
Research on classification systems...
1978, Stockholm: Swed Counc Build Res
WELLISCH, H.H.:
Indexing and abstracting: an international bibliography
1980, Santa Barbara: ABC-Clio

45/47 - Information retrieval - technical means and methods

Manual retrieval. Card index. Peek-a-boo cards. Indexes. Computerized indexes. KWIC and KWOC indexes. Permutated indexes. Offline and online retrieval. Information retrieval systems. Personal documentation systems. (Databases and online systems see also in 41).

ADAMS, A.L.:
Planning search strategy for maximum retrieval from bibliographic data bases
1979, Online Rev 3(4)373-379
ASHFORD, J.H.:
Information management packages on minicomputers
1980, J Inf Sci 2(1)23-28
BARKER, P.G.:
BINSYS - a personal information retrieval system
1978, J Inf Sci 2(1)34-51
BELL, C.; JONES, K.P.:
Towards everyday language information retrieval systems via minicomputers
1979, J Am Soc Inf Sci 30(6)334-339
BIVINS, K.T.:
REFLES, An individual microcomputer system for fact retrieval
1980, Online Rev 4(4)357-365.
BIVINS, K.T.; ERIKSSON, L.:
REFLINK: a microcomputer information retrieval system
In: Proc Nat Online Meet 1981
1981, Medford: Learn Inf p. 73-80
BOURNE, C.P.:
On-line systems: history, technology, and economics
1980, J Am Soc Inf Sci 31(3)155-160
CAWKELL, A.E.:
A personal microcomputer system [PRIMATE] for office use
In: 4th Int Online Inf Meet London 1980
1980, Oxford: Learned Inf - p. 377-385
1980, J Am Soc Inf Sci 31(3)155-200
CUADRA, C.A.:
Directory of online databases
1979, Santa Monica: Cuadra Assoc.
DATABASES IN EUROPE
a directory of machine-readable data bases and data banks
1977 (3rd ed.), London: ASLIB
DATABASES ONLINE
[cost of searching, subject coverage]
1980, Online Rev 4(1)101-115
DAVIES, G.W.P.:
Euronet DIANE: origins, goals and present status
1980, Int Forum Inf Doc 5(1)29-34
DE JAEGER, H.K.:
The great information providers: organizations generating, announcing or repackaging information
1978, Ghent (Belg.): Astrid - 24 microfiches

ENCYCLOPEDIA
of information systems and services
1978 (3rd ed.), Detroit: Gale Res (4th ed. pending)
EUSIDIC (ed.):
Information trade directory - an international directory of information products and services
1979, Oxford: Learn Inf - 278 p.
FARRADANE, J.:
A comparison of some computer-produced permuted alphabetical subject indexes
1977, Int Classif 4(2)94-101
FENICHEL, C.H.; HOGAN, T.H.:
Online searching - a primer
1981, Oxford: Learn Inf - 152 p.
GARFIELD, E.:
The Permuterm subject index: an autobiographical review
1976, J Am Soc Inf Sci 27(5-6)288-291
GÖTTING, R.:
Information-Retrieval-Systeme mit Sichtlochkarten [Information retrieval systems by means of peek-a-boo cards]
1974, Z Dok 25(5)201-209
HAIMES, A.R.:
IV-3 as a private viewdata system
In: Videotex, Viewdata [see 48] p. 323-335
HALL, J.L.:
On-line bibliographic data bases 1979 directory
1979, London: Aslib - 94 p.
HALL, J.L.:
On-line information retrieval sourcebook
1977, London: ASLIB - 268 p.
HALL, J.L. (ed.):
On-line information retrieval 1965-1976 (bibliography)
1977, London: ASLIB - 126 p.
HALL, J.L.; DEWE, A.:
Online information retrieval 1976-1979 - an international bibliography
1980, London: ASLIB - 230 p.
HAWKINS, D.T.:
Online information retrieval bibliography
1978, Online Rev 2(1)63-109
HAWKINS, D.T.:
Online information retrieval bibliography: third update
1980, Online Rev 4(1)61-100
HENRY, W.H.; LEIGH, J.A.; TEDD, L.A.:
Online searching - an introduction
1980, London: Butterworths - 210 p.
HOUGHTON, B.; CONVEY, J.:
On-line information retrieval systems - an introductory manual to principles and practice
1977, London: Shor String Press - 160 p.
HUBER, W.; MAHON, B.:
Euronet DIANE Dienstleistungsangebot und Möglichkeiten der Nutzung [...services and applications]
1979, Nachr Dok 30(4/5)153-159
JOLLEY, J.L.:
Progress in documentation: punched feature [peek-a-boo] cards
1975, J Doc 31(3)199-215
LEGGATE, P. et. al.:
An on-line system for handling personal data bases on a [DEC] PDP-11/20 minicomputer
1977, ASLIB Proc 29(2)56-66
LUHN, H.P.:
Keyword-in-context index for technical literature (KWIC index)
1959, Yorktown Heights: IBM
PARKER, I.M.; THORPE, P.:
GRIP - a personal online indexing system using a microcomputer
1979, Program 13(1)14-22
SCHMITZ-ESSER, W.:
A review of the world press information banks
in: 2nd Int Online Inf Meet p. 243-250
1978, Oxford: Learn Inf
SCHRODE, A.:
PLIDOS - Ein Beispiel für die Nutzung des Microcomputers in IuD [PLIDOS - an example of the use of a microcomputer in information and documentation]
1980, Nachr Dok 31(6)210-216
SEMTURS, F.:
STAIRS/TLS - a system for 'free text' and 'descriptor' searching
In: Inf Age in Perspect - Proc ASIS Ann Meet 1978, vol.15,p.295-297
SHARP, G.:
Online business information
1977, Online 2(1)33-40
SLADE R.; KELLY, A.M.:
Sources of popular literature online:

New York Times information bank and the magazine index
1979, Database 2(1)70-83
STERNBERGER, P.:
Using personal home computers to retrieve information from online databases
In: 4th Int Online Inf Meet London 1980
1980, Oxford: Learn Inf p. 79-84
TEITELBAUM, H.H.; HAWKINS, D.T.:
Data base subject index
1978, Online 2(2)16-21
TOMBERG, A.(ed.):
Data bases in Europe (3rd ed.)
1977, London: ASLIB - 74 p.
TOMBERG, A.(ed.):
EUSIDIC database guide 1980
1979, Oxford: Learn Inf - 172 p.
WANGER, J.; LANDAU, R.N.:
Nonbibliographic on-line data base services
1980, J Am Soc Inf Sci 31(3)171-180
WILLIAMS, M.(ed.); ROUSE, S.H.(ed.):
Computer-readable bibliographic data bases - a directory and data sourcebook
1976, Washington: ASIS - 814 p.

48 - Viewdata

Videotex. Teletext. Viewdata

CRINER, K.; JOHNSON-HALL, M.:
Videotex: threat or opportunity
1980, Spec Libr 71(9)379-385
HOOPER, R.:
Applications of Viewdata
In: 3rd Online Meet London 1979, p. 283-288
1979, Oxford: Lern Inf
IFRA symposium on electronic publishing:
The 'new media' and the newspaper industry
1980, Newspaper Tech 4-35
KARLGREN, H.:
Viewdata - something to be crazy about ?
1979, Int Classif 6(3)172-176
REID, A. (ed.):
Prestel 1980
1980, London: Post Off Telecommun - 110 p.
REYNOLDS, R.:
Typographical and design considerations with Viewdata
in: 3rd Int Online Meet, London, Dec.1979, p. 289-300
1979, Oxford: Learn Inf
SIGEL, E. (ed.):
Videotex, the coming revolution in home/office information retrieval
1980, White Plains: Knowl Ind - 154 p.
STRAUCH, D.; VOWE, G. (ed.):
Bildschirmtext - Facetten eines neuen Mediums [Viewdata - facets of a new medium]
1980, München: Oldenbourg - 216 p.
WHITE, M.S.:
Viewdata - a review
1978, Inf Sci(entist) 12(4)145-153
VIDEOTEX
and its potential impact in Europe - a multiclient study
1979, Butler Cox - vol. 1,2,3
VIDEOTEX,
Viewdata and Teletext
1980, London: Online Publ - 623 p.
VIEWDATA
a review and bibliography
1978, Online Rev 2(3)217-224
WILLIAMS, M.:
Viewdata systems could form worldwide network
1980,05.12 Financ Times p. 13
WINSBURY, R.(ed.):
Viewdata in action: a comparative study of Prestel
1981, London: McGraw-Hill - 238 p.
WOOLFE, R.:
Videotex: the new television/telephone information service
1980, London: Heyden - 178 p.

50 - Word and text processing

Word and text processing in general. Traditional technical means. Typewriting. Typewriters. Electronic typewriters. Dictating. Dictating equipment. Word processing. Word processors. Personal computers and terminals as word processors. Use of word processors in correspondence and special applications. Camera-ready publishing. Phototypesetting. Further general sources cited in chapter 5.

BERGERUD, M.; GONZALES, J.:
Word processing - concepts and carriers
1978, New York: Wiley - 232 p.

BOBBEY, J.:
Selecting a word processing microcomputer
1980, Pers Comput 4(4)66-67

BUCKLAND, L.F.:
Book composition by authors - system and equipment considerations
In: Proc 1st Ann Meet Soc Scholar Publ 1979 Boston
1980, Washington: SSP - p.49-53

BURNS, C.:
Information storage and display
1981, J Am Soc Inf Sci 32(2)141-147

CARRIGAN, B.:
Automated text editing [bibliography of NTIS reports]
1980, NTIS rep PB80-806714 - 240 p.

CECIL, P.B.:
Word processing in the modern office
1980, Menlo Park: Benjamin-Cunnings - 350 p.

CHERRY, G.W.:
Evaluating word-processing software
1981, Mini-Micro Syst 14(4)123-129

DE VOLPI, A. et al.:
Computerized technical-document preparation (TXT users manual)
1980, Argonne Nat Lab (NTIS rep. DOE-TIC-11216) - 74 p.

DISPLAY WRITER
introduced by IBM
1980, Word Process Syst 7(8)37

DODSON, R.T.:
Fast input for fast output
in: Word processing..1979, London; Uxbridge: Online p.145-150

FRANKENTHALER, M.R.:
Utilizing the computer to prepare a manuscript
1976, Scholar Publ 7(2)161-168

FRITZ, E.:
Bürosatz = schreiben + setzen [Office typesetting = type + set]
1980, BTA/BTO Bürotech 28(9)806-813

HAIDER, K.:
Office automation and word processing
1978, Amidenhead (GB) Infotech Int p. 161-172

HANSEN, J.R.:
Perspective on word and data processing [incl. a list of features]
1980, Small Syst World (12)21-22,54

HOGBEN, J.E.; IZZARD, B.A.:
Chosing a word processing system
1977, Data Syst n.v.(7)6-13

INTRODUCING
a sound approach to dictation
1981, Which Word Processor 2(5)27-28

MCGIRR, C.J.:
Application of word processing to engineering documentation
n.d., St Petersburg: Gen Electr (NTIS rep GEPP-TIS-519)

PATERSON, A.:
Successful word processing
1980, n.p., Logica - 206 p.

REINDL, E.:
Anforderungen an bildschirmorientierte Textsysteme [Requirements for VDU text systems]
1980, Online Adi Nachr (11)892-898

ROCHESTER, N. et al.:
The chord keyboard [one-hand operated microtypewriter]
1978, Computer 11(12)57-63

RODWELL, P.:
Choosing a word processor
1981, Pers Comput World 4(4)81-83,86

ROSEN, A.; FIELDEN, R.:
Word processing

1977, Englewood Cliffs: Prentice-Hall - 354 p.
RUNGE, G.:
Textverarbeitung und Fotosatz - Imprinta 79 [Text processing and phototypesetting - Imprinta 79 exhibition]
1979, BTA/BTO Bürotech 27(6)684-688
SCHRAMM, H.F.W.:
Trends bei Datendruckern: für jede Aufgabe eine breite Auswahl [Trends in data printers: a large assortment for every task]
1980, Online Adi Nachr (11)872-876
STIBIC, V.:
De computer en word processor helpen de schrijver van een technische of wetenschappelijke publicatie [The computer and word processor help the author of a technical or scientifical publication]
1980, Informatie (Neth.) 22(5)410-419
TASCHENDIKTIERGERÄTE
[Pocket dictating machines]
1981, BTA/BTO Bürotech 29(2)164-170
TELEFON-DIKTIERANLAGEN:
Das Diktat über den schnellen Draht [Telephonedictating equipment: dictating via a line]
1980, BTA/BTO Bürotech 28(1)45-46
TEXED
Comprehensive TEXED offers exceptional value
1980, Which Computer 4(8)31-36
WOHL, J.D.:
Replacing the pad and pencil
1980, Datamat 26(6)169-176
WORD PROCESSING
a guide for office management
n.d., Luton: Macintosh - 120 p.
WORD PROCESSING:
current practices and future development
1980, North Wood Hills: Middles - 328 p.
WORD PROCESSING:
selection, implementation and useage
1979, Uxbridge: Online Publ - 316 p.

60 - Personal computing

Personal computing in general. Pocket calculators. Programmable pocket calculators. Personal computers. Terminals and mainframes. Programming of personal computers. Personal software. Personal applications. Further general sources cited in chapter 6.

ARANDA, R.:
Personal office computing - information networks and videotex as pathways to office automation for professionals and managers
1981, Carnforth: Savant Inst - 190 p.
BOON, K.:
Programmeren met de pocket calculator [Programming a pocket calculator]
1980, Deventer: Kluwer
BRUMBAUGH, K.E.:
Personal computing for informational professionals
In: Proc ASIS Ann Meet 1979 vol. 16 p.286-288
1979, New York: Knowl Ind Publ
BULTHUIS, K. et al.:
Ten billion bits on a disk
1979, IEEE Spectrum 16(8)26-33
BURGE, F.(ed.):
What is happening in the personal computer market ?
1980, Anaheim, Cal.: Wescon - 14 p.
CHEKROUN, A.:
BASIC - programmation des microordinateurs [BASIC - the language of microcomputers]
1981, Paris: Dunod - 96 p.
ELLIS, C.:
Intelligent workstations for electronic mail
in: Bus Telecommun Online Conf 18-19 June 1980, London
ENTICKNAP, N.:
The Philips guide to business computers and the electronic office

1979, Purley: Input Two-Nine - 130 p.
GIBSON, G.A.; LIU, Y.Ch.:
Microcomputers for engineers and scientists
1980, Englewood Cliffs: Prentice-Hall - 480 p.
GRAVINA, R.M.:
SMALLTALK and the personal computer
1980, Comput Educ (GB) (35)9-13
GRAY, P.; CARLSON, F.R. Jr.:
Analyzing the future impact of personal computers
1980, IEEE Trans vol SMC 19(8)484-496
GREEN, D.R.; LEWIS, J.:
Science with pocket calculators
1978, London: Wyckham - 300 p.
HANDEL, J.:
The new literacy: programming languages as languages
1981, Byte 6(3)300-307
HAYES, J.P.:
Technology changes in personal computers
1980, IEEE Trans vol SMC 10(8)476-480
HOFFMAN, J.:
Personal computing
1979, Reston: Reston Publ - 262 p.
HOLMEN, M.G.:
Who is using personal computers ?
1980, IEEE Trans vol SMC 10(8)480-484
ISAACSON, P.; JULIUSSEN, E.:
Window on the 80's [prospects of computer hardware and software]
1980, Computer 13(1)4-6
KAY, A.C.:
Microelectronics and the personal computer
1979, Sci Am 237(3)230-244,262
KAY, A.; GOLDBERG, A.:
Personal dynamic media [Dynabook of Xerox]
1977, Computer 10(3)31-41
LARRECHE, J.-C.:
BASIC - une introduction à la programmation
1981, Paris: Edit Eyrolles (7th ed.) - 120 p.
MITTMAN, B.; BORMAN, L.:
Personalized data base systems
1975, Los Angeles: Melville - 312 p.
MULLISH, H.:
The complete pocket calculator handbook
1976, New York: Collier
NILLES, J.M.:
Personal computers in the future: an overview
1980, IEEE Trans vol. SMC 10(8)474-476
RASKIN, J.; WHITNEY, T.:
Perspectives on Personal Computing
1981, Computer 14(1)62-73
RUGG, T.; FELDMAN, P.:
32 Basic programs [for the TRS-80 level II computer][for the PET computer][for the Apple computer]
n.d., Portland: Dilithium Press 270/270/280 p.
SAVUSCH, M.:
1001 things to do with your personal computer
1980, Blue Ridge Summit (Pa): Tab Books - 334 p.
SCHOICHET, S.:
Personal work stations: a concept evolves into a booming industry
1981, Mini-Micro Syst 14(4)98-99,102-104,107,113
SEDMAN, E.C.:
The use of MicroCobol for telesoftware
In: Videotex, Viewdata.. [see 48] p. 399-411
STEK, R.J.:
Personal computing: past, present and future
1979, Proc 7th Ann Can Conf Inf Sci, p. 268-277
STOTTS, G.A.:
Name-address and sort program
1980, Interface Age 5(11)81-82,140-141
UTTAL, B.:
The comming struggle in personal computers
1981, Fortune 103(13)84-92
WALLS, B.:
Personal computers
1978, New York: Trafalgar House - 193 p.
WEBER, K.:
BASIC für Anfänger [BASIC for beginners]
1979, Bern: Haupt

70 - Graphical presentation

Graphical methods. Graphs. Line, bar and pie charts. Special graphs. Gantt charts. 'Z' diagrams. Organizational diagrams. Decision tables. Flowcharts. Hymans charts. Venn diagrams. Technical means for graphical presentation. Plotters. Digitizers. Graphical displays. Further general sources cited in chapter 6.

BUTLAND, J.; BUTLAND, S.D.:
An easy-to-use graph drawing package
1980, Computer 13(2)69-80

ERBESDOBLER, R. et al.:
Entscheidungstabellen-Technik [The techniques of the decision tables]
1976, Heidelberg: Springer - 166 p.

GERZON, F. et al.:
DIRECT information retrieval system - experiment
1970, Eindhoven: Philips ISA (int. rep.) - 114 p.

HARTMAN, W. et al.:
Information systems handbook ('ARDI' handbook)
1968, Apeldoorn: Philips - ca 400 p.

HERDEG, W.:
Diagrams - the graphic vizualization of abstract data
1976, Zürich: Graphis - 184 p.

KALUSH, A.G.:
Drawing pictures using printer plotting
1981, Creat Comput 7(1)136,138,140

KIRBY, P.:
Desktop graphics [friendly computer graphics]
1979, Datamat 25(5)164-167,170

KOMMEREN, G.J.:
Boolean-matrix applications for design/programming activities
1976, Eindhoven: Philips-ISA (int.rep. IDT/AS/GK/760409)

LEWIS, B.N. et al.:
Flow charts, logical trees and algorithms for rules and regulations
1967, London: HSMO - 28 p.

LOMBAERS, H.J.M. (ed.):
Project planning by network analysis
1969, Amsterdam: North-Holland - 456 p.

LONDON, K.R.:
Decision tables
1972, Princeton: Auerbach - 205 p.

MACHOVER, C.:
A brief, personal history of computer graphics
1978, Computer (USA) 11(11)38-45

MCDANIEL, H.:
An introduction to decision logic tables
1968, New York: Wiley - 96 p.

MCDANIEL, H. (ed.):
Applications of decision tables
1970, Princeton: Brandon - 226 p.

MORITZ, B.:
Diagramm-Techniken für den EDV Praktiker [Graphical techniques for the ADP professionals]
1977, n.p.: Klausdorf - 90 p.

NORDSIECK, F.:
Die schaubildliche Erfassung und Untersuchung der Betriebsorganisation [Graphical presentation and analysis of business organisation]
1931 (5th ed. 1955), Stuttgart: Poeschel - 160 p.

PFERD, W. et al.:
Interactive graphics teleconferencing
1979, Computer 12(11)62-72

POLLACK, S.L.:
Analysis of the decision rules in decision tables
1963, US Dept Commerce (NTIS rep. AD-407719) - 70 p.

POLLACK, S.L. et al.:
Decision tables - theory and practice
1971, New York: Wiley - 180 p.

ROLLING, L.:
The role of graphical display of concept relationship in... a thesaurus of documentation terms
1965, Bruxelles: Euratom - 30 p.

TURNBULL, A.T.; BAIRD, R.N.:
Graphics of communication - typography layout design
1964, New York: Holt - 342 p.

WOELFLE, R.M. (ed.):
A guide for better technical presentations
1975, New York: IEEE Press - 230 p.
WOLFE, G.W.:
Plotting data or functions - a BASIC subroutine for plotting via line printe
1980, Kilobaud Microcomput 4(3)167-169
ŽLÁBEK, K.:
Diagramy 'Z'
1940, Praha: Cesta - 116 p.

80 - Communication in general

Communication in science, technology and management. Means of communication. Traditional means of communication. Progressive techniques. Future prospects. Office of the future. Further general sources cited in sections 80 and 81.

ARTANDI, S.:
Man, information and society: new patterns of interaction
1979, J Am Soc Inf Sci 30(1)15-18
ASIS:
The information age in perspective; proceedings of ASIS annual meeting
1978, New York 13-17 Nov 1978
1978, White Plains: Knowl Ind - 382 p.
BLECHMAN, F.:
Program your phone calls to dial... time... rate... re-call
1980, Interface Age 5(10)74-76,78,132
DE MENTHON, S.:
Mieux utiliser le téléphone un media sur votre bureau [Better usage of the telephone]
1979, Paris: Éditions d'organisation - 142 p.
GRUNSTEIDL, W.:
The office of the future
1978, Informatie (Neth) 20(4)231-234
KOCHEN, M.:
Technology and communication in the future
1981, J Am Soc Inf Sci 32(2)148-157
MAHON, B.:
The potential impact of telecommunication networks on information systems intelligence
1980, Inf Process Manage 16(6)305-311
PAUSCH, R.:
Integrierte Bürokommunikationssysteme [Integrated office communication systems]
1979, BTA/BTO Bürotech 27(12)1427-1429
PERSON-TO-PERSON
networks [computer conferencing and electronic information exchange]
1978, Bull Am Soc Inf Sci 4(5)9-23
RAITT, D.I.:
Recent developments in telecommunications and their impact on information services
1982, ASLIB Proc 34(1)54-76
RHODES, W.L. Jr.:
Office of the future - light years away ?
1981, Infosyst 28(3)40-41
SHORT, J.; WILLIAMS, E.; CHRISTIE, B.:
The social psychology of telecommunications
1976, London: Wiley - 194 p.
THE NEW OFFICE LOOK
1981, Which Computer 5(2)47-53
THOMA, G.R.:
Transmission of information: an overview
1981, J Am Soc Inf Sci 32(2)131-140
UHLIG, R.P.; FARBER, D.J.; BAIR, J.H.:
The office of the future - communication and computers
1979, Amsterdam: North-Holland - 380 p.
UNESCO:
Many voices, one world - communication and society today and tomorrow
1980, Paris: UNESCO - 312 p.

82 - Electronic mail

Telex. Teletex. Electronic mail. Further general sources cited in section 82.

CAMERASS, R.:
Viewdata: a practical medium for electronic mail
In: Videotex, Viewdata.. [see 48] p. 173-184

GLEISBERG, H.:
Können Telebrief und Teletex den Briefverkehr entlasten ? [Can the teleletter and teletex relieve the post ?]
1980, BTA/BTO Bürotech 28(11)1132-1135

GRAY, J.:
All set to spread the word by electronic mail service
1980,06,05 Electron Times p. 28

HOUSMAN, E.M.:
Online communication by computer conferencing and electronic mail
In: 4th Int Online Inf Meet London 1980, p. 129-135
1980, Oxford: Learn Inf

KLAN, G.:
Telebrief-Dienst [The Telebrief service]
1981, BTA/BTO Bürotech 29(4)439-440

POTTER, R.J.:
Electronic mail
1977, Science 195(4283)1160-1164

REES, J.:
Unreal ideas of change [by electronic mail and office of the future]
1981, Computing 9(3)16-17

REICHWALD, R.:
Bürokommunikation im Teletex-Bereich [Office communication by teletex services]
1981, BTA/BTO Bürotech 29(4)430, 433-438

RIVERS, D.A.:
Electronic mail: alternatives for document distribution
1981, Word Proces & Inf Syst 8(1)20-53

RÜGGEBERG, R.:
Erste Erfahrungen im Teletex-Dienst der Deutschen Bundespost [First experience of the German PTT with the Teletex service]
1981, BTA/BTO Bürotech 29(12)1190-1193

SCHMINCKE, H.:
Verandert Teletex die Büroarbeit ? [Will office work be changed by teletex ?
1981, BTA/BTO Bürotech 29(6)641-645

ZÁVADA, D.:
Satzlexikon der Handelskorrespondenz - New commercial dictionary
1972, Wiesbaden: Brandstetter - 334 p.

83/85 - Conferences. Presentations. Education

Conferences, congresses and meetings. Computer conferencing. Presentations. Lectures. Technical means. Audiovisual media. Projection. Overhead projection. Slides. Slide shows. Films. Programmed learning. Further general sources cited in sections 83 to 85.

BROWN, M.:
PRESTEL and education - a viewdata telesoftware system for education
In: 4th Int Online Inf Meet London 1980
1980, Oxford: Learn Inf p. 115-118

COMMUNICATING
through poster sessions
1979, IEEE Trans PC-22(3)137-140

EDUCATIONAL FILM LOCATOR
1978, Ann Arbor: Bowker

EDWARDS, M.:
Stay-at-home conferences: more than just an energy-saver
1981, Infosystems 28(8)48-54
EISENHOWER, D.D.:
Crusade in Europe
1948, Exeter: Heinemann
EISENSCHITZ, T.S.:
Poster sessions as a medium of scientific communication
1979, J Res Commun Stud 1(3)235-242
FAETHERINGHAM, T.:
Computerized conferencing and human communication
1977, IEEE Transact PC-20(4)207-213
FOX, M.S.; BEBEL, D.J.; PARKER, A.C.:
The automated dictionary
1980, Computer 13(7)35-48
GOLD, E.M.:
Attitudes to intercity travel substitution
1979, Telecommun Policy 3(2)147-149
GOLDBERG, A.:
Educational uses of a Dynabook
1979, Comput & Educ 3(4)247-266
GROGONO, A.W.:
Graphic color slides
1980, Byte 5(11)126-144
HILTZ, S.R.; TUROFF, M.:
The network nation: human communication via computer
1978, Reading (Mas.): Addison-Wesley Publ - 528 p.
KEHRBERG, K.T.; POLLACK, R.A.:
Videodisc in the classroom: an interactive economics course
1982, Creat Comput 8(1)98-102
LAWRY-CORRY, E.:
A basic guide to conference organizing
1978, ASLIB Proc 30(7)260-270
MAMBERT W.A.:
Presenting technical ideas: A guide to audience communication
1968, New York: Wiley - 216 p.
MANTEN, A.A.:
Symposia and symposium publications
1976, Amsterdam: Elsevier - 168 p.
NADLER, L.; NADLER, Z.:
The Conference book [Guide to designing, planning and running conferences]
1977, Houston: Gulf Publ, 267 p.
OSBORNE, A.F.:
Applied imagination [principles of brainstorming]
1953, New York: Scribner
RASCHE, H.O.:
Austattung von Seminar- und Vortragsräumen einschliesslich Organisation von Veranstaltungen [Equipment of seminar and lecture rooms and the organization of presentations]
1978, Baden-Baden: FBO Göller - 36 p.
SHORT, J. et al.:
The social psychology of telecommunications
1976, London: Wiley - 194 p.
TOMCZYK, M.S.:
The future of personal computers in education
in: Burge, F.: What is happening in the personal computer market
1980, Wescon, Anaheim, Cal - 10(3)1-6

86/87 - Publishing

Publishing. Writing. Layout. Legibility of printed and displayed text. Technical means. New methods of publishing. Terse publishing. On demand publishing. Paperless publishing. Further general sources cited in sections 86 and 87.

ANSI:
Synoptics - ANSI standard Z39.34 [terse publishing]
1977, New York: ANSI
ANTHONY, L.J.(ed.):
EURIM IV - A European conference on innovation in primary publication
1980, Luxemburg: CEC
ASHBY, P.; CAMPBELL, R.:
Microform publishing
1979, London: Butterworths - 190 p.

BAILEY, H.S.Jr.:
The limits of on-demand publishing
1975, Scholarly Publ 6(4)291-298

BALKIN, R.:
A writer's guide to book publishing
1977, New York: Hawthorn - 236 p.

BARRASS, R.:
Scientists must write - A guide for better writing for scientists, engineers and students
1978, New York: Chapman & Hall - 176 p.

BERKOWITCH, I.:
Building a science magazine within PRESTEL [weekly magazine SCITEL]
1979, Psychol Technol 10(1)1-3

BERNIER, C.L.:
Terse-literature viewpoint of wordage problem - amount, languages, access
1972, J Chem Doc 12(2)81-84

BRUSAW, C.T. et al.:
The business writer's handbook
1976, New York: St Martin's Press - 522 p.

CAWKELL, A.E.:
The paperless revolution
1978, Wireless World (GB) 84(1512) 69-74

CRAIG, J.:
Phototypesetting: a design manual
1978, London: Pitman - 224 p.

CUADRA, C.A.:
A brief introduction to electronic publishing
1981, Electron Publ Rev 1(1)29-34

DE BOER, et al.:
Schriftelijk raporteren [Report writing]
1974, Utrecht: Aula - 328 p.

ELECTRONIC PUBLISHING:
an introductory guide
1981, London: Publisher's Assoc - 33 p.

GREASER, C.U.:
Alternatives to traditional forms of scientific communication
1976, Santa Monica: Rand - 22 p.

HARTLEY, J.; BURNHILL, P.:
Fifty guide-lines for improving instructional text
1977, Program Learn Educ Technol 14(1)65-75

KATZEN, M.:
The visual impact of scholarly journal articles
1977, Leicester: Primary Commun Res Cent Univ Leicester

KING, D.W.; RODERER, N.K.:
The electronic alternative to communication through paper-based journals
In: Inf Age in Perspect - Proc ASIS Ann Meet vol.15, p.180-182

KNIGHT, G.N.:
Indexing, the art of: a guide to indexing of books and periodicals
1979, London: Allen & Unwin - 218 p.

LANCASTER, F.W.:
Towards paperless information systems
1978, New York: Acad Press - 180 p.

LEONOV, V.P.:
On the concept of automated encyclopedia
1979, Int Forum Inf Doc 4(1)6-11

MANN, P.H.:
The publishing of scholarly monographs
1980, J Doc 36(1)1-10

MAURICE, M. et al. (ed.):
The impact of new technologies on publishing - Proc Symp Luxemburg 1979
1980, München: Saur - 195 p.

MAXWELL, R.:
Data retrieval and international publishing
1982, ASLIB Proc 34(1)38-45

MCGRAW-HILL:
The Mcgraw-Hill's authors book
1968, New York: McGraw-Hill - 74 p.

MITCHELL, J.T.:
Writing for professional and technical journals
1968, New York: Wiley - 406 p.

MONTGOMERY, M.; STRATTON, J.:
The writer's hotline handbook - a guide to good usage and effective writing
1981, New York: New Amer Libr - 384 p.

MORGAN, C.:
What's wrong with technical writing today ?
1980, Byte 5(12)6-12

O'CONNOR, M.(ed.):
Model guidelines for the preparation of camera-ready typescripts by authors...
1980, London: CIBA - 48 p.

O'HARE, M.H.:
Future roles for synopsis publication
1980, Luxemburg: CEC - 43 p.

PESTEL, H.C.; RUBIN, S.A.:
Electronic handbook - fact or fiction
1977, Online 1(4)84-87

REYNOLDS, L.:
Legibility studies: their relevance to present-day documentation methods
1979, J Doc 35(4)307-340

ROISTACHER, R.C.:
The virtual journal
1978, Comput Networks (Neth) 2(1) 18-24

RUSSAK, B.:
Publishing primary scientific journals during the next decade
1977, IEEE Trans Prof Commun PC-20(2)51-54

SENDERS, J.:
An online scientific journal
1977, Inf Sci(entist) 11(1)3-9

SÖRGEL, D.:
An automated encyclopedia - a solution of the information problem?
1977, Int Classif 4(1/2)4-10,81-89

STAINTON, E.M.:
A bag for authors
1977, Scholar Publ 8(4)335-345

SUTHERLAND, W.R.:
Impact of technology on scientific publishing
1977, IEEE Trans Prof Commun PC-20(2)56-58

UNESCO:
Guidelines for editors of scientific and technical journals
1979, Paris: UNESCO - 36 p.

VANDERBORGHT, G.:
Guidelines for preparation of texts of dissertations for their presentation and publication
1976, Paris: UNESCO - 18 p.

WELLS, H.G.:
The work, wealth and happiness of mankind
1932, London

WENDT, D.; PLATA, W.:
Increasing the legibility of journals
1981, J Res Commun Stud 2(4)237-254

WILEY:
A guide for Wiley authors in the preparation of manuscripts and illustration
1973, New York: Wiley - 66 p.

WRIGHT, P.:
Presenting technical information: a survey of research findings
1977, Instr Sci 6(-)93-134

INDEX

By the same author:

Personal Documentation for Professionals - Means and Methods

1980, North-Holland, xii + 214 pages, 119 fig., 232 ref., Dfl 80 or US $ 35

* second printing 1981
* Spanish translation (ATE, Barcelona), 1982
* Japanese translation pending (Ohmsha, Tokyo)

Every professional person - scientist, researcher, manager, technician, teacher - owns his personal collection of documents (books, reports, journals, cuttings, photocopies, slides, microfiches, drawings, etc.) that must be well organized and accessible at any time. He needs his own personal documentation system.

This book describes the organization of such personal files, their structure, content, classification and indexing, as well as the technical means that can be employed for filing the original documents and for retrieval. The retrieval instruments, ranging from the simple card systems and peek-a-boo cards, to the computerized indexes, use of computer terminals, and personal computers, are characterized and evaluated. The advantages and weak points of these techniques are explained and demonstrated via many examples. Four case histories show the practice of personal documentation.